Wildlife Photographer of the Year

PORTFOLIO SEVEN

Designed by
GRANT BRADFORD

Project Co-ordinator
SHEELAGH COGHLAN

Captions Editor
STEPHEN YOUNG

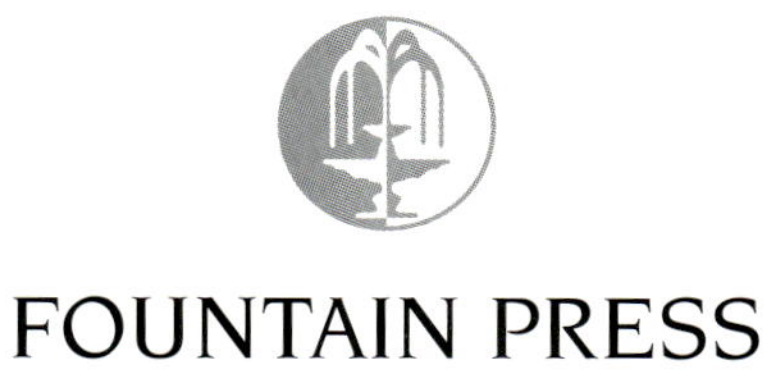

FOUNTAIN PRESS

Published by
FOUNTAIN PRESS LIMITED
Fountain House
2 Gladstone Road
Kingston-upon-Thames
Surrey KT1 3HD
England

Picture Editor
Design & Layout
GRANT BRADFORD

Project Co-ordinator
SHEELAGH COGHLAN

Captions Editor
STEPHEN YOUNG

Page Planning
REX CARR

Colour Origination
Foreart
Hong Kong

Printing & Binding
Die Keure n.v.
Belgium

ISBN 0 86343 347 2

Foreword

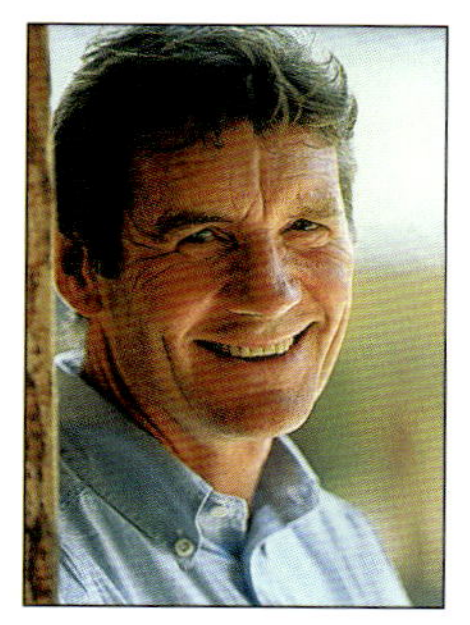

Ever since photographs showed us how a horse's legs really move when they gallop, we have relied on the split-second precision of the camera shutter to extend our knowledge of the natural world. This latest collection of prize-winning and commended images from the 1997 BG plc Wildlife Photographer of the Year Competition shows the extraordinary and undiminished power of the well-aimed camera to enrich our knowledge and dazzle our senses.

There have been many times on my travels when I wish I could have held on to a millisecond of beauty or turned a fleeting glimpse of the drama of nature into something permanent and unforgettable.

Thank goodness, then, for photographers like these, who, together with those who make their cameras and the film they use and those who print and process the results seem to produce work of more surpassing brilliance each year. In a single frame, these photographers not only capture what the human eye so often misses, but what the human eye will never be able to see. They turn a fraction of a second of life into something that combines art and mystery with an extraordinary and valuable amount of information.

This collection offers not just a staggering display of patience and precision but the thrilling prospect that the horizons of wildlife photography seem as boundless as ever.

Michael Palin London 1997

Contents

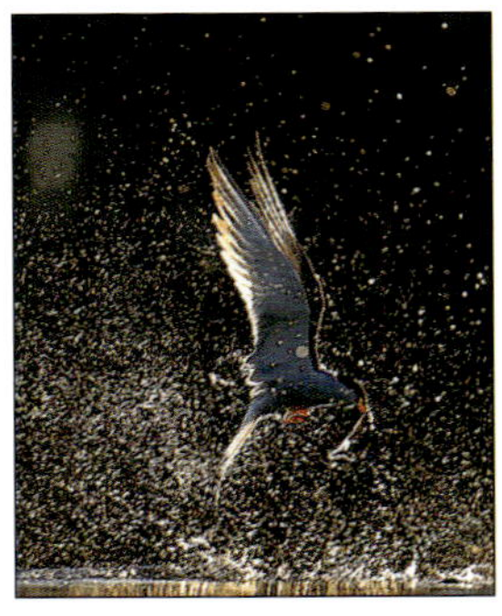

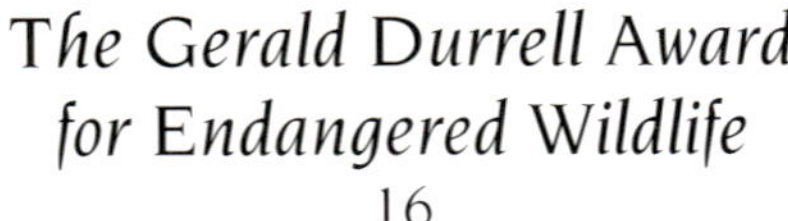

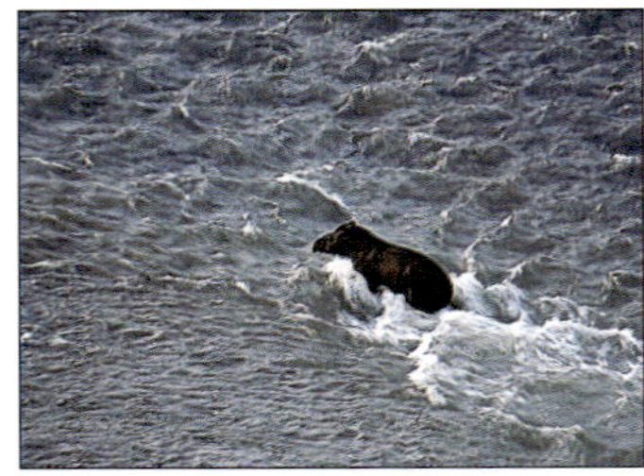

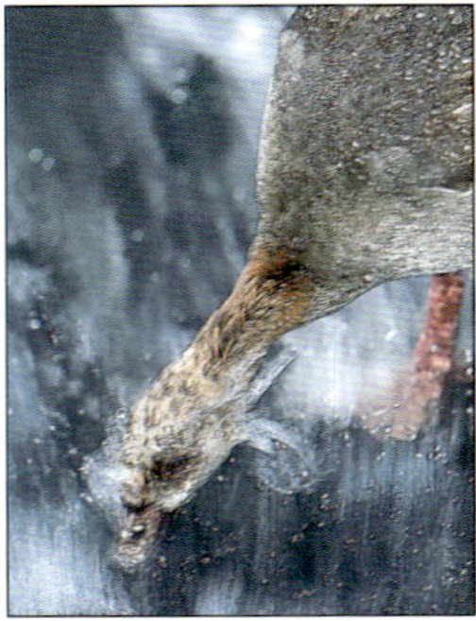

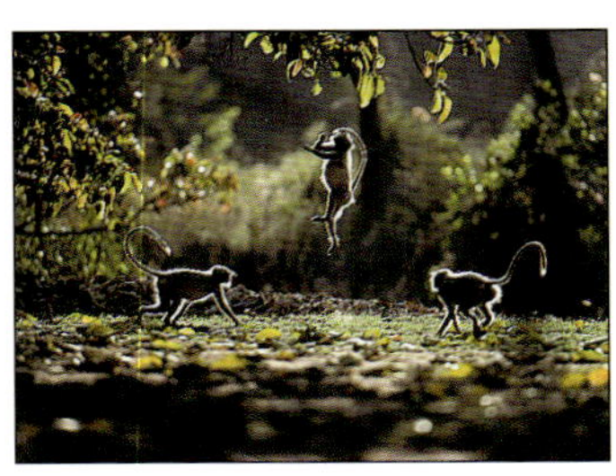

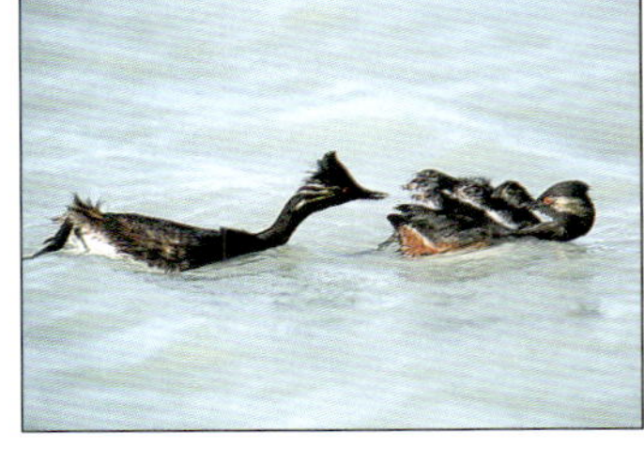

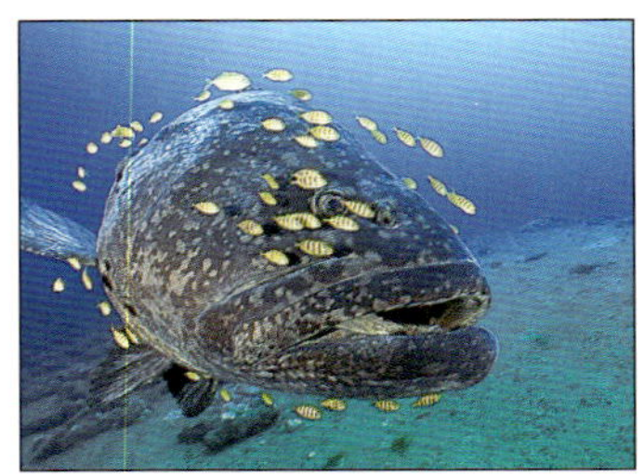

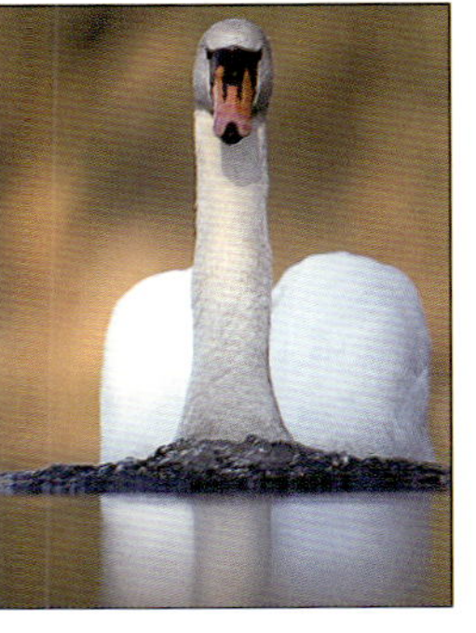

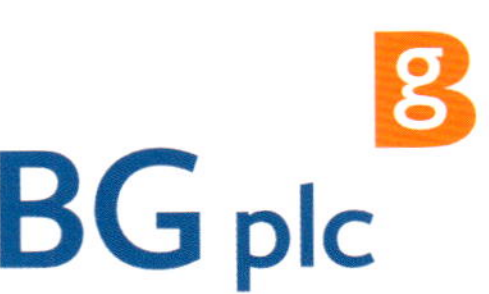

Wildlife Photographer of the Year

1997

"BG plc - formerly named British Gas plc - is proud to continue the company's long association with the Wildlife Photographer of the Year Competition.

Operating as British Gas International overseas and as Transco, the gas pipeline and storage business in the UK, BG is committed to minimising the impact of its activities on the environment. Wherever we work, we are determined to stay at the forefront of best practice.

These photographs are a reminder of the beauty and fragility of the natural world. They drive home to us how much we all have to do if we are to preserve this precious heritage for future generations."

David Varney
Chief Executive
BG plc

WILDLIFE PHOTOGRAPHER OF THE YEAR 1991-1996

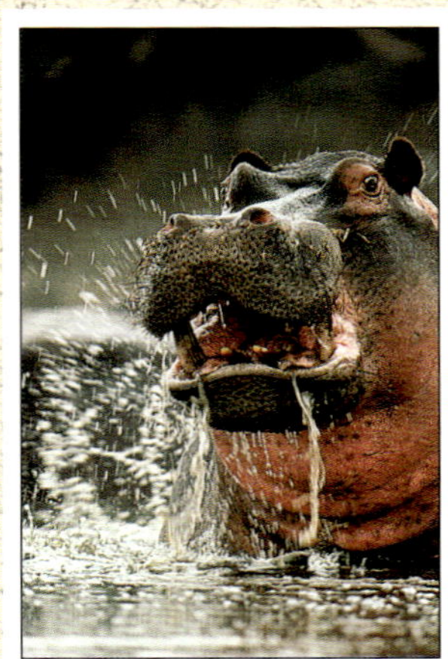

PORTFOLIO ONE
Frans Lanting
The Netherlands
1991

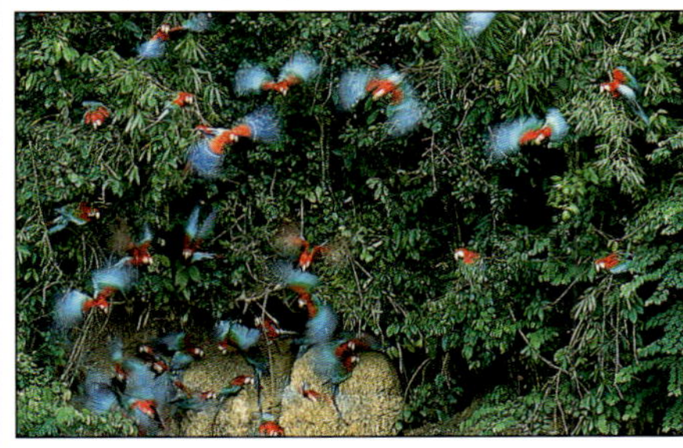

PORTFOLIO TWO
André Bärtschi
Liechtenstein
1992

PORTFOLIO THREE
Martyn Colbeck
United Kingdom
1993

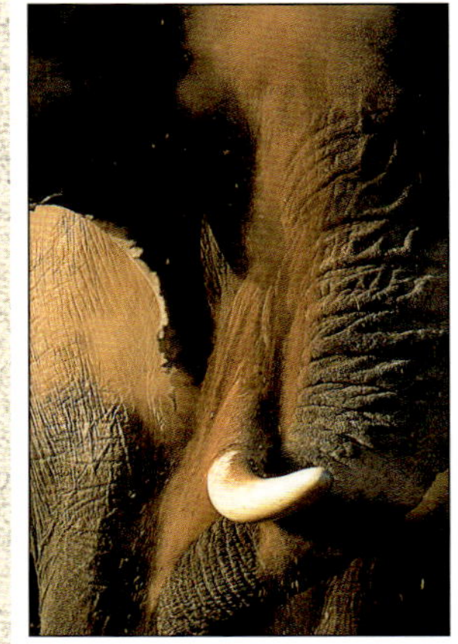

INTRODUCTION

THE JUDGES

Bruce Pearson
Wildlife artist

Heather Angel
Wildlife photographer

Dr Giles Clarke
Head of Exhibitions and Education, The Natural History Museum, London

Rosamund Kidman Cox
Editor, BBC Wildlife Magazine

Bob Bodman
Picture editor, The Daily Telegraph

Simon King
Wildlife film maker

Jonathan Scott
Wildlife photographer

This book displays the winning and commended images from the 1997 Wildlife Photographer of the Year Competition, which has been organised for the fourteenth year by BBC WILDLIFE Magazine and The Natural History Museum, London, and sponsored for the eighth year by BG plc.

The competition exists to encourage amateur and professional photographers around the world to record and document the beauty and wonder of the natural world. Each year the number of entries grows. This year over 19,000 slides were entered by photographers in 65 countries.

Photographs, which have to be colour slides, are entered in 12 different categories which each carry a first prize of £500 and a runner-up prize of £250. Where competition is particularly fierce the judges award a specially commended, or third prize. Some of the photographs that reach the final stages of the judging are highly commended. There are two special awards: The Eric Hosking Award for the best portfolio of pictures by a photographer aged 26 years or under, and The Gerald Durrell Award for Endangered Wildlife. There is also a Young Wildlife Photographer of the Year Competition for photographers aged 17 years and under.

The winning photographers are brought to The Natural History Museum in October for the presentation of the main awards and the official opening of the exhibition of winning and commended images. Three travelling sets of the exhibition tour the UK, visiting some 36 different galleries, museums and nature centres. Framed sets of the exhibition go on display in Australia, France, Germany, Holland, Japan and the USA, amongst other countries.

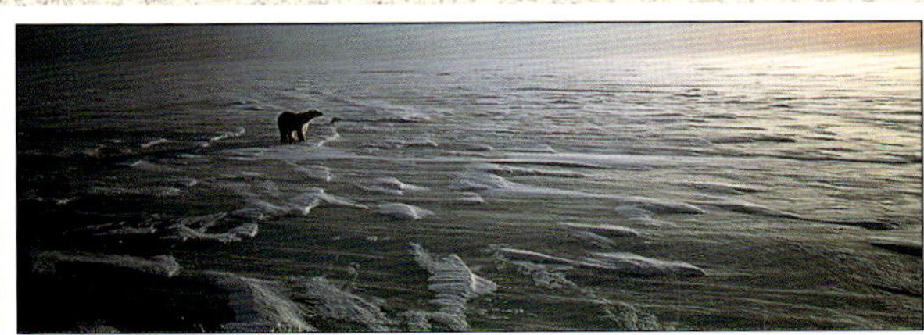

PORTFOLIO FOUR
Thomas D Mangelsen
United States of America
1994

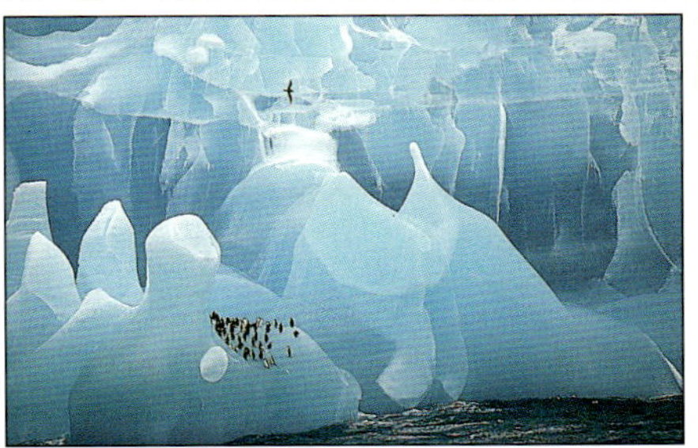

PORTFOLIO FIVE
Cherry Alexander
United Kingdom
1995

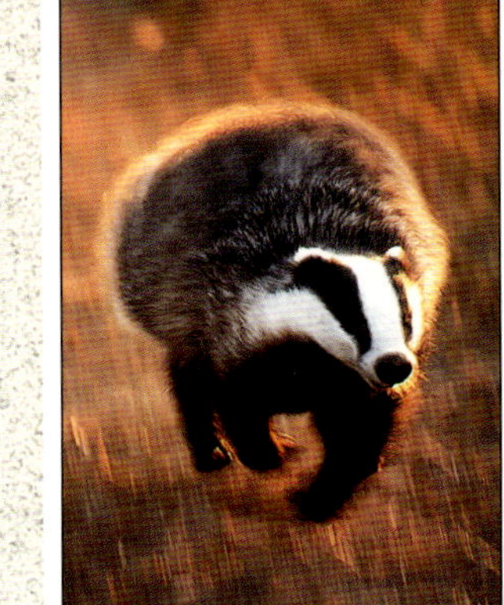

PORTFOLIO SIX
Jason Venus
United Kingdom
1996

Wildlife Photographer of the Year

The 'Wildlife Photographer of the Year' title was awarded for the single image judged to be the most striking and memorable of all the photographs entered for the competition. The 1997 winner Tapani Räsänen, received the BG plc award - a bronze trophy of an ibis - and a cheque for £2,000.

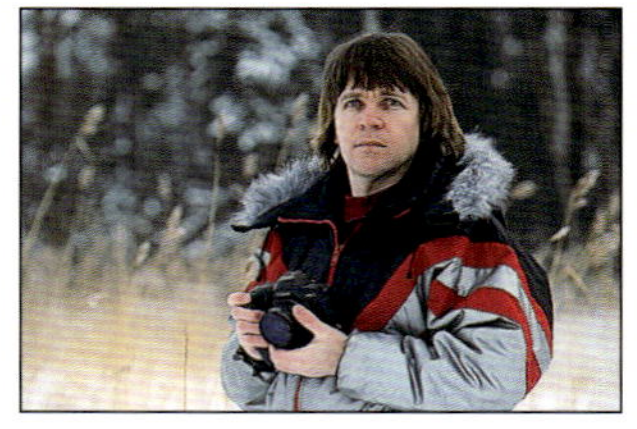

Tapani Räsänen

Tapani is a professional photographer from Finland who first became interested in photography during his time at university. He particularly enjoys photographing birds and takes most of his pictures within a 40 kilometre radius of his home, which is surrounded by lakes and forests. He has published three books and contributed to many others, and arranges lectures and exhibitions of his work all over Finland and abroad. He has won many prizes for his photography and in 1991 he was the Finnish Nature Photographer of the Year.

Tapani Räsänen

Finland

WILDLIFE PHOTOGRAPHER OF THE YEAR 1997

Common tern fishing

"Common terns are my favourite birds and I have been photographing them for eleven years now. But they can be difficult subjects, especially when they're fishing, because they dive so rapidly and are quickly in the air again. In this picture, taken at Lake Saimaa, southern Finland, the evening sun beautifully highlights the outline of the bird."

Canon EOS 1NRS with 300mm lens; 1/1000 sec at f4.5; Fujichrome Provia 100 rated at 200

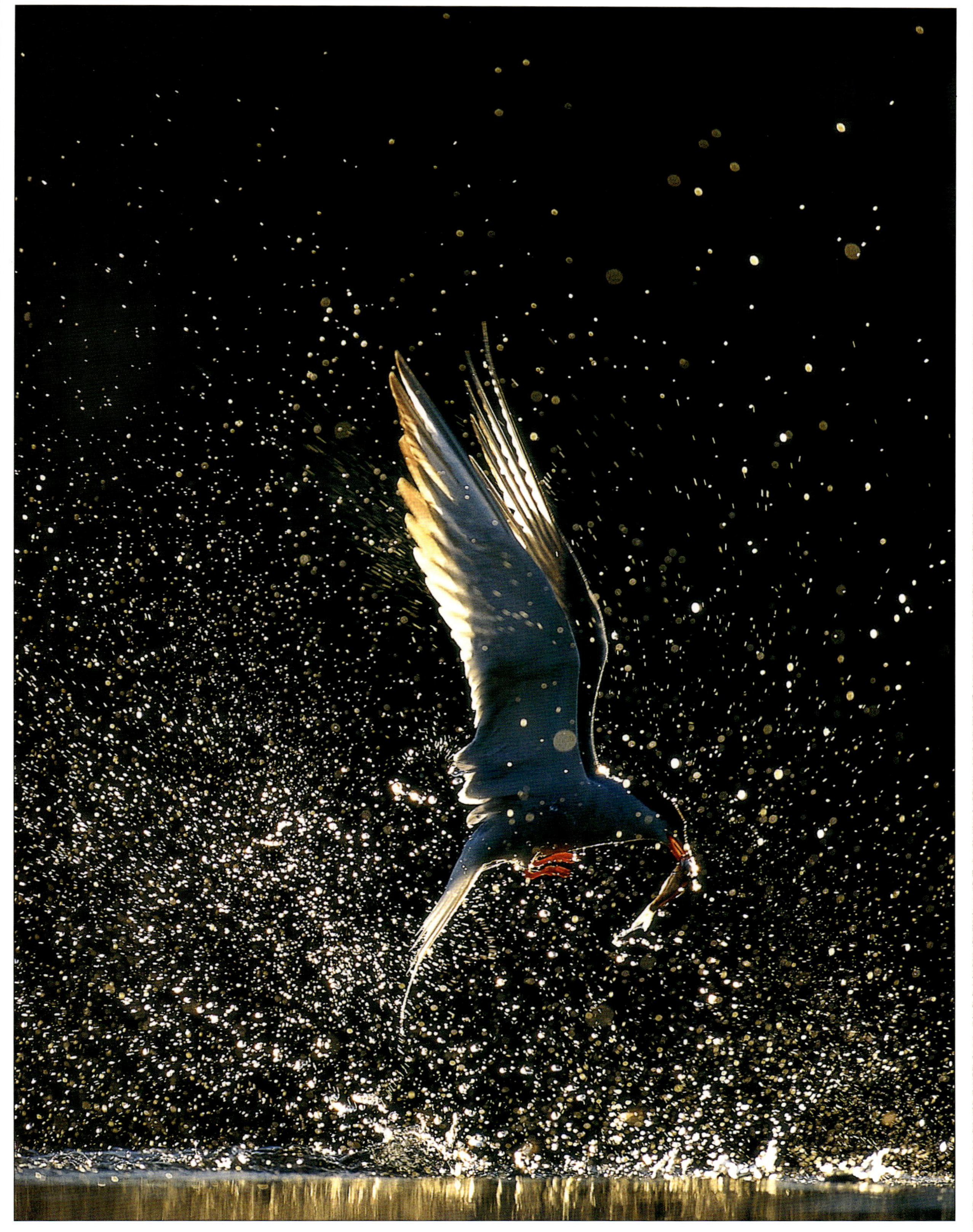

The Eric Hosking Award

This award goes to the best portfolio of six images taken by a photographer aged 26 or under. The award was introduced in 1991 in memory of Eric Hosking - Britain's most famous bird photographer. Eric was a supporter of the competition from its earliest days. The prize is a specially commissioned trophy and a cheque for £1,000.

The 1997 winner, Heinrich van den Berg from South Africa, also won the award in 1996. He comes from a family of enthusiastic wildlife photographers, and won his first photographic competition when he was 14 years old. He is a civil engineer but spends most of his holidays and weekends in the wild or game reserves taking pictures. He likes to find innovative and creative ways of capturing aspects of animal behaviour, and has a particular interest in birds. Heinrich is a fellow of the Photographic Society of South Africa.

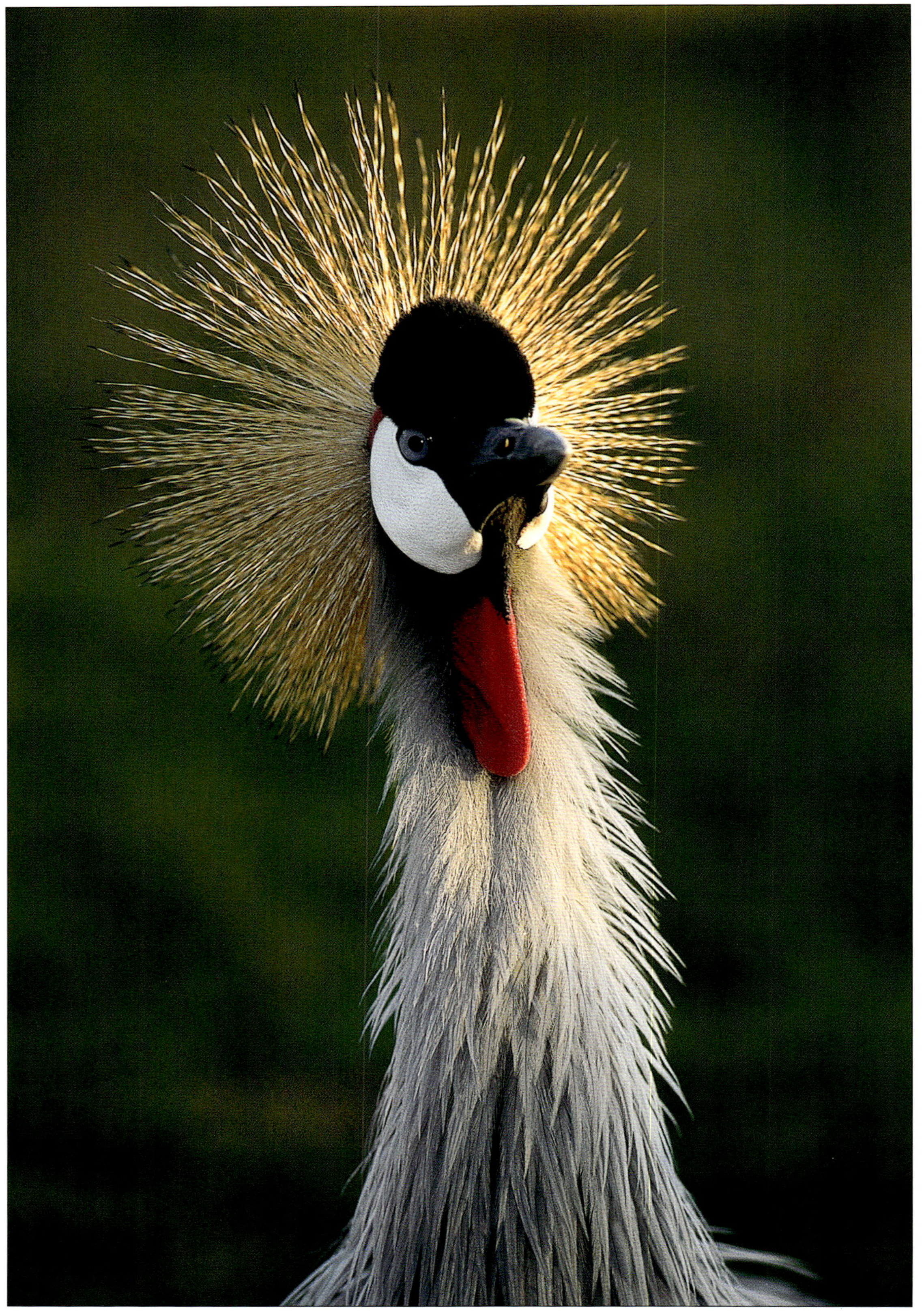

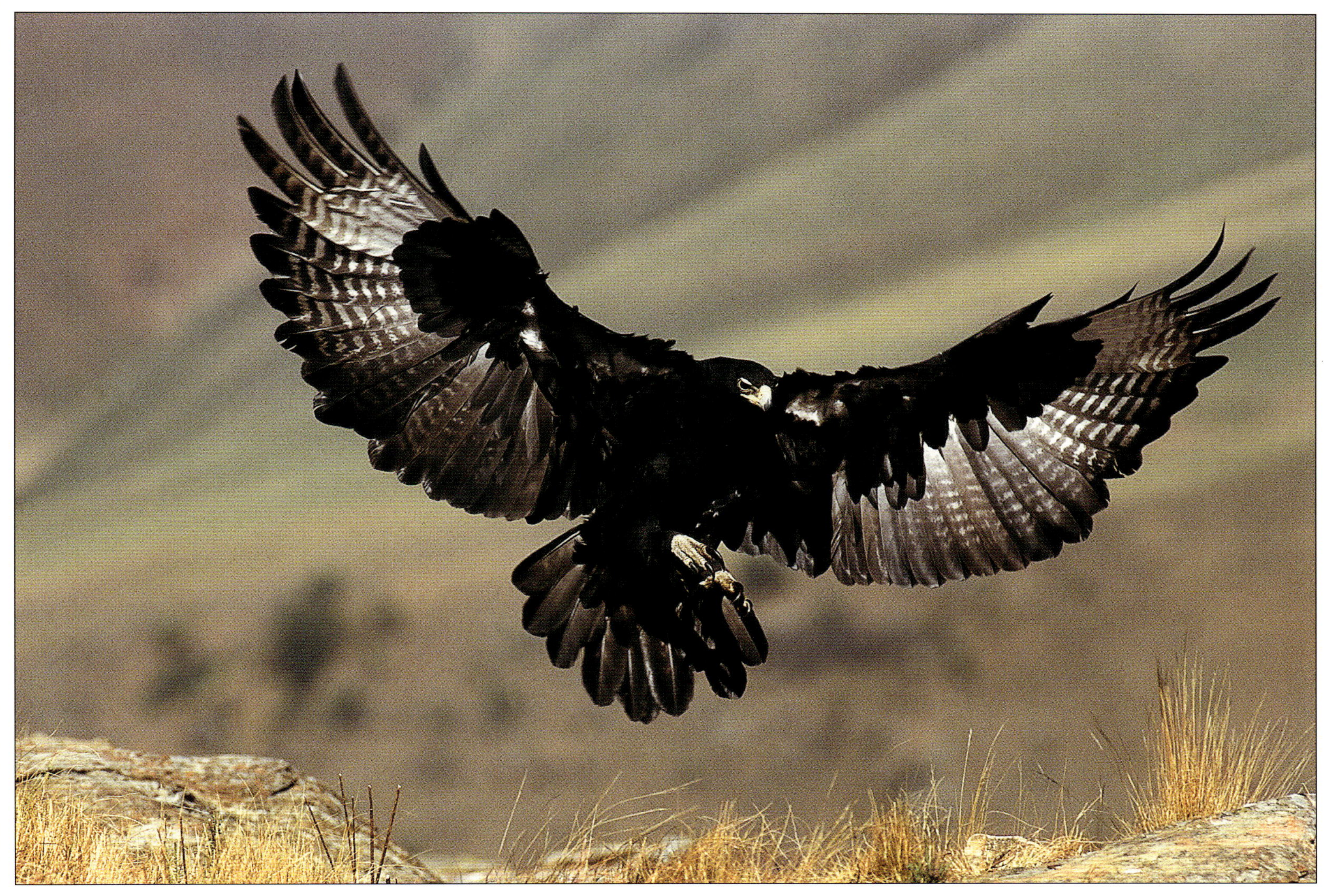

Heinrich van den Berg
South Africa

Crowned crane portrait

"Normally these cranes are very difficult to get close to, but this one, from the Kwa-Zulu Natal Midlands, was inquisitive. I chose backlighting because it accentuated the bird's crown."

Canon F1 with 300mm lens and x1.4 converter; flash; 1/90 sec at f5.6: Fujichrome Velvia

Heinrich van den Berg
South Africa

Black eagle landing

"We tried to photograph bearded vultures from a hide in the Drakensberg mountains, but while black eagles were around, no bearded vulture would come down. Majestic, acrobatic and cheeky, the black eagle is the self-proclaimed king of the mountains."

Canon F1 with 300mm lens and x1.4 converter; 1/500 sec at f5.6; Fujichrome Provia

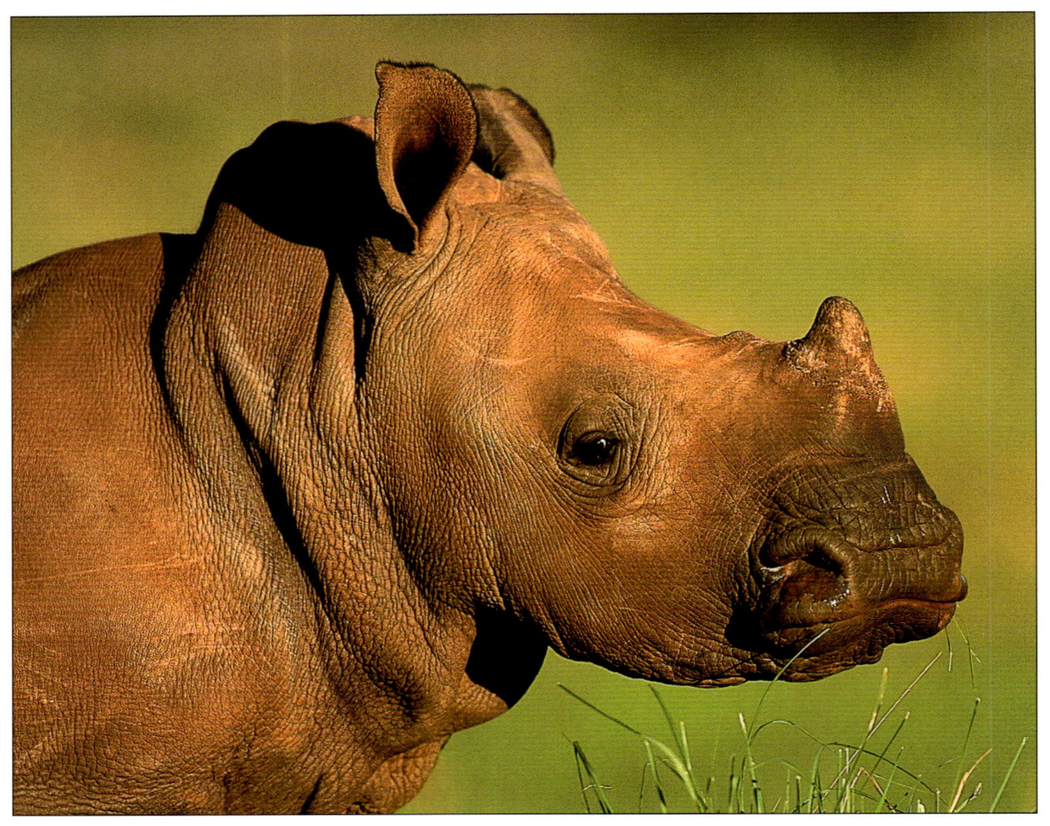

Heinrich van den Berg
South Africa

Young white rhino

"Unlike its mother, this little rhino felt very threatened by our presence. It mock charged us a few times, almost like a child throwing a tantrum. I photographed it in a game reserve in Gauteng, South Africa."

Canon T90 with 500mm lens: 1/350 sec at f6.3:
Fujichrome Velvia

Heinrich van den Berg
South Africa

Springbok in flight

"On the previous day, we'd witnessed three cheetah chases in this part of the Kalahari Gemsbok National Park. In one of the chases, the cheetahs had caught a young springbok from this herd. Now the whole herd seemed tense, sprinting away at full speed for no reason."

Canon F1 with 500mm lens; 1/750 sec at f4.5;
Fujichrome Velvia

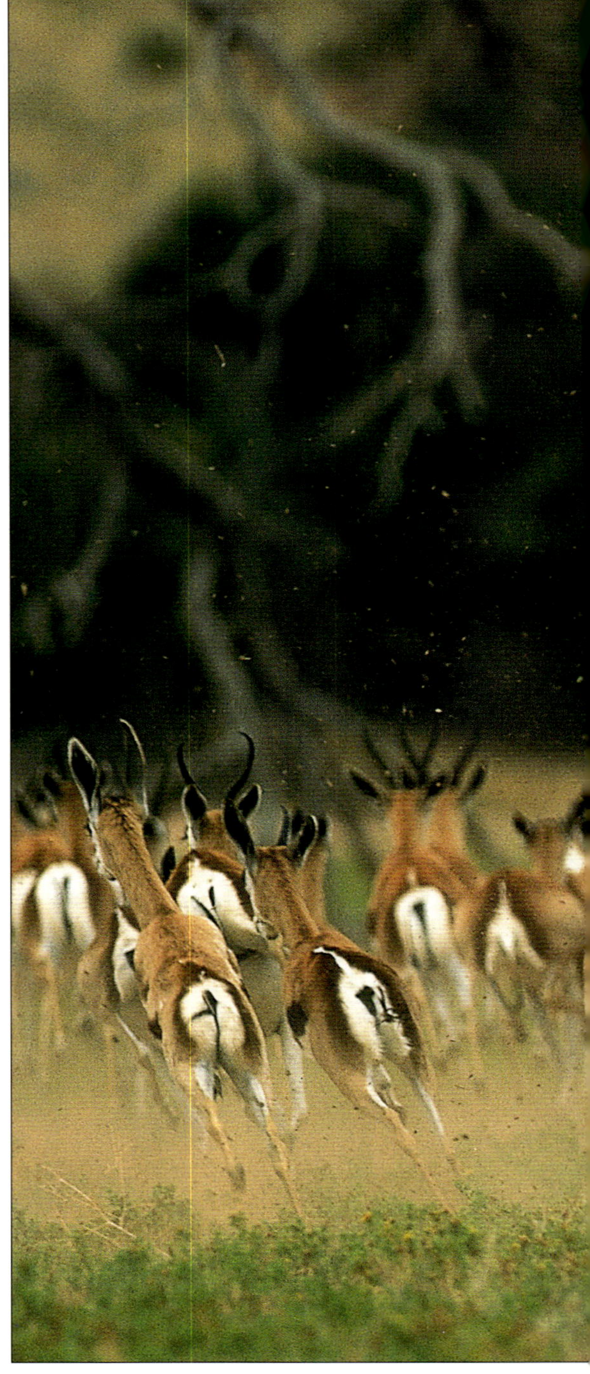

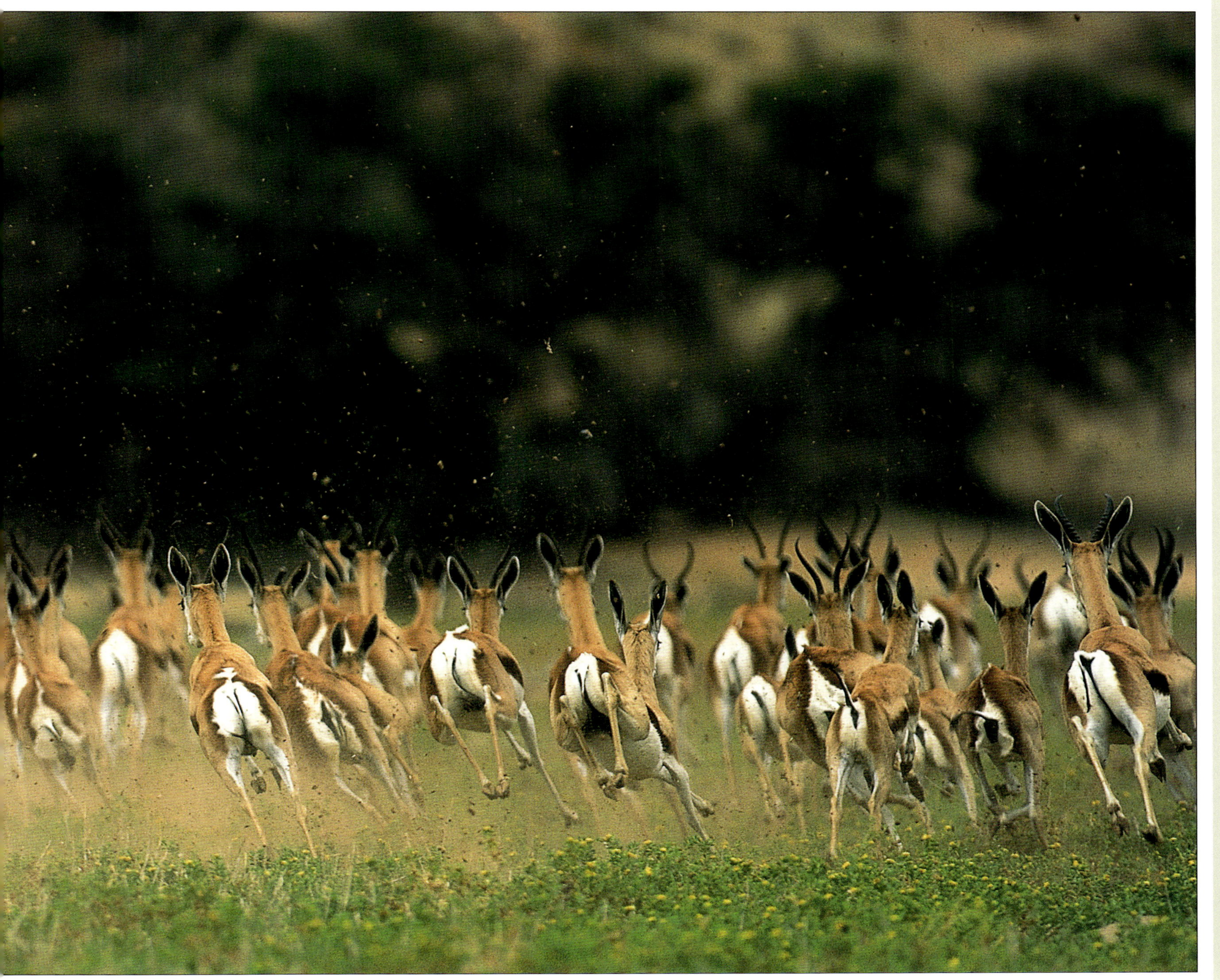

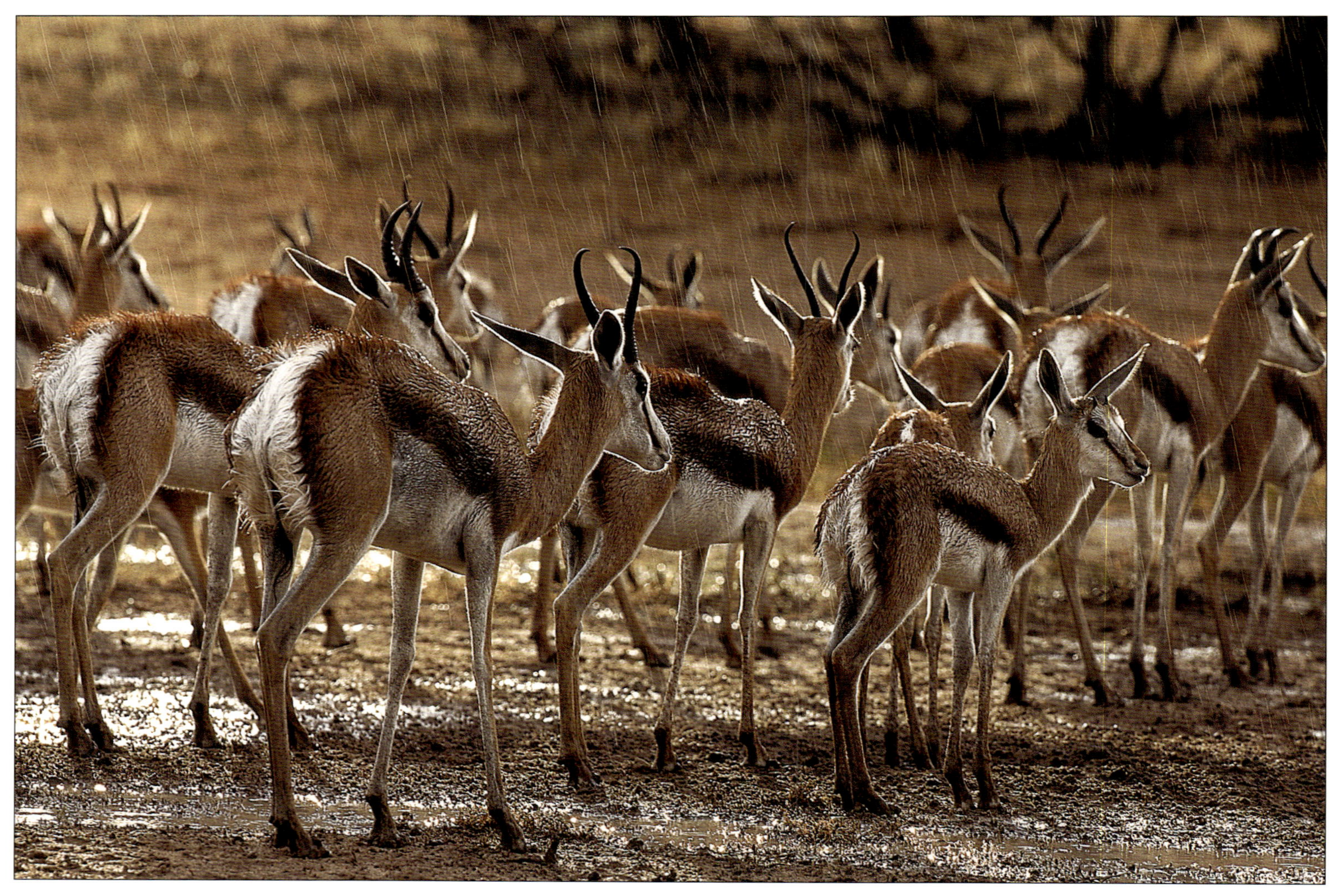

Heinrich van den Berg
South Africa

Springbok in rain storm

"We were fortunate to witness a rain storm in the Kalahari Gemsbok National Park. The springbok hated it, turning their backs to the wind and starting to run with every lightning bolt. It must have been the first rain the young in the herd had experienced."

Canon EOS 50 with 300mm lens and x1.4 converter; 1/250 sec at f4; Fujichrome Velvia

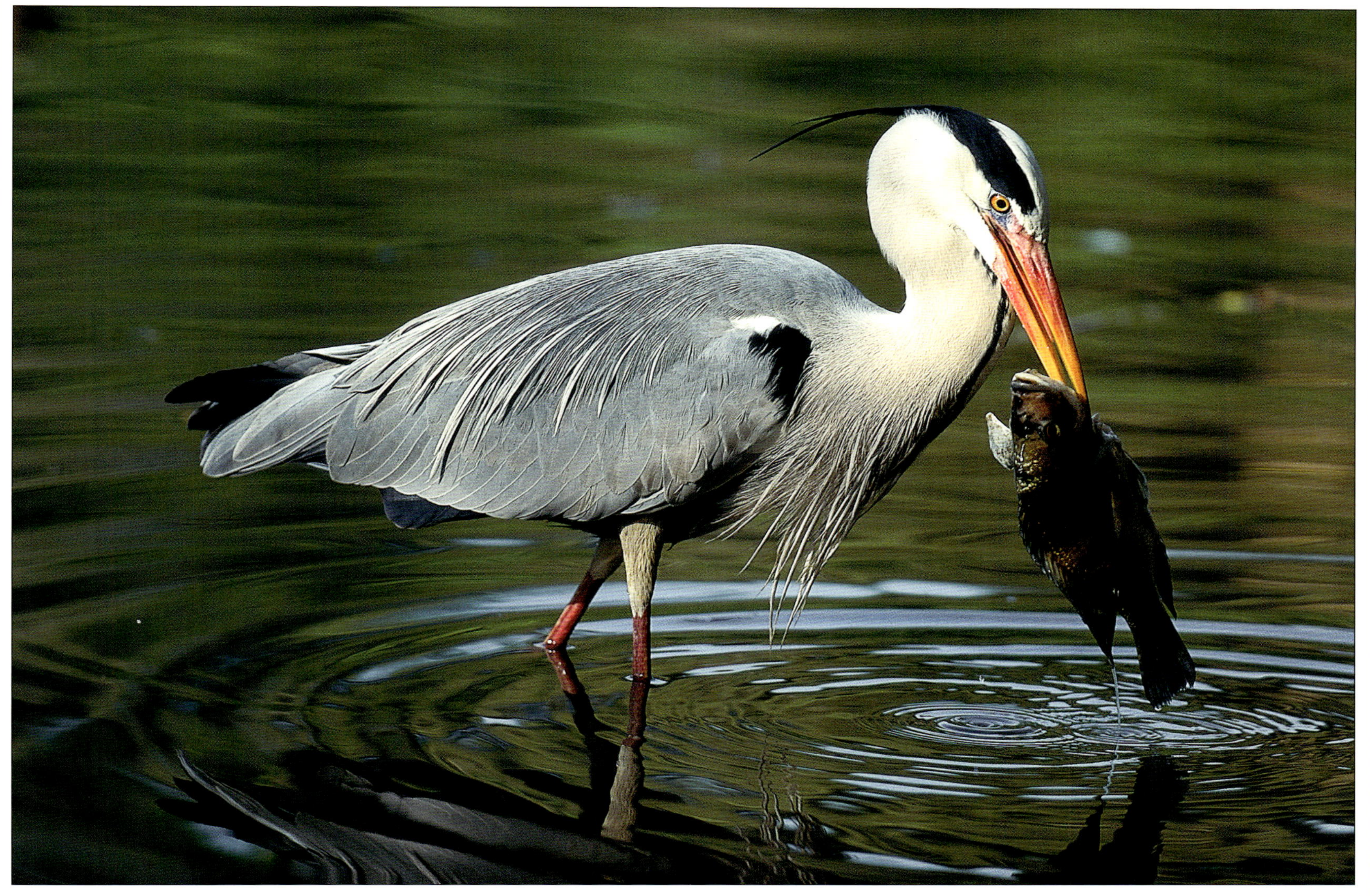

Heinrich van den Berg
South Africa

Grey heron

"I spent many hours with the lens focused on this heron, waiting for it to catch a fish. On this occasion I spotted it only after it had caught the fish. Fortunately for me, the fish was exceptionally big and the heron couldn't swallow it at the first attempt."

Canon T90 with 300mm lens; 1/250 sec at f4; Fujichrome Velvia

The Gerald Durrell Award for Endangered Wildlife

This award was introduced in 1995 to commemorate Gerald Durrell's long-standing involvement with the Wildlife Photographer of the Year Competition and his work with endangered species. The subjects illustrated must be officially listed as endangered or threatened at an international or national level. The winner, Kevin Schafer, received a specially commissioned trophy and a cheque for £1,000.

Kevin Schafer is an internationally renowned wildlife photographer from the United States. He originally trained as a biologist and his work appears in many international publications such as National Geographic and GEO. He has published a number of books, the most recent being a major photographic study on the national parks of Costa Rica.

Kevin Schafer
United States of America
WINNER

Brazilian tapir

"I was photographing macaws from a cliff top hide near the Tambopata River, Peru, when a solitary tapir emerged from the forest. As it was crossing the wide, shallow river, it paused mid-stream, allowing me to take the photo."

Nikon N90s with 500mm lens; 1/15 sec at f8; Fujichrome Velvia

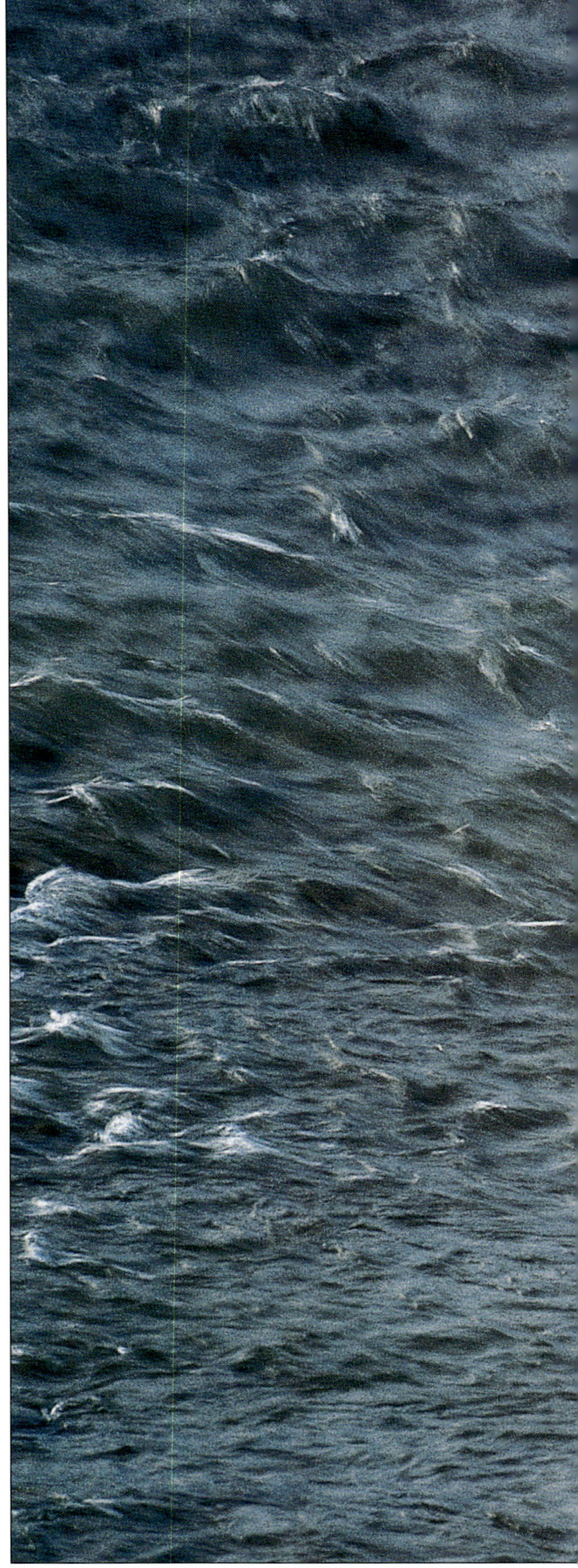

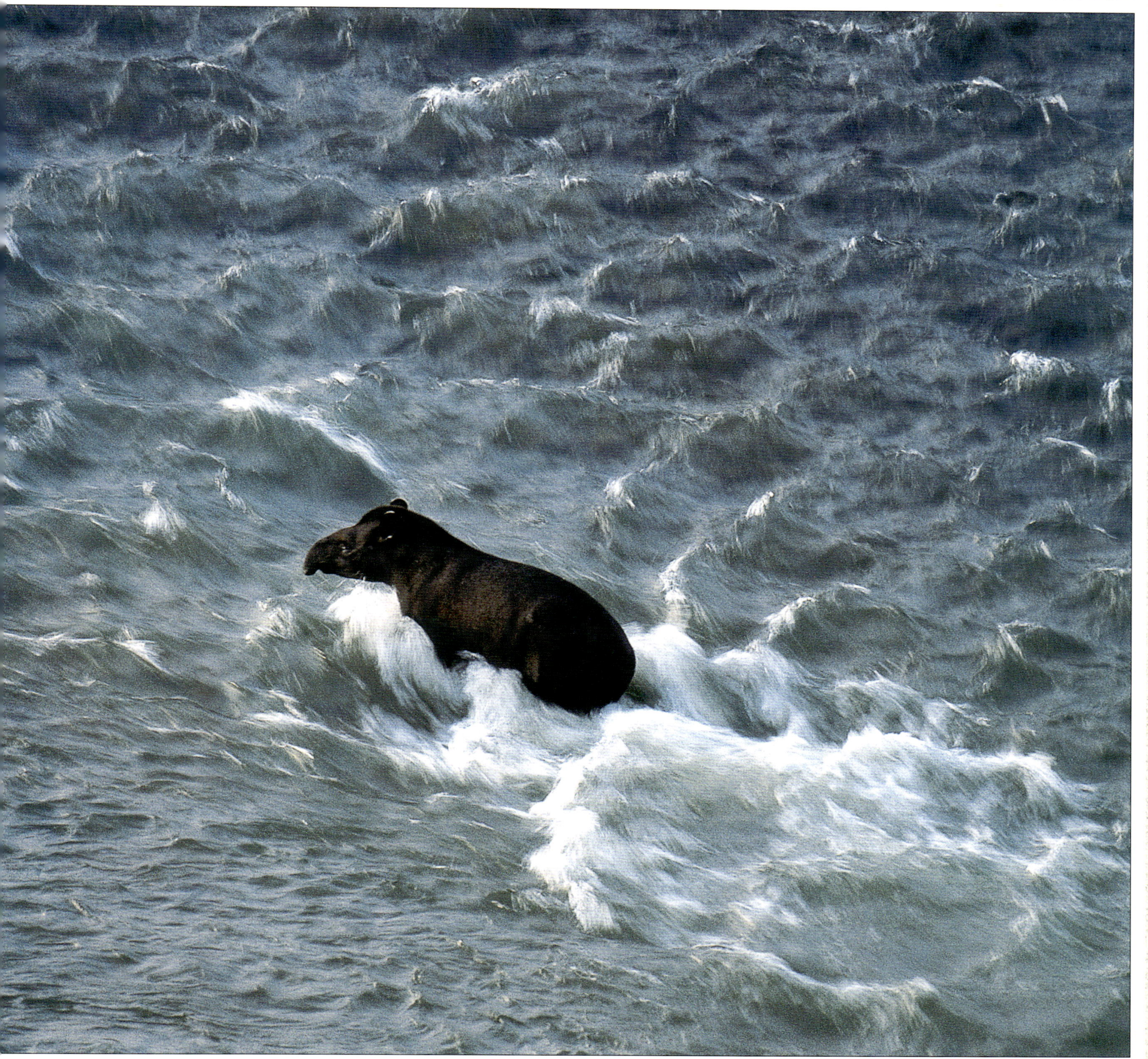

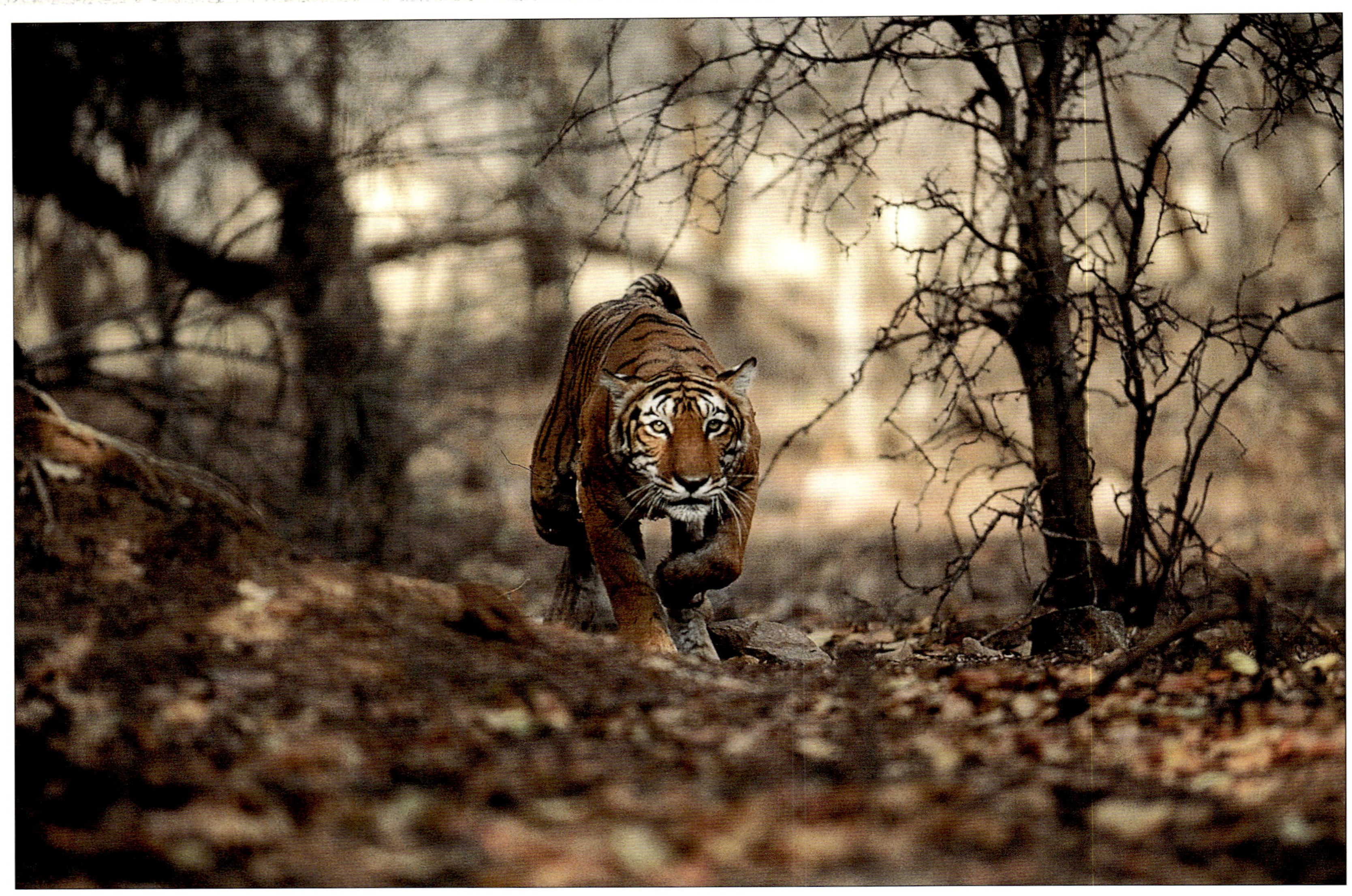

Anup Shah
United Kingdom
RUNNER-UP

Tiger chasing bird

"This drama took place in Ranthambore National Park, India. The tigress had killed a wild boar and retired to rest in the shade. But she was alert to the presence of scavengers and noticed that a tree-pie, a carnivorous bird, had landed on the carcass. In a flash she was up and charging."

Canon EOS 600 with 600mm lens; 1/30 sec at f5.6; Kodachrome

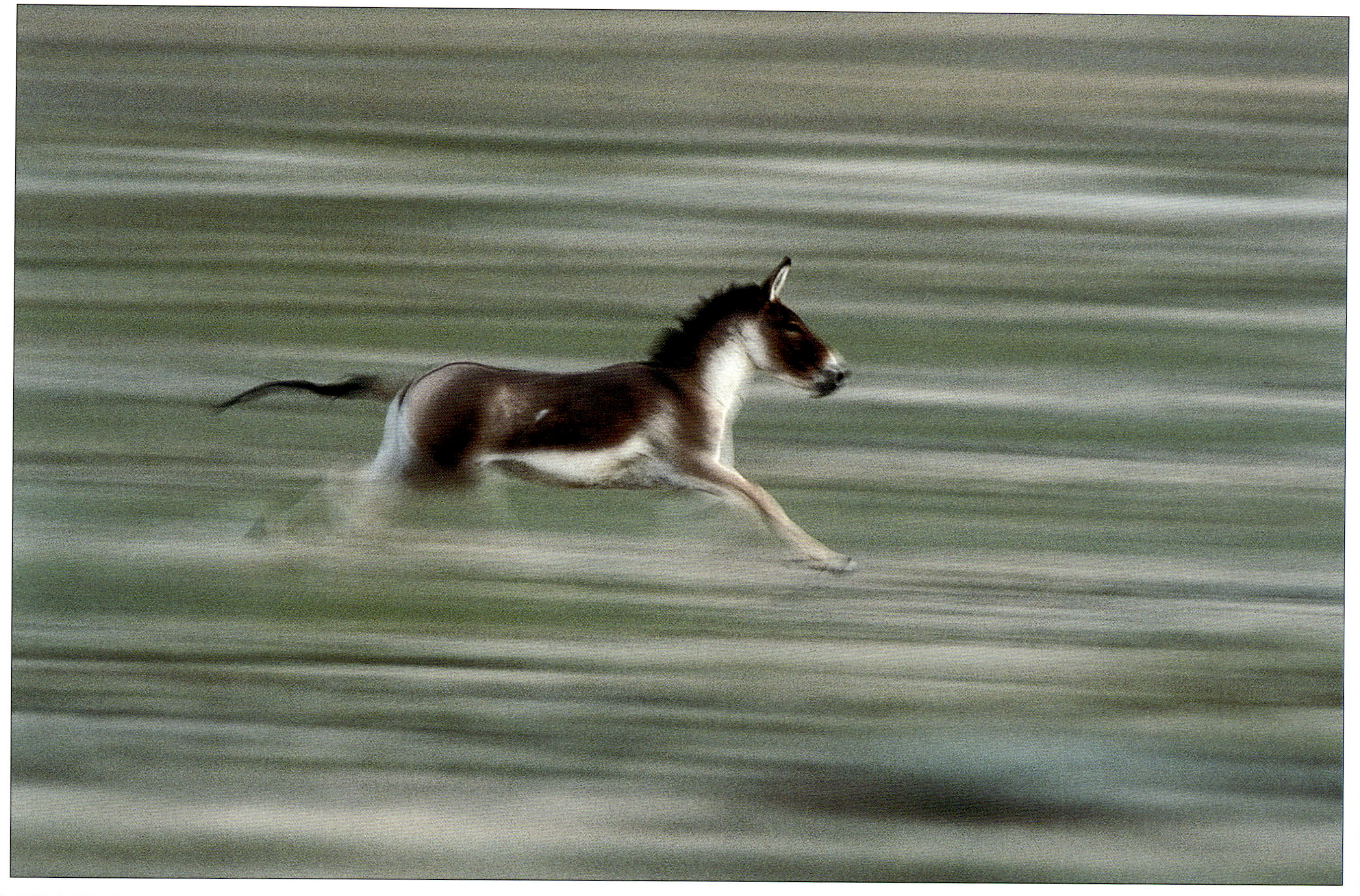

Gertrud & Helmut Denzau
Germany
HIGHLY COMMENDED

Kiang

"While defending his territory during the mating season, this kiang (Tibetan wild ass) had to run long distances over the high mountain plains in the Indo-Tibetan border area. Neighbouring stallions tried to chase mares out of his territory and into their own."

Nikon F4 with 600mm lens; tripod; 1/15 sec at f4; Fujichrome Sensia

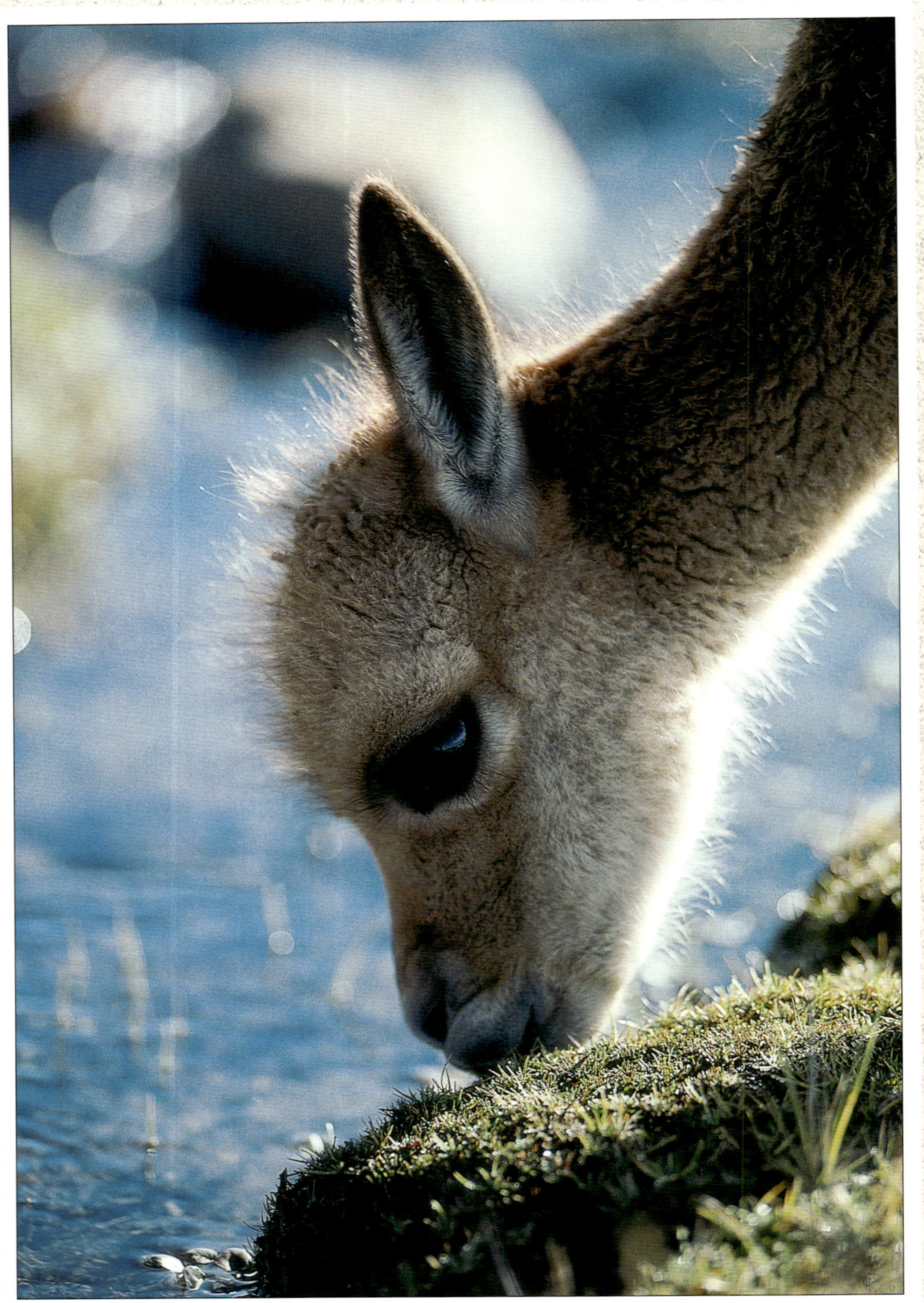

André Bärtschi
Liechtenstein
HIGHLY COMMENDED

Young vicuña feeding on herbs

"One morning I was watching a group of vicuñas beside a small river in Ulla Ulla Biosphere Reserve, Bolivia, when they came close to drink and graze at the river's edge. In this picture, the extreme fineness of the young vicuña's fur is emphasised by backlighting."

Nikon F4 with 300mm lens and x1.4 teleconverter; tripod; Kodachrome 64

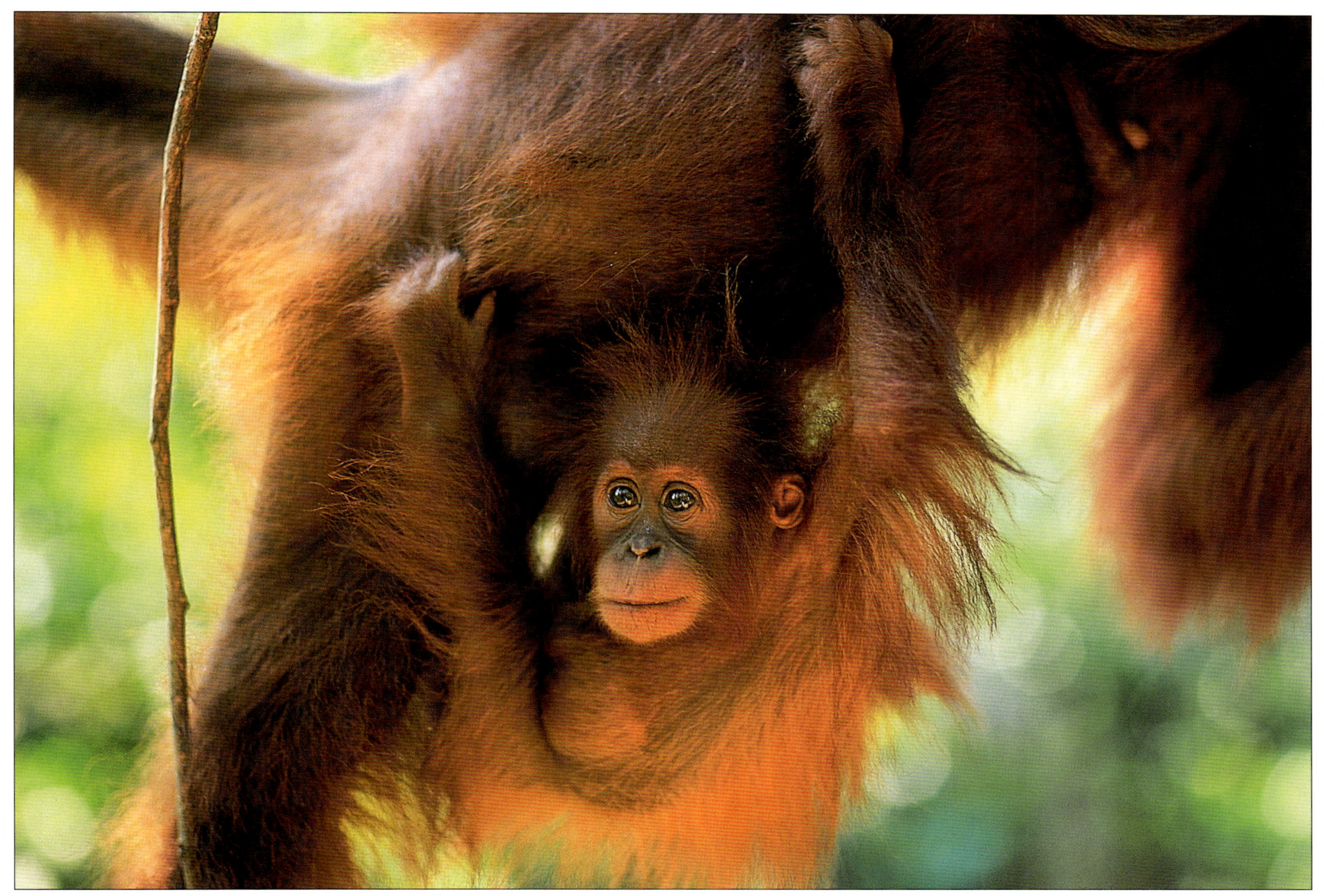

Manoj Shah
United Kingdom
HIGHLY COMMENDED

Orang-utan swinging

"This wild orang-utan mother and baby had come to visit a feeding station at a rehabilitation centre in Leuser National Park, Indonesia. The baby was less than a year old. I had a lucky break, because the sun broke through the clouds and forest canopy to backlight the scene."

Canon EOS 1N with 300mm lens; 1/60 sec at f4;

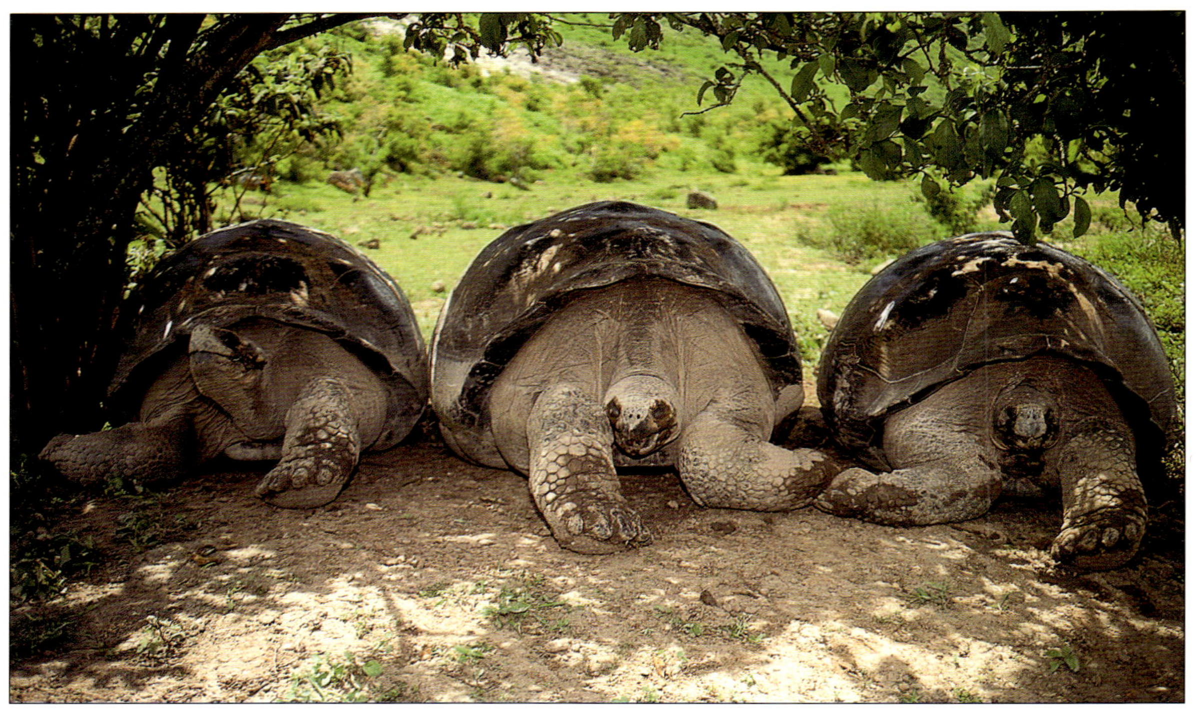

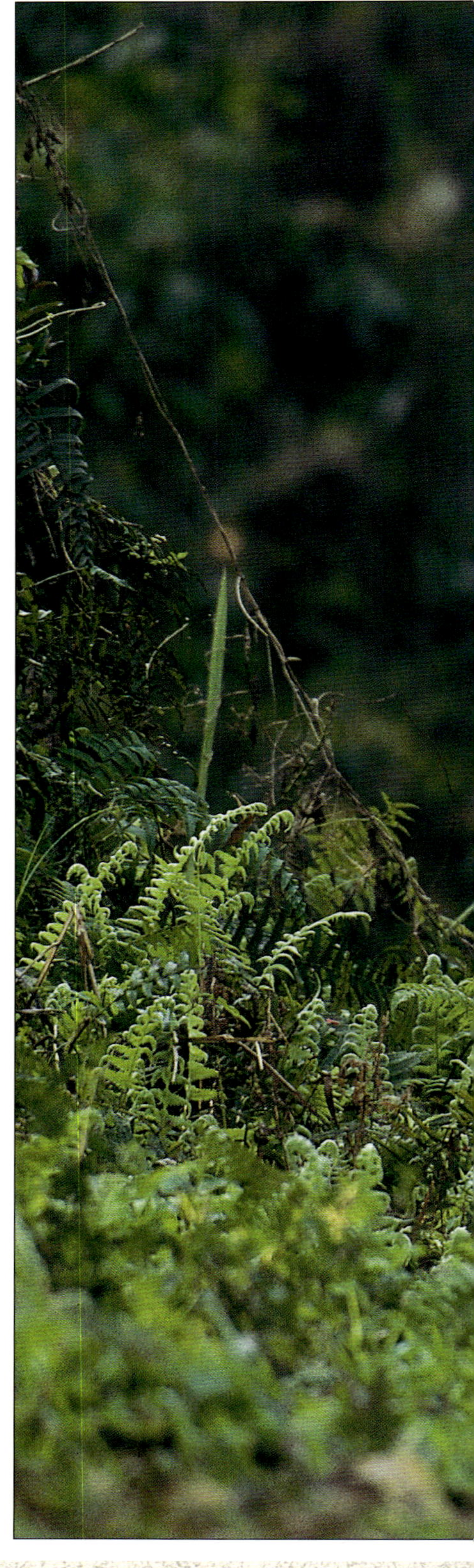

Jonathan R Green
United Kingdom
HIGHLY COMMENDED

Giant tortoises

"This photograph was taken on the crater floor of Alcedo volcano, Galapagos Islands, where giant tortoises, such as these three males, congregate during the rainy season. Sometimes the males are aggressive towards each other, but this is forgotten when the need to find a shady spot becomes a priority."

Minolta Dynax 700i with 80-200mm lens; 1/250 sec at f11; Fujichrome 100

Uwe Anders
Germany
HIGHLY COMMENDED

Greater one-horned rhino

"This rhino appeared from dense forest in Kaziranga National Park, India. When it glanced back over its shoulder it seemed to be saying goodbye, not only as an individual but also as a species. I was deeply impressed and I hope this never becomes a reality."

Canon EOS 1N with 600mm lens; tripod; 1/8 sec at f11; Fujichrome Sensia 100

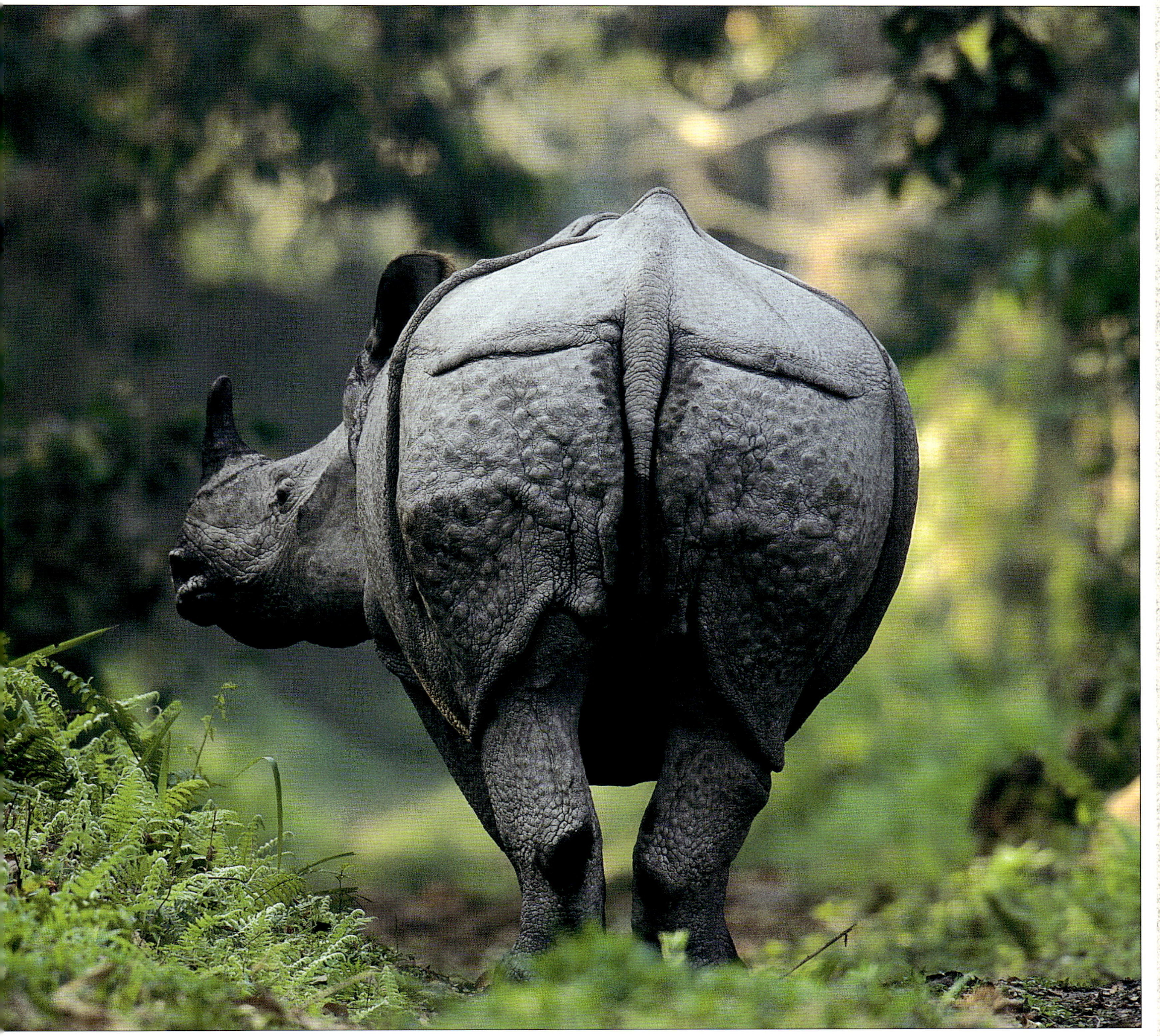

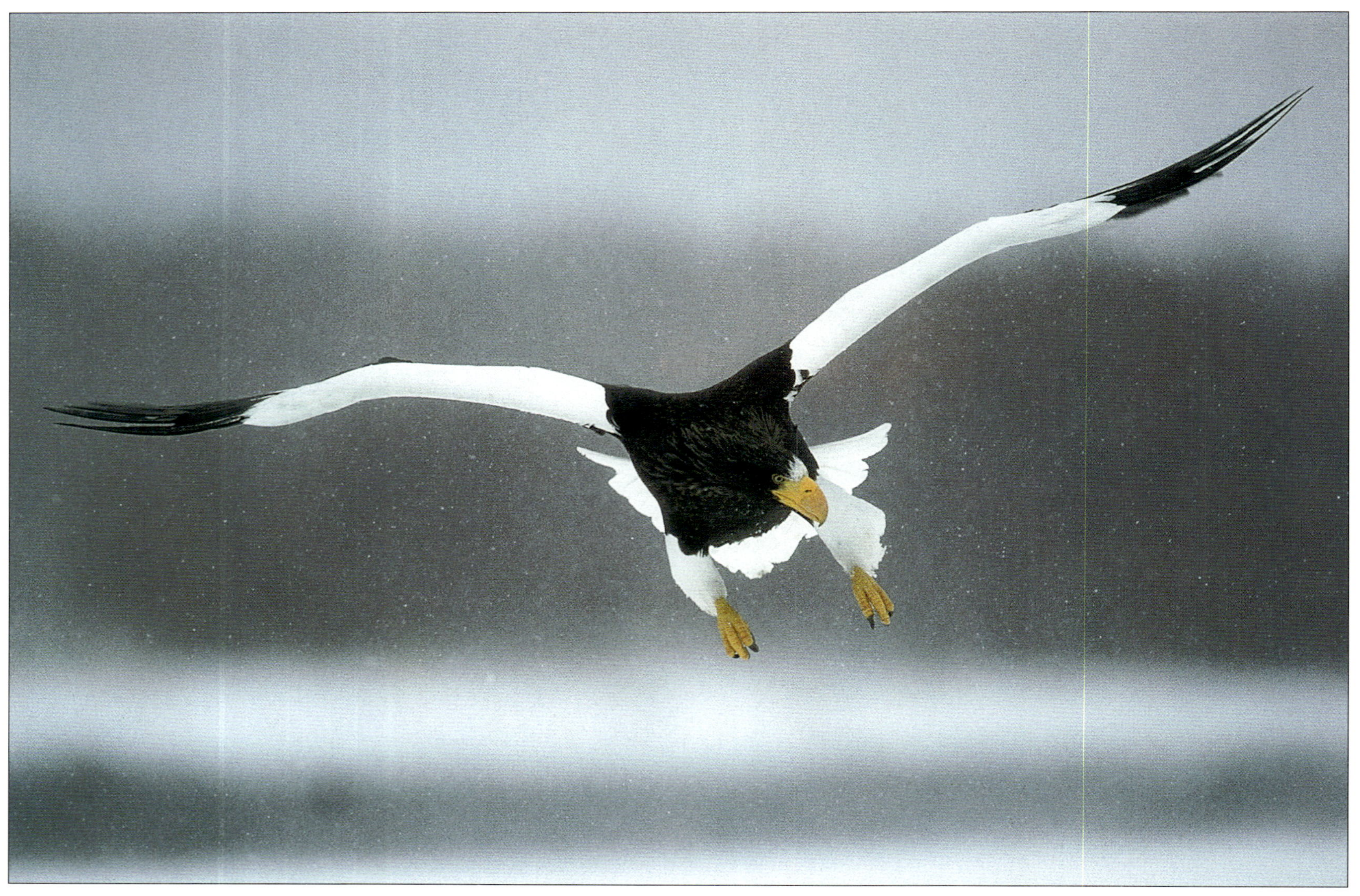

Klaus Nigge
Germany
HIGHLY COMMENDED

Steller's sea eagle

"To take pictures of Steller's sea eagles, I built an igloo on the bank of a river in Kamchatka, where the birds come to feed on dying salmon. Sometimes more than ten eagles gathered in front of my igloo, fighting over a single fish. This one was hovering above such a group."

Nikon F90x with 600mm lens; Fujichrome Sensia 100

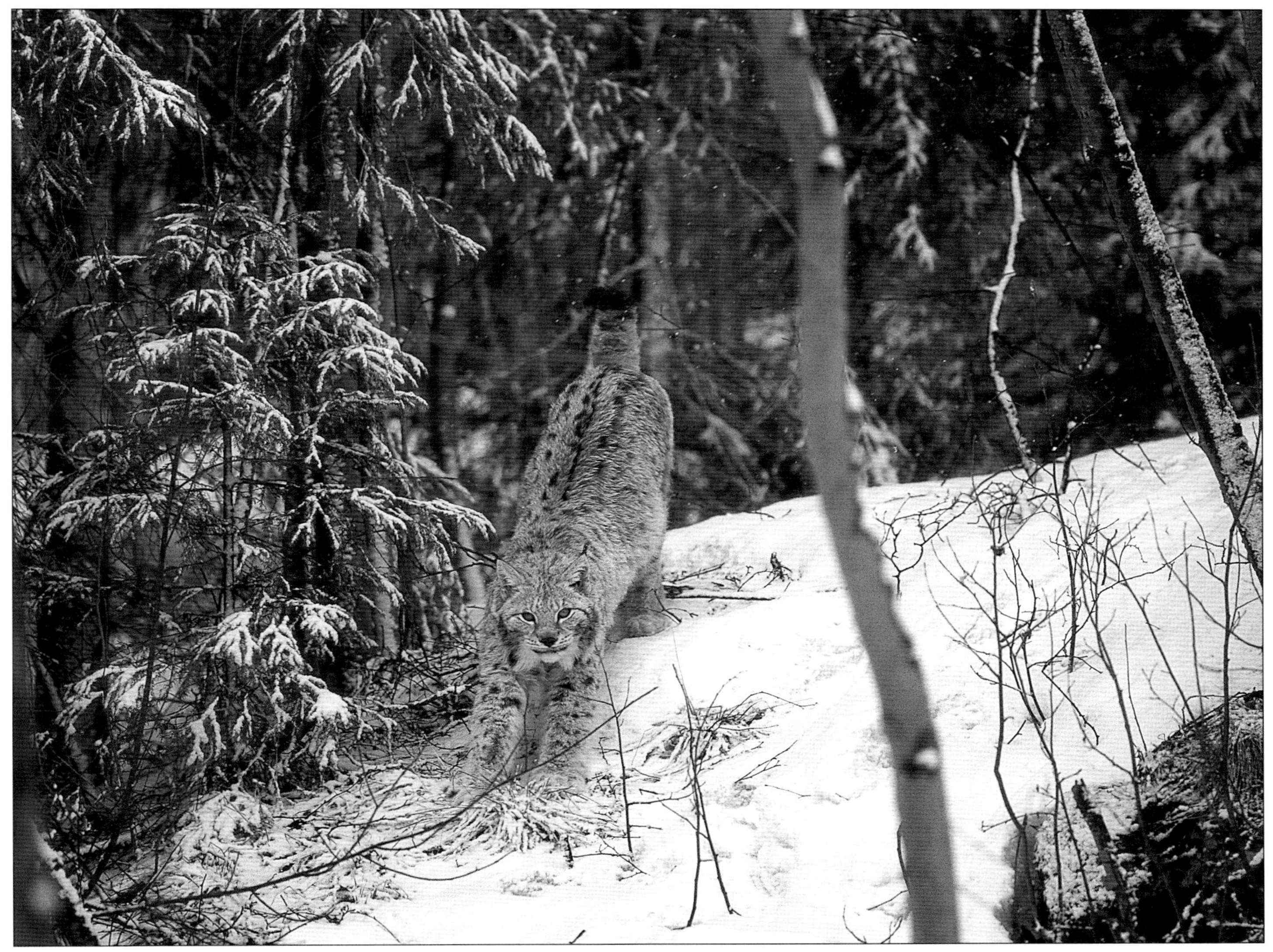

Kjell Ljungström
Sweden
HIGHLY COMMENDED

Lynx

"This Swedish lynx has just arrived from its resting place and is stretching before dining on a freshly killed roe deer. Lynx are shy and elusive, and their presence is often revealed only through tracks in the snow. Glimpses of them are rare."

Nikon F4s with 180mm lens; 1/125 sec at f2.8; Fujichrome Sensia

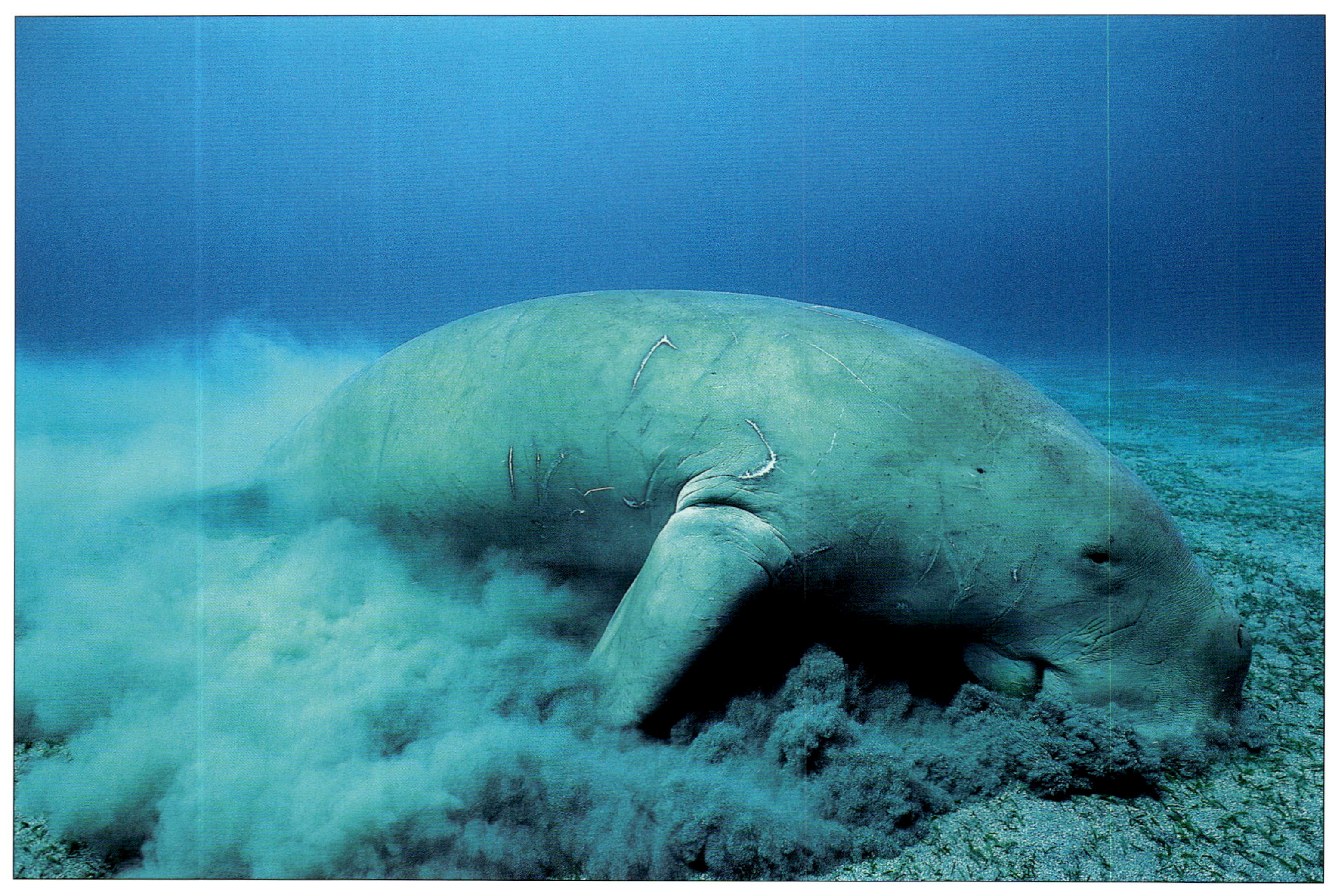

Kelvin Aitken
Australia
HIGHLY COMMENDED

Dugong feeding

"The scars on this male dugong are the result of battles with other males over females and territory. I spotted him off an isolated island in Vanuatu just half an hour before I was due to leave for the airfield. I fired off one film before swimming back to shore and flopping into my vehicle with dripping cameras and dive gear."

Nikonos V with 15mm lens; 1/60 sec at f4; Kodachrome 64 rated at 80

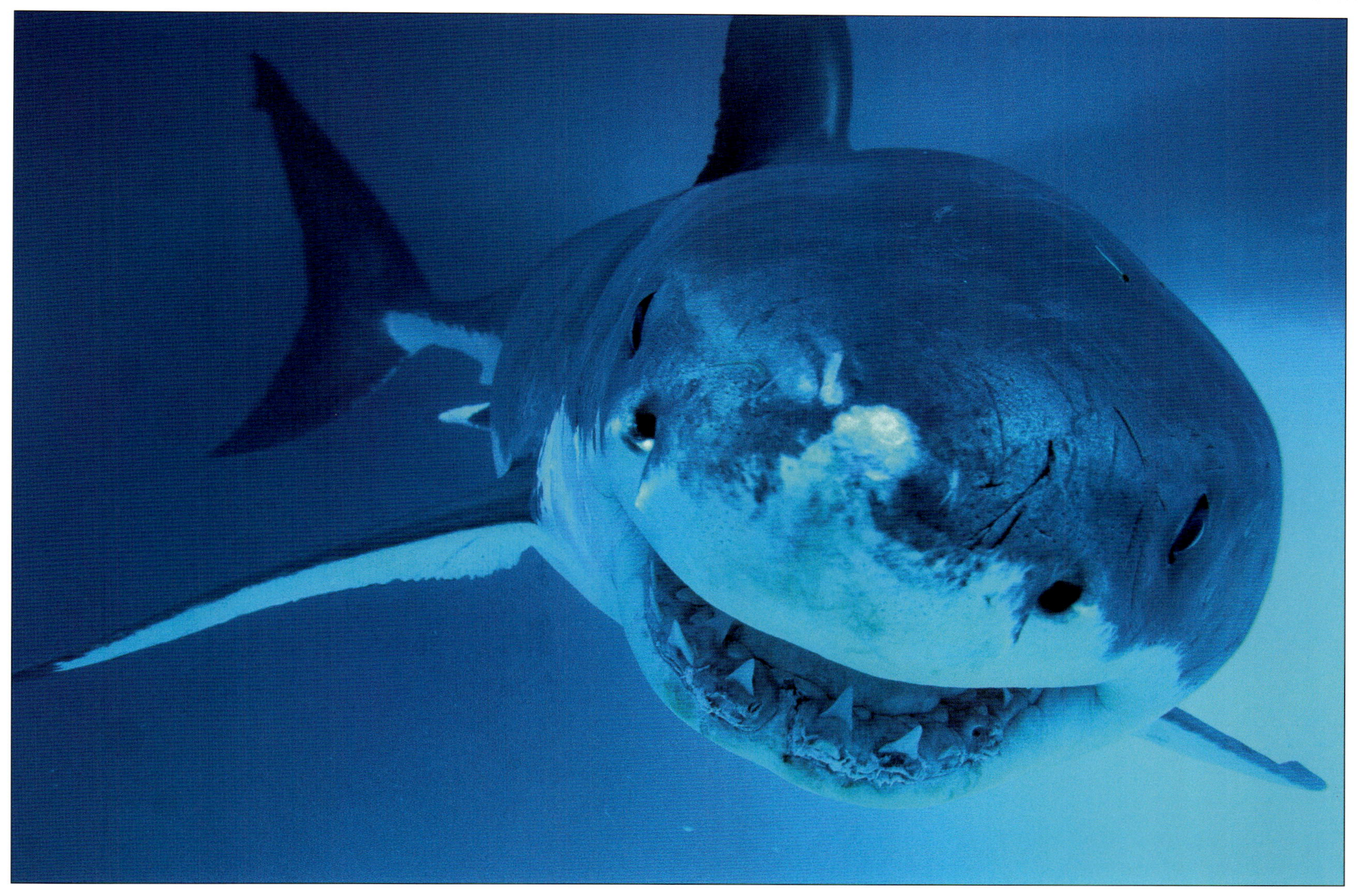

David B Fleetham
Canada
HIGHLY COMMENDED

Great white shark

"This picture was taken during a great white shark expedition last year off the South Neptune Islands. We were protected by an aluminium shark cage, but on this last shot of the series the shark's nose pushed the camera right back into the cage."

Canon EOS 10S with 35-200mm zoom lens; underwater housing; Kodak LPZ rated at 200

Animal Portraits

The photographs entered in this category should show the subjects in close-up.

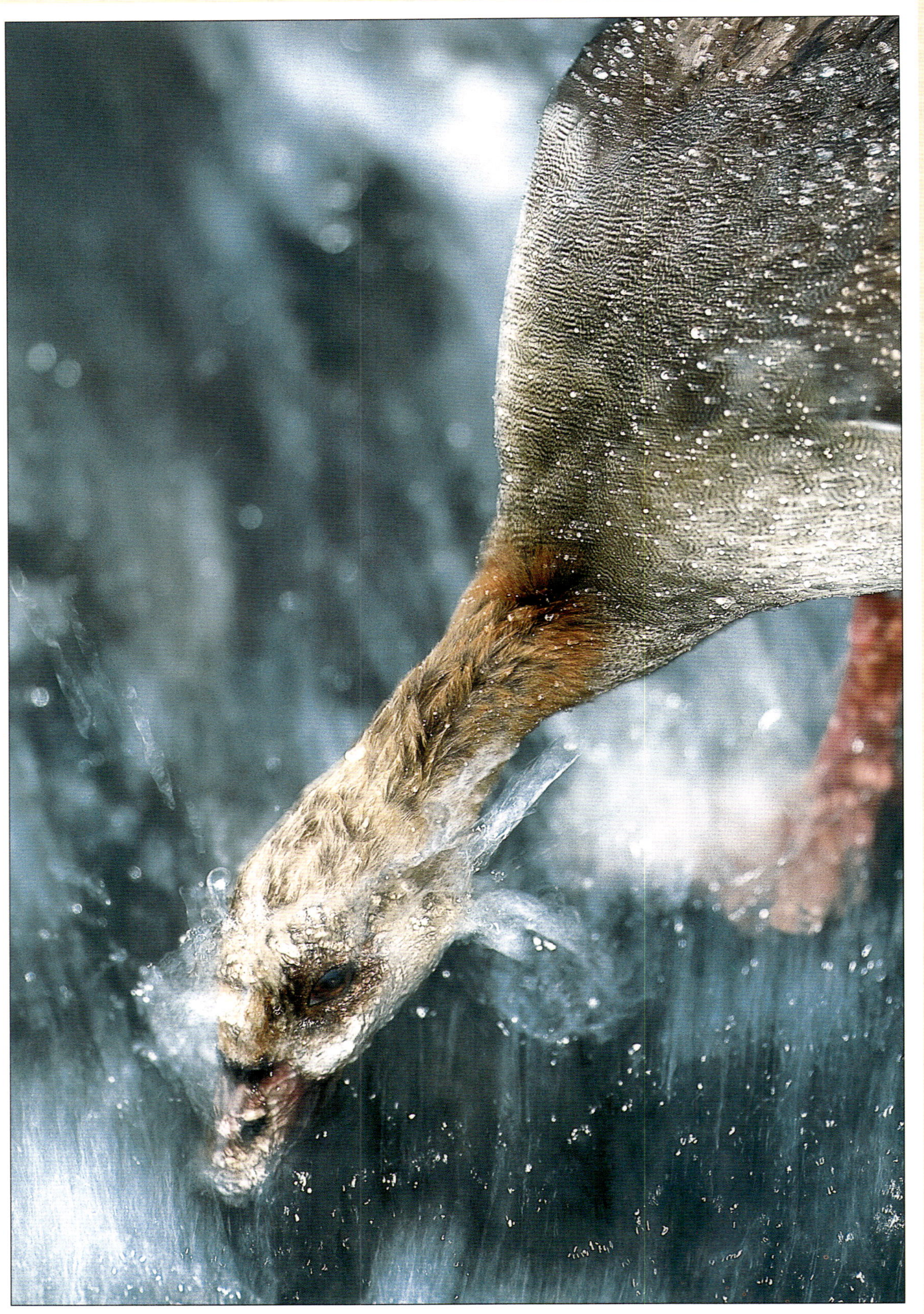

Richard du Toit
South Africa
WINNER

Egyptian goose

"Late one afternoon a family of Egyptian geese arrived at the Sabie River, Kruger National Park, and one of them started feeding on underwater algae growing on the rocks. When the goose submerged its head, spectacular cascades of water sprayed over its body."

Canon EOS 5 with 500mm lens; beanbag; flash; 1/60 sec at f4.5; Fujichrome Velvia

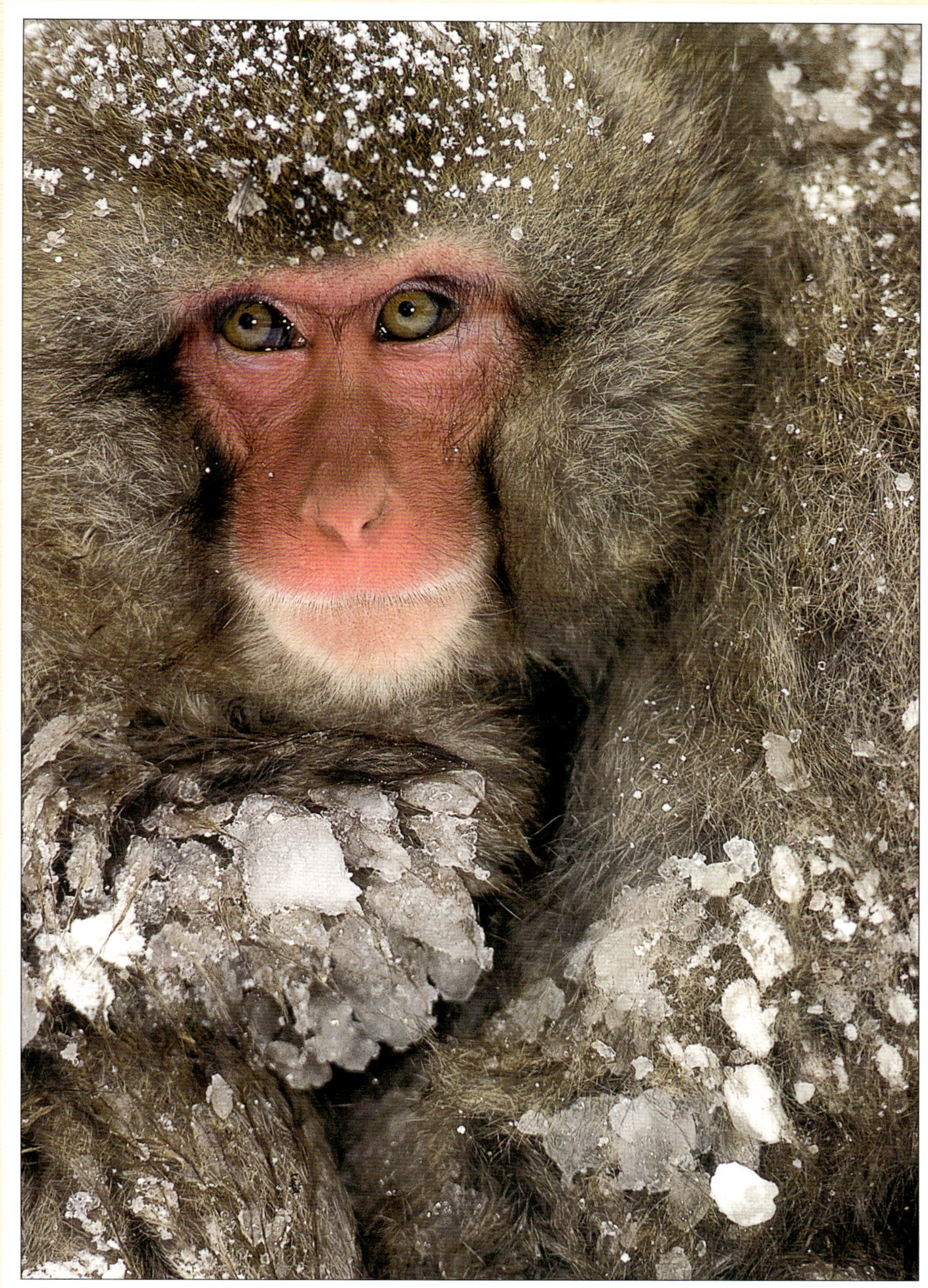

Daniel J Cox
United States of America
RUNNER-UP

Snow monkey

"This photo was taken at Jigokudani, where Japanese red-faced macaques spend many hours basking in the warm waters of thermal springs. It was a cold snowy day, but the snow was wet and it clung to the monkey's fur."

Nikon F5 with 80-200mm lens; tripod; Fujichrome Provia

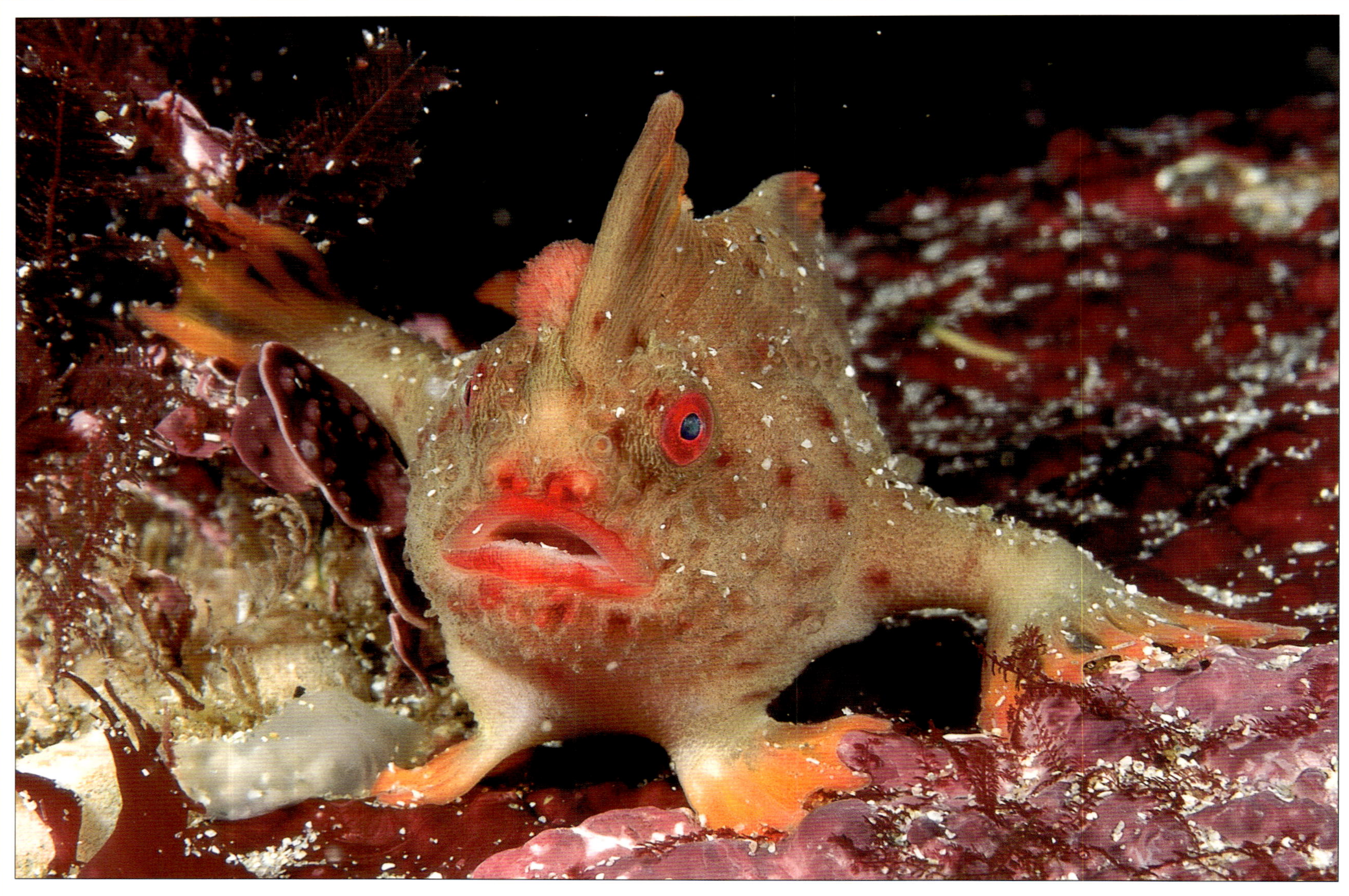

Fred Bavendam
United States of America
SPECIALLY COMMENDED

Red handfish

"In 1995 I went to Tasmania with the intention of photographing handfish. Tasmania is one of the few places in the world where these relatives of anglerfish are reliably found at depths suitable for divers. This is one of two species I was able to photograph."

Nikon F4 with 105mm macro lens in underwater housing; two strobes; 1/125 sec at f22; Fujichrome Sensia

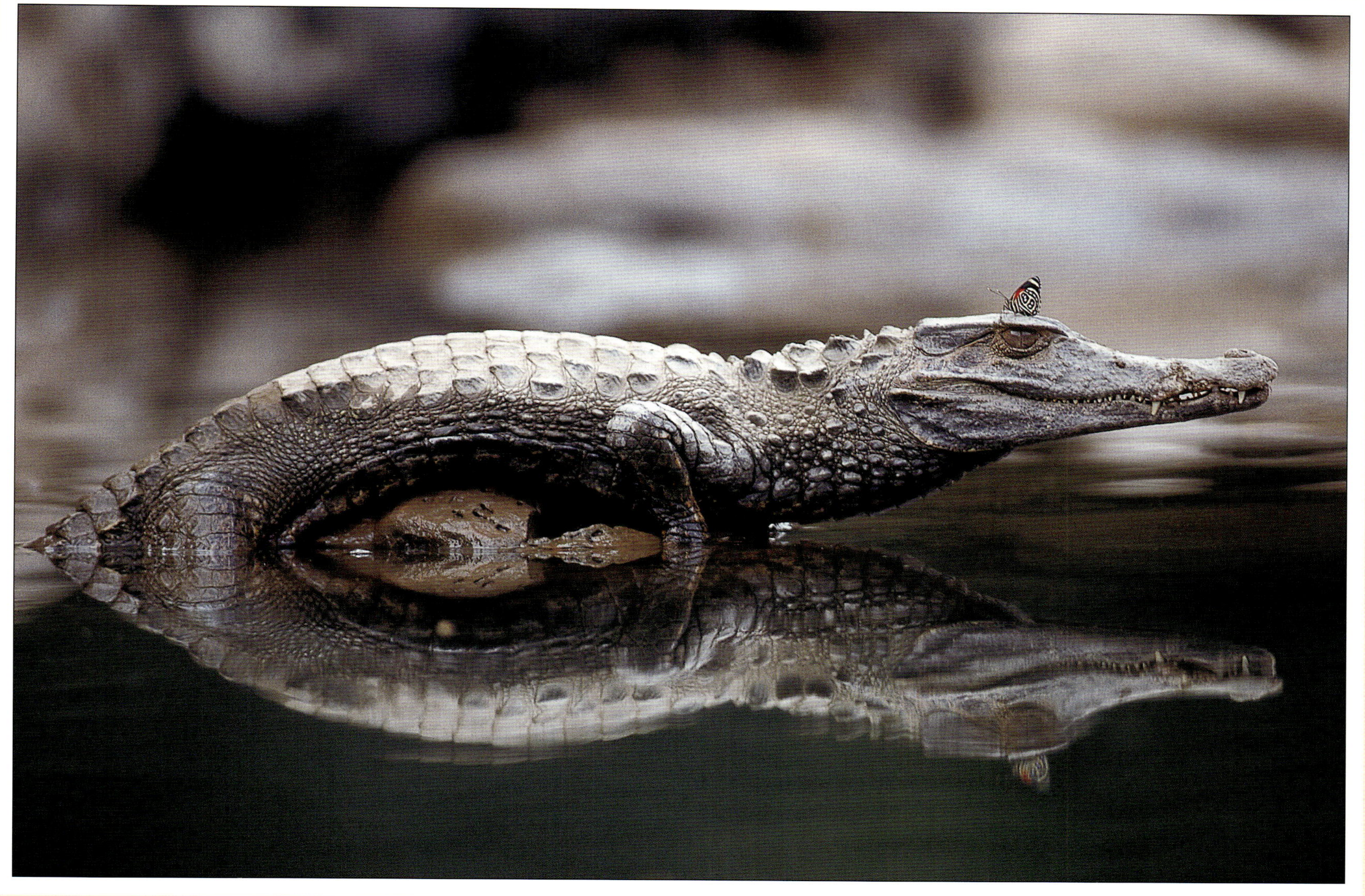

André Bärtschi
Liechtenstein
SPECIALLY COMMENDED

Caiman with butterfly

"I found this Schneider's dwarf caiman basking on a rock on the shore of the Távara River, Peru. I had taken a couple of photographs, when a nymphalid butterfly fluttered into the scene and dipped down to sip salty fluids from the caiman's eye."

Nikon F4 with 300mm lens; 1/250 sec at f2.8; Fujichrome Provia

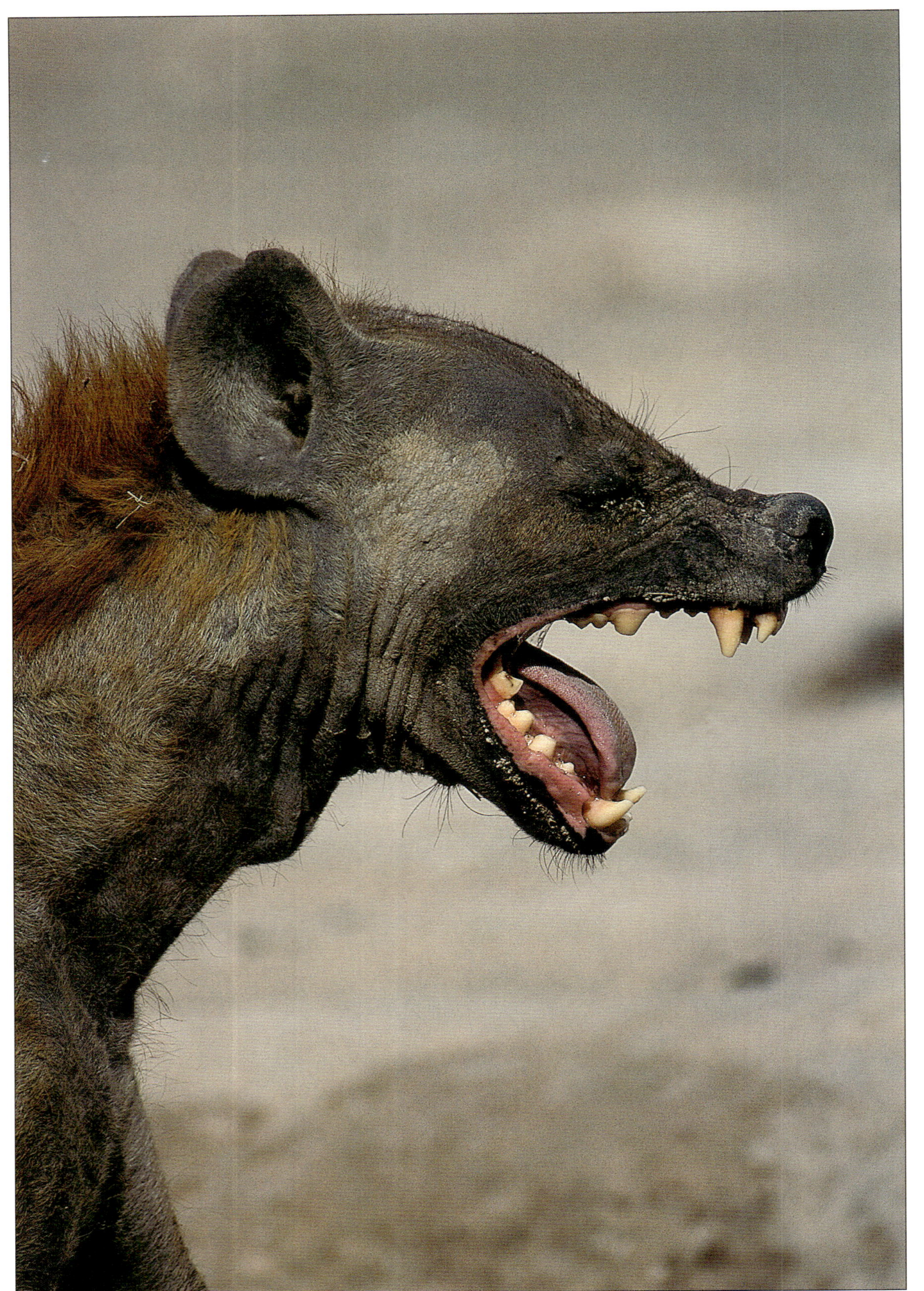

Karl Ammann
Switzerland
HIGHLY COMMENDED

Spotted hyena

"Spotted hyenas often lie outside their dens in the late afternoon. When I drove up to this one in the Serengeti, it sat up and looked around without focusing on me. I was just ready when the yawn came, but I have to admit that I would have preferred a head-on view."

Nikon F4 with 800mm lens; window mount; 1/90 sec at f5.6; Fujichrome Velvia

Heinrich van den Berg
South Africa
HIGHLY COMMENDED

Lion cub carrying bone

"We followed a party of lions as they walked down a dry riverbed in Kalahari Gemsbok National Park. Only when they crossed the road did we notice that this proud cub was carrying part of a wildebeest's leg, perhaps as a trophy, or as food for the journey."

Canon EOS 5 with 300mm lens and x1.4 converter; 1/500 sec at f4; Fujichrome Velvia

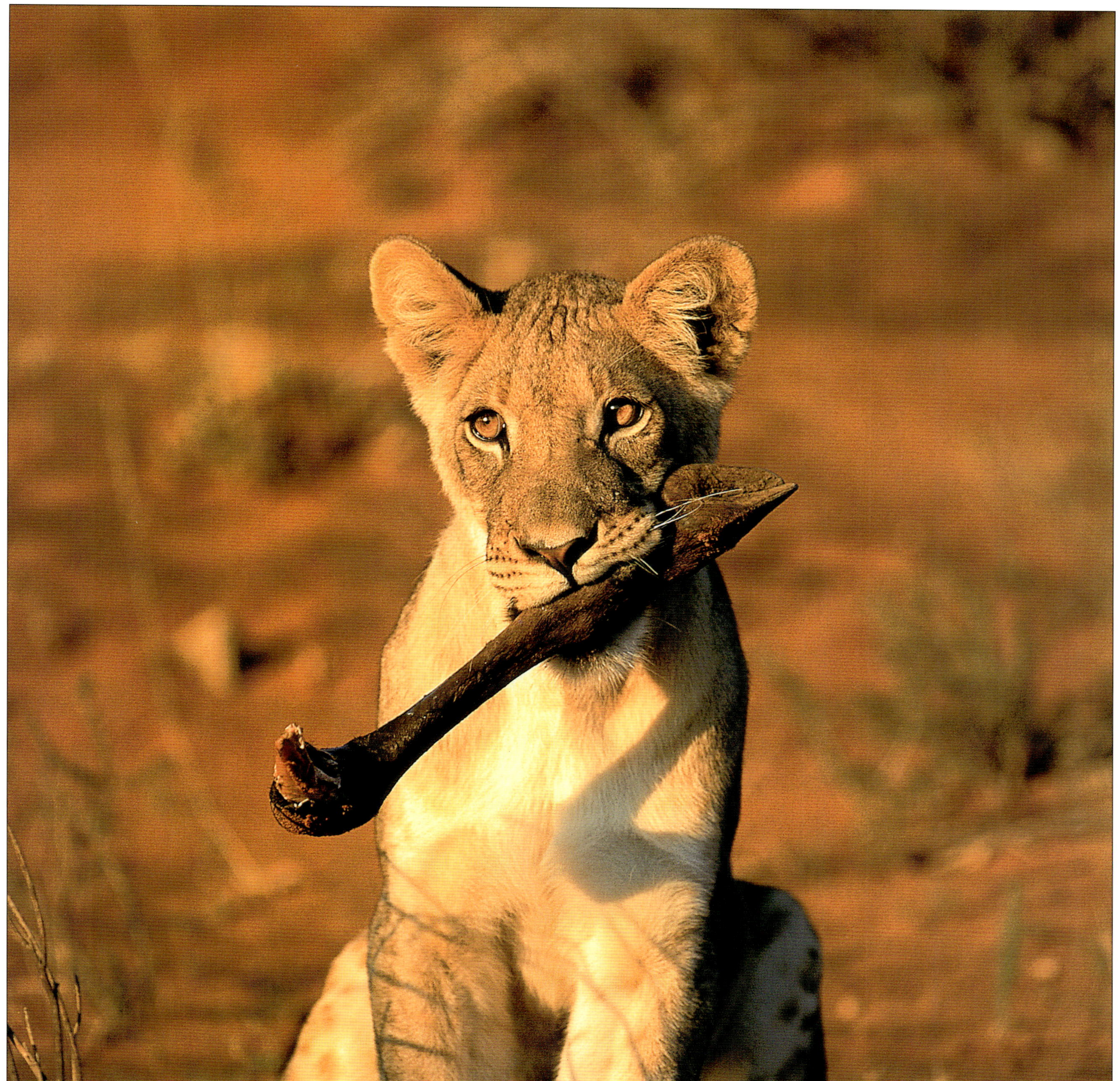

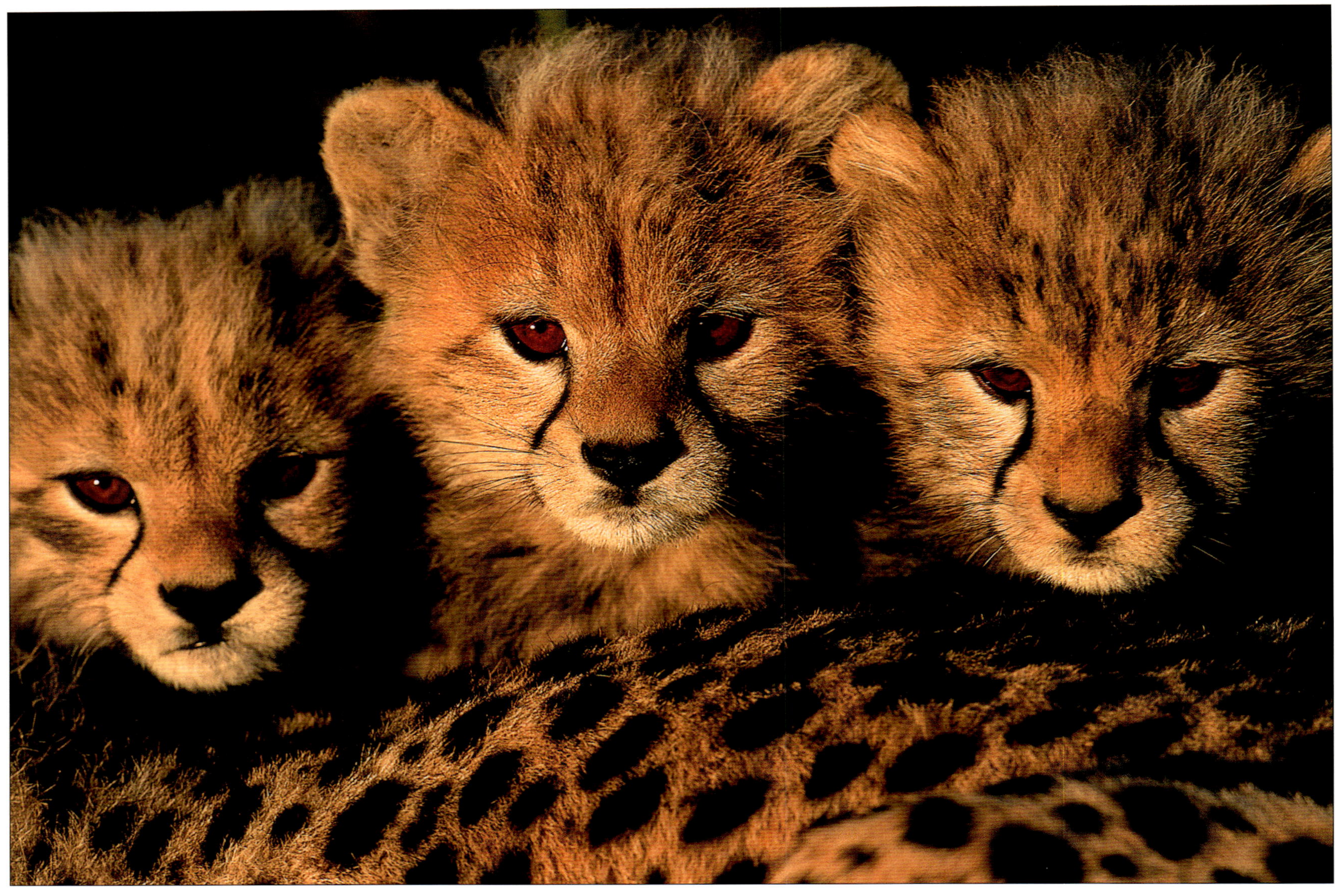

Anup Shah
United Kingdom
HIGHLY COMMENDED

Cheetah cubs

"I took this photograph just after daybreak in Kenya's Maasai Mara Reserve. The three cheetah cubs rested their faces on their mother's warm belly, perhaps because they were feeling the cold."

Canon EOS 1N with 600mm lens; 1/125 sec at f4;

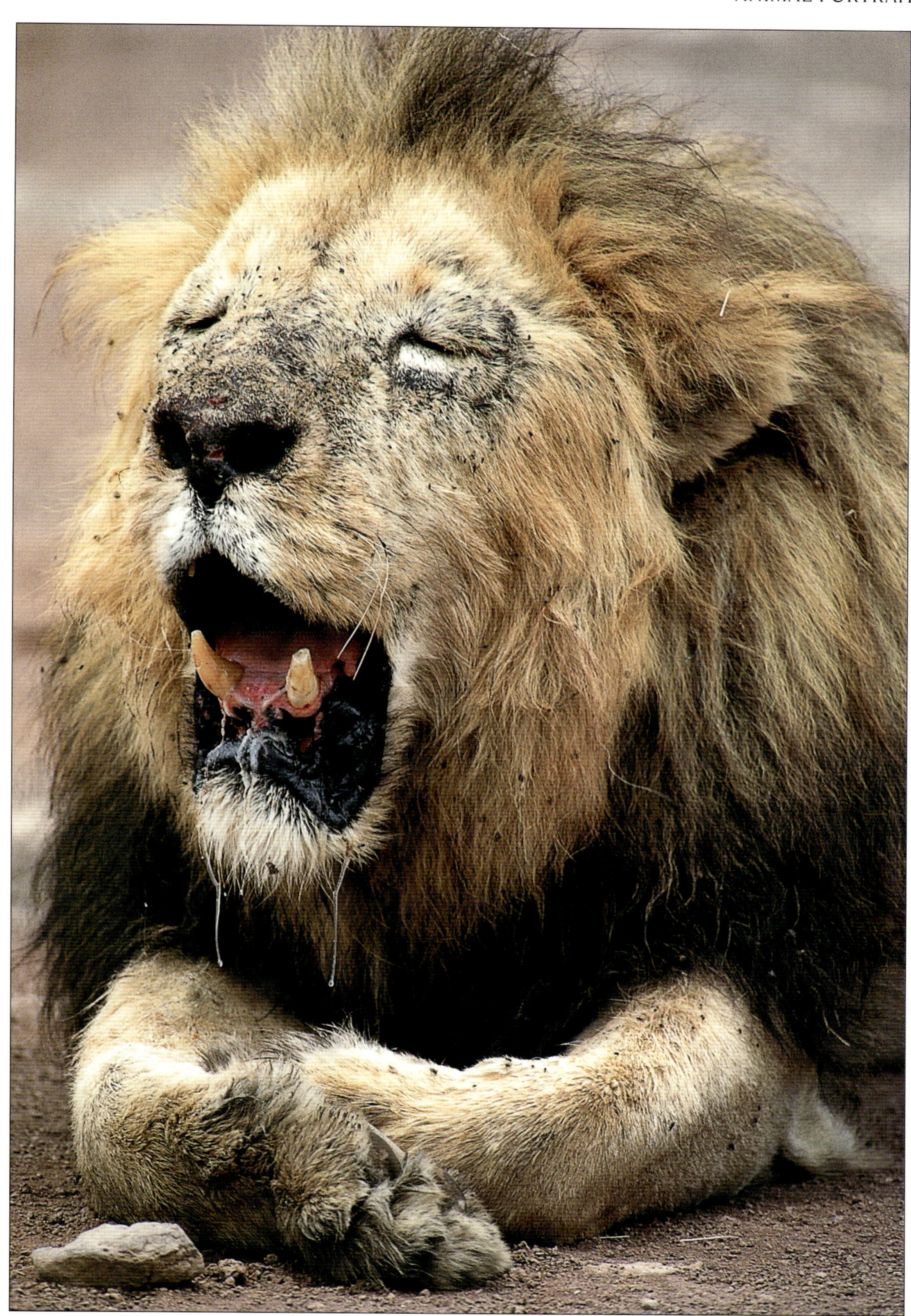

Romain Grisius
Luxembourg
HIGHLY COMMENDED

Old lion

"I was on a game drive across the Ngorongoro Crater, Tanzania, when I caught sight of this lion. I came to the conclusion that he was old because he had a marked, dark mane and because his canine teeth were rather worn out."

Canon A1 with 300mm lens; 1/250 sec at f5.6; Fujichrome Sensia 100

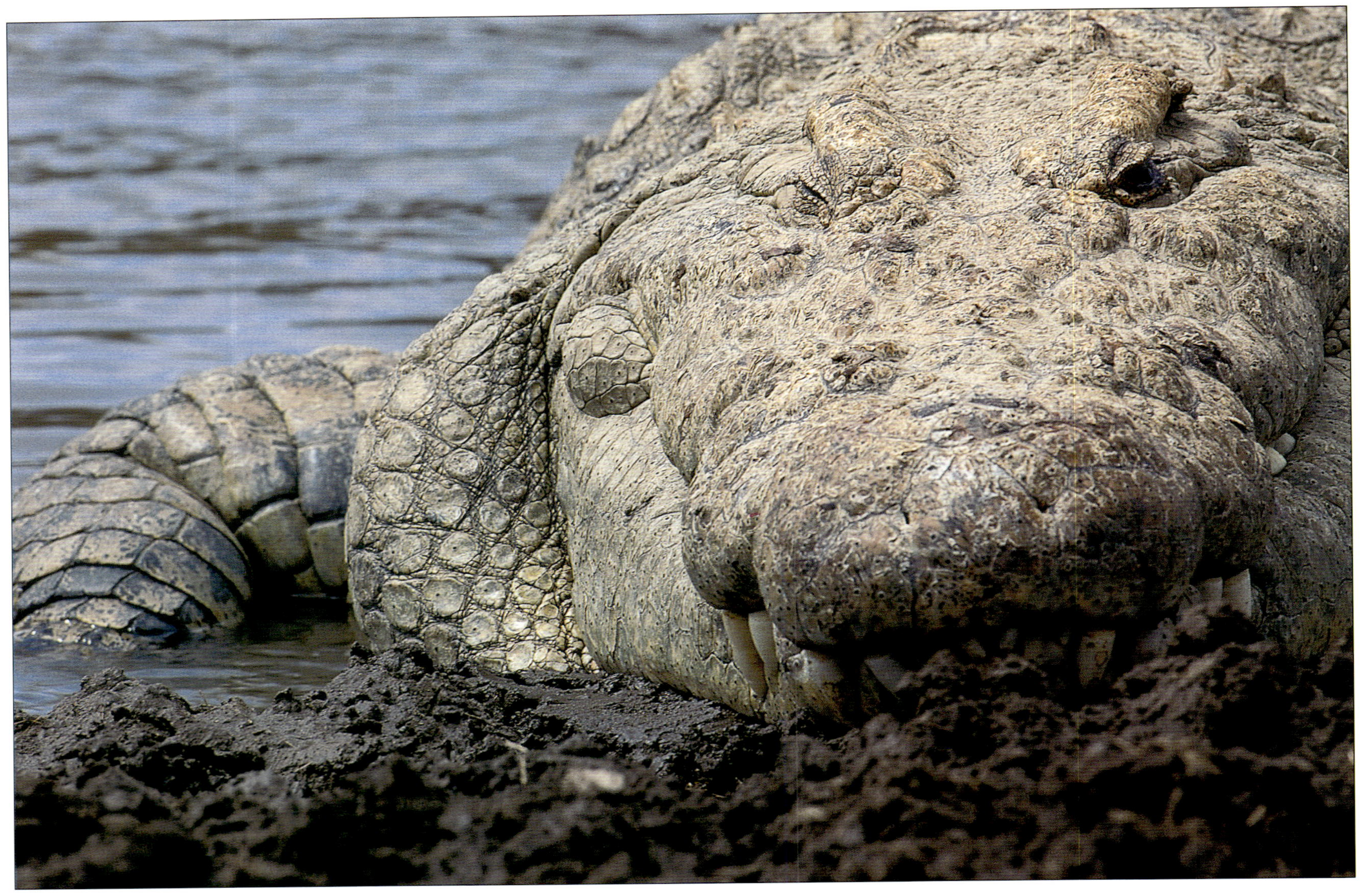

Peter Blackwell
United Kingdom
HIGHLY COMMENDED

Nile crocodile

"I encountered this crocodile at the Mara River, Kenya. It kept a watchful eye on me as I took this photograph."

Nikon N90 with 500mm lens; 1/250 sec at f8; Fujichrome Velvia rated at 80

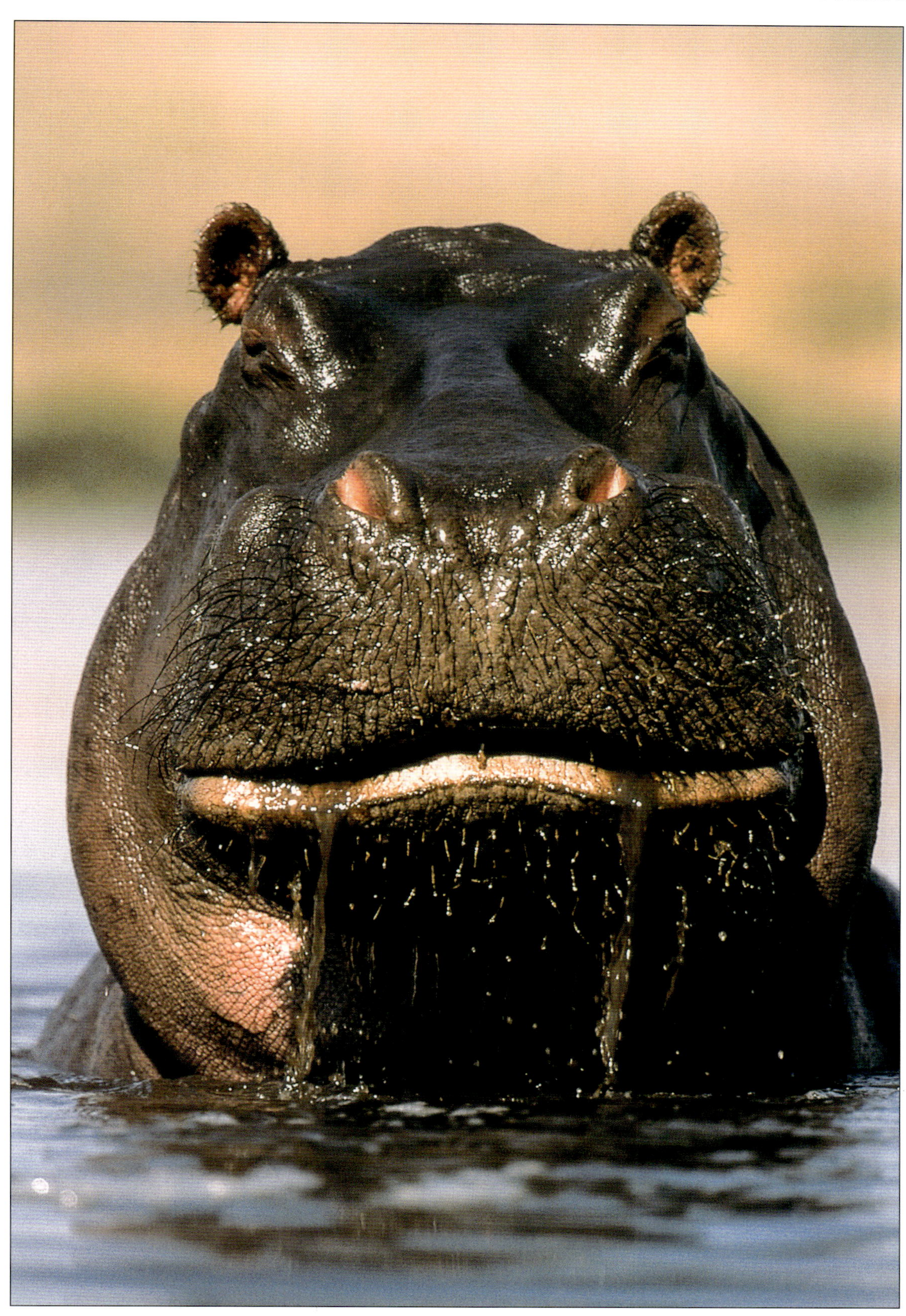

John Conrad
United States of America
HIGHLY COMMENDED

Hippo

"We were watching a pod of hippos from the safety of our vehicle, when this big fellow began to charge. I managed to take this grab shot before our driver retreated."

Canon EOS 5 with 35-350mm lens; 1/500 sec at f5.6; Fujichrome 100

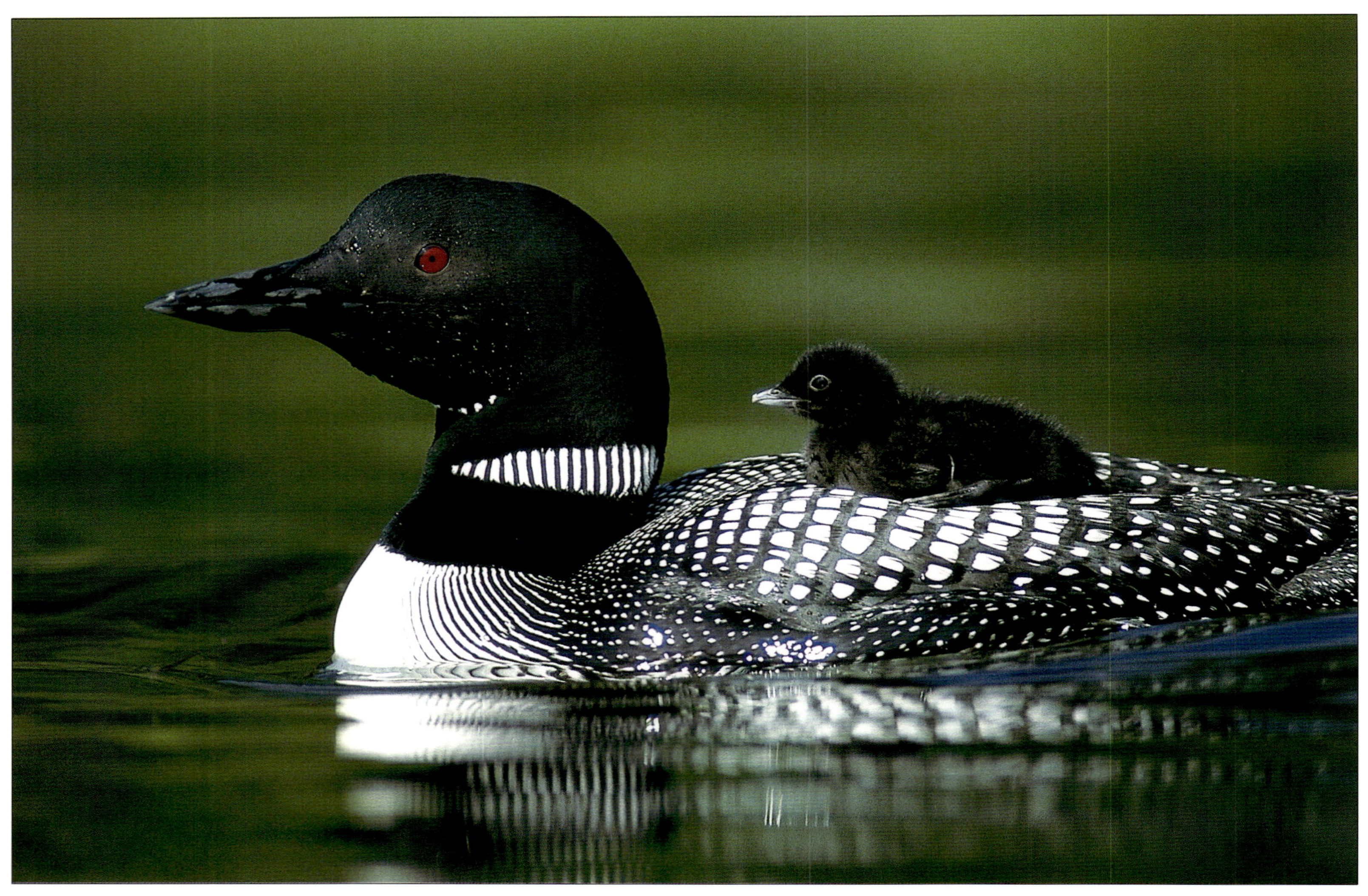

Gary L Lackie

United States of America

HIGHLY COMMENDED

Common loon and chick

"For a number of years loons have been nesting at this lake near Anchorage, Alaska, despite the fact that it is used as a floatplane landing and take-off area. The chicks ride on their parents' backs for only about a week, knowing when they were going to hatch was a crucial part of getting the photo."

Canon 10s with 400mm lens and x1.4 extender; monopod; 1/250 sec at f4; Fujichrome Velvia

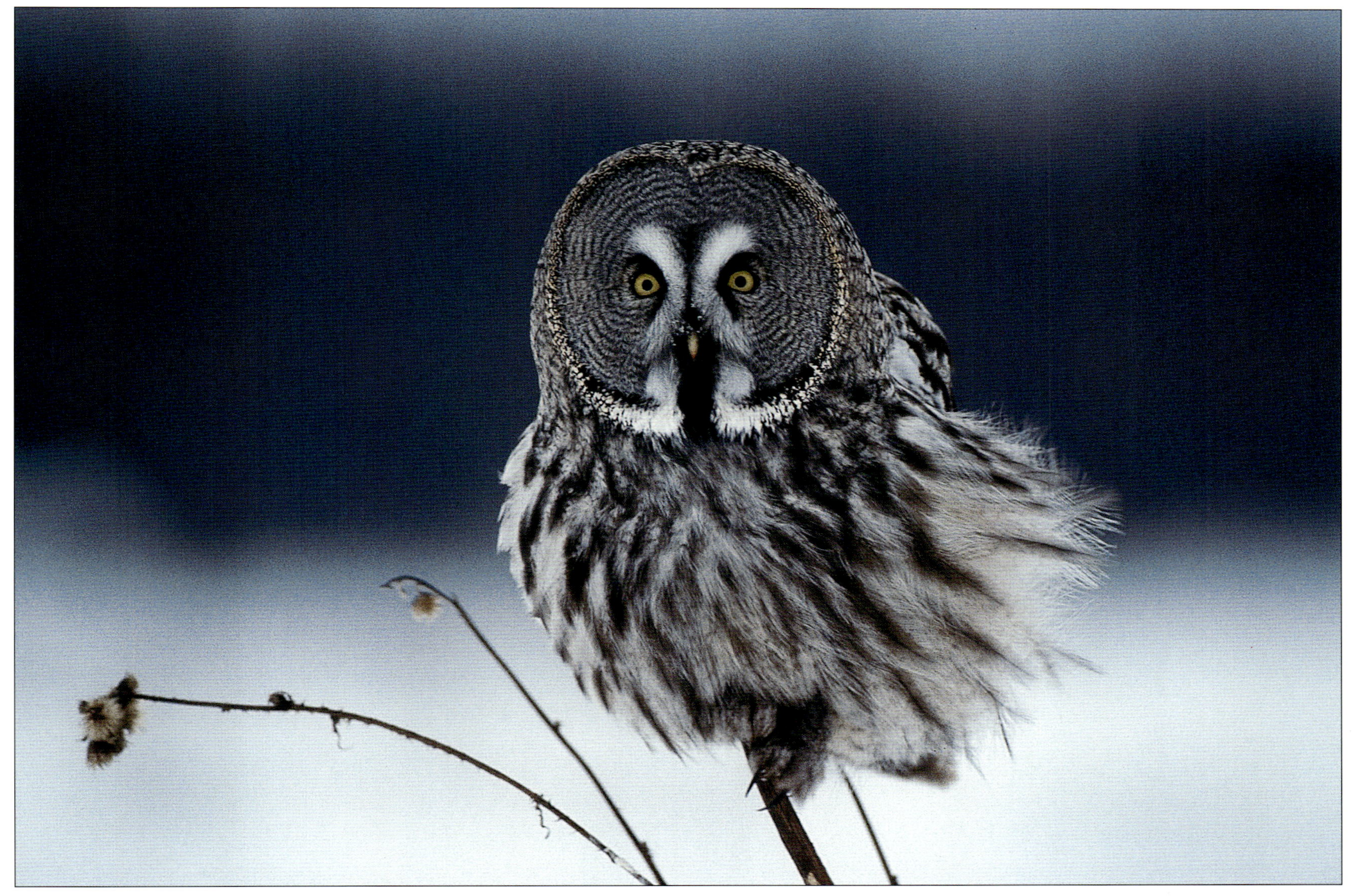

Tero Niemi
Sweden
HIGHLY COMMENDED

Great grey owl

"Great grey owls are birds of the cold Northern forests. This one was hunting voles outside Skellefteå in the Västerbotten region of Northern Sweden."

Nikon F90 with 500mm lens; Fujichrome 100

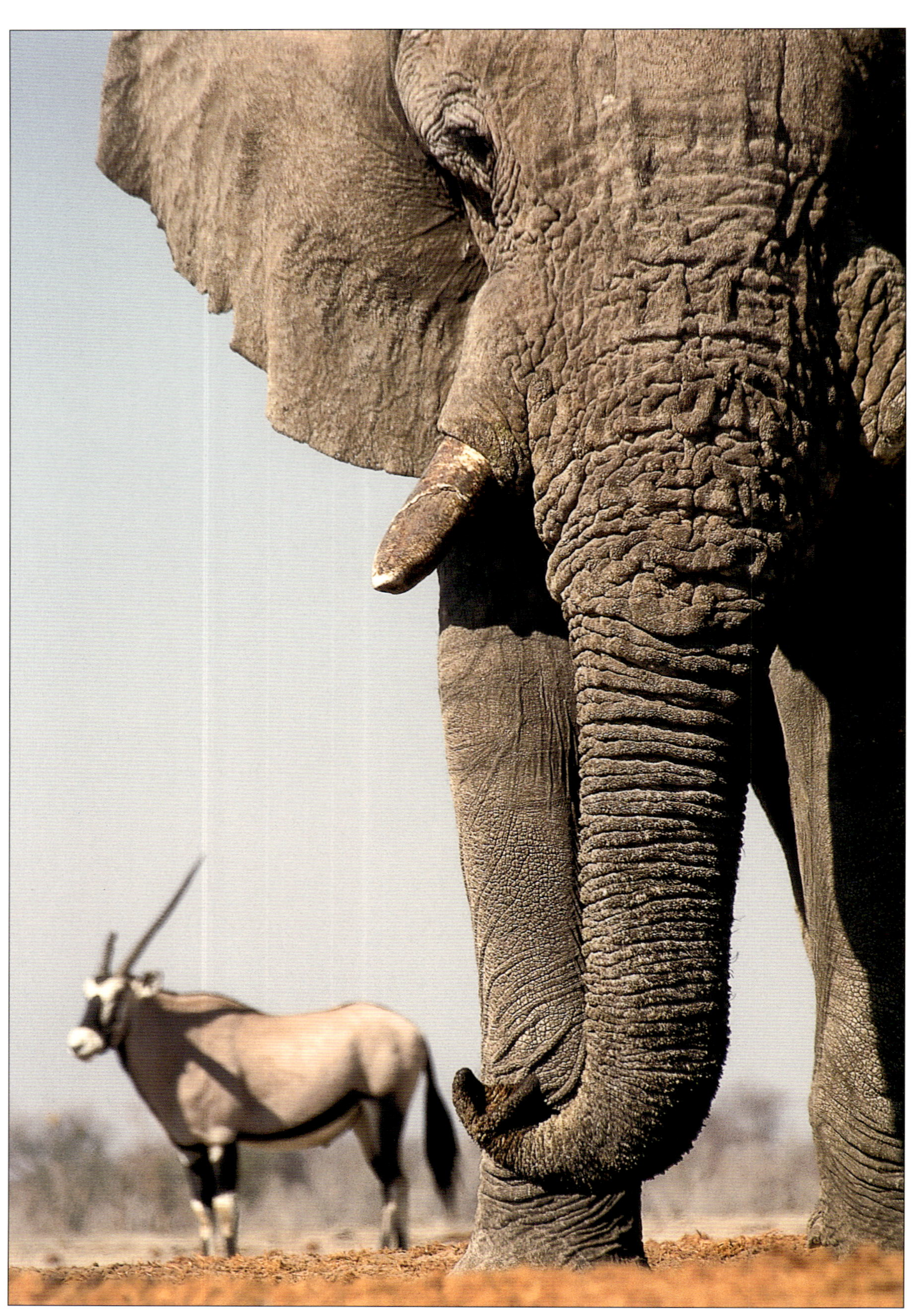

Jill Sneesby
& Barrie Wilkins
South Africa
HIGHLY COMMENDED

Elephant and gemsbok

"We waited by a water hole at Etosha Pan, Namibia, and photographed this elephant with different animals as they came to drink. This picture was our favourite, as it emphasised the power of the elephant."

Canon EOS 1N with 100-300mm lens; 1/250 sec at f11; Fujichrome Provia 100

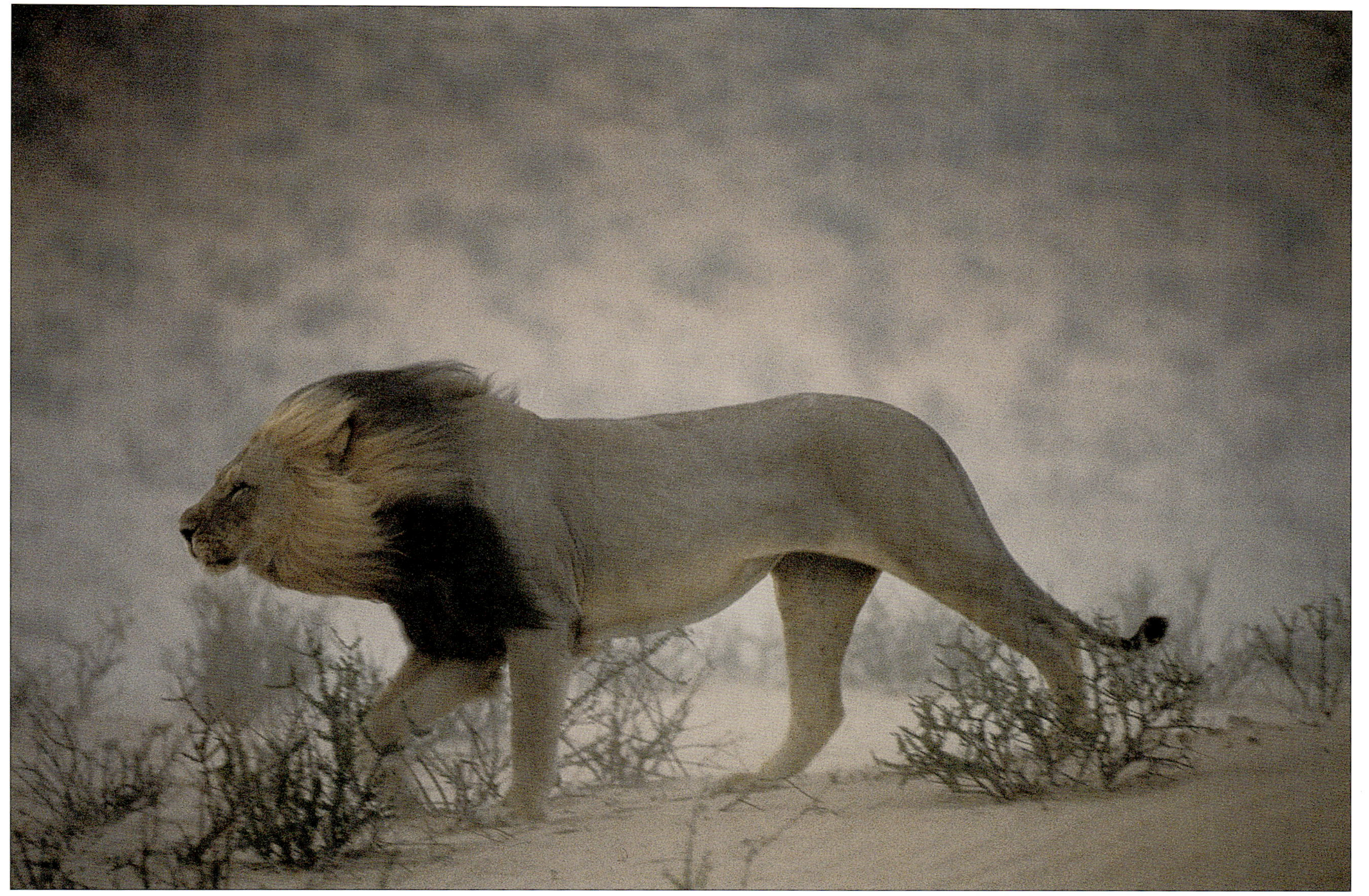

Chris Johns
United States of America
HIGHLY COMMENDED

Lion in sandstorm

"I searched for this lion in the dry bed of the Nossob River, Kalahari Gemsbok National Park, guessing that he might be seeking relief from the blowing sand and thunderstorm. To me, the picture represents the power and beauty of Africa."

Nikon; Fujichrome Provia

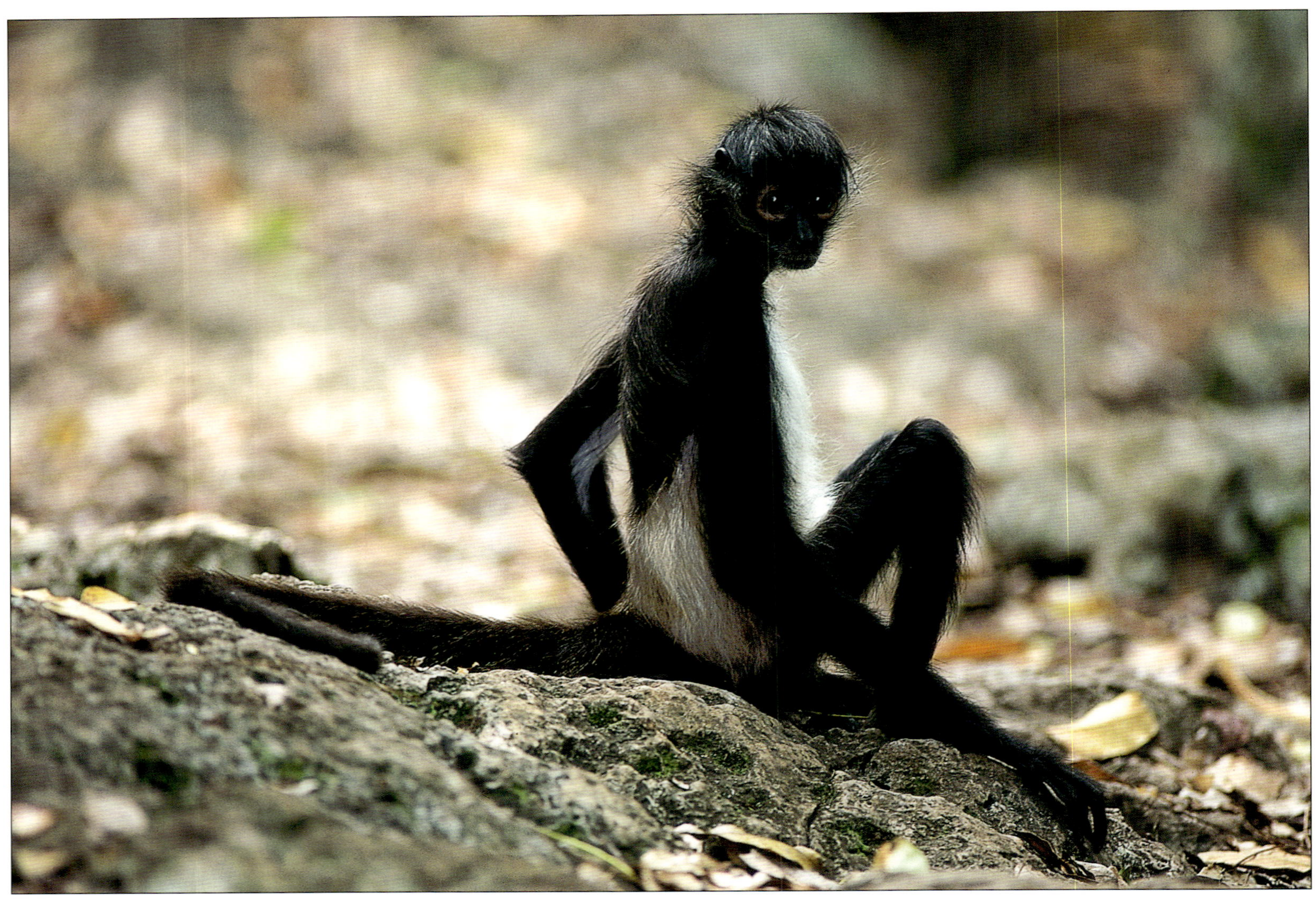

Iñaki Relanzón
Spain
HIGHLY COMMENDED

Spider monkey

"I recently spent five days working with biologists who are studying spider monkeys on the Yucatán Peninsula, Mexico. During a photographic session, one of the monkeys came down to the ground, and I was able to take this picture just as it looked in my direction."

Nikon F4s with 300mm lens; 1/250 sec at f2.8; Fujichrome Velvia

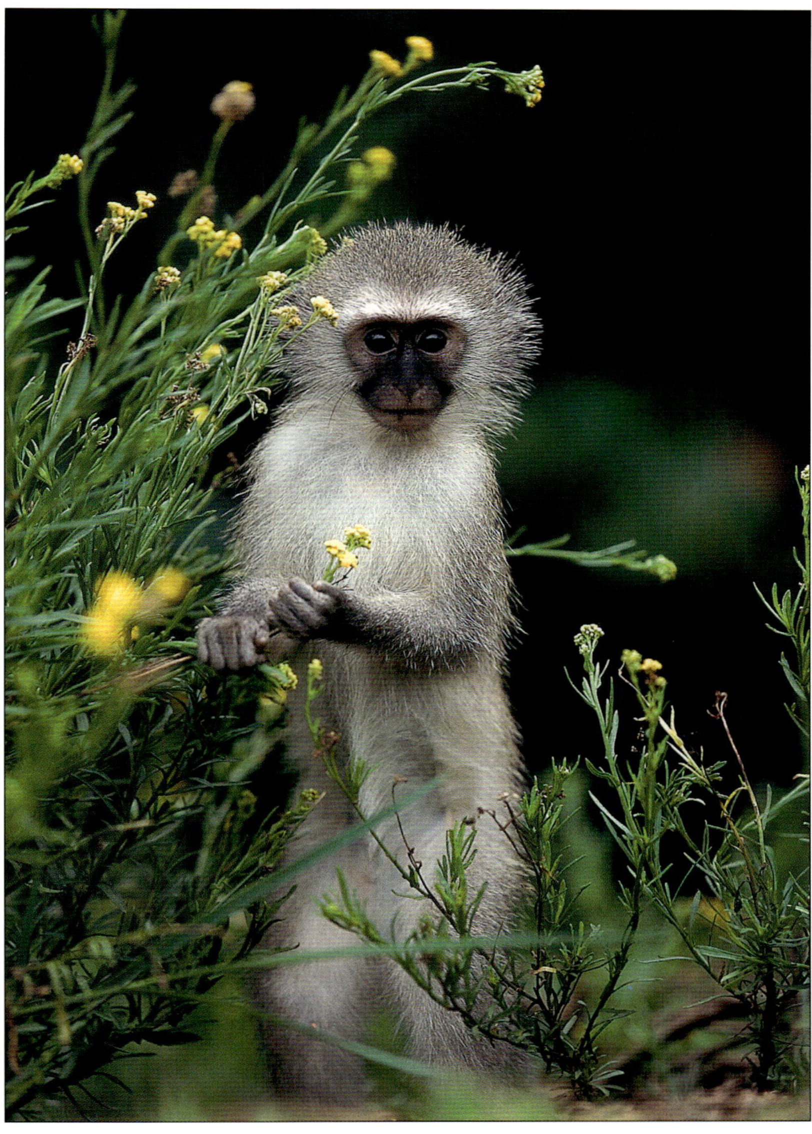

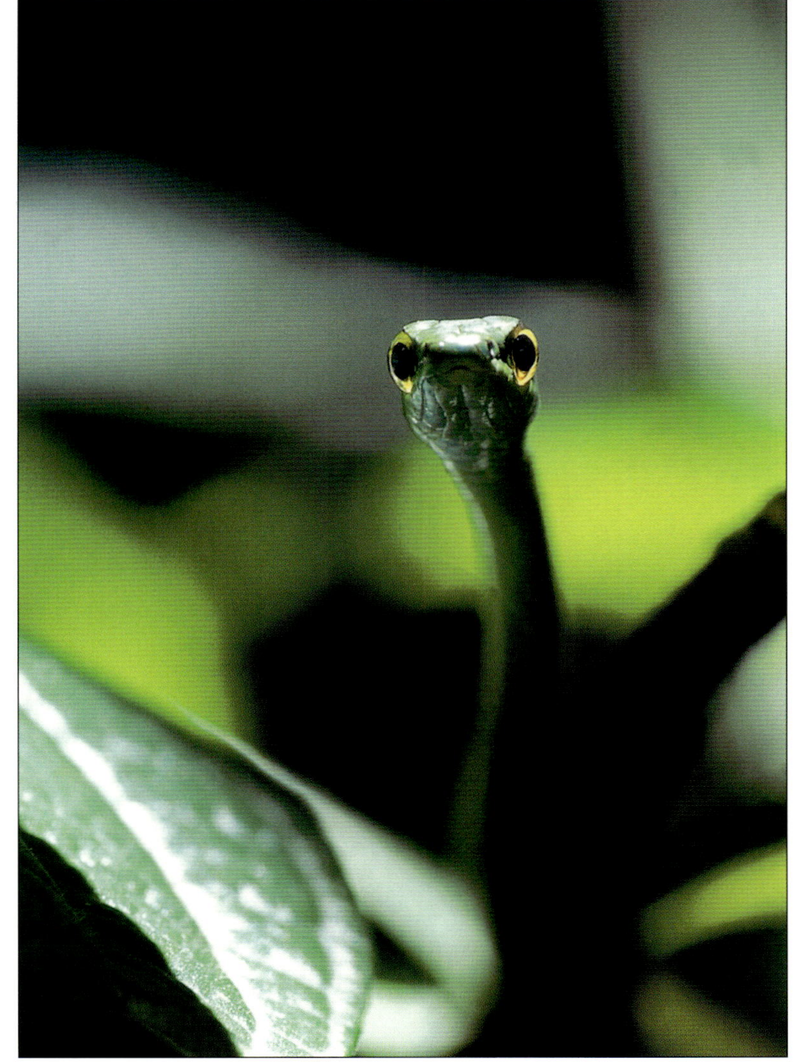

Heinrich van den Berg
South Africa
HIGHLY COMMENDED

Young vervet monkey

"Vervet monkeys eat virtually anything, even flowers. This one belonged to a family that lived in the mangroves on the east coast of South Africa. One day it just ventured out into the open and picked a flower."

Canon EOS 50 with 70-200mm lens; 1/250 sec at f2.8; Fujichrome Velvia

Jim Stamates
United States of America
HIGHLY COMMENDED

Vine snake

"I was hiking in a remote jungle in Costa Rica looking for poison dart frogs, when I was attracted by movement in the thick brush. The vine snake seemed curious as I got on my knees to view it at eye level. Every time it moved closer I had to reposition myself and my gear."

Nikon F4s with 80-200mm lens and extension tube; tripod; flash; Fujichrome Provia

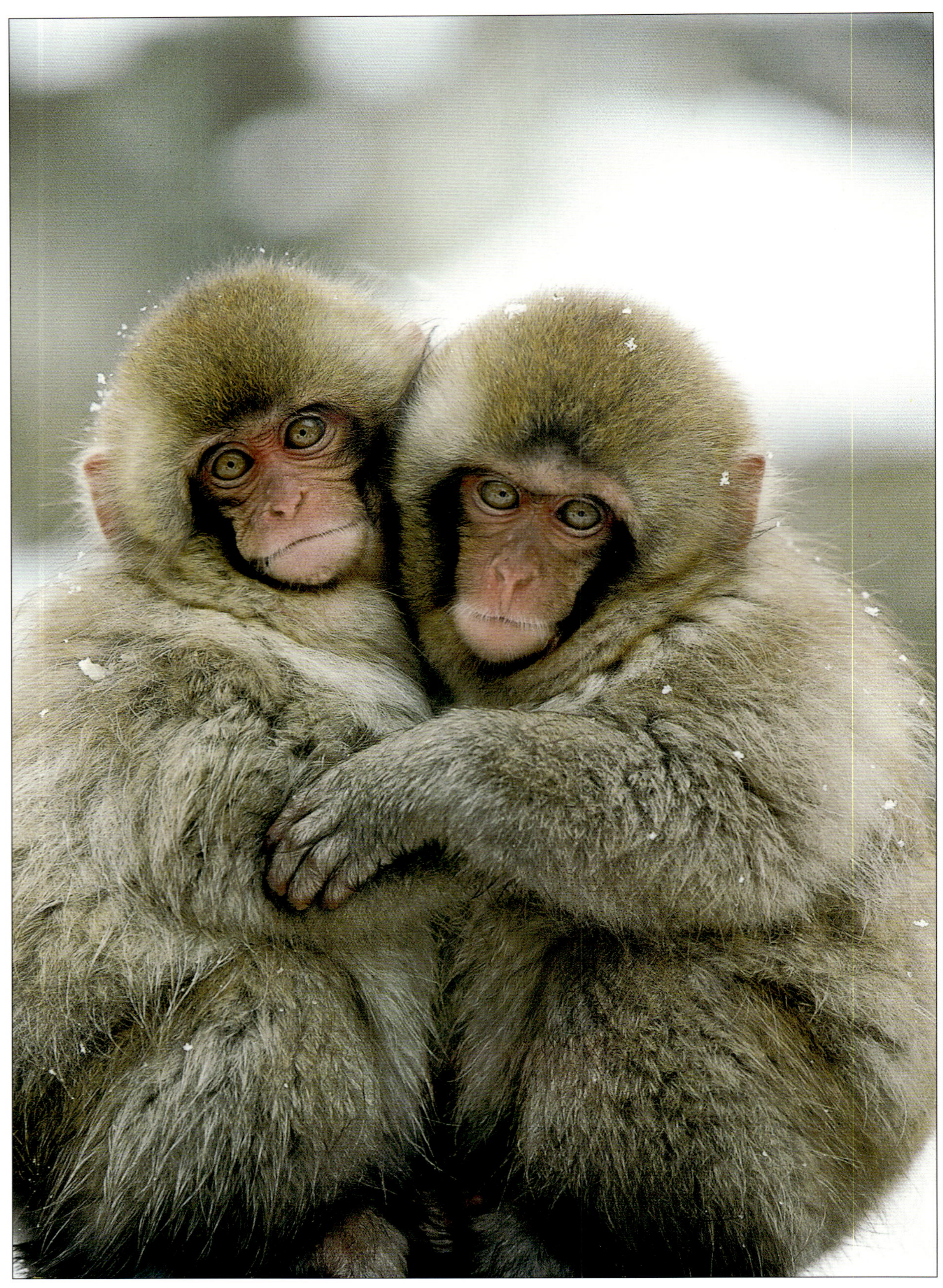

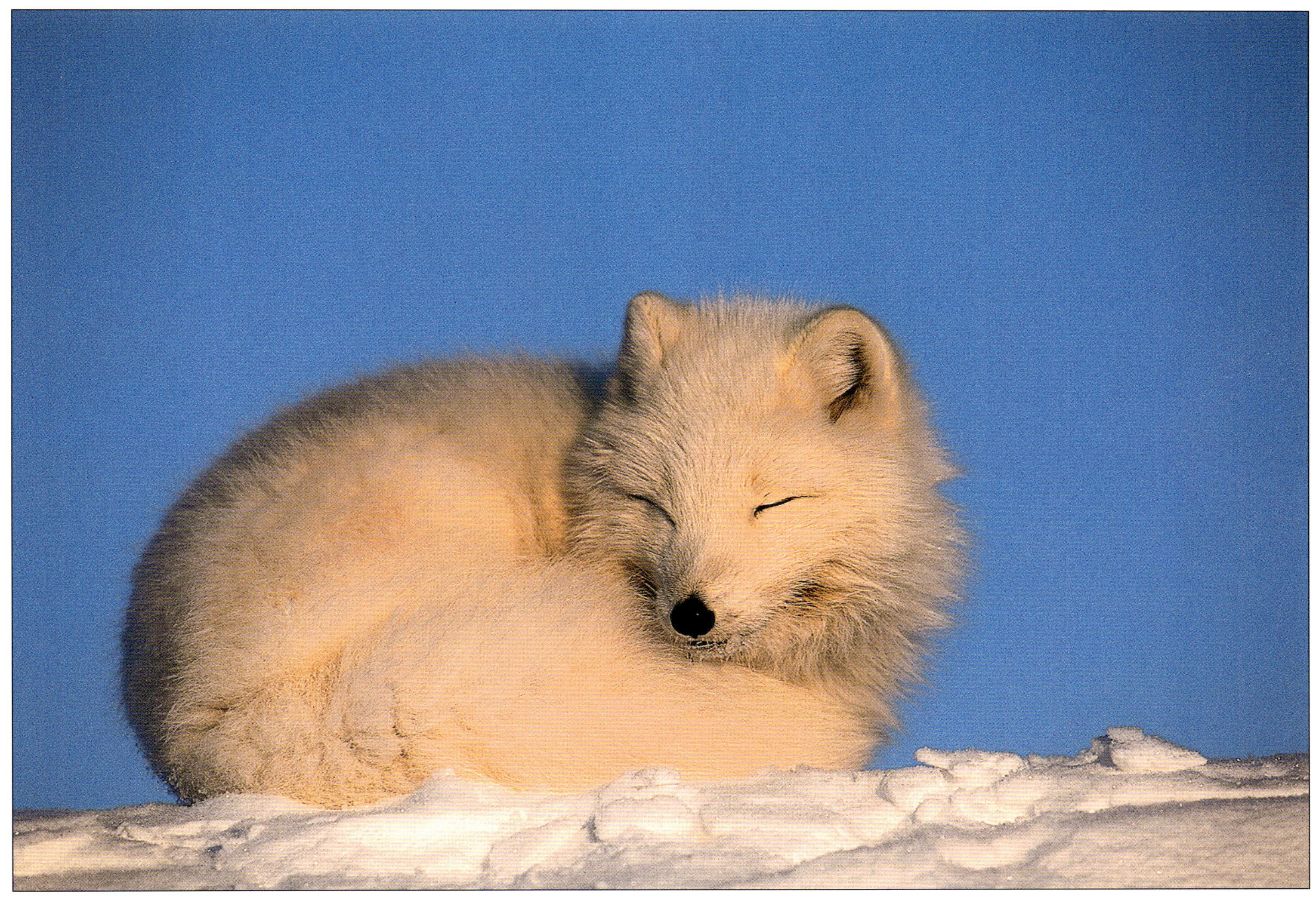

Konrad Wothe
Germany
HIGHLY COMMENDED

Young snow monkeys cuddling

"In January 1997 I visited the Japanese red-faced macaques living in the Japanese Alps, near Nagano. These social monkeys are attracted to hot springs in cold weather. They also keep warm by cuddling, as demonstrated by these two youngsters."

Canon EOS 1N with 70-200mm lens; Kodak Ektachrome 100S

Staffan Widstrand
Sweden
HIGHLY COMMENDED

Arctic fox asleep

"This fox was one of five that followed me for several days on Ellesmere Island, Canada. One day he just curled up in front of me, closed his eyes and went to sleep. I never figured out whether the foxes were waiting for leftovers from my food, or expecting me to die in the bitter cold."

Nikon F4 with 105mm micro lens; 1/125 sec at f4; Fujichrome Velvia

Animal Behaviour

- MAMMALS -

The subjects should be actively doing something. Pictures are judged on their interest value as well as their aesthetic appeal.

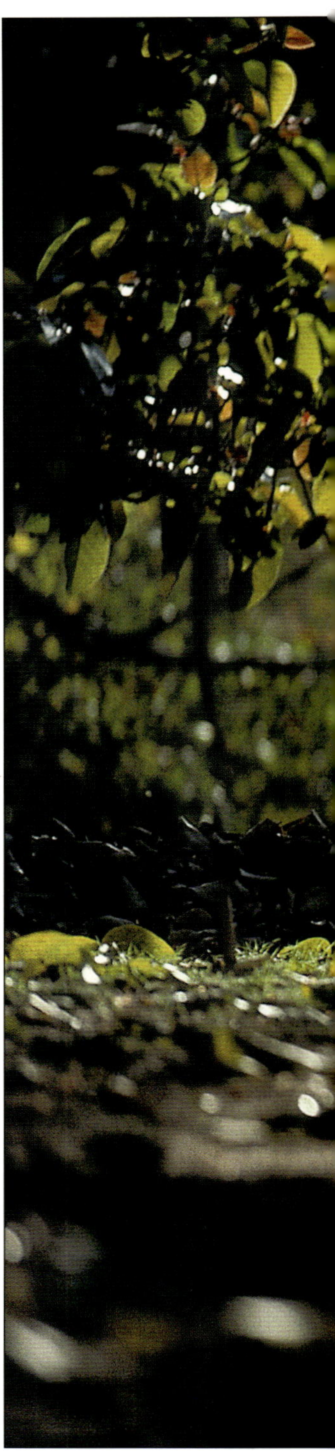

Anup Shah
United Kingdom
WINNER

Langur monkeys playing

"A troop of langur monkeys often gathers around a huge banyan tree in its territory. While the adults rest and forage, the adolescents play around the tree, as in this scene from Ranthambore National Park, India. Sometimes the youngsters devise games on the spur of the moment, like jumping up to catch leaves."

Canon EOS 600 with 200mm lens; 1/500 sec at f4; Kodachrome

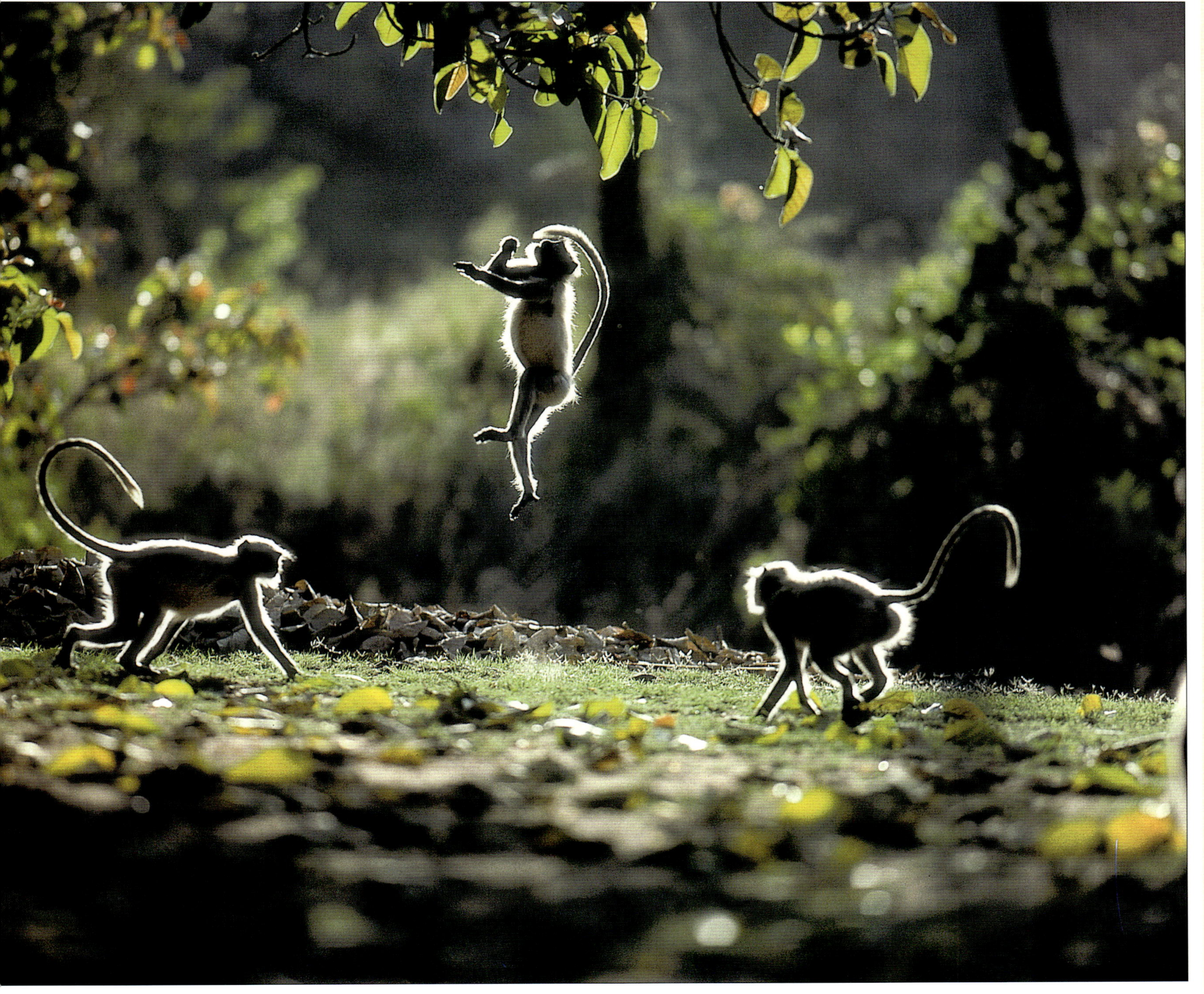

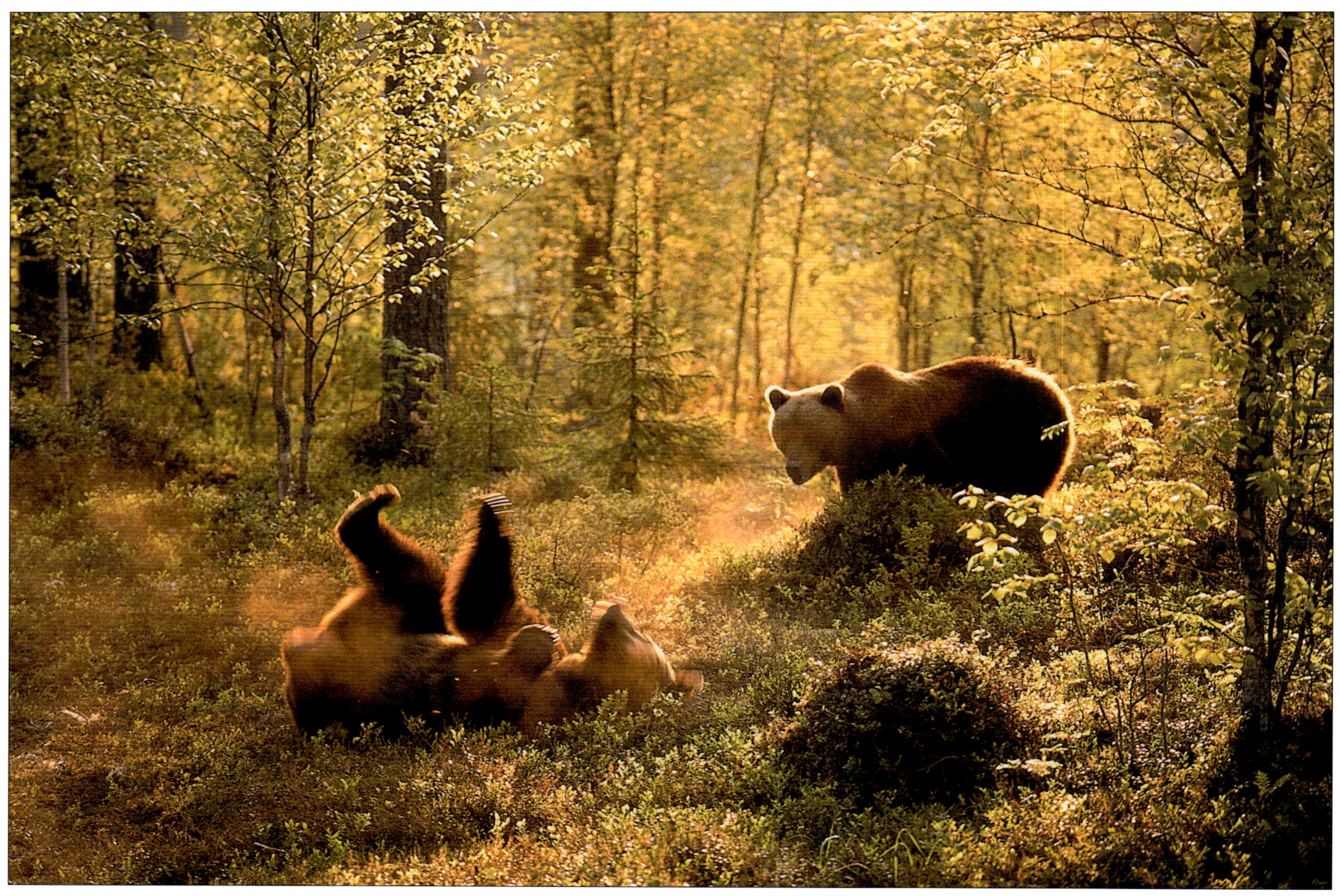

Eero Kemilä
Finland
RUNNER-UP

Bear couple

"I was following some bear couples during the mating season, when I saw this male rolling on a piece of meat used as bait. His behaviour would have given him the smell of a freshly killed animal and made him more attractive to the female. I took the picture near Lieksa, close to the Russian border."

Nikon F4 with 80-200mm lens; 1/60 at f5.6; Fujichrome RDP100

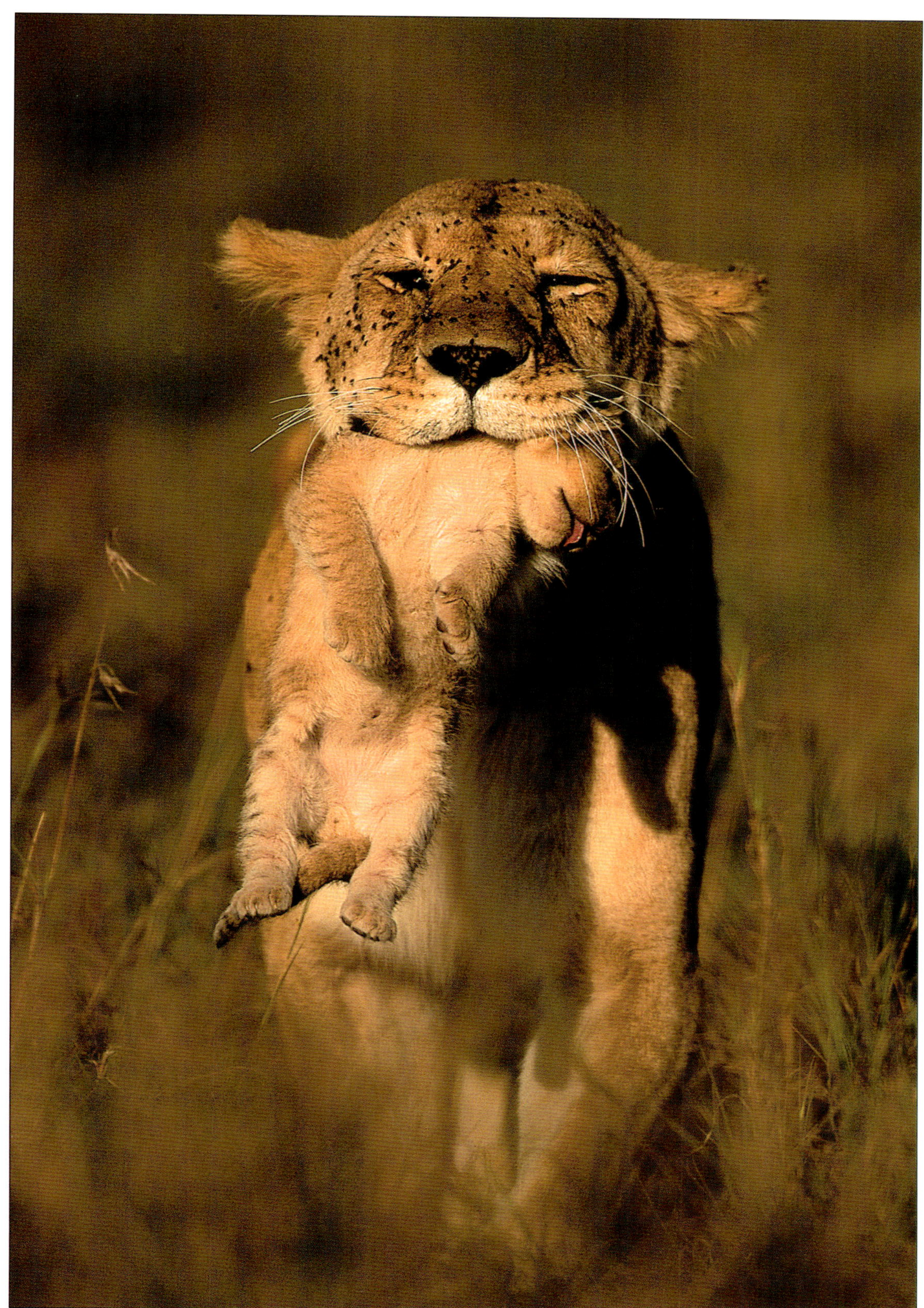

Kevin Schafer
United States of America
HIGHLY COMMENDED

Lion carrying cub away from fire

"As fire raged over the grassy plains, this Kenyan lioness carefully moved her three-week-old cubs away from danger. She carried each of the three cubs half a mile to a new hiding place, stoically ignoring the many flies gathered on her face."

Nikon N90s with 500mm lens; 1/500 sec at f4; Fujichrome Velvia

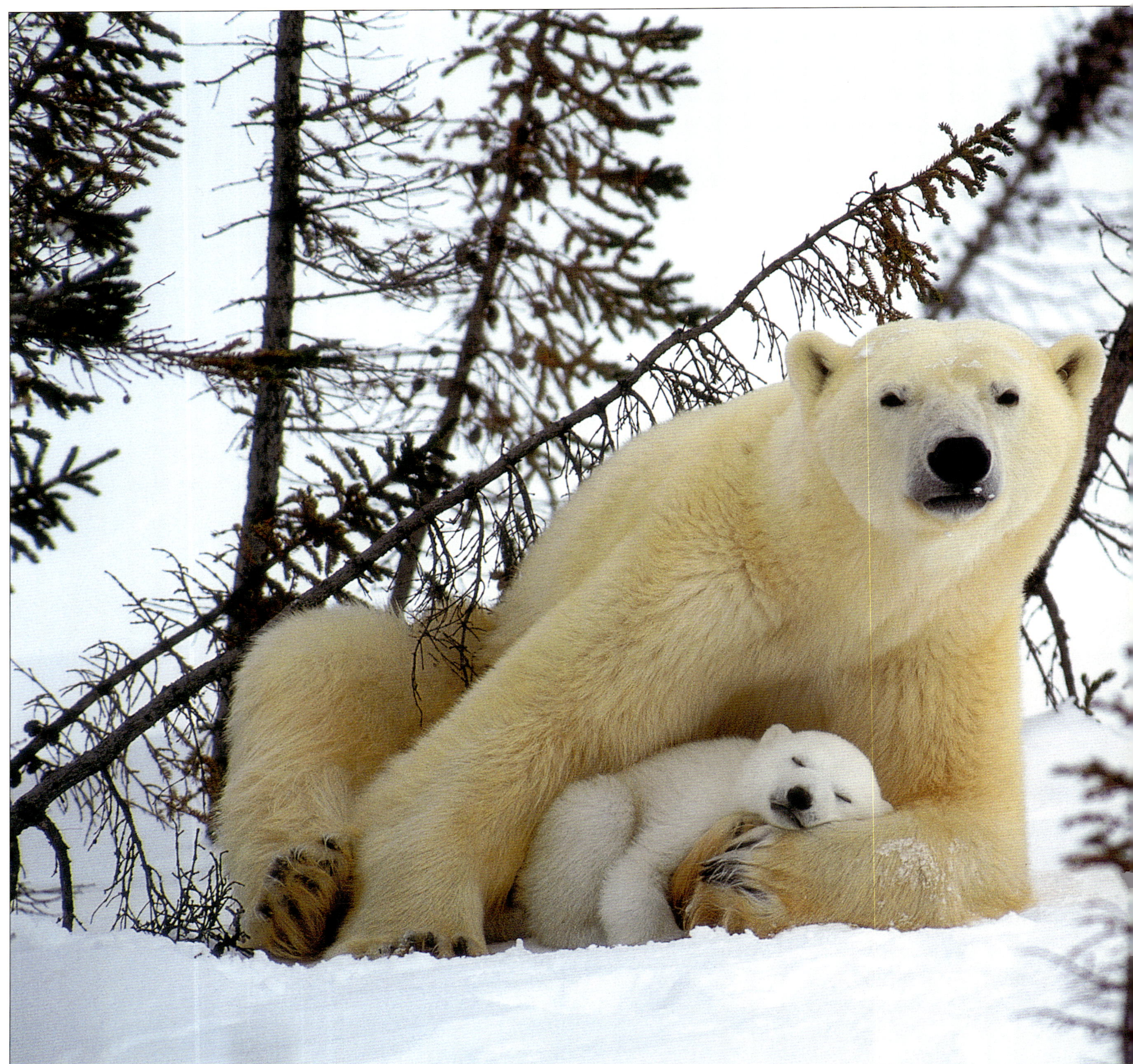

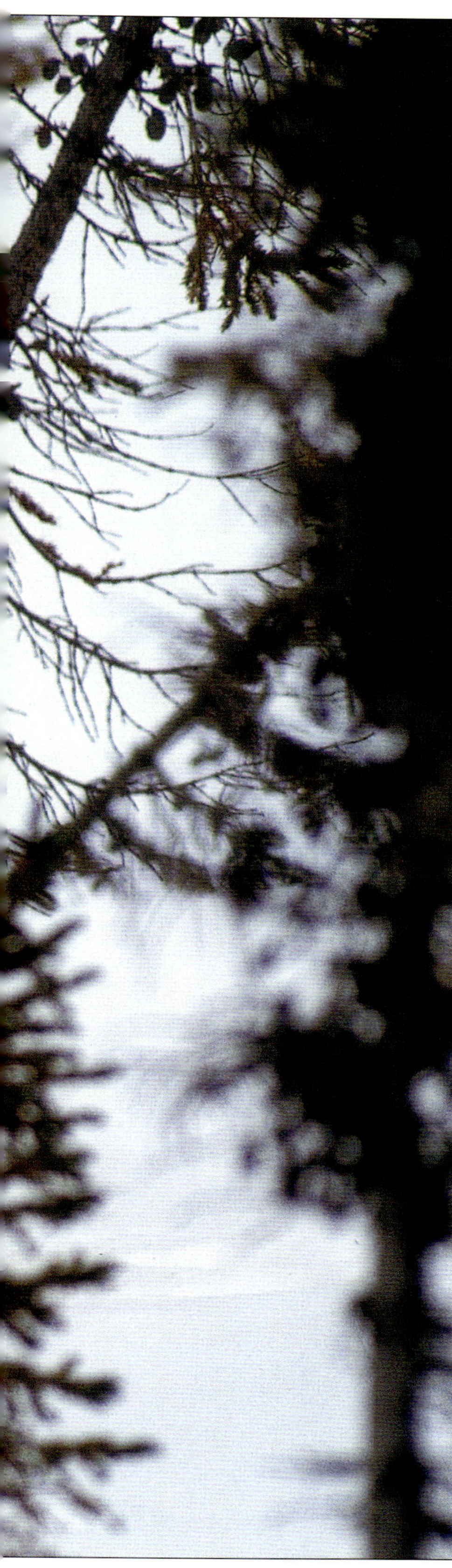

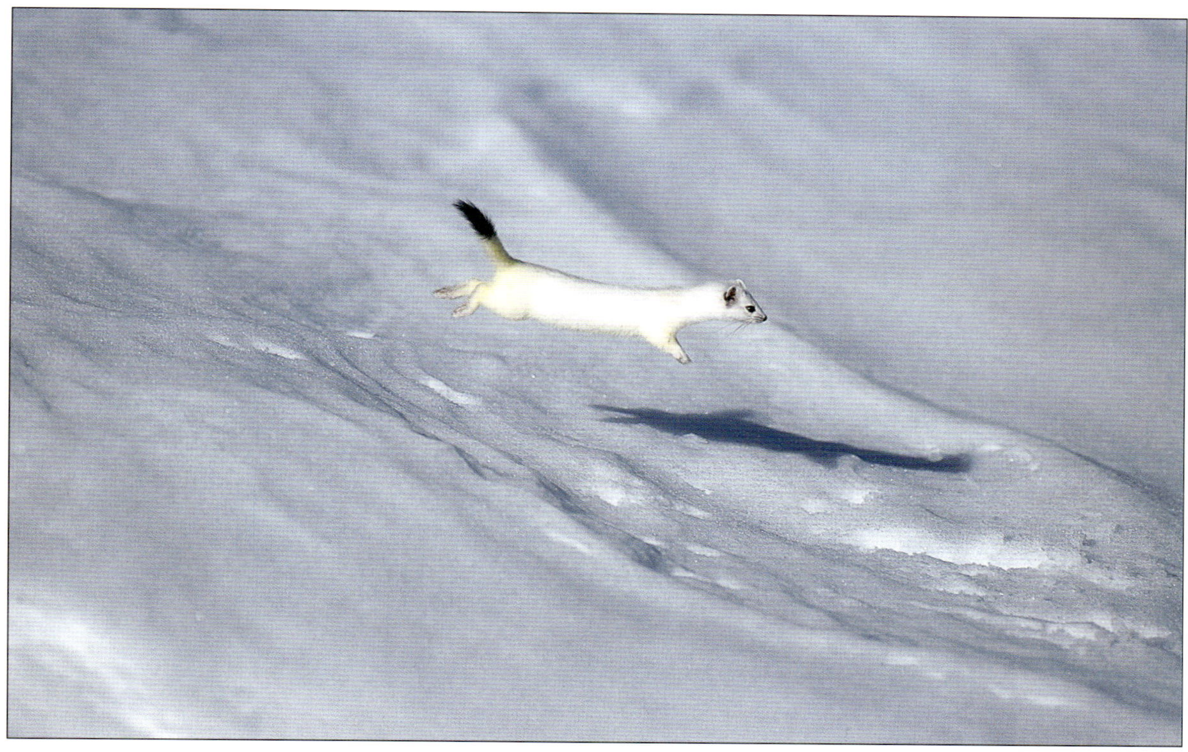

Wayne R Bilenduke
Canada
HIGHLY COMMENDED

Polar bear mother and cub

"After travelling for many kilometres by snowmobile in Wapusk National Park, Manitoba, I finally came upon this mother with her two newborn cubs. She cradled one cub on her front paw, while the other one snuggled out of sight against her warm body."

Nikon 801s with 500mm lens and x1.4 extender; 1/125 sec at f5.6; Fujichrome Velvia rated at 100

Elio Della Ferrera
Italy
HIGHLY COMMENDED

Fast ermine

"Of all the animals I have photographed, the ermine is the most difficult to catch on film. It is small, runs very fast and its movements are hard to predict. I took this photo at an altitude of 2,700 metres in Stelvio National Park, Italy, as the ermine was racing from one hole to another."

Canon EOS 1N with 300mm lens; 1/1600 sec at f3.5; Fujichrome Provia 100

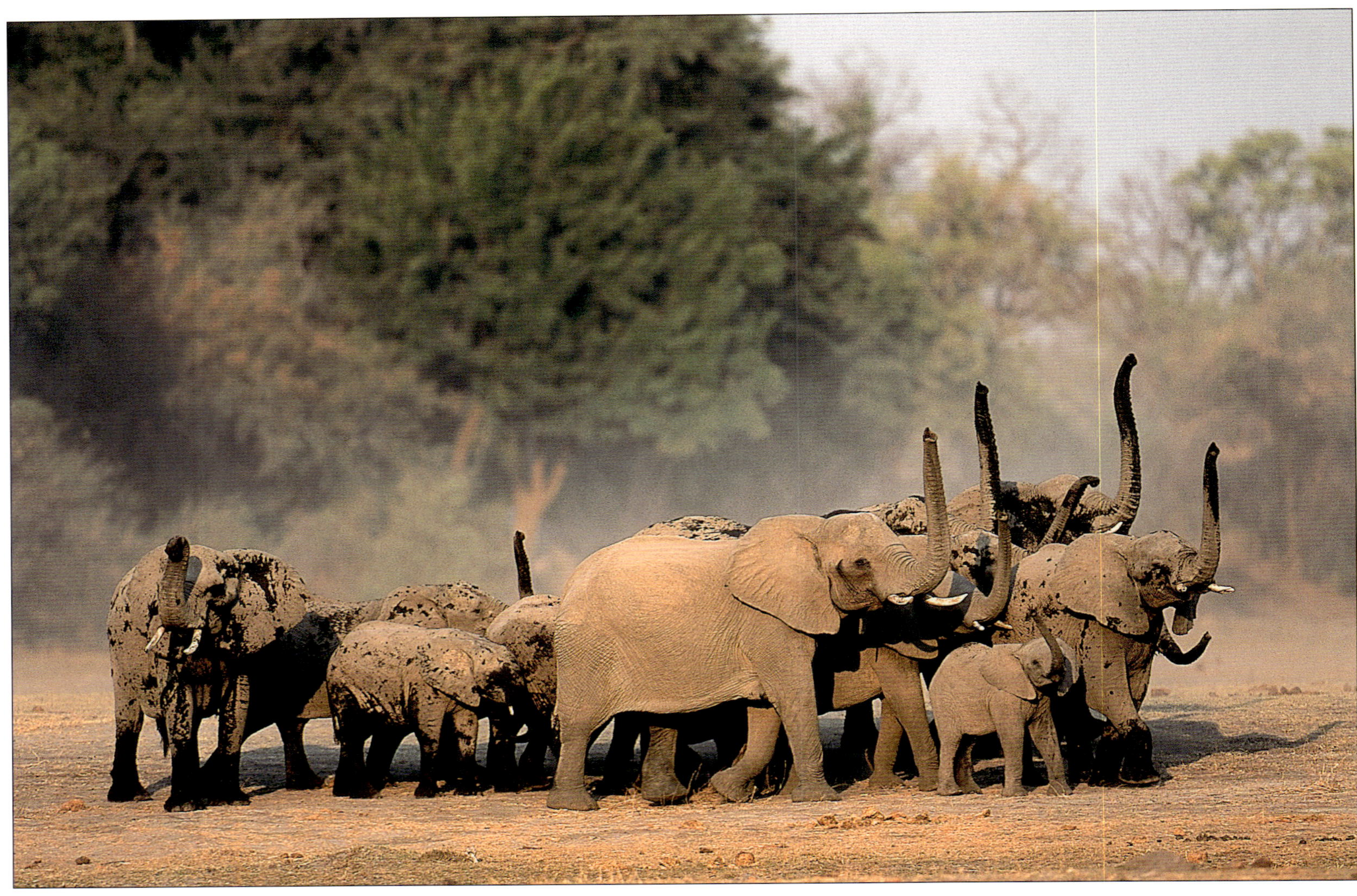

Beverly Joubert
Botswana
HIGHLY COMMENDED

Elephants smelling for danger

"This photo was taken in a part of Botswana that has been hunted heavily for years. The elephants are shy and the slightest change can make them suddenly alert, testing the air for any hint of danger. This herd decided that they'd picked up a false alarm, despite the fact that I was lying on the ground no more than 150 metres away."

Canon EOS 1 with 600mm lens; beanbag; Fujichrome Velvia

Nigel J Dennis
South Africa
HIGHLY COMMENDED

Chacma baboon with water lily

"I've noticed vervet monkeys feeding on water lily tubers on several occasions, but I've only once seen baboons exploiting this food source. The baboons, from Kruger National Park, became so engrossed that they seemed oblivious to the danger of crocodiles."

Canon EOS 5 with 600mm lens; Fujichrome Velvia

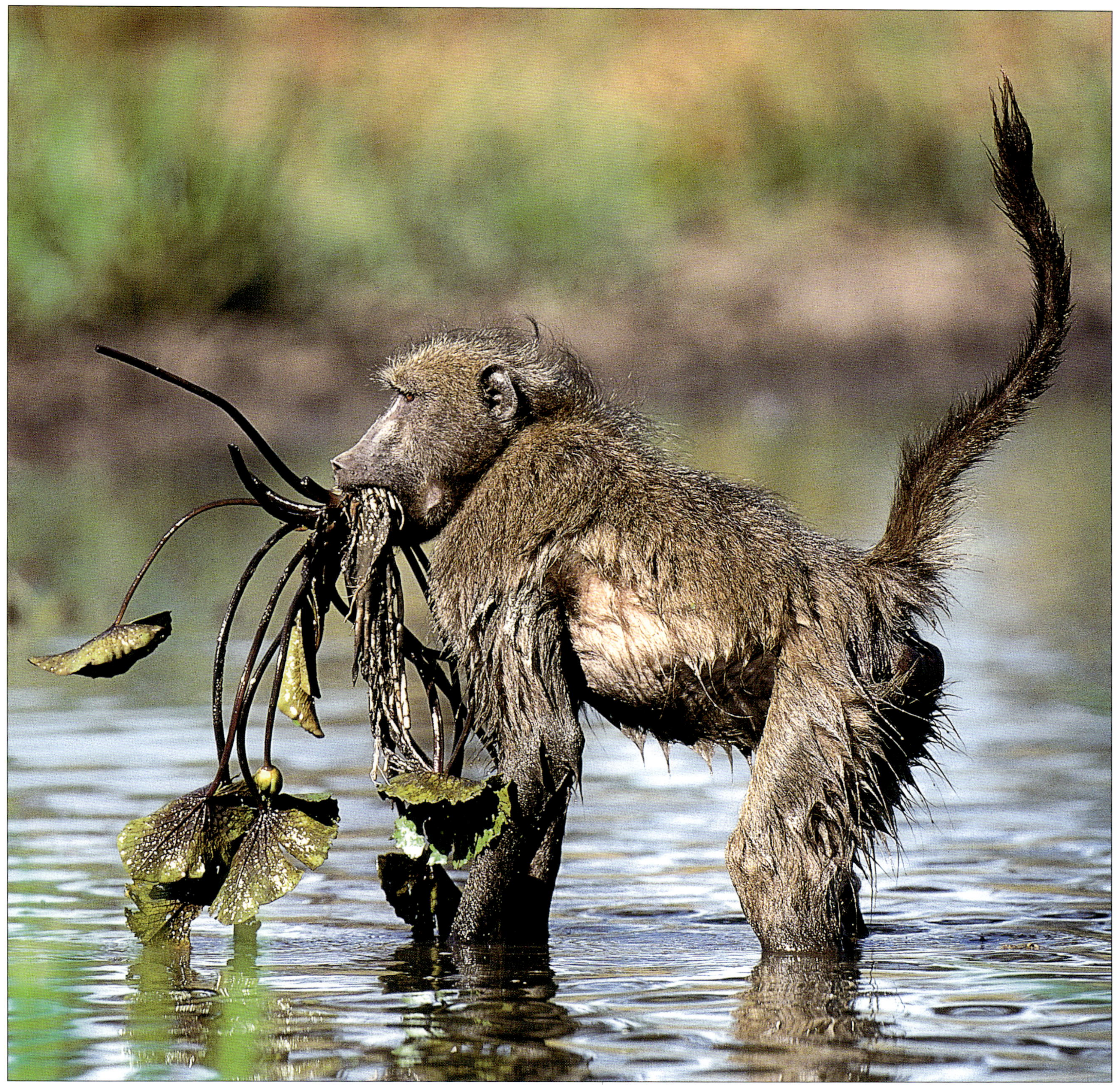

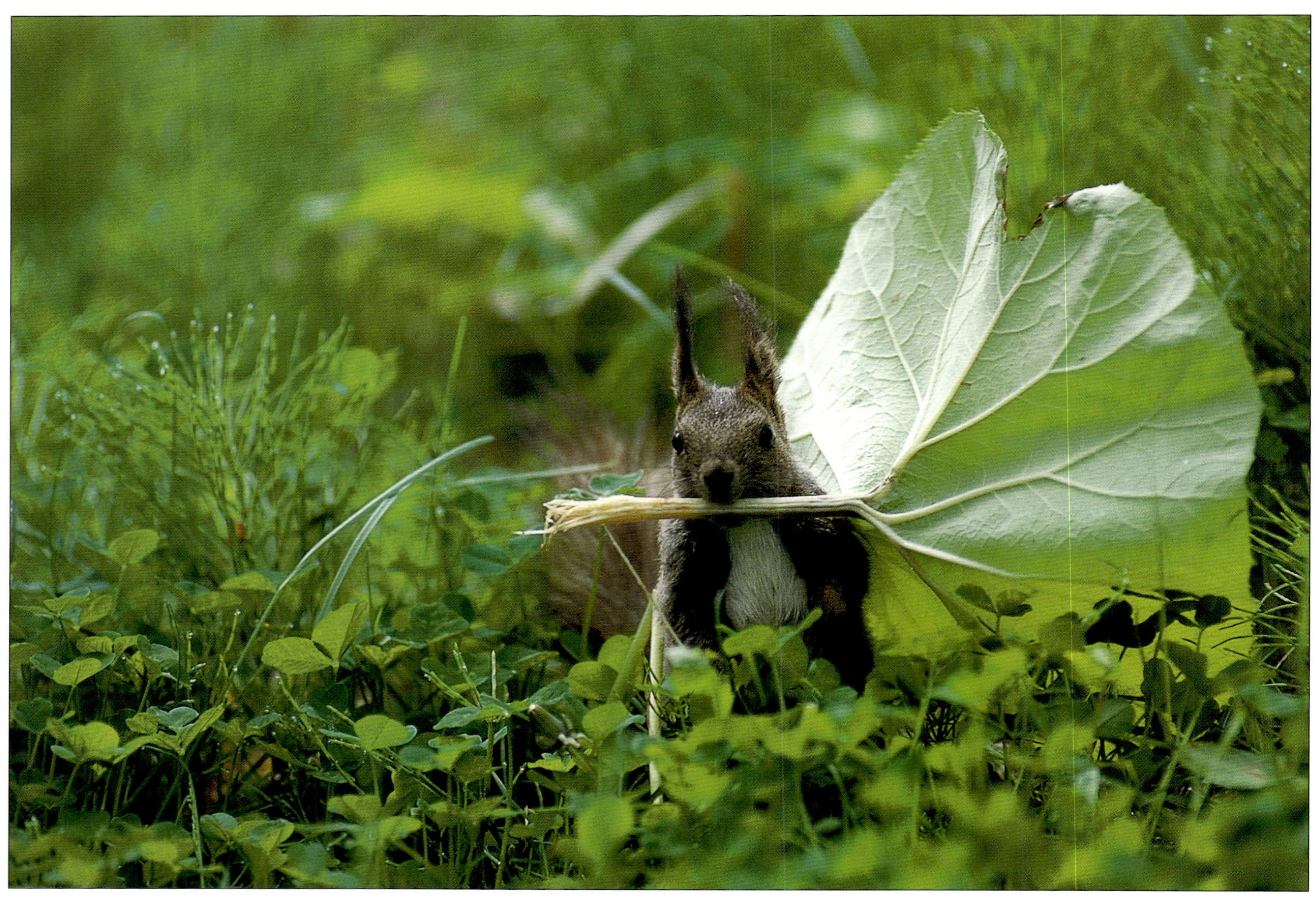

Kotaro Sano

Japan

HIGHLY COMMENDED

Squirrel with leaf

"I was camping out in my vehicle at Otofuke in Hokkaido, when I had this surprising encounter. The squirrel had found an edible plant called 'fuki' and was carrying it off so he could eat it in a safe place. Fuki isn't a main dish for squirrels, but they often eat the delicious stems."

Canon F1 with 400mm lens; tripod; auto at f2.8; Fujichrome Provia 100

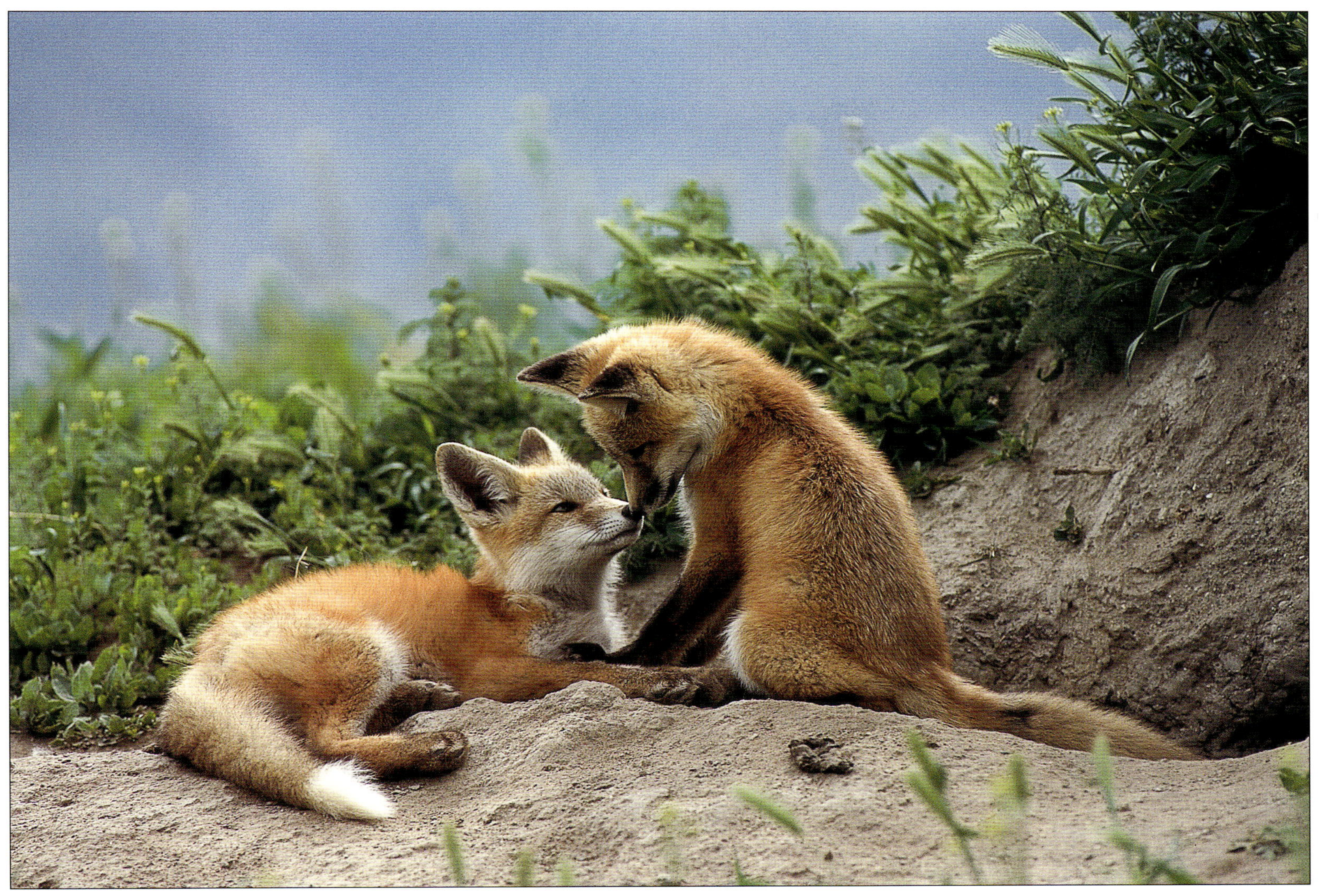

David N Olsen
United States of America
HIGHLY COMMENDED

Red fox cubs

"Many foxes make a living around the shores of the Great Salt Lake in Utah, feeding on the bird life of this highly productive marshy area. I spent about three months studying one den on the shore of the lake, where I captured this intimate moment."

Nikon F4 with 300mm lens; 1/500 sec at f2.8; Fujichrome Velvia

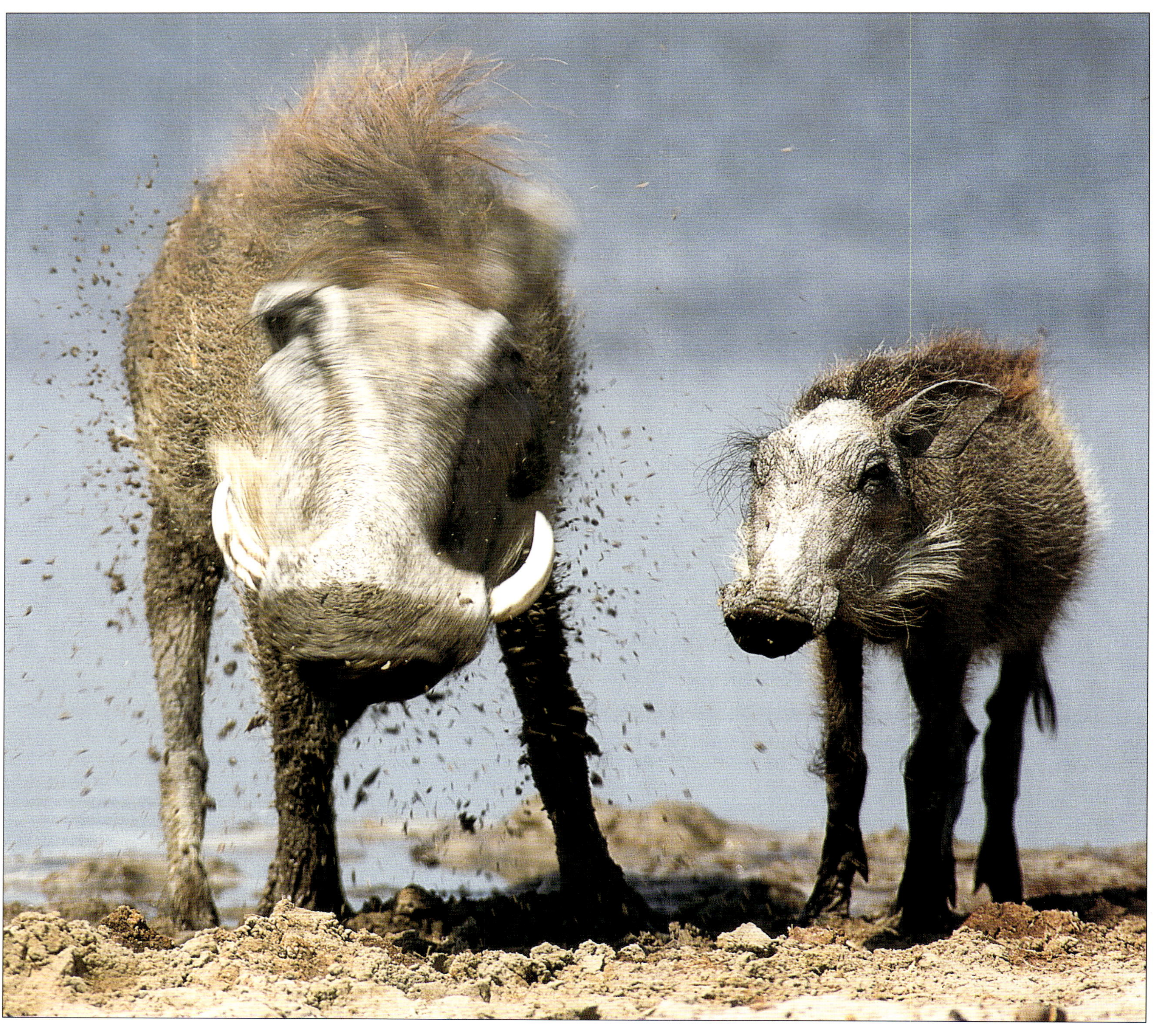

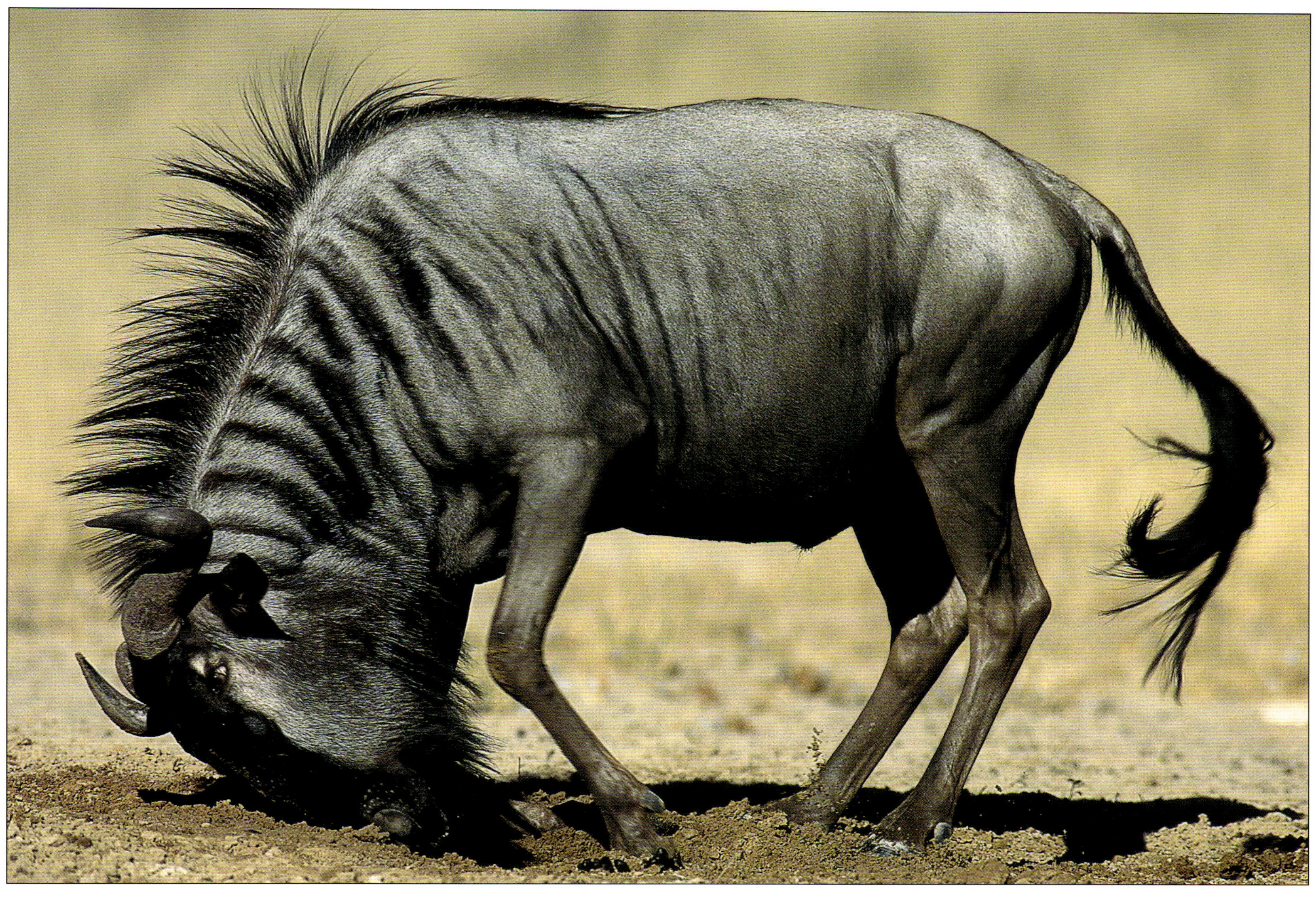

Tony Heald
United Kingdom
HIGHLY COMMENDED

Warthogs

"I came across these warthogs at Mashara water hole in Etosha National Park, Namibia. The mother was shaking mud from her coat."

Nikon F90x with 600mm lens; 1/320 sec at f5.6; Fujichrome Provia 100

Gil Lopez-Espina
United States of America
HIGHLY COMMENDED

Blue wildebeest rolling in mud

"I spotted this wildebeest early one winter morning in the Kalahari Gemsbok National Park, South Africa. First he satisfied his thirst at a water hole, then he decided to take a roll in the mud."

Nikon F4 with 600mm lens; cambrac; 1/250 sec at f4; Fujichrome Velvia rated at 40

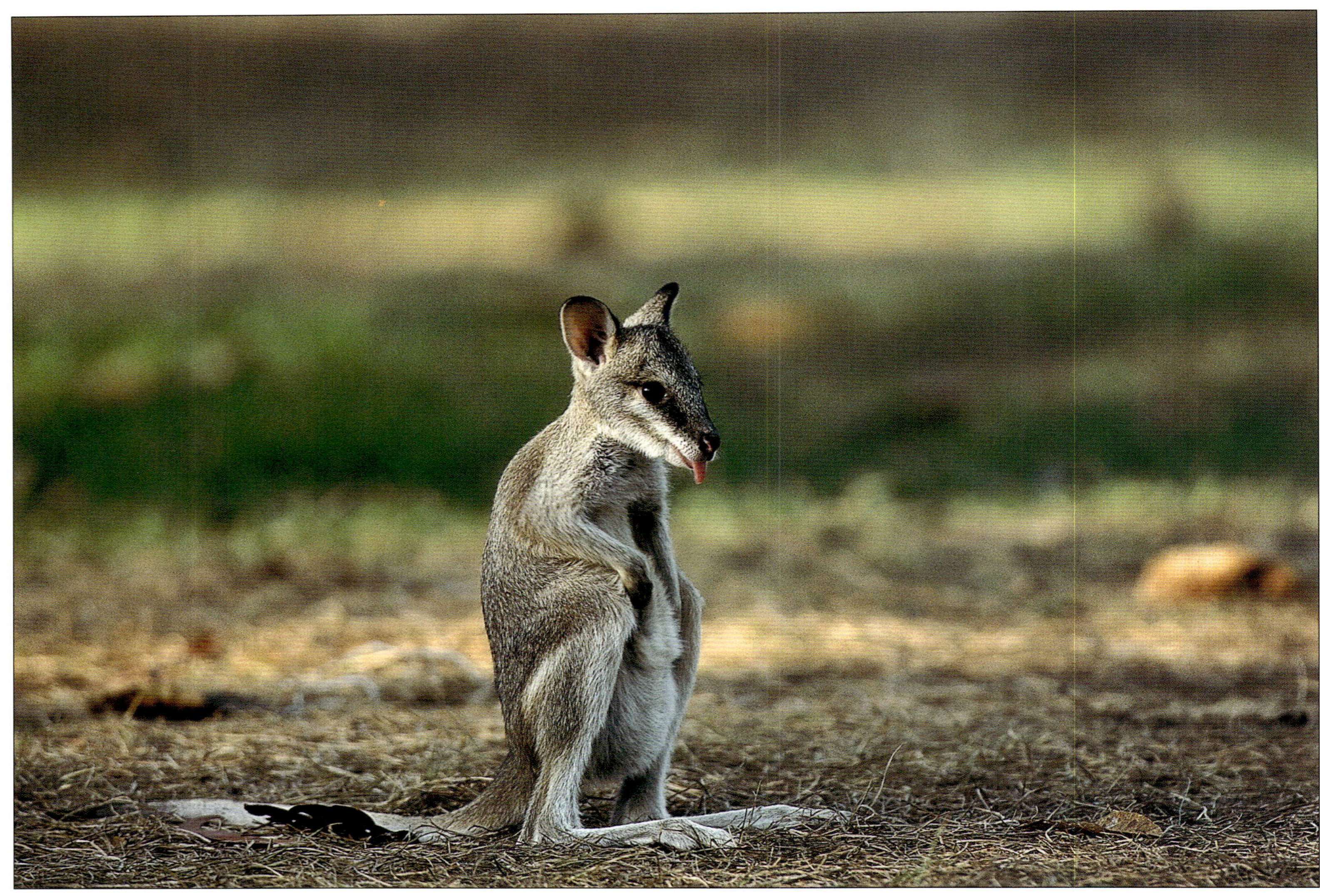

Jörg Hauke
Germany
HIGHLY COMMENDED

Baby agile wallaby

"I encountered this baby agile wallaby in Kakadu National Park, North Australia. It was standing near to its mother and cleaning itself. While looking at me, it stuck out its tongue. It looked so funny that I just pressed the release button."

Canon EOS 1N with 500mm lens; tripod; programme at f5; Fujichrome 100

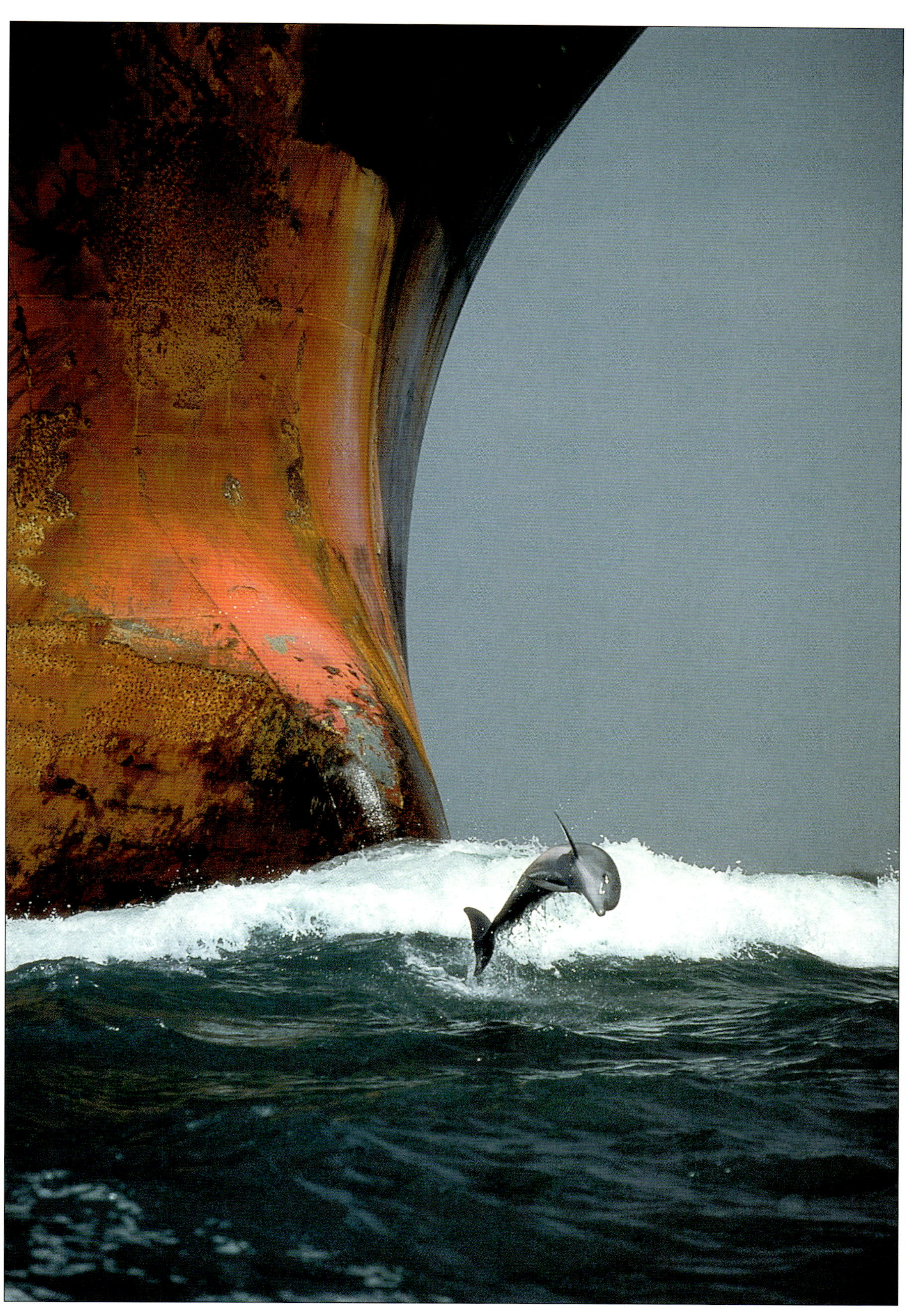

Michel Denis-Huot
France
HIGHLY COMMENDED

Bottle-nosed dolphin and tanker

"Dolphins like playing in the waves created by ships, such as this huge oil tanker at Port Aransas in Texas. The picture was taken from a speedboat following the tanker."

Canon EOS 1NRS with 300mm lens; 1/500 sec at f4; Fujichrome 100

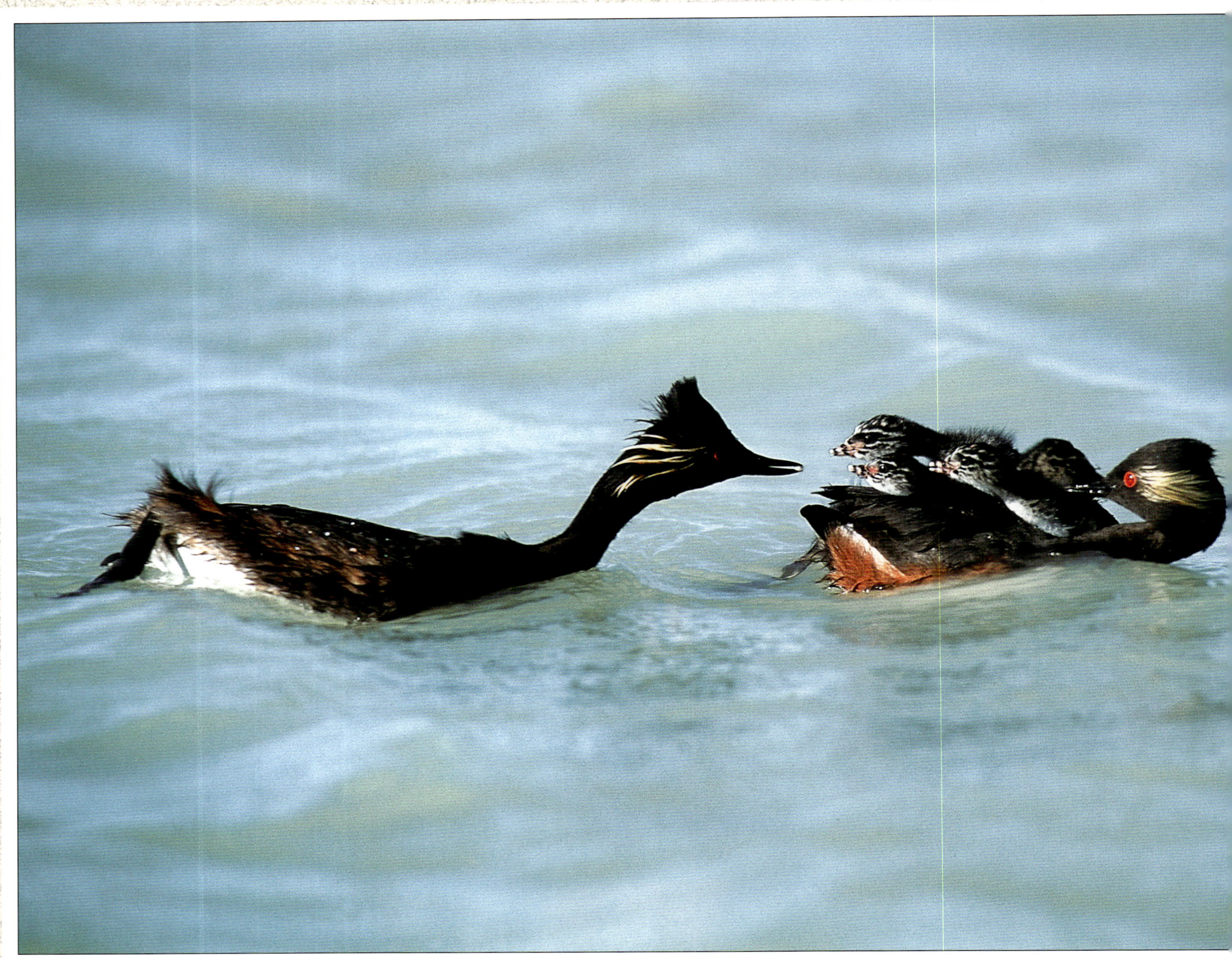

Animal Behaviour

- BIRDS -

The birds should be actively doing something. Pictures are judged on their interest value as well as their aesthetic appeal.

Torsten Brehm
Germany
WINNER

Black-necked grebes

"When I noticed that some grebes were nesting in the Etosha Pan, Namibia, I thought about getting a dream shot like this. A little while later, I was waiting by the edge of the Pan in my car when the grebes moved towards me. So I seized the opportunity and took the shot."

Canon EOS 5 with 400mm lens and x2 converter; Fujichrome Velvia

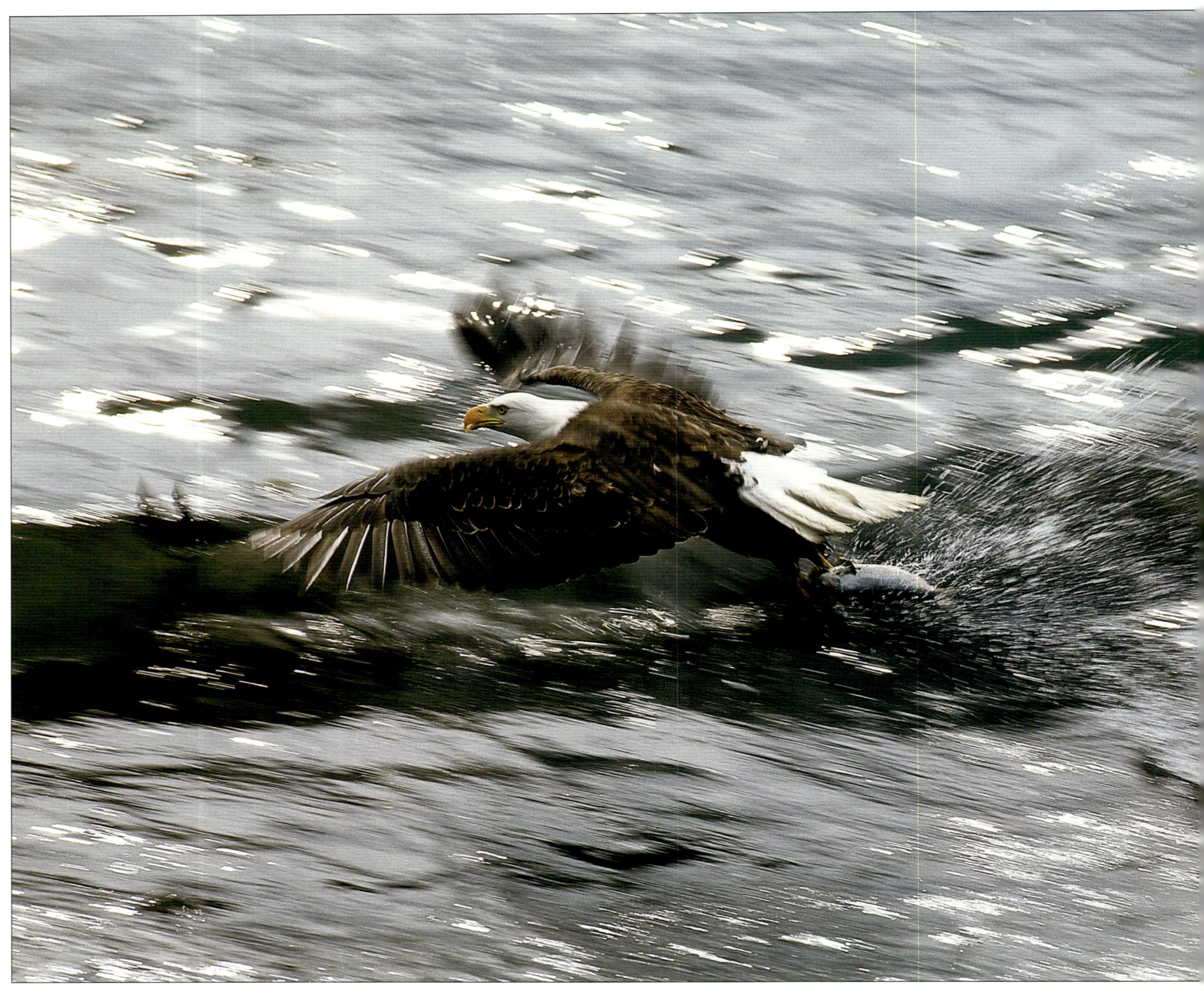

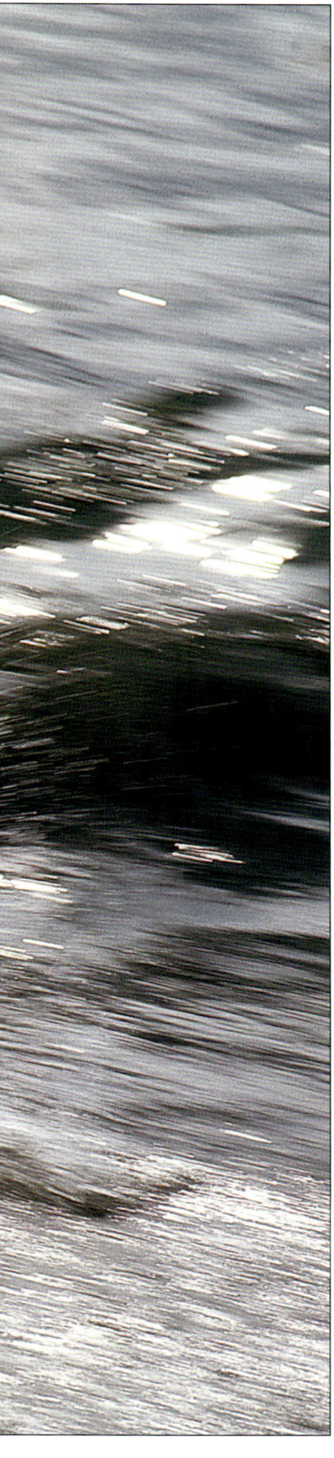

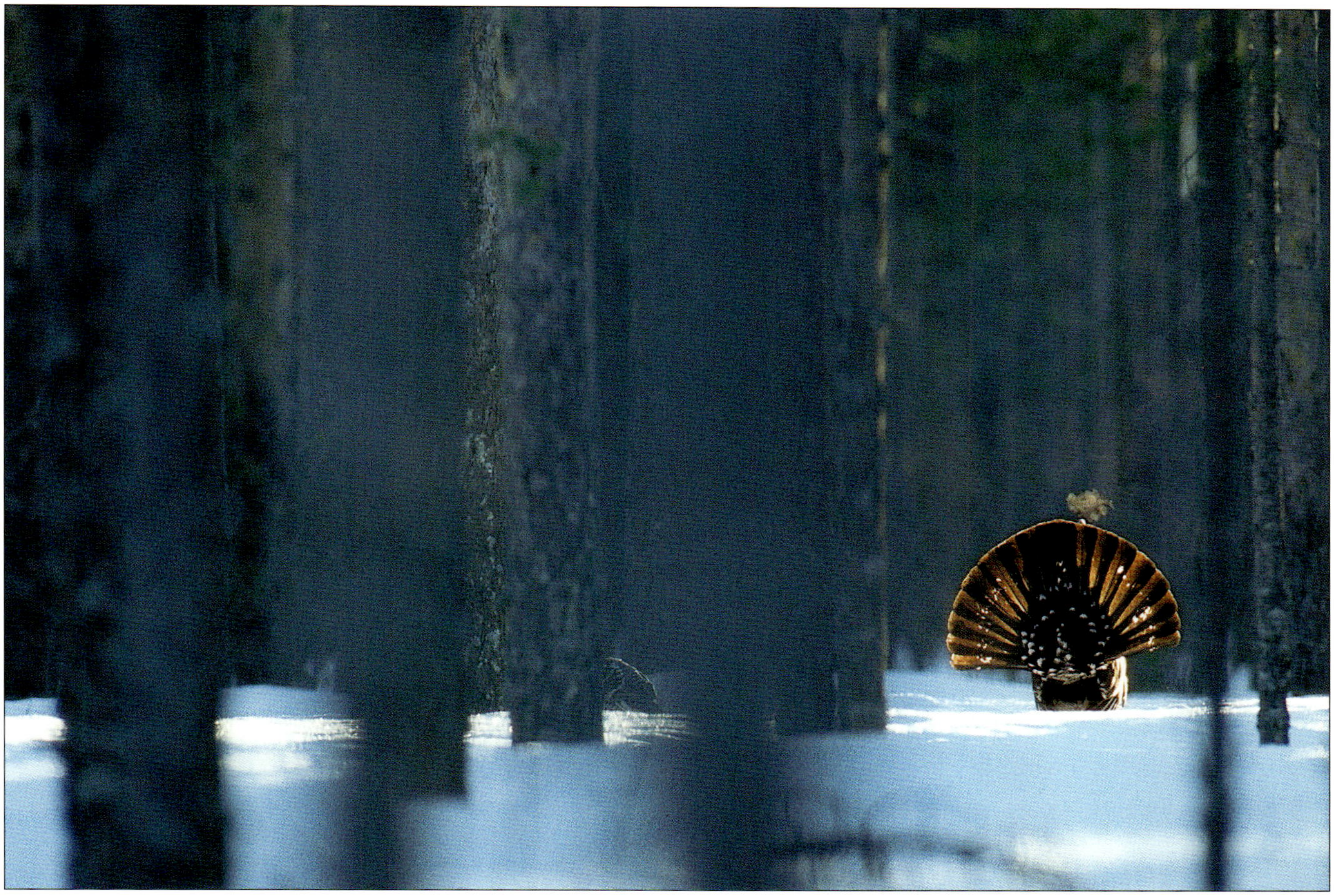

Thomas D Mangelsen
United States of America
RUNNER-UP

Bald eagle catching fish

"Bald eagles winter and nest in the forests surrounding Kachemak Bay, southeast Alaska, where this photograph was taken. The bay keeps the birds supplied with fish, their principal food."

Nikon F5 with 600mm lens; 1/500 sec at f4; Fujichrome Velvia

Eero Kemilä
Finland
SPECIALLY COMMENDED

Capercaillie

"The winter in Finland was cold and exceptionally long this year and there was a metre of snow on the ground in early May. That meant I could dig a hole in the snow and watch the capercaillie on its display site against the rising sun."

Nikon F5 with 600mm lens; tripod; 1/500 sec at f4; Fujichrome

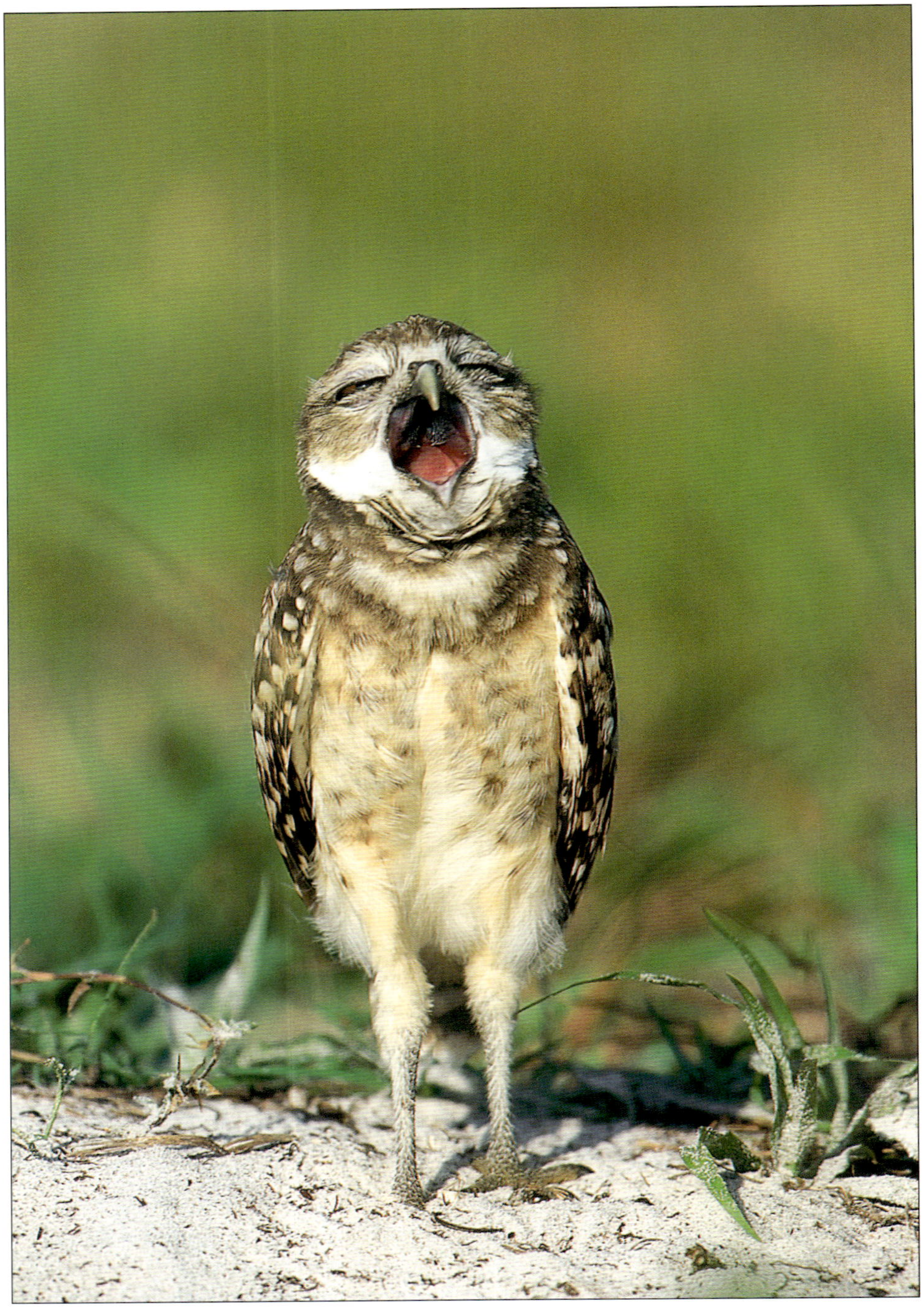

Dr Mamoru Yoshida
United States of America
HIGHLY COMMENDED

Burrowing owl yawning

"After I'd loaded my third roll of film, this Florida burrowing owl yawned, as if to let me know that it was getting bored of being photographed. I captured this cute behaviour on film, thanked the bird for a wonderful photo session and left."

Canon EOS A2 with 500mm lens and x1.4 extender; tripod; 1/125 sec at f6.7; Fujichrome Velvia

Peter Blackwell
United Kingdom
HIGHLY COMMENDED

Seven little bee-eaters

"I was in the Maasai Mara, Kenya, when I found this group of brightly coloured bee-eaters. They were sunning themselves in the early morning."

Nikon N90 with 500mm lens; tripod; 1/30 sec at f4; Fujichrome Velvia rated at 80

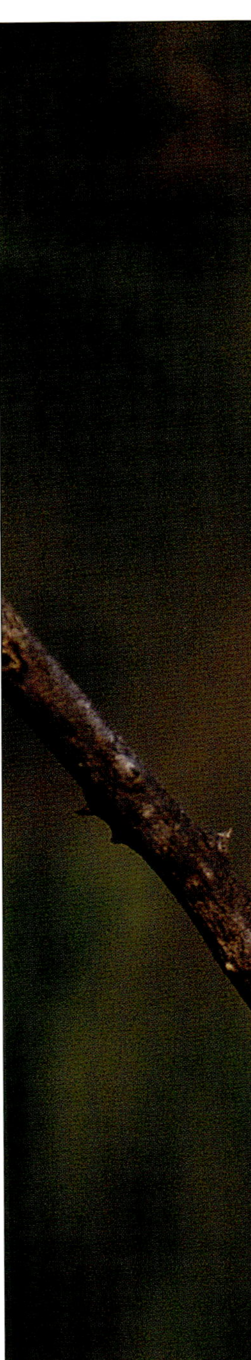

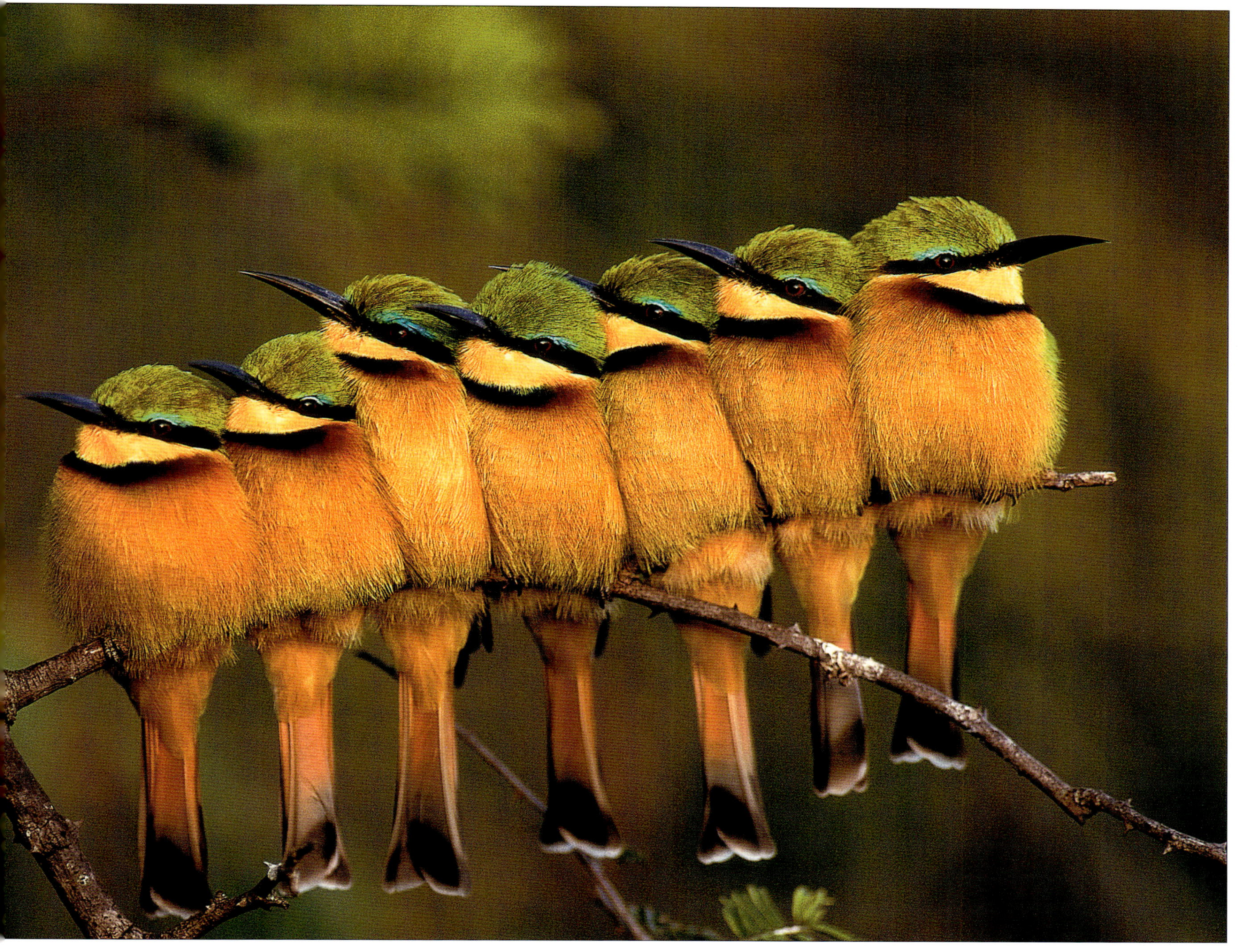

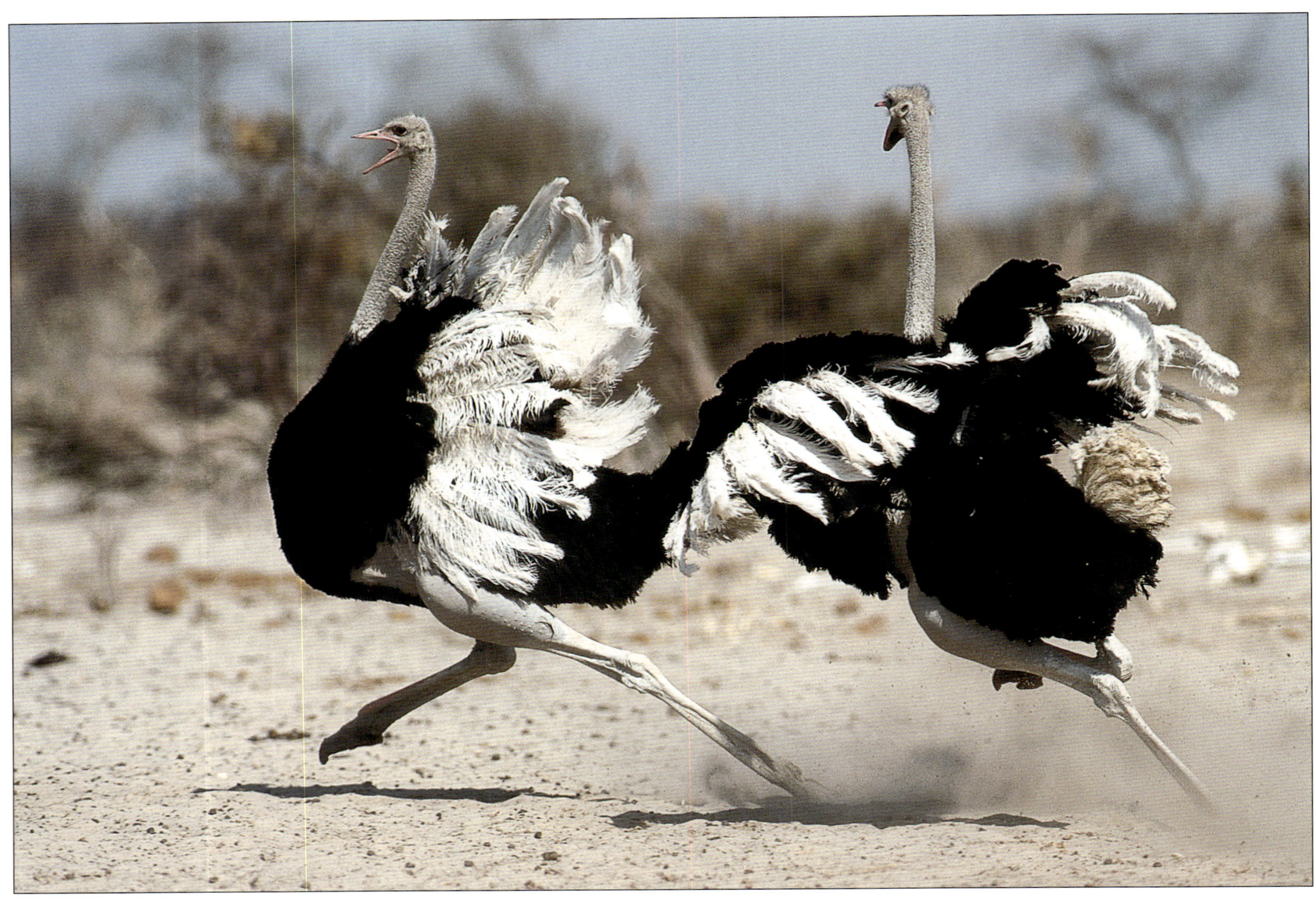

Tony Heald

United Kingdom

HIGHLY COMMENDED

Ostriches

"This picture shows one male ostrich chasing another in a dispute over dominance at Mashara water hole in Namibia's Etosha National Park. There was a receptive female nearby."

Nikon F90x with 600mm lens; 1/400 sec at f5.6; Fujichrome Provia 100

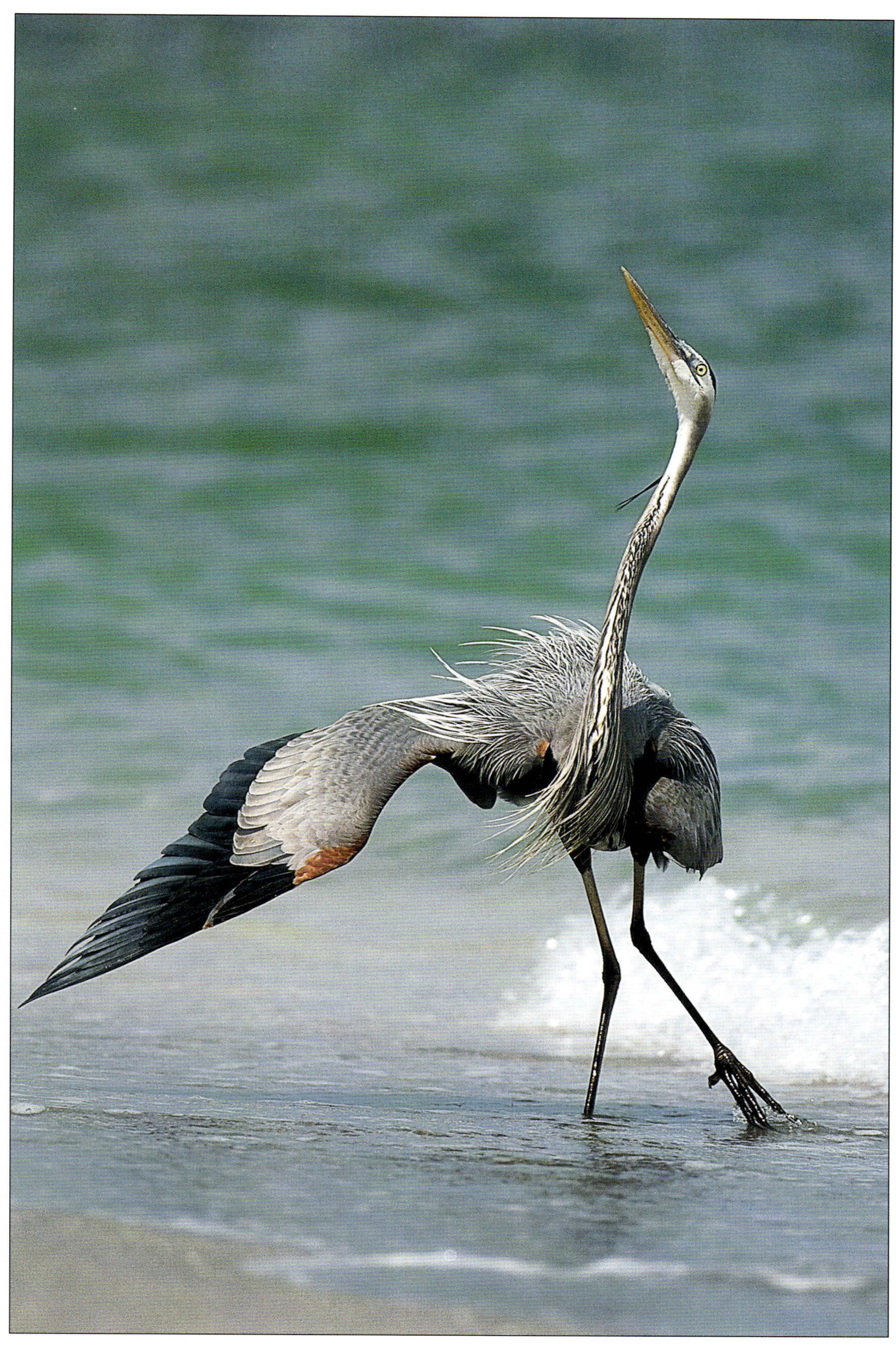

Arthur Morris
United States of America
HIGHLY COMMENDED

Great blue heron threat display

"I was photographing a great blue heron as it waited for a fisherman's hand-outs on Captiva Island, Florida. Suddenly it took off and flew 300 yards, landing near to another bird. The two herons began sky pointing, strutting, and dropping and spreading their wings. I ran to get in on the action."

Canon EOS A2 with 400mm lens; 1/750 sec at f5.6; Fujichrome Velvia rated at 100

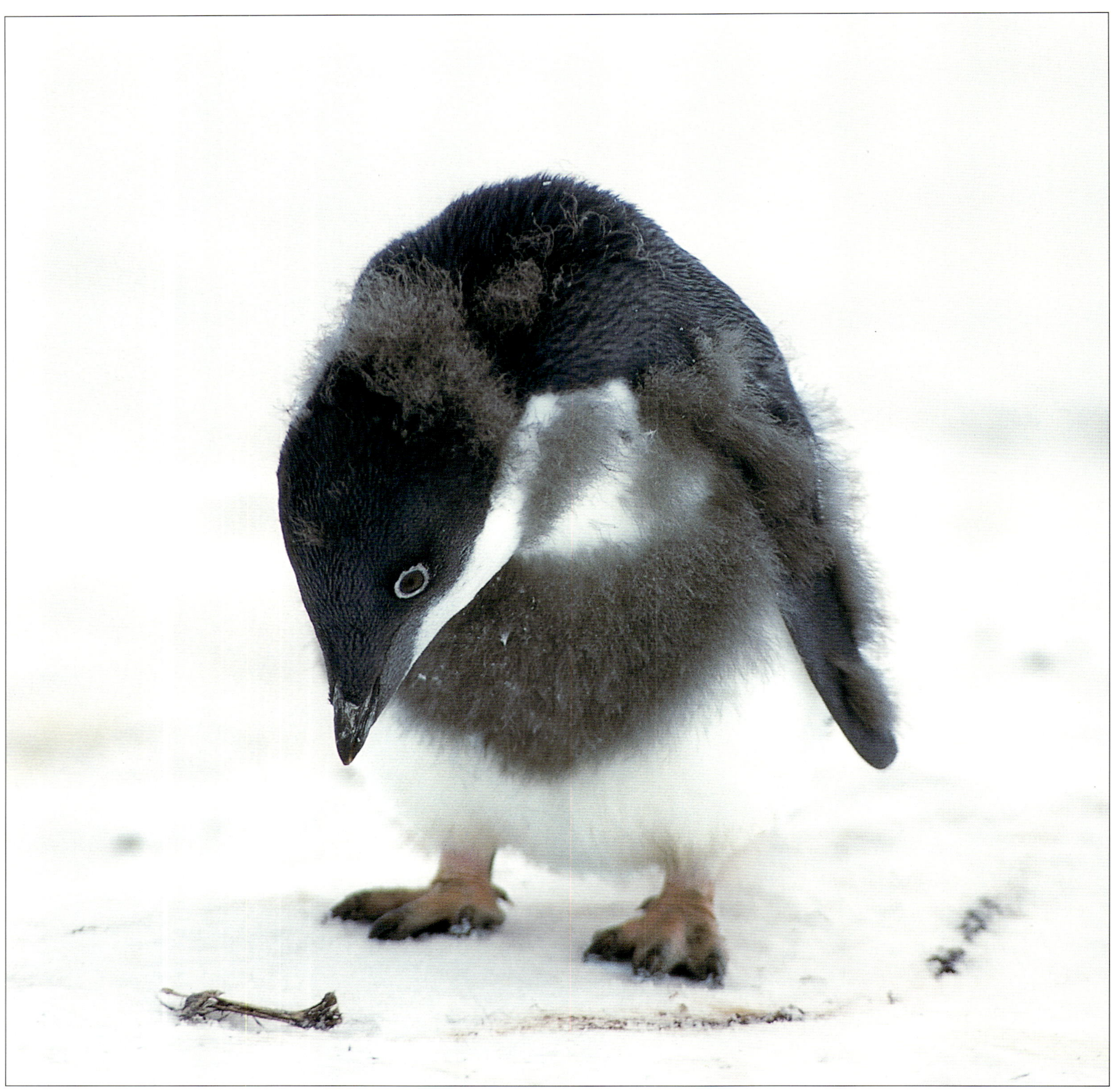

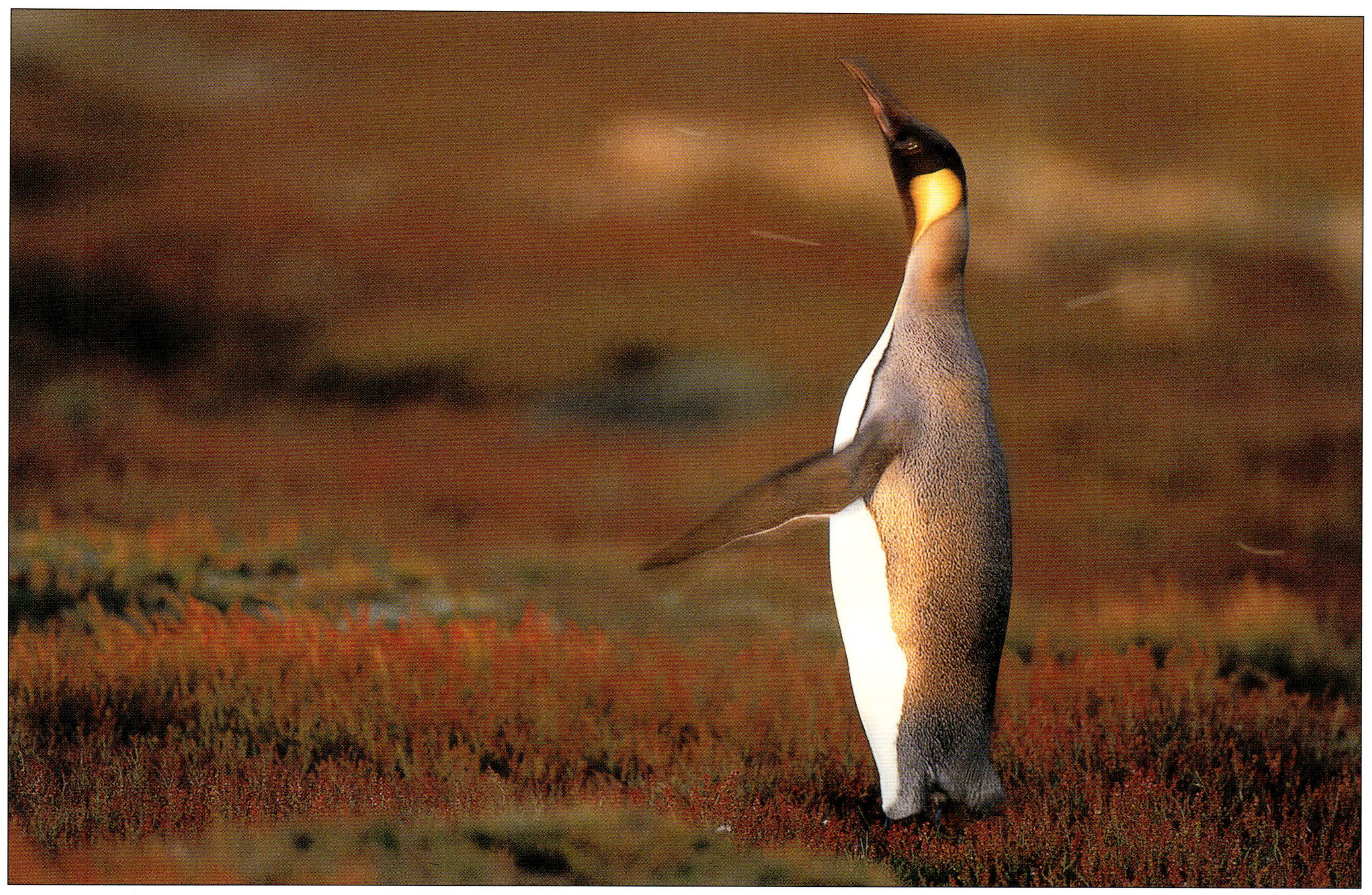

Dr Charles Tyler
United Kingdom
HIGHLY COMMENDED

Young Adelie penguin

"Life can be tough for young Adelie penguins at Cape Hallett, Antarctica. They are highly vulnerable to attack from skuas, who often eat only the liver and leave the rest of the carcass to decay. The penguin in this picture was investigating a bone that may have come from one of its relatives."

Canon T90 with 300mm lens; tripod; Fujichrome 100

Rich Kirchner
United States of America
HIGHLY COMMENDED

King penguin shaking off feathers

"In February 1997, on Sea Lion Island in the Falklands, there were two moulting king penguins in the middle of thousands of Magellanic penguins. I photographed this one as it shook off loose feathers in the first light of morning."

Nikon N90s with 500mm lens; 1/60 sec at f4; Fujichrome Velvia rated at 80

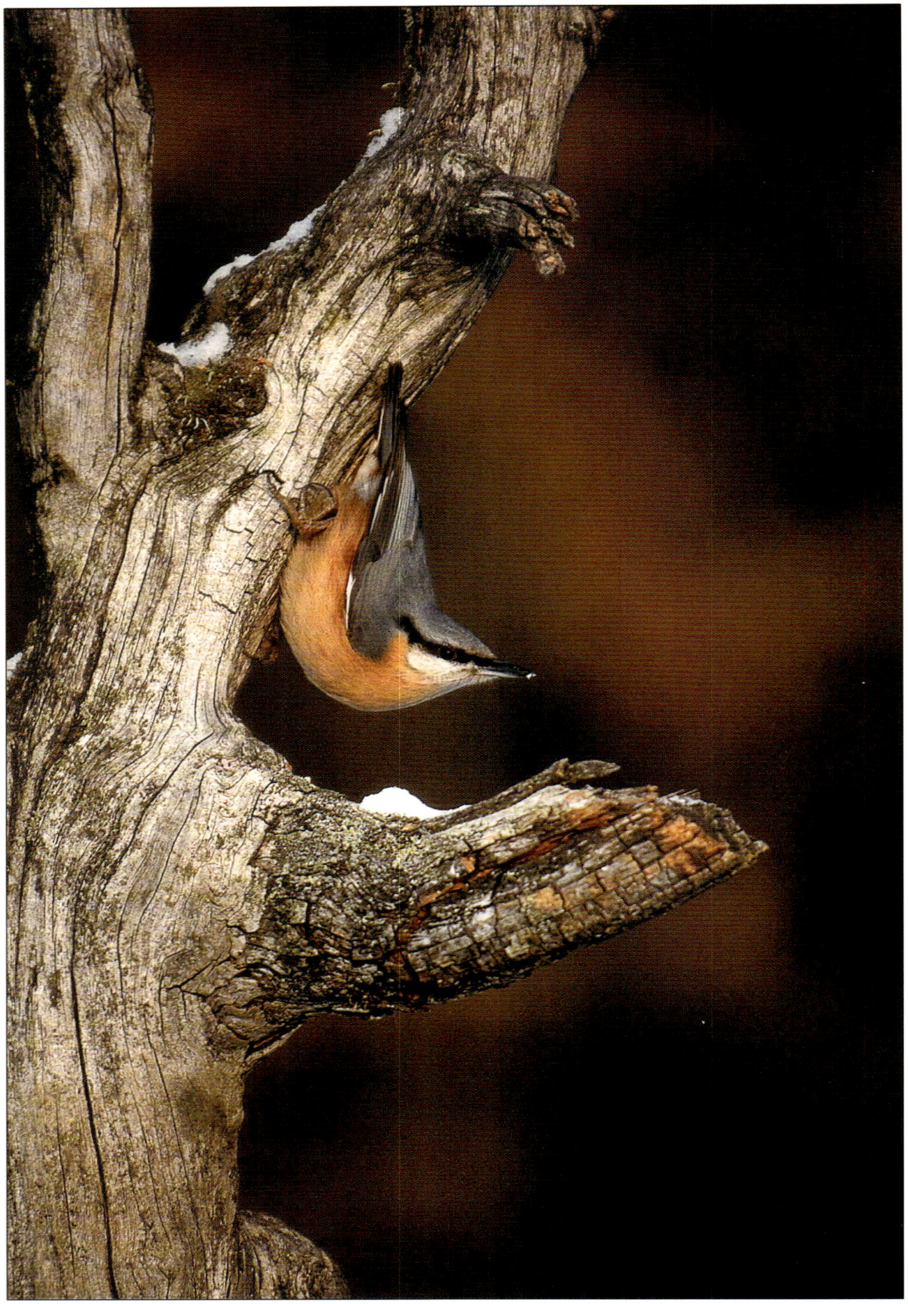

Ewald Neffe

Austria

HIGHLY COMMENDED

Nuthatch on tree

"Nuthatches often come down trees head first, looking for insects and other food. Even so, I had to spend many hours in a hide in bitterly cold weather to get this shot, which was taken in Styria, Austria."

Canon EOS 100 with 35-350mm lens; tripod; 1/250 sec at f5.6; Fujichrome Sensia

Hannu Hautala

Finland

HIGHLY COMMENDED

Siberian jay

"The Korouoma river canyon in Finland is one of my favourite places and the Siberian jay is one of my favourite birds. Everything came together on this sunny day in March, when one side of the canyon was in shadow and a blanket of snow reflected light onto the bird."

Canon EOS 1N with 70-200mm lens; tripod; auto at 1/1000 sec; Fujichrome 400

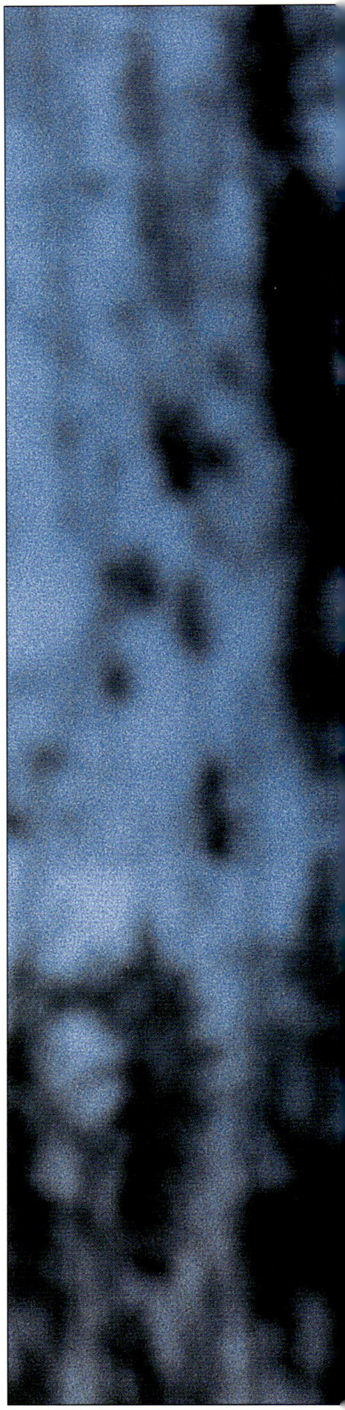

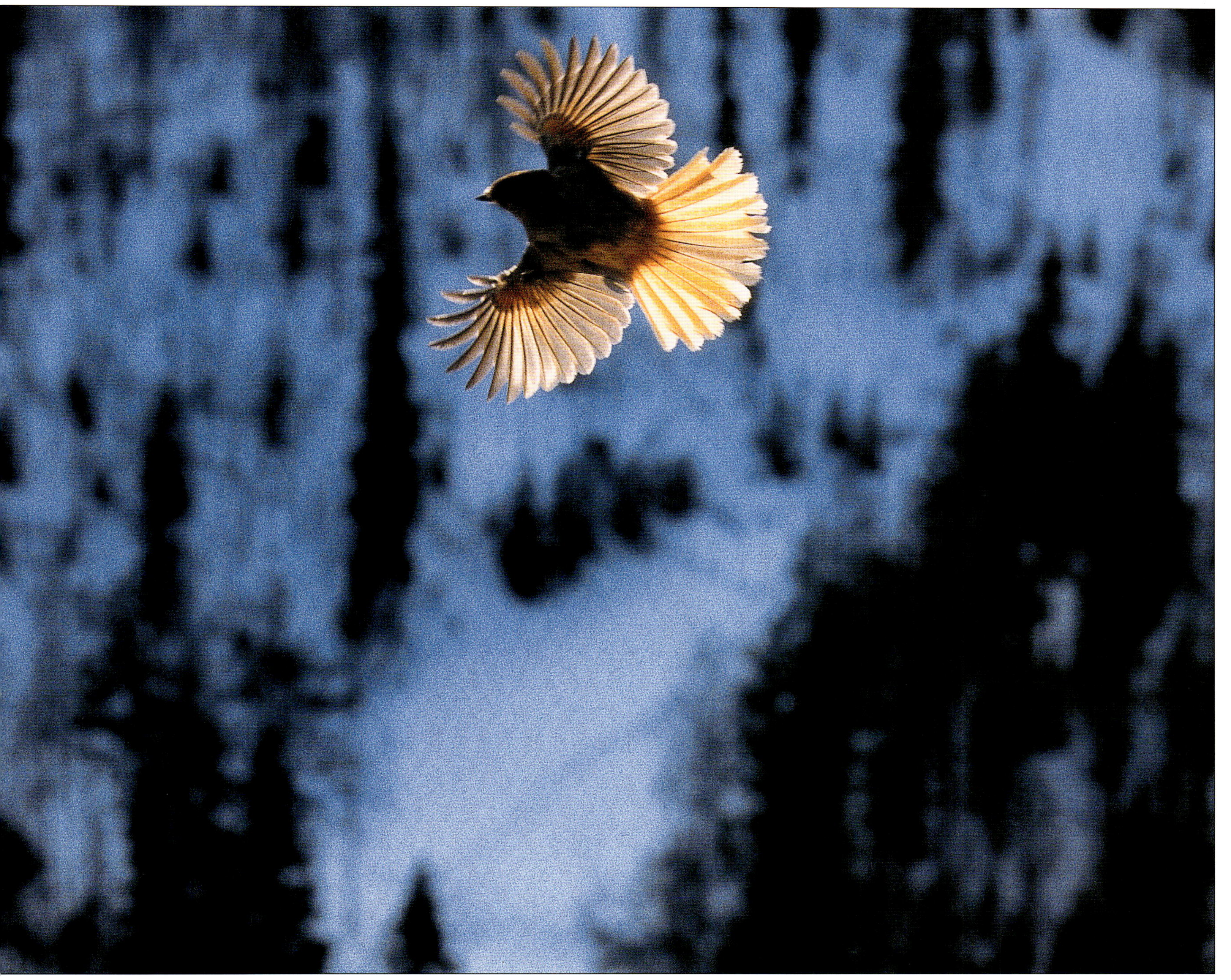

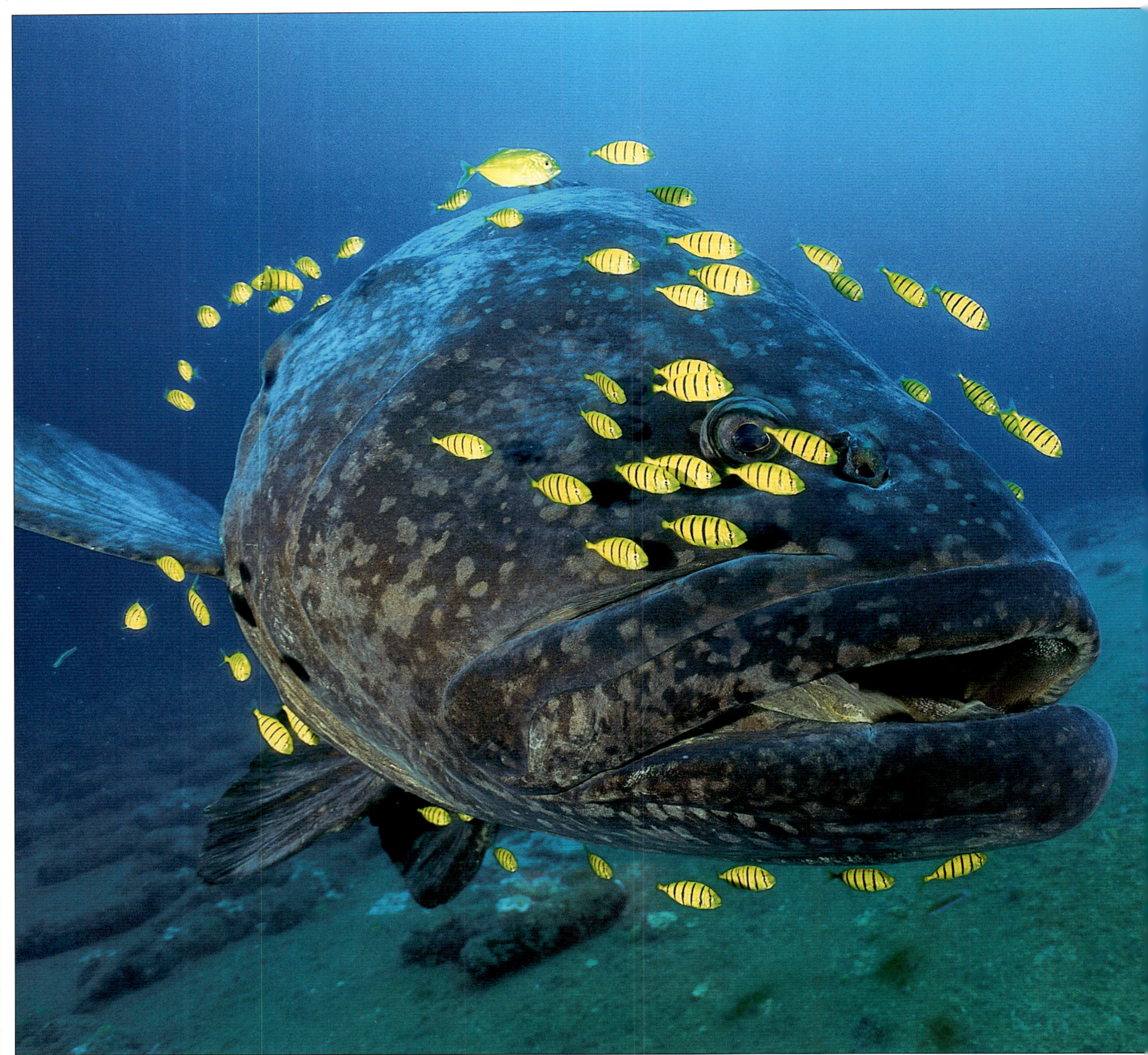

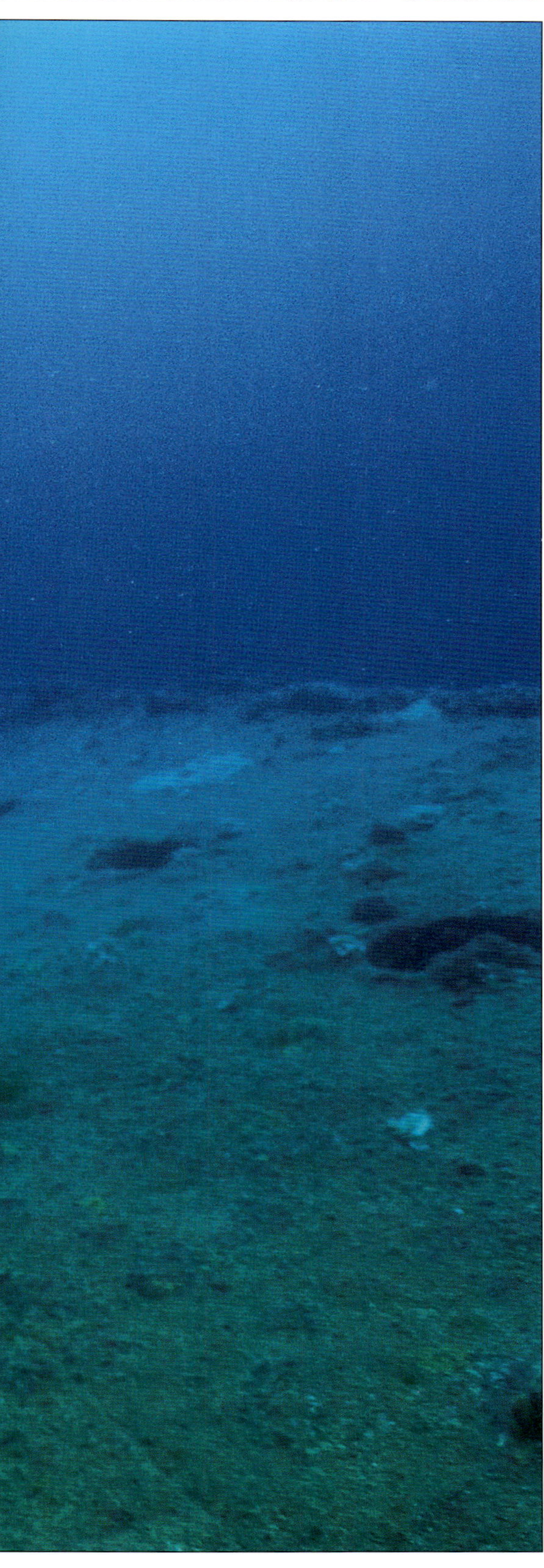

Animal Behaviour

- ALL OTHERS -

The photographs entered in this category should show the subject actively doing something. Pictures are judged on their interest value as well as their aesthetic appeal.

Andy Belcher
New Zealand
WINNER

Grouper with followers

"My first dive on the wreck of the 'President Coolidge', off Vanuatu, was very exciting, especially my meeting with Boris, the resident grouper. Determined to get more time with this 400 kilogram giant, I returned to the wreck two years later. Boris came so close I had to back up to focus the lens. He circled again and again, and I kept on pressing the shutter release."

Nikon F-801s with 20mm lens in underwater housing; two strobes; 1/60 sec at f8; Fujichrome Velvia rated at 100

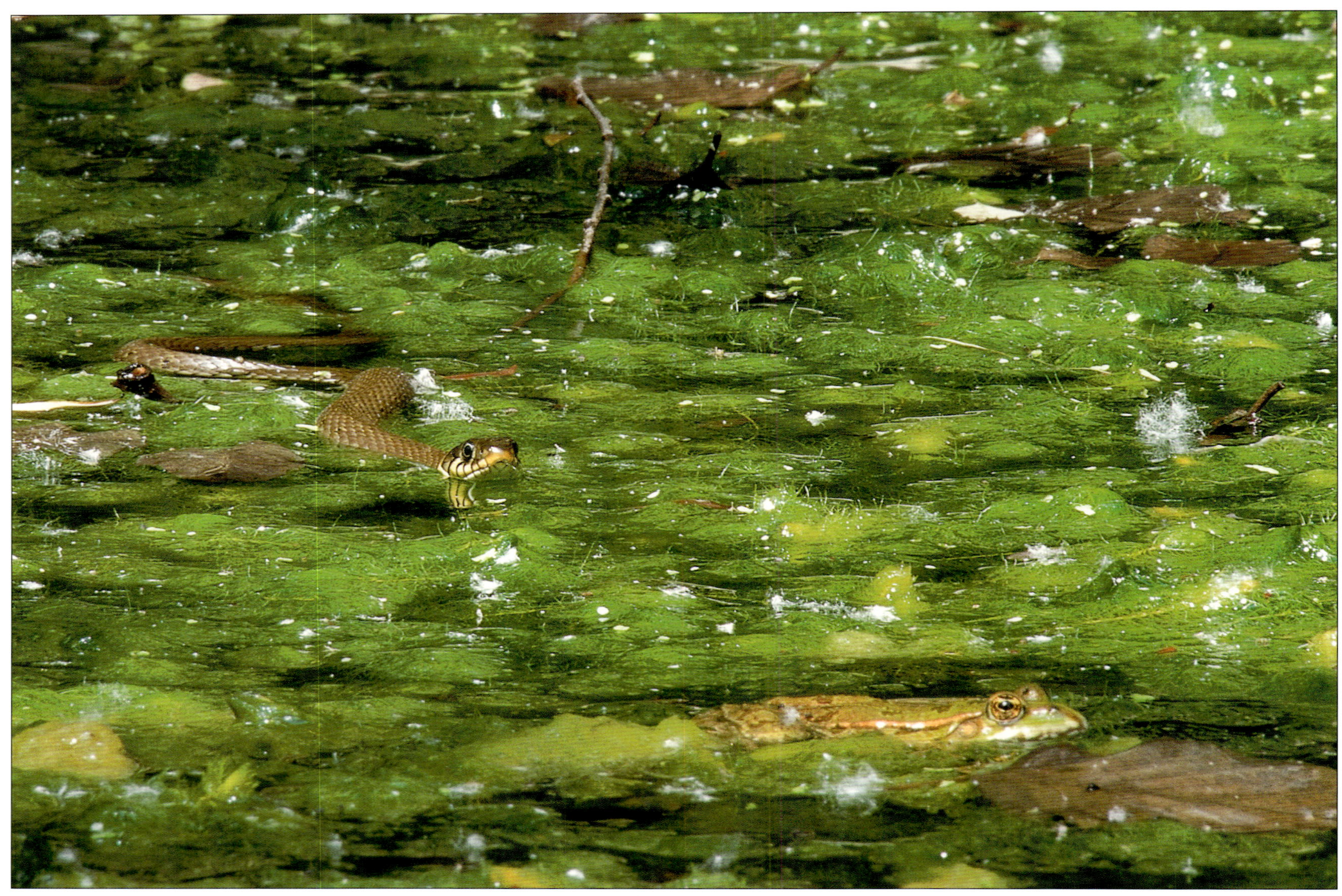

Frank Neumann
Germany
RUNNER-UP

Grass snake hunting frog

"Several grass snakes live at this pond in an old quarry near Stuttgart and I have spent many weekends watching them. The snake in this picture was stalking the frog in slow motion, but it wasn't successful and the frog escaped."

Canon EOS 5 with 300mm lens and x2 converter; tripod; auto at f32; Fujichrome Sensia 100

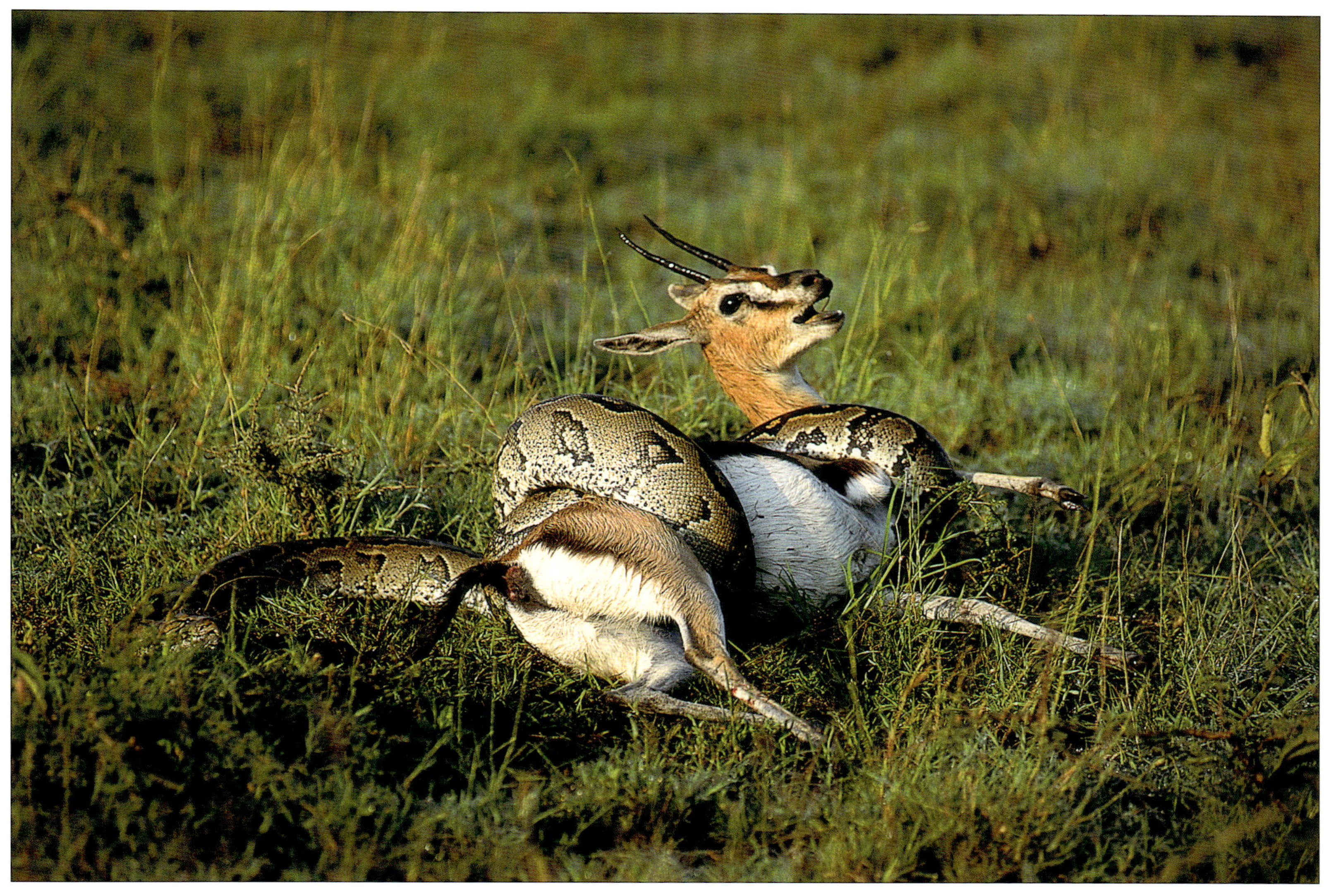

Peter Blackwell
United Kingdom
HIGHLY COMMENDED

Python and gazelle

"This Thomson's gazelle from the Maasai Mara had been captured by an African rock python. But with a last burst of energy, and a little luck, it kicked the python on the head. The snake was dazed and the gazelle managed to get away."

Nikon 8008s with 80-200mm lens; beanbag; 1/250 sec at f5.6; Fujichrome Velvia rated at 80

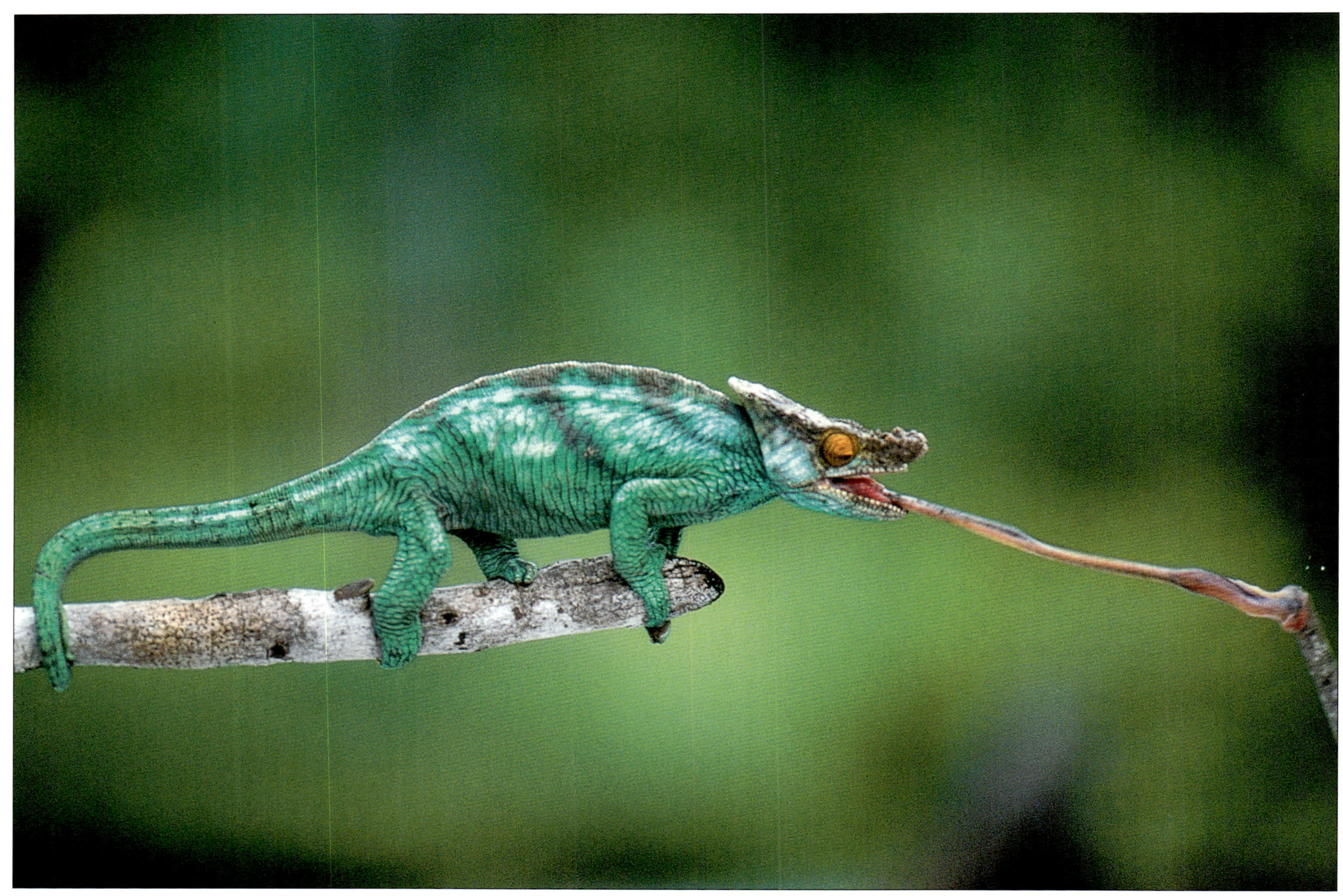

Dr Hermann Brehm

Germany

HIGHLY COMMENDED

Parson's chameleon catching prey

"Parson's chameleon is the largest chameleon in the world and its hunting technique is highly effective. I have never seen one fail to catch its prey. The tongue is too fast for the eye to follow, but modern cameras can catch it on film, as this shot, taken in Madagascar, shows."

Canon EOS RS with 300mm lens; tripod; Fujichrome Velvia

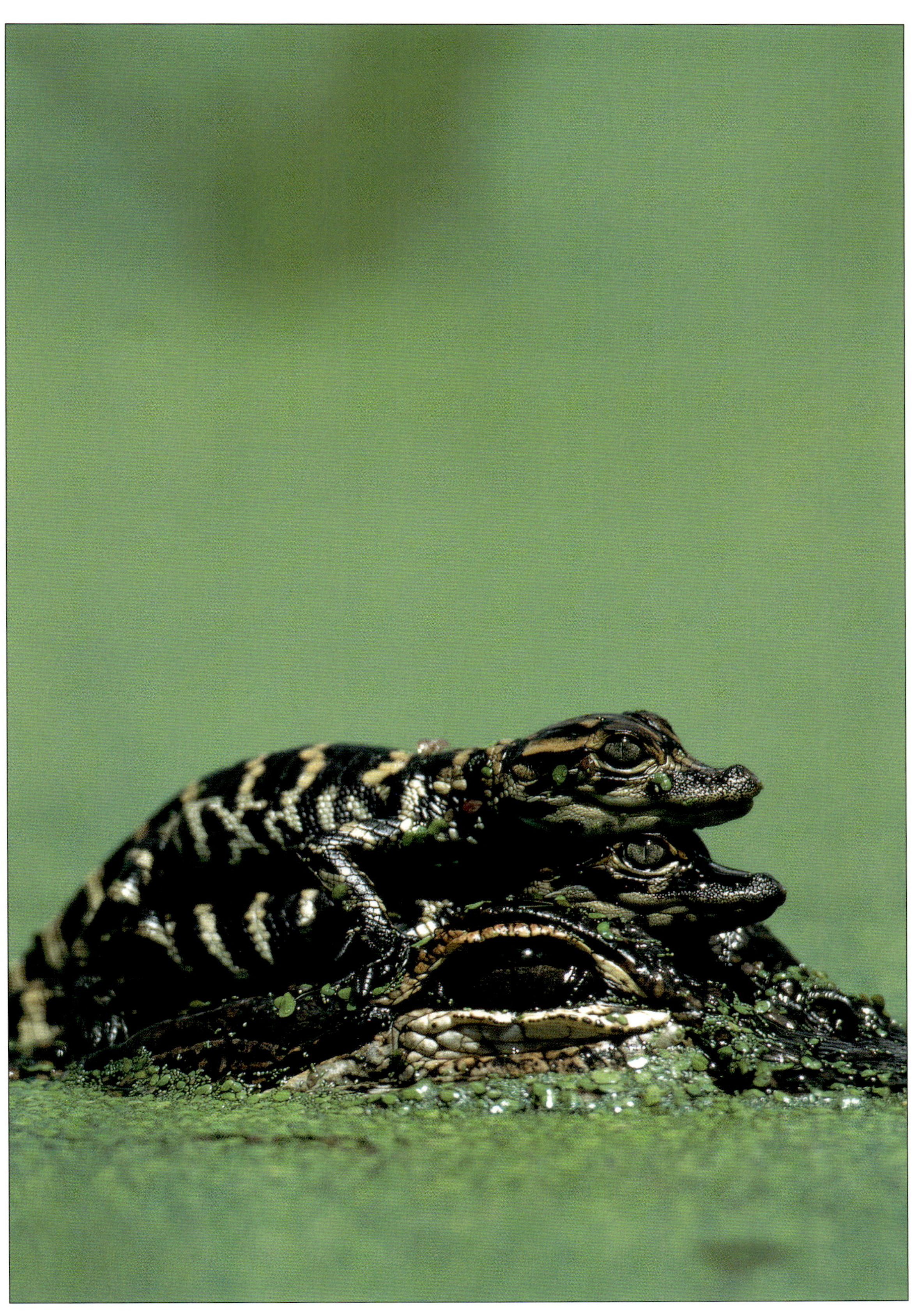

Chris Johns
United States of America
HIGHLY COMMENDED

Newborn alligators

"When baby alligators first hatch, they aren't very good swimmers. These youngsters, from the Everglades National Park, Florida, have found a safe perch on their mother's head."

Nikon; Kodachrome 64

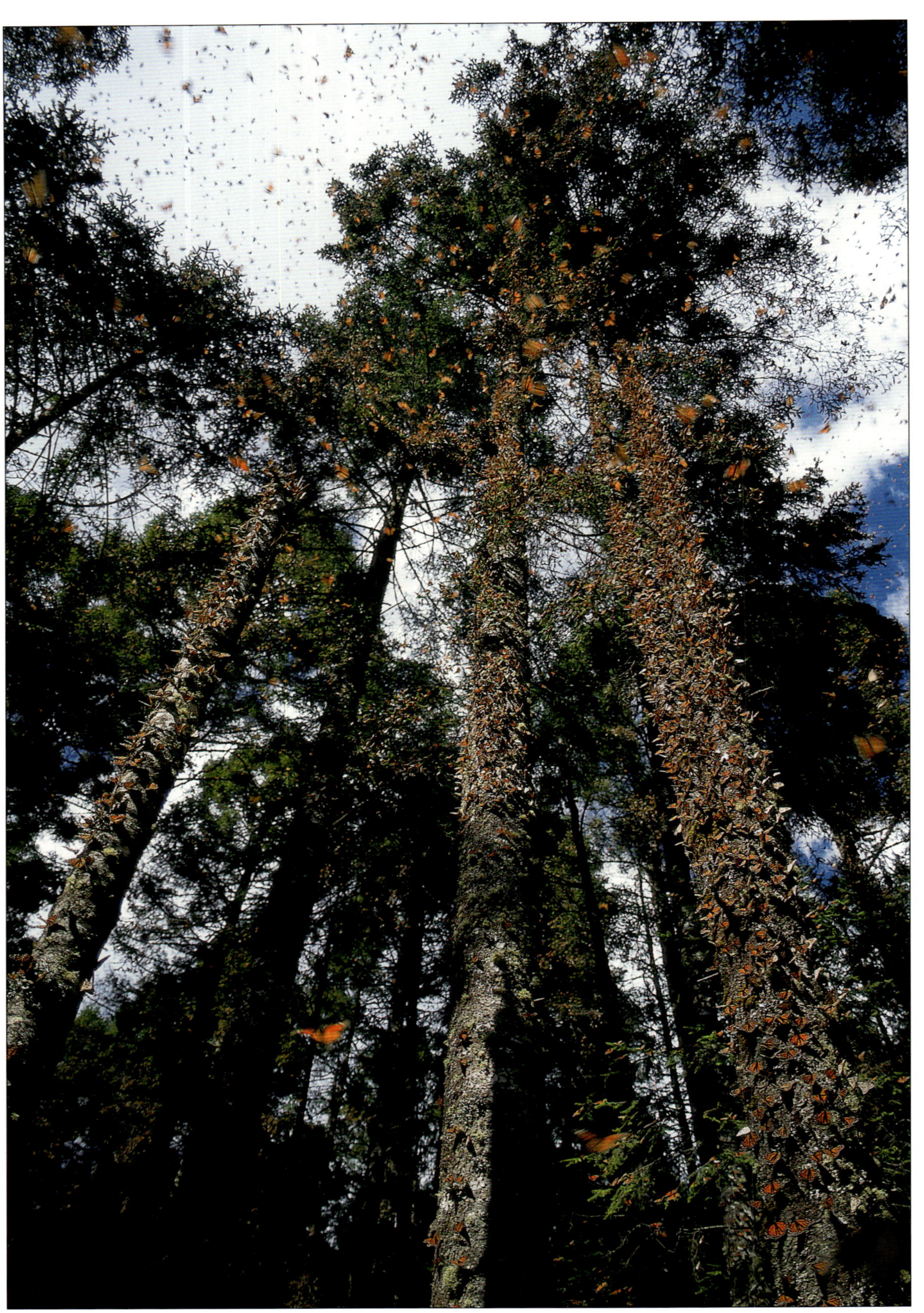

Iñaki Relanzón
Spain
HIGHLY COMMENDED

Monarch butterflies

"Every winter huge numbers of migratory monarch butterflies arrive in Michoacán State, Mexico. In the mornings, warmed by the rising sun, the monarchs become highly active and the sky turns into a spectacular blue and orange mosaic."

Bronica ETRSi with 40mm lens; tripod; polarising filter; 1/60 sec at f5.6; Fujichrome Velvia

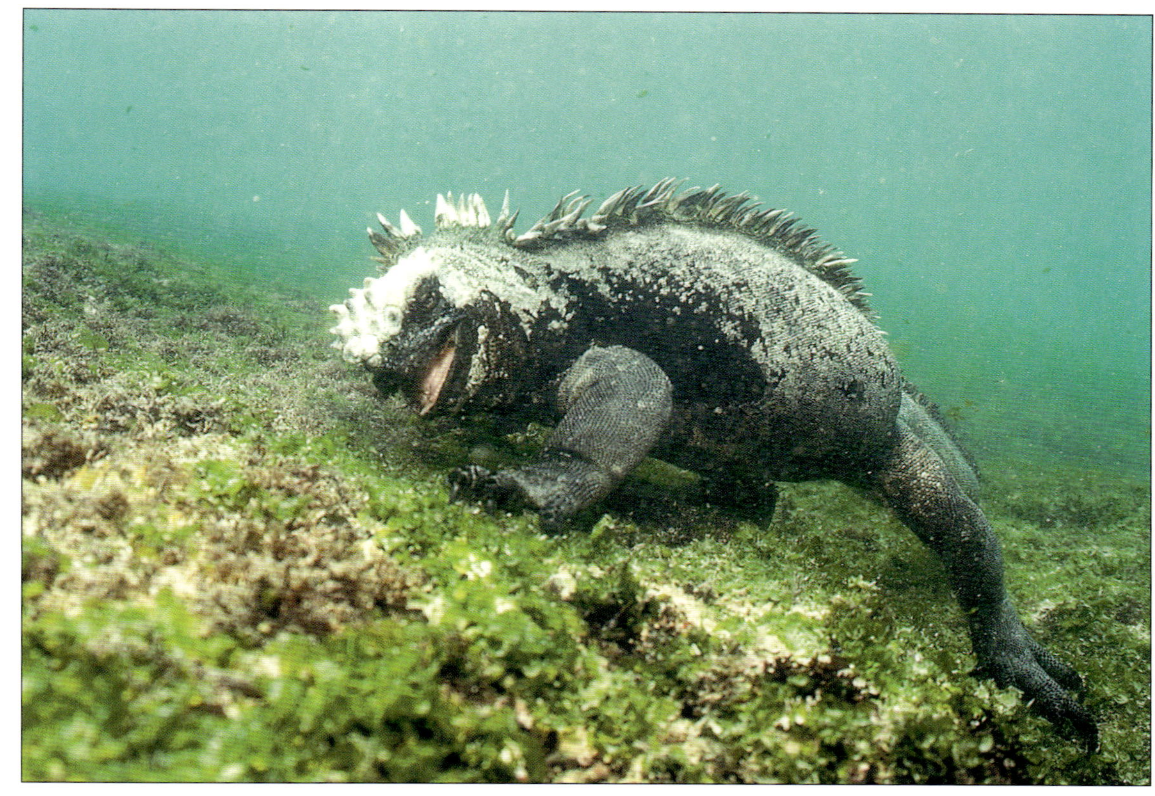

Jonathan R Green
United Kingdom
HIGHLY COMMENDED

Marine iguana feeding underwater

"This male marine iguana from the Galapagos Islands was feeding on algae in about ten feet of water. Once feeding, iguanas become oblivious to divers. They may remain underwater for around 45 minutes before returning to land to warm up and digest their food."

Nikonos V with 20mm lens; flash; 1/125 sec at f8; Fujichrome Provia 100

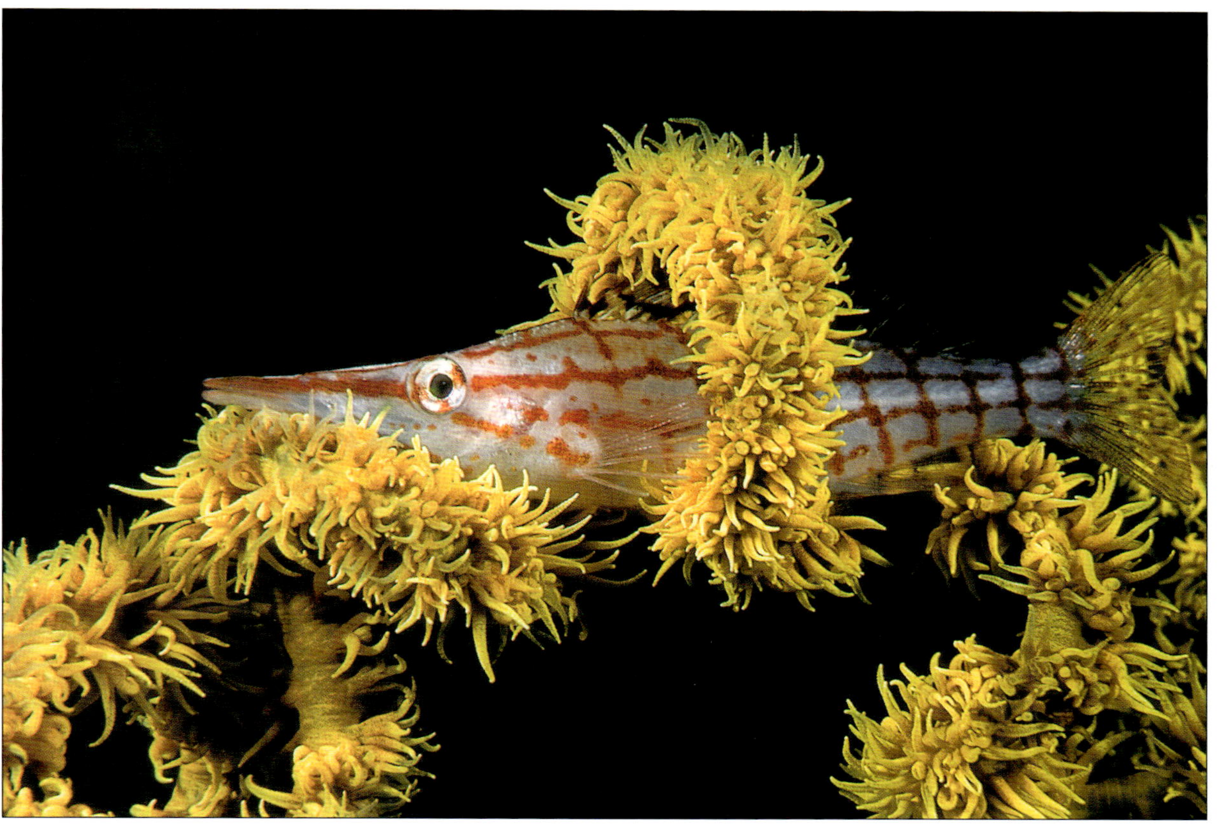

John Olsen
Australia
HIGHLY COMMENDED

Longnose hawkfish in spiral black coral

"Imagine my surprise on a night dive off the island of Komodo, Indonesia, to find this fish inside a coil of coral, just like a serviette in a ring. Longnose hawkfish are usually seen on red gorgonian coral, but here they have learned to find shelter among the stinging cells of this bright yellow species."

Nikonos V with 35mm lens and extension tube; twin flash; 1/60 sec at f22; Fujichrome Velvia rated at 32

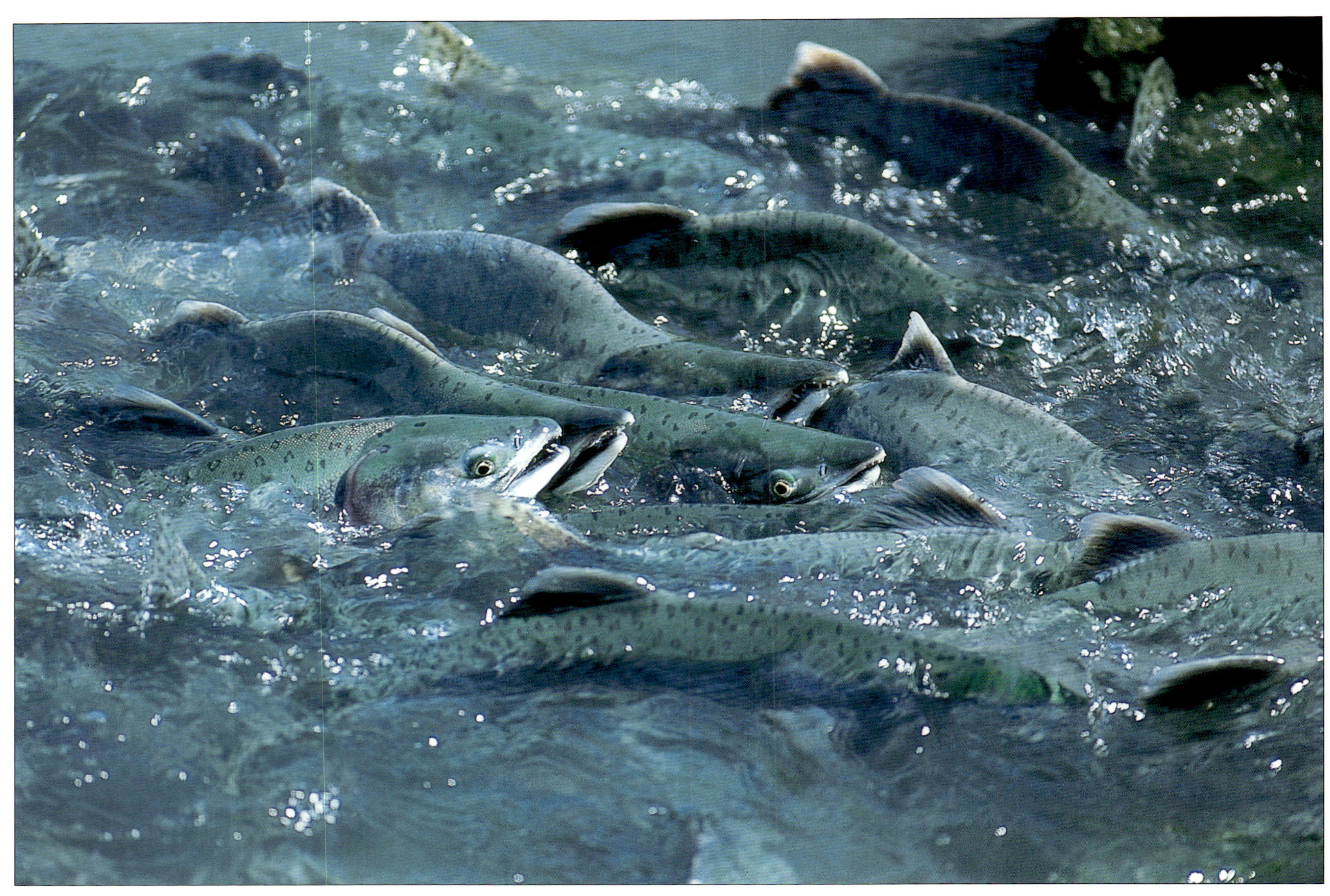

Rich Kirchner

United States of America

HIGHLY COMMENDED

Salmon spawning in small stream

"Large numbers of spawning pink salmon were crowding into this small stream near Valdez, Alaska. Eventually the stream was solid salmon."

Nikon F4 with 500mm lens; 1/250 sec at f8; Fujichrome Velvia

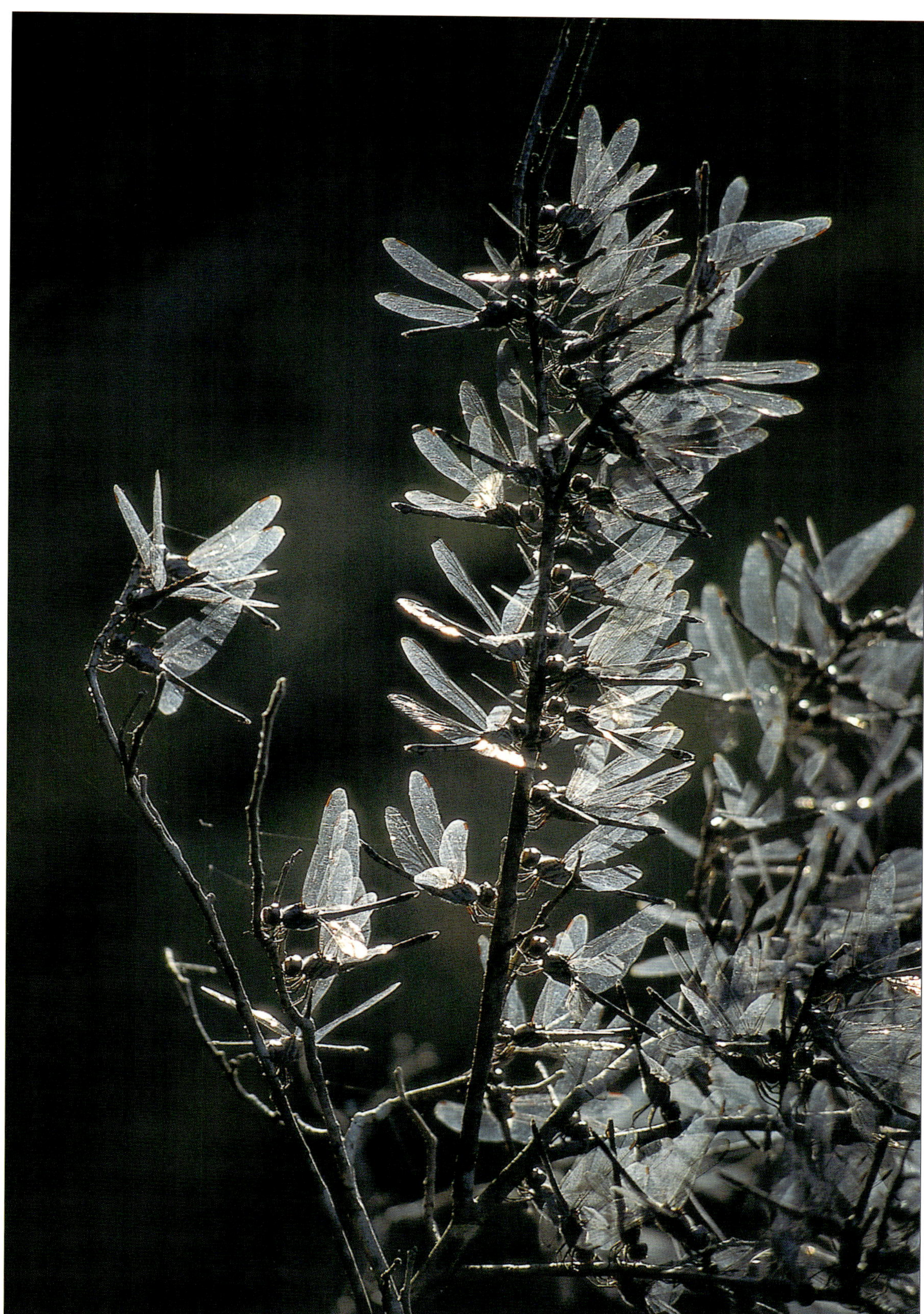

Axel Gomille
Germany
HIGHLY COMMENDED

Dragonflies

"Earlier this year I was working as a naturalist in Kanha Tiger Reserve, India. One morning, while taking a guest for an elephant ride, I came across this sleeping community of dragonflies. It was very difficult to take pictures from the back of the elephant because he wouldn't stand still."

Nikon F-801s with 70-210mm lens; shoulderpod; 1/30 sec at f5.6; Fujichrome Sensia 100

British Wildlife

Entries must feature wild plants or animals, which can be in wild or urban settings.

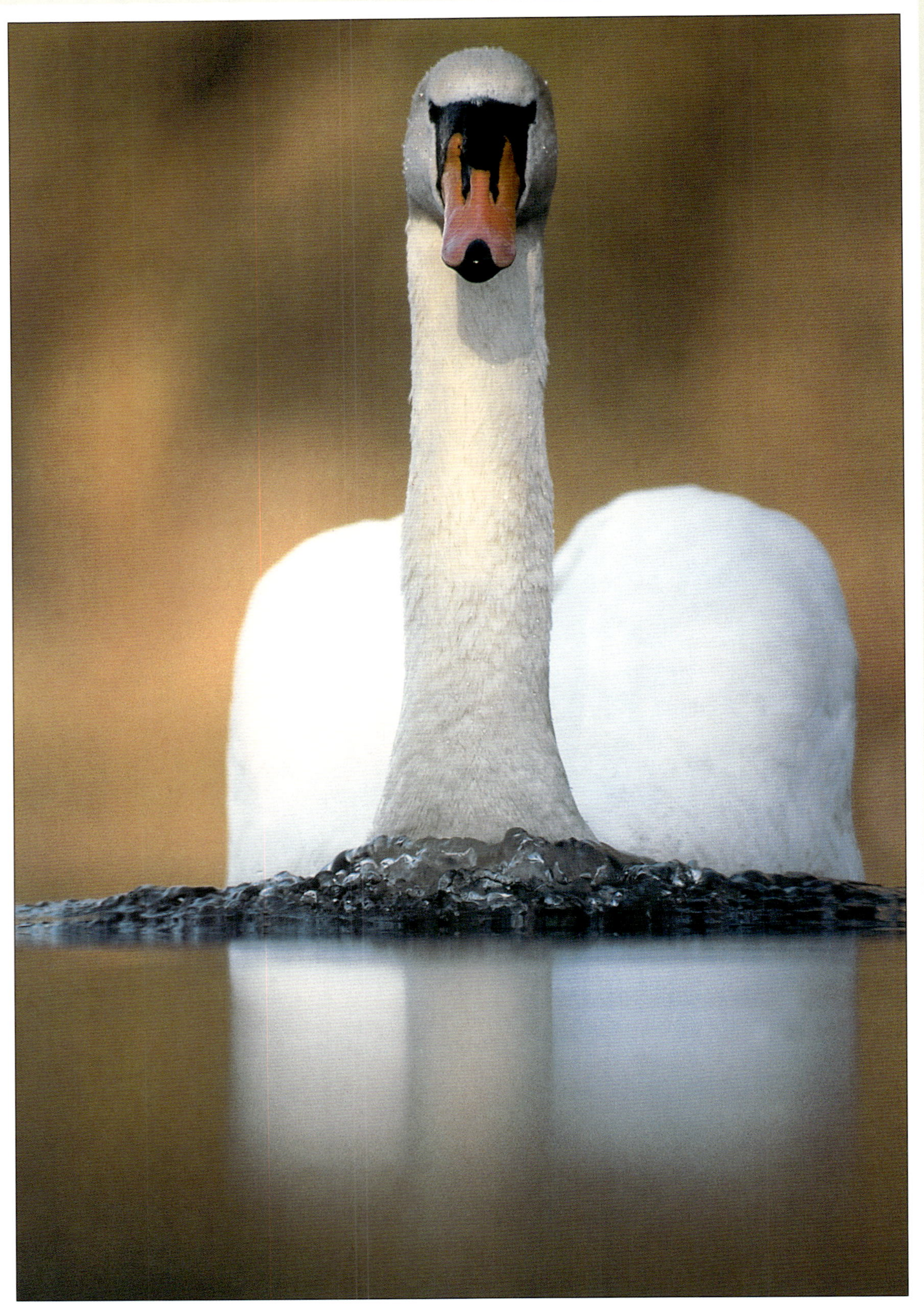

Russell Hartwell
United Kingdom
WINNER

Mute swan

"I photographed a pair of mute swans at a Buckinghamshire lake over several sessions in January 1997. For this portrait I stood downstream from a waterfall, positioned the lens level with the lake's surface and waited for the swan to investigate the strange creature in the water."

Nikon F4 with 500mm lens; 1/500 sec at f5.6; Fujichrome Provia 100 rated at 200

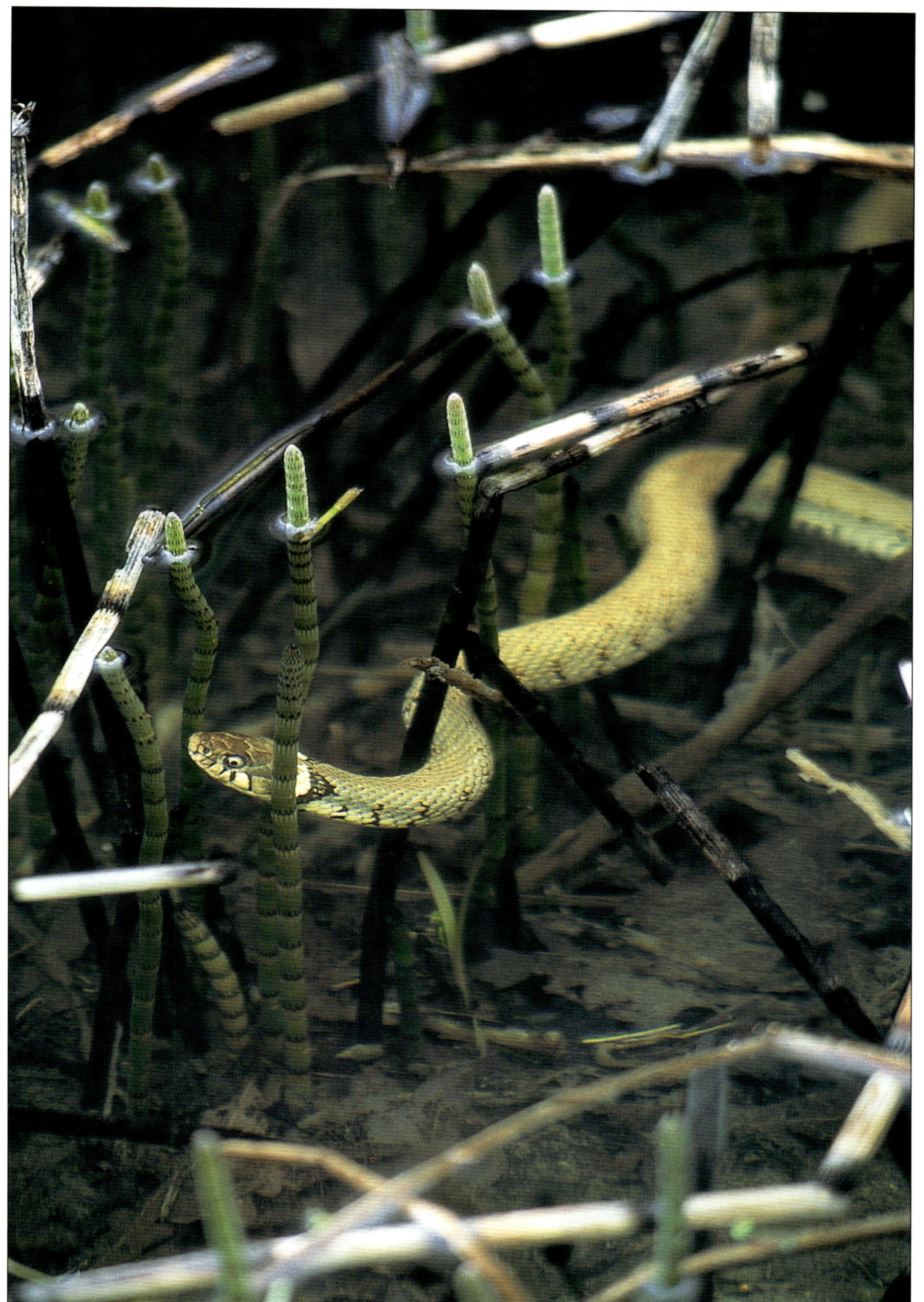

Dr David J Slater
United Kingdom
RUNNER-UP

Grass snake swimming

"This snake caught my attention at a pond in an Oxfordshire forest. As soon as I moved to photograph it, it saw me and came closer, ignoring the many sticklebacks and frogs in the pond. It appeared to be hunting me and I held its interest by waving my hands while focusing."

Canon EOS 50E with 80-200mm lens; tripod; polarising filter; 1/30 sec at f2.8; Fujichrome Velvia

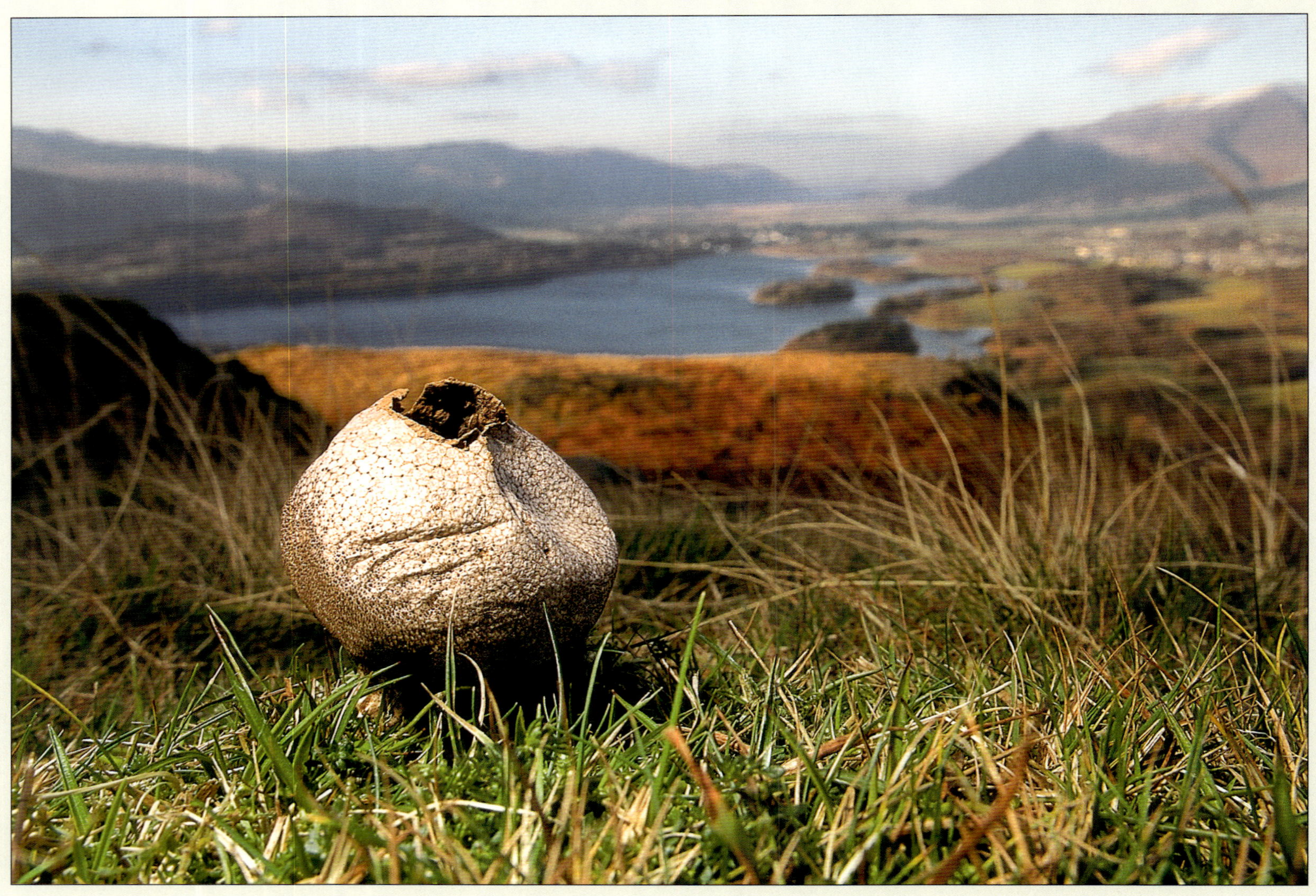

Michael Hutchinson
United Kingdom
HIGHLY COMMENDED

Puffball fungus

"This fungus (Lycoperdon foetidum) was a surprise find near the top of a fell in the Lake District. Before my trip, I had the idea for the shot, but I didn't expect to get the opportunity in mid-December. I had left my reflector at home and had to use a white shopping bag as a substitute."

Canon EOS 5 with 24mm lens and close-up lens; flash; f22; Fujichrome Velvia

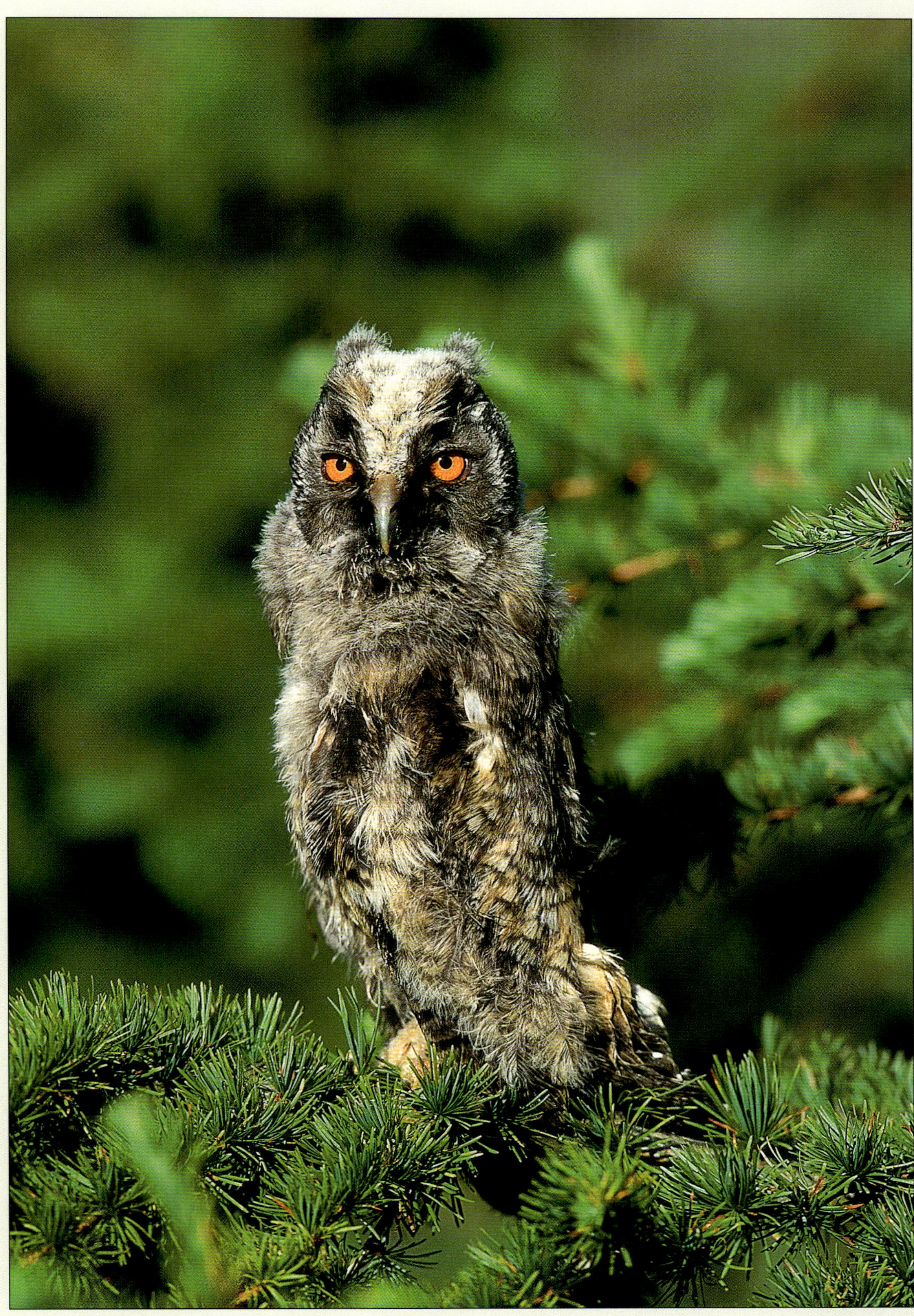

Alan Ross
United Kingdom
HIGHLY COMMENDED

Long-eared owl chick

"I was photographing roe deer in a forestry plantation in southwest Scotland, when I suddenly noticed two long-eared owl chicks. Once the deer family had moved on, I carefully photographed each chick in turn. This was the first time long-eared owls had been known to nest in this particular area."

Canon T90 with 300mm lens;
Fujichrome 50 rated at 64

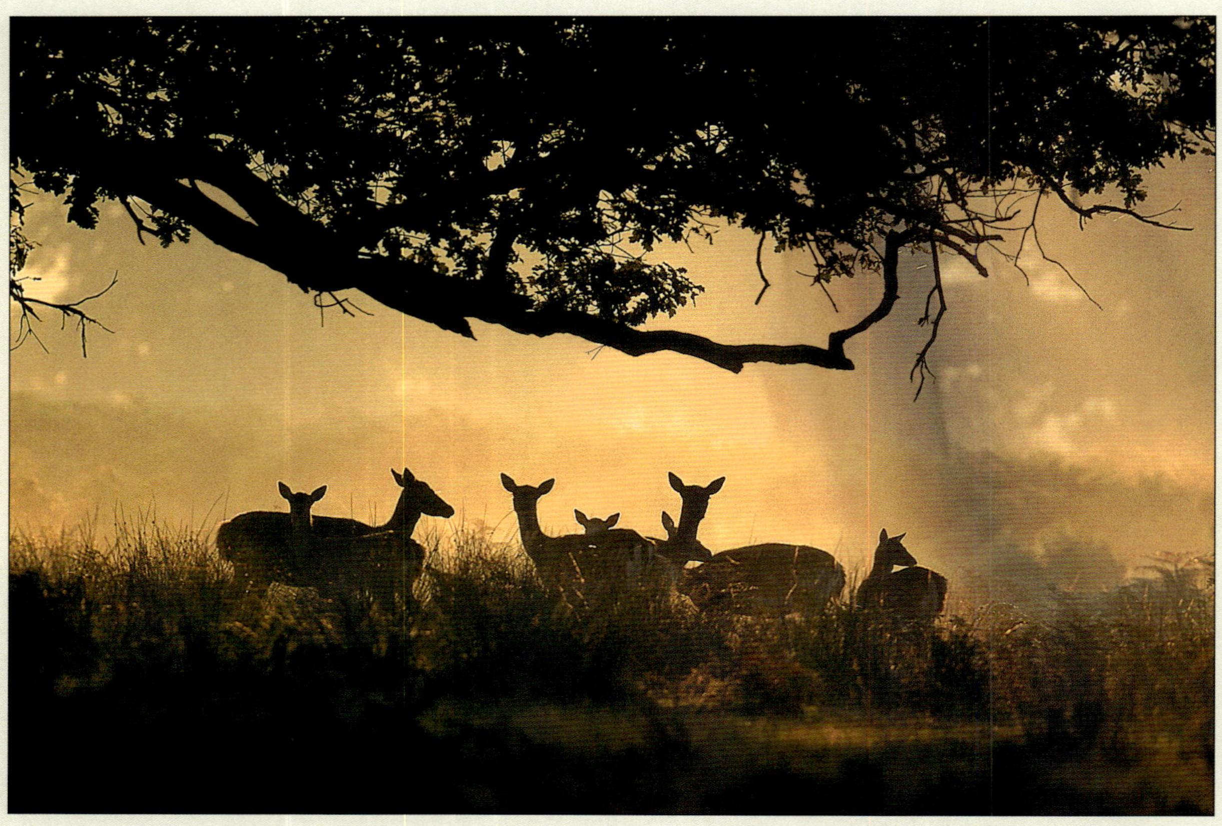

Mark Hamblin
United Kingdom
HIGHLY COMMENDED

Fallow deer group

"I'd arrived at Bradgate Park in Leicestershire just before dawn. As I made my way into a clearing I suddenly spotted these fallow deer, but they began to wander away. When they reached the tree, the entire scene was immediately lit up with wonderfully soft backlighting."

Canon T90 with 500mm lens; 1/250 sec at f6.7; Fujichrome Sensia 100

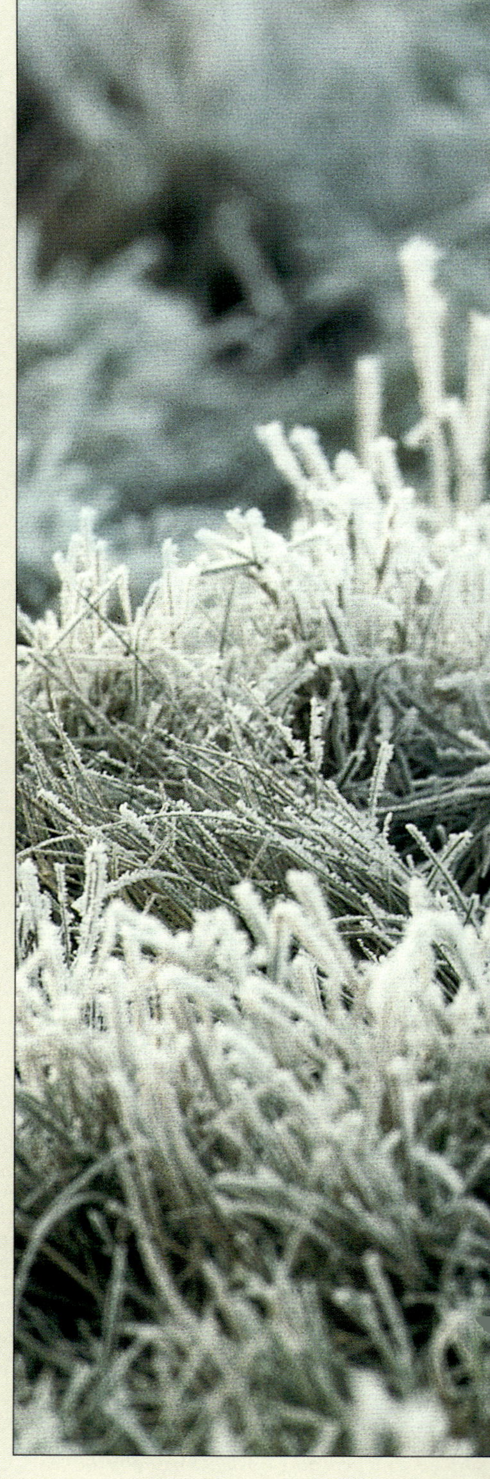

Ernie Janes
United Kingdom
HIGHLY COMMENDED

Hare in hoar frost

"When I discovered this hare's regular lying-up place, I tried to drive past most days so that the animal would get used to my Landrover. Two months later, the hare was taking little notice of me, and I was able to take the photograph at dawn on a very frosty morning."

Canon EOS 1 with 500mm lens; beanbag; 1/30 sec at f4.5; Kodachrome 64

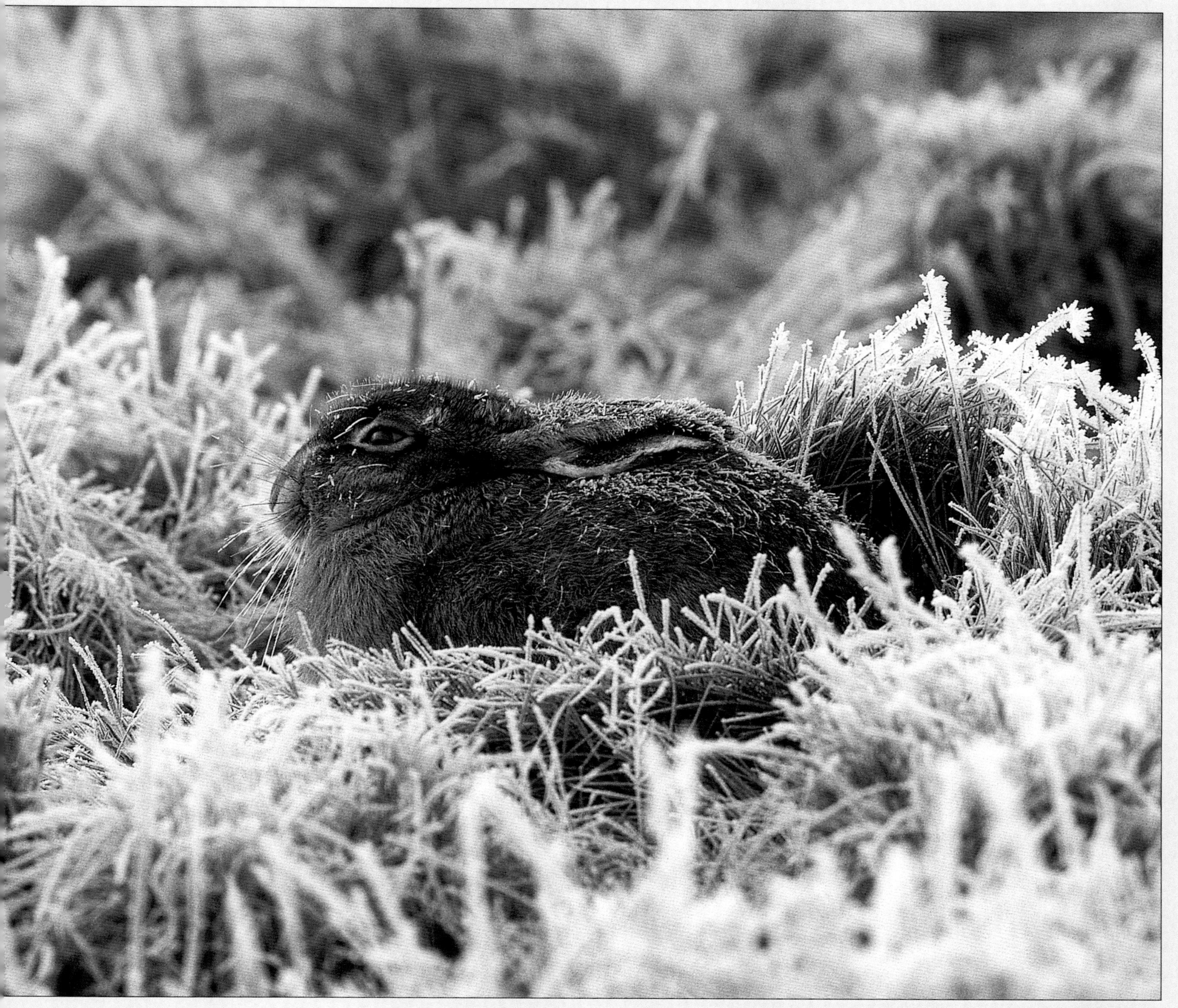

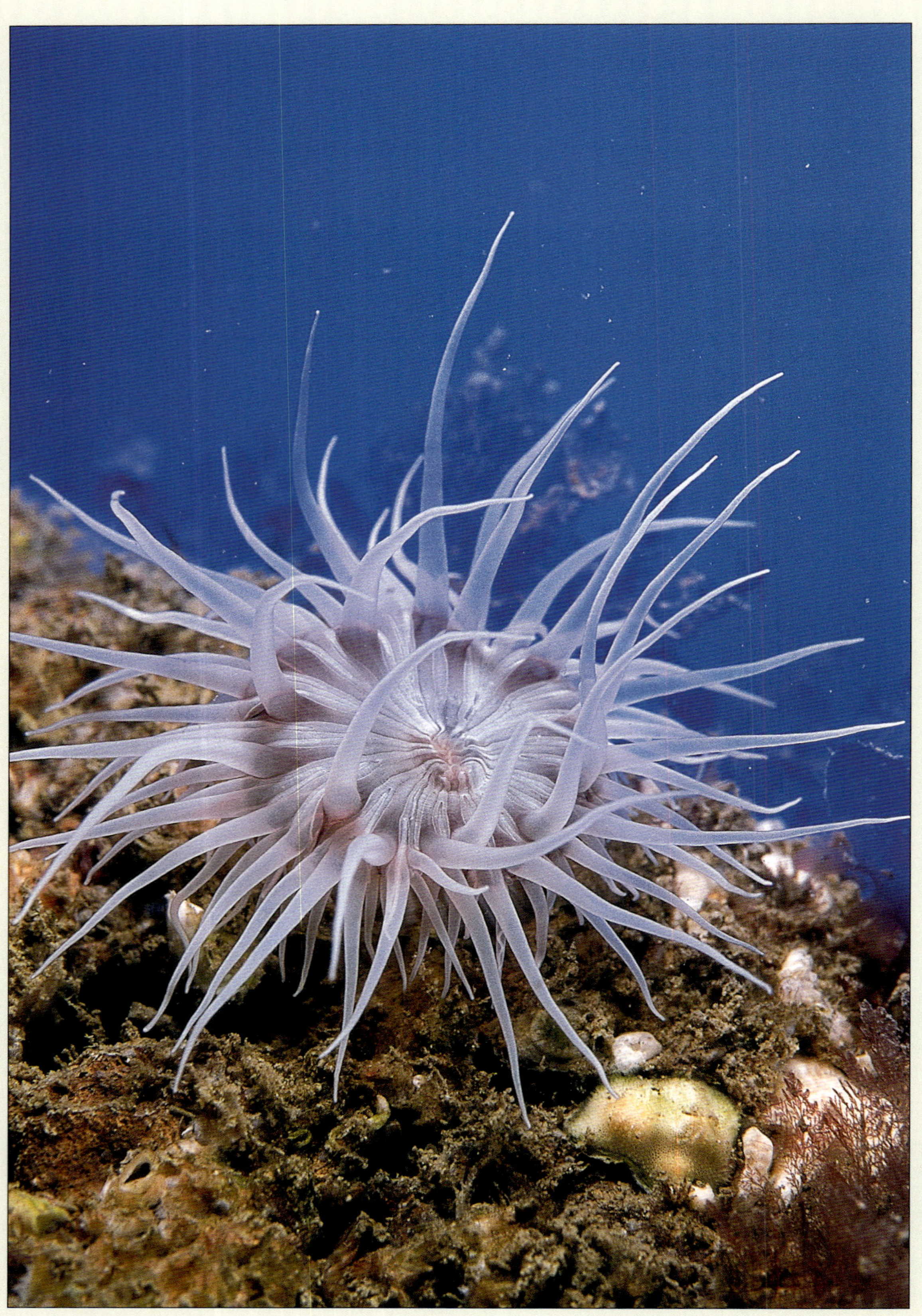

Mark Webster
United Kingdom
HIGHLY COMMENDED

Dahlia anemone feeding

"These anemones are common on shallow water reefs and in rock pools throughout the southwest. At slack water they are often found as unattractive blobs on the rock. But when a tidal current is flowing they extend their tentacles to capture passing plankton."

Nikon 801 with 60mm micro lens in underwater housing; flash; 1/60 sec at f16; Fujichrome Velvia

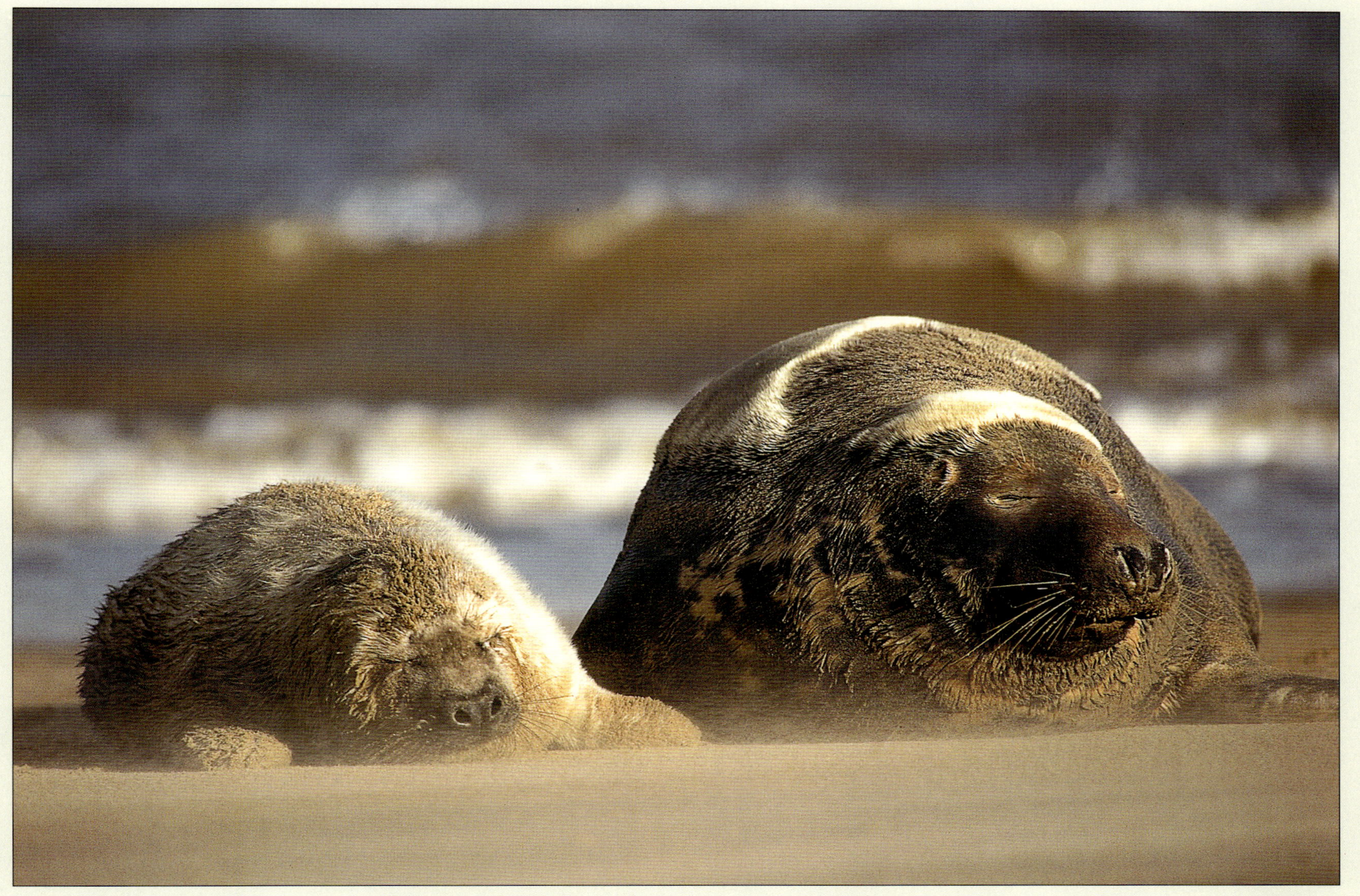

Allan Potts
United Kingdom
HIGHLY COMMENDED

Grey seals in sandstorm

"These grey seals were so preoccupied with the wind and blowing sand on the Lincolnshire coast that they didn't realise I was there. With camera on tripod I approached very slowly, so as not to disturb them, and I was able to get within five metres. A memorable occasion to say the least."

Nikon F4 with 500mm lens; tripod; 1/250 sec at f4.5; Ektachrome 100

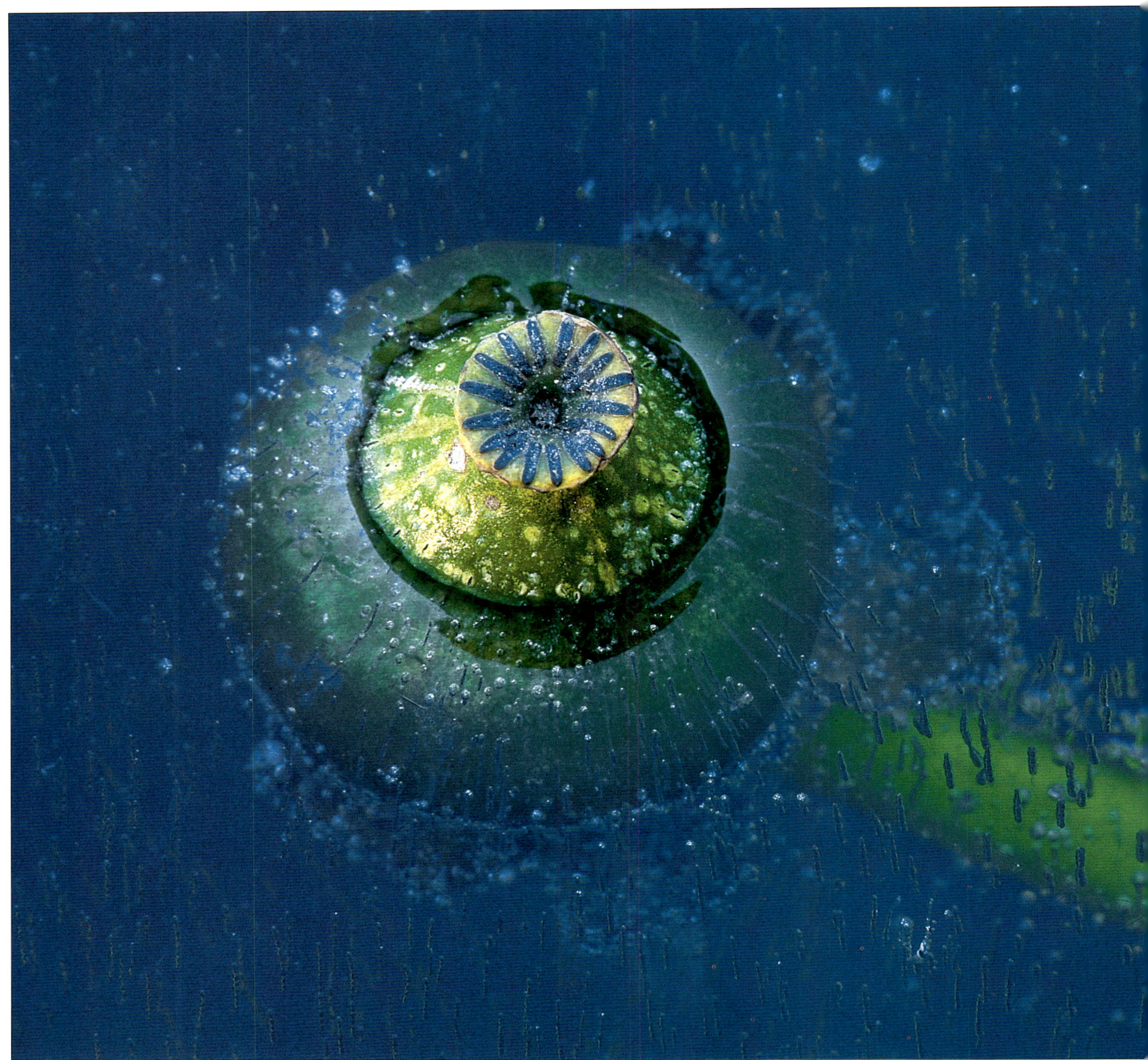

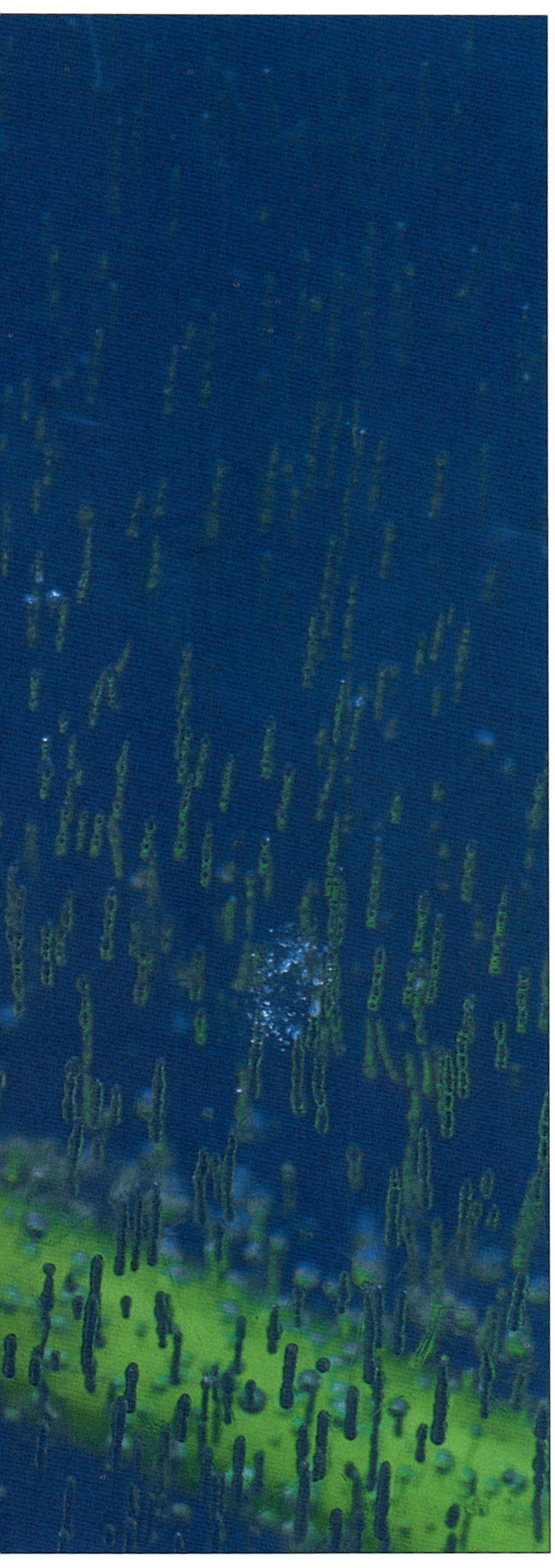

In Praise of Plants

Pictures should highlight the beauty and importance of flowering and non-flowering plants.

Paavo Hamunen
Finland
WINNER

Water lily in frozen pond

"One evening in October I was jogging near my home in Kuusamo, Finland, when I noticed water lily leaves in the pond beside the track. The temperature dropped to −7 degrees Celsius that night, and so in the morning I went back to the pond with my camera."

Nikon F4 with 105mm micro lens; 1/2 sec at f22; Fujichrome Velvia

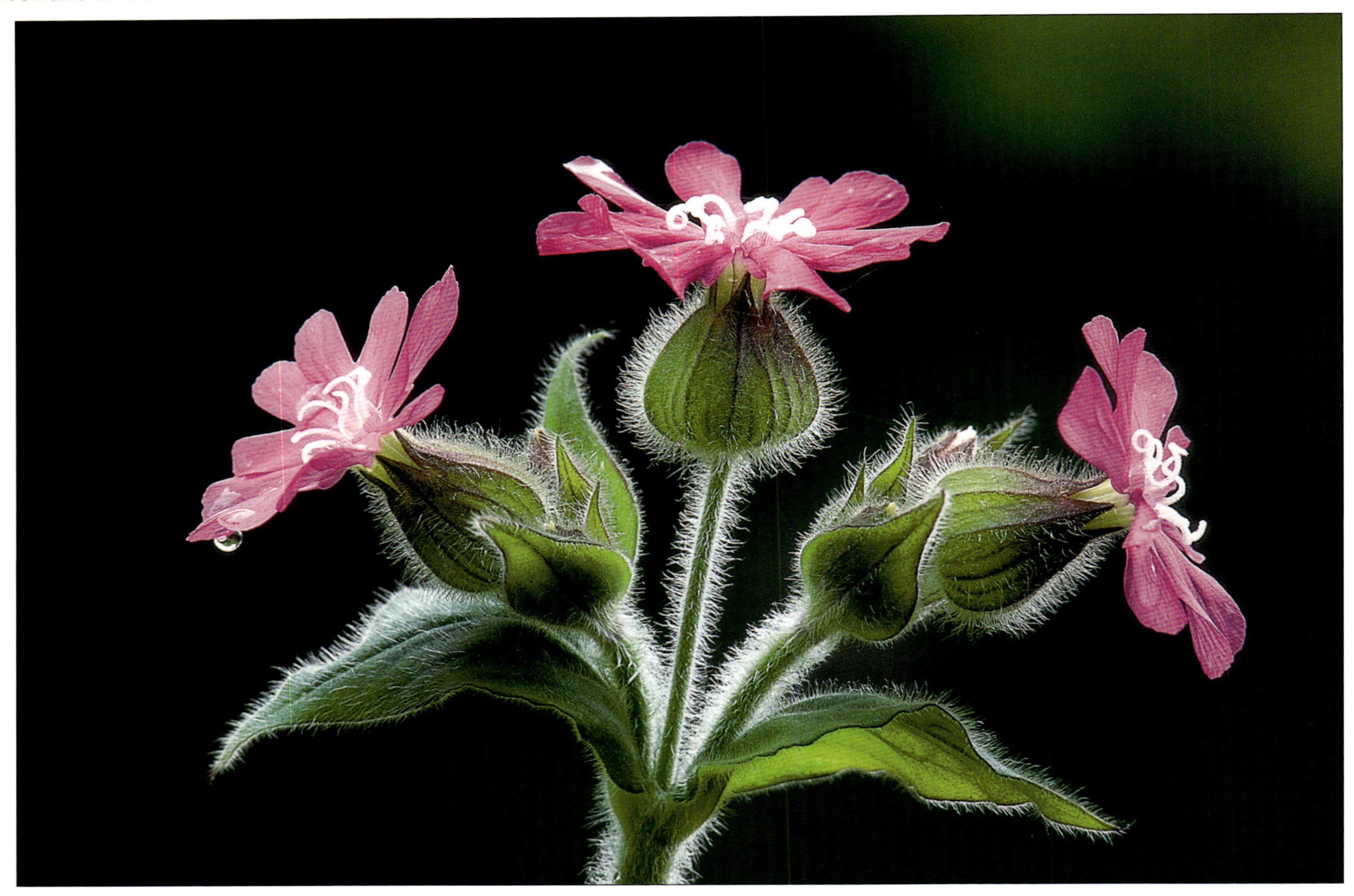

Laurie Campbell
United Kingdom
RUNNER-UP

Red campion

"Red campion is a common plant in woodland close to where I live in Berwickshire. Because I had so many subjects to choose from, it was relatively easy to find just the composition I wanted."

Nikon F3 with 200mm macro lens; tripod; 1/4 sec at f16; Fujichrome Velvia

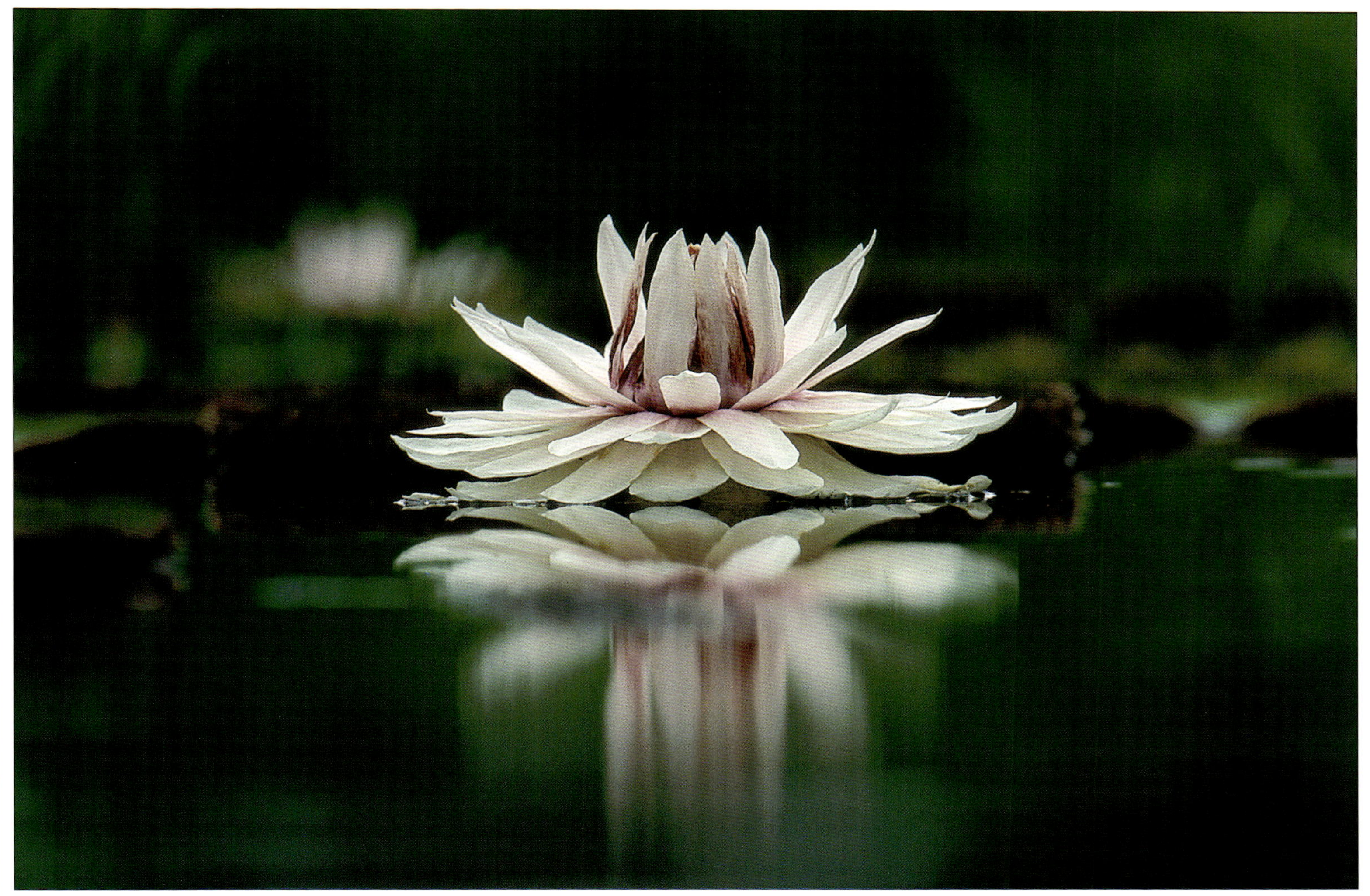

Jan Vermeer
Netherlands
HIGHLY COMMENDED

Giant water lily

"Earlier this year I went on an expedition to Guyana. One day I was waiting for a group of giant otters to appear when it started raining. There were several giant water lilies (Victoria amazonica) growing in the pond in front of me, and so I put the camera close to the water line and captured this image."

Canon EOS 5 with 300mm lens; beanbag; Fujichrome Velvia

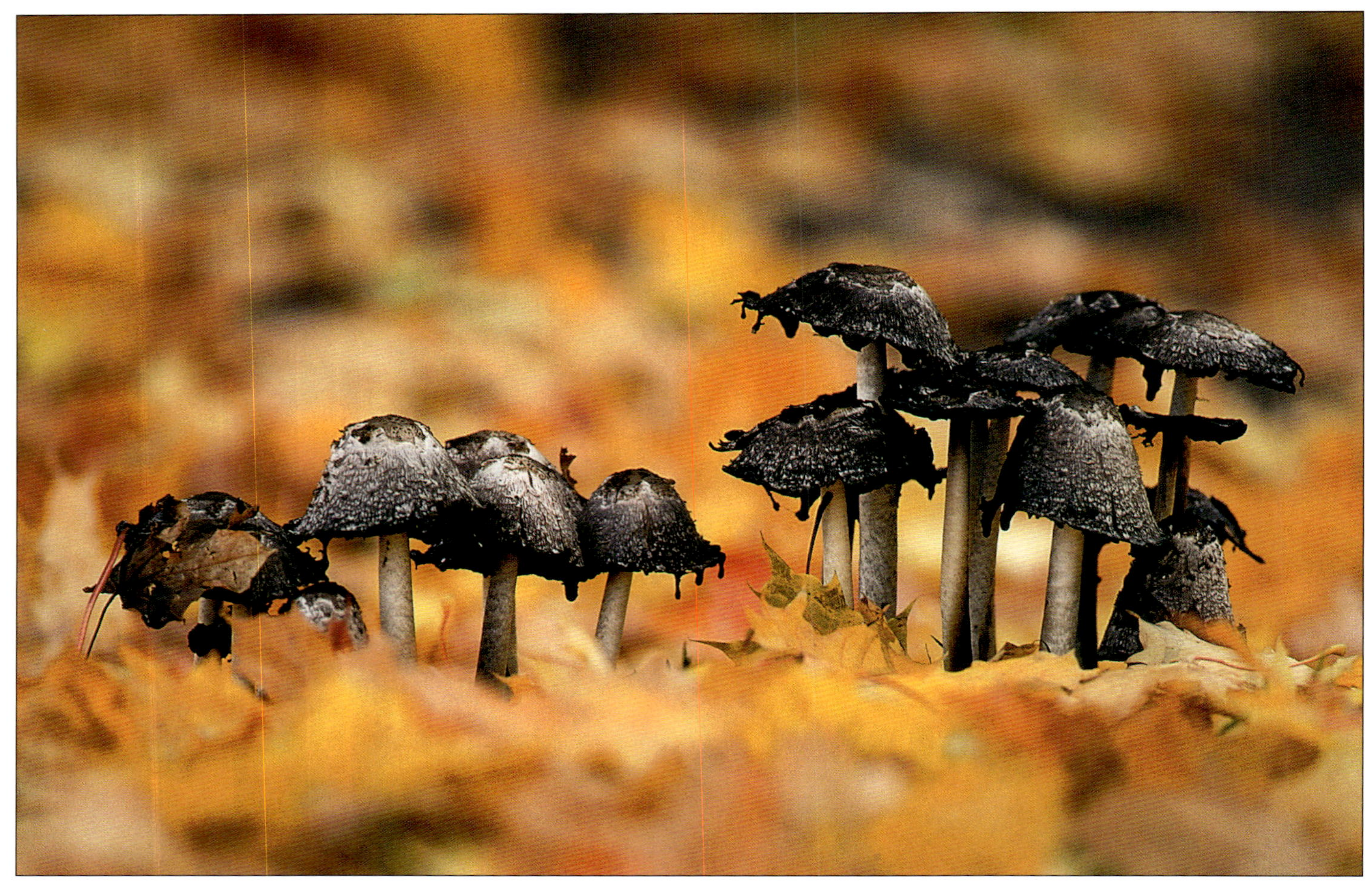

Sten Björklund
Sweden
HIGHLY COMMENDED

Shaggy cap

"Fungi of this species are white when they first appear, but they turn black as they age. The photograph was taken at an old ironworks in Gysinge, Sweden."

Nikon 801 with 300mm lens; tripod; Kodak Elite 100

Maurizio Biancarelli
Italy
HIGHLY COMMENDED

Dog rose

"In winter I often go to Monte Cucco in the Central Apennines to photograph the snowy woods and frozen beeches. On this occasion I wasn't so lucky because the weather was dull and foggy, but my eye was drawn by these bright red rose fruits, which were the only splashes of colour in a white landscape."

Hasselblad 553 ELX; tripod; Fujichrome Velvia

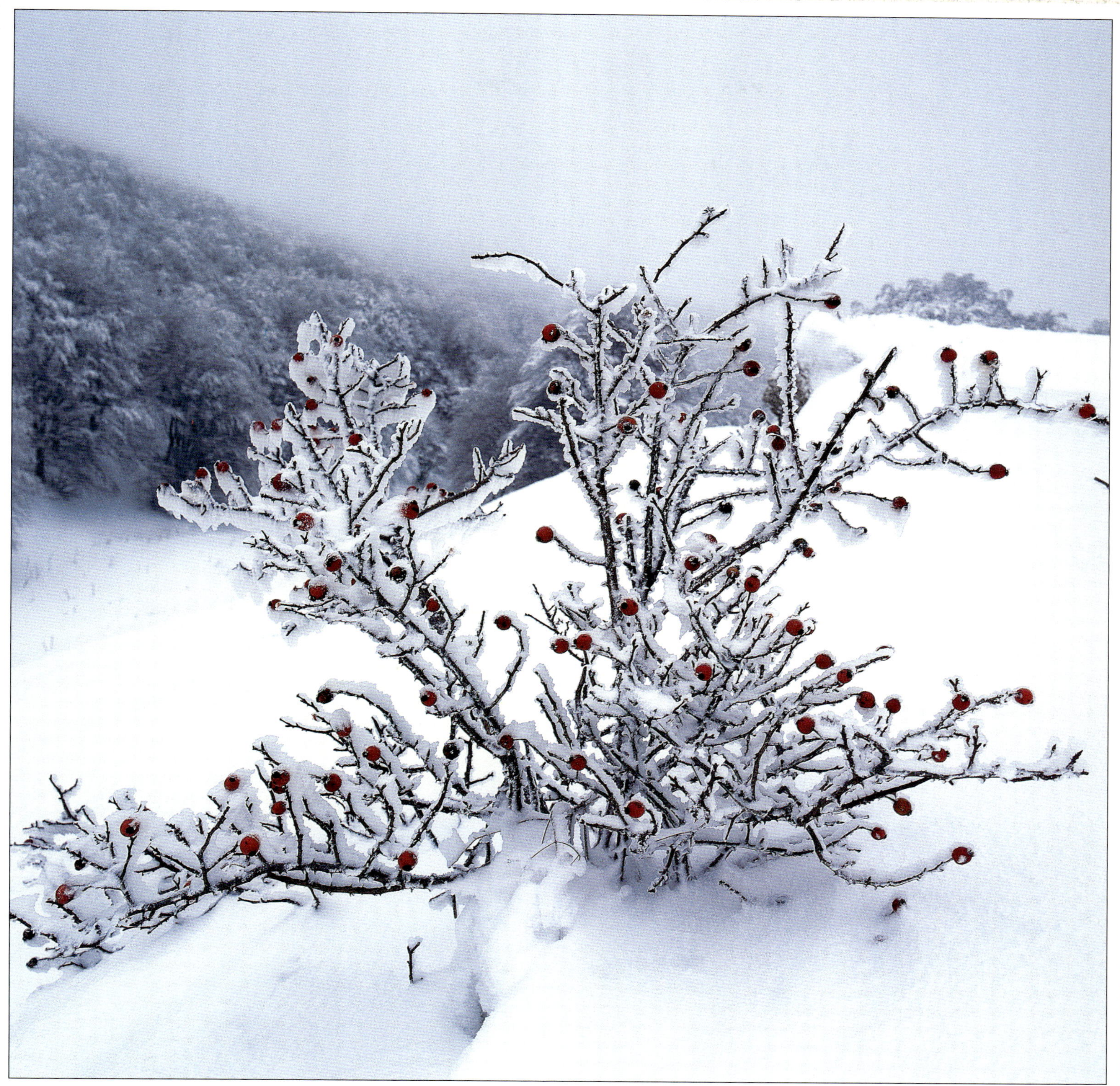

The Underwater World

Pictures, which must have been taken under water, can illustrate any marine or freshwater subject. A special prize was awarded for the best picture of a coral reef or reef species, to mark the International Year of the Reef 1997.

Reinhard Dirscherl
Germany
WINNER

Turtle eating jellyfish

"I was diving in a channel between two islands in the Maldives, when I saw this big jellyfish. The turtle arrived just as I did, but it ignored me and started circling the jellyfish, looking for a suitable place to take a bite. I waited until it opened its mouth, then pressed the trigger."

Nikon RS with 13mm fisheye lens; 1/125 sec at f11; Kodak Elite II 100

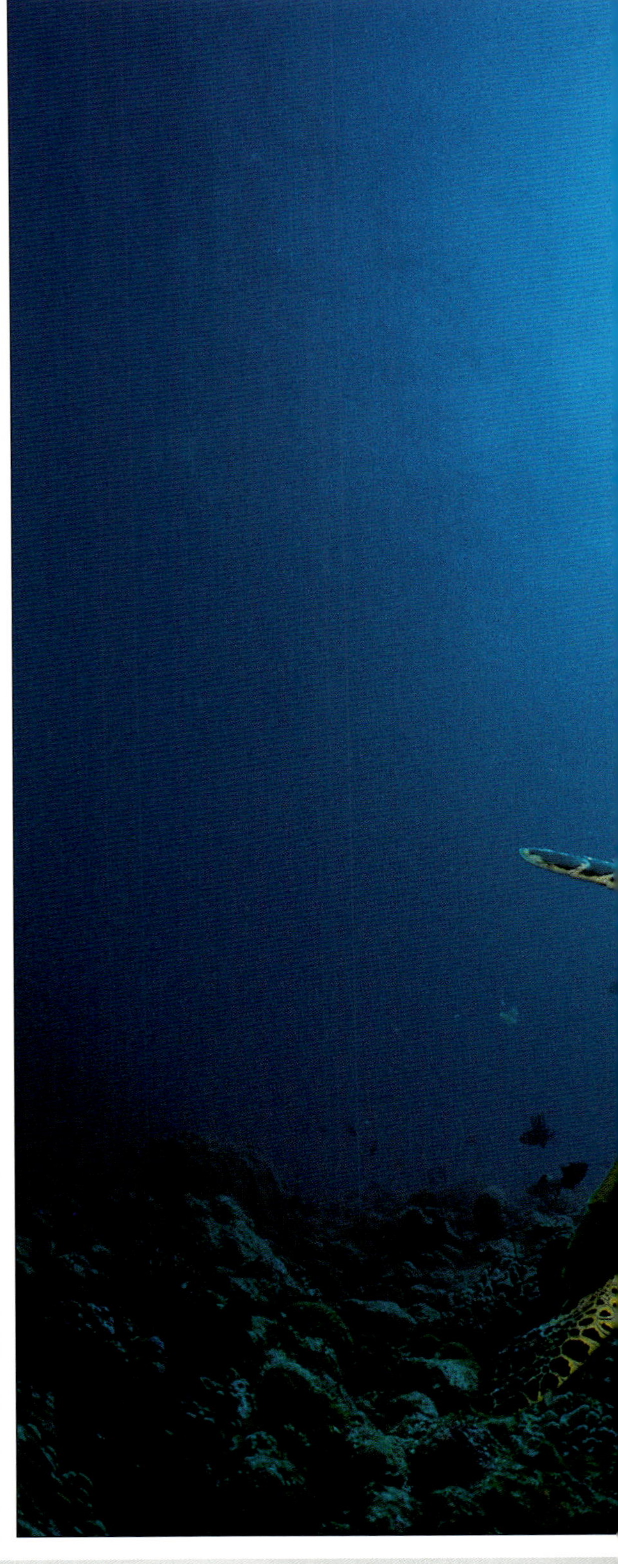

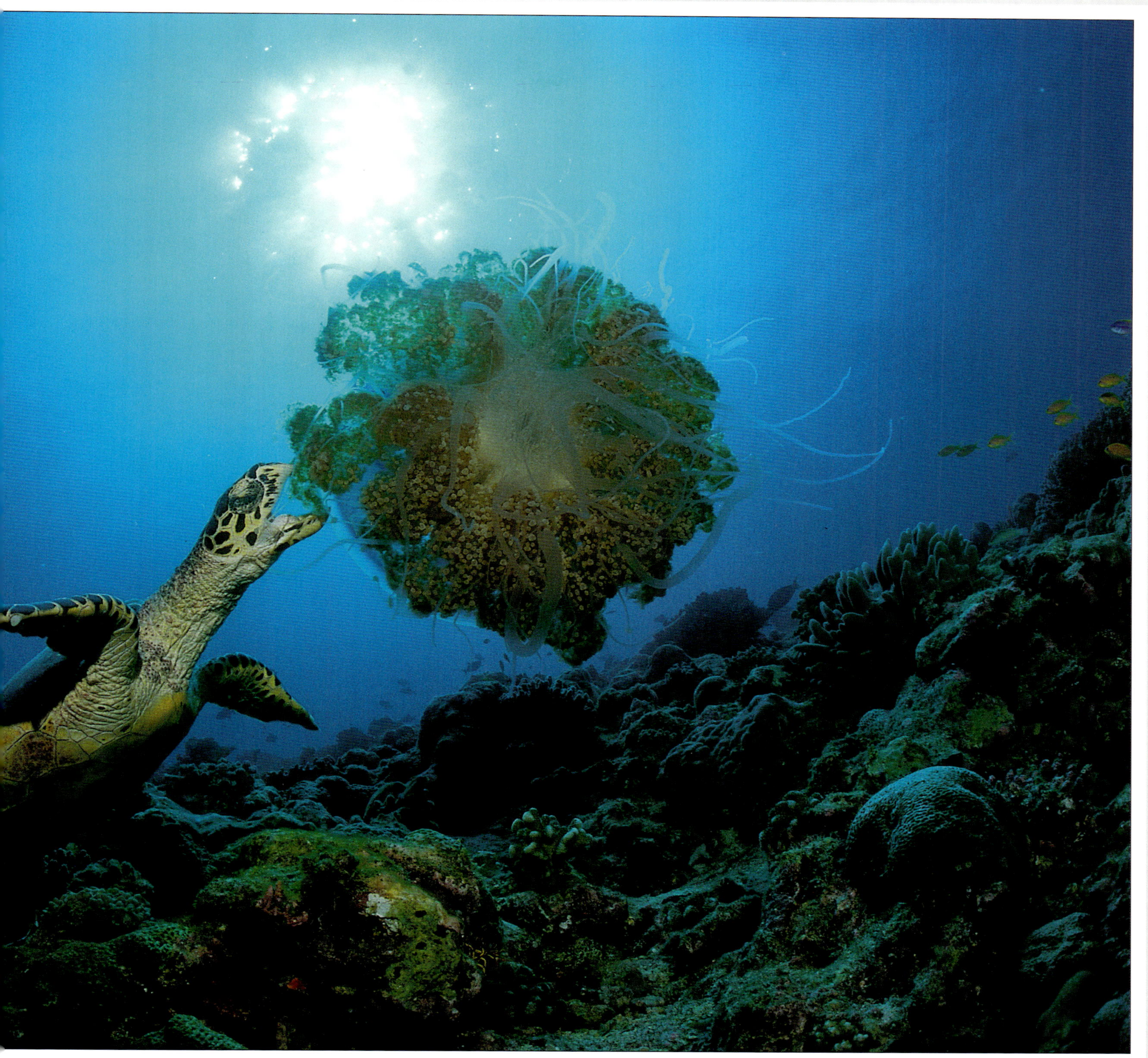

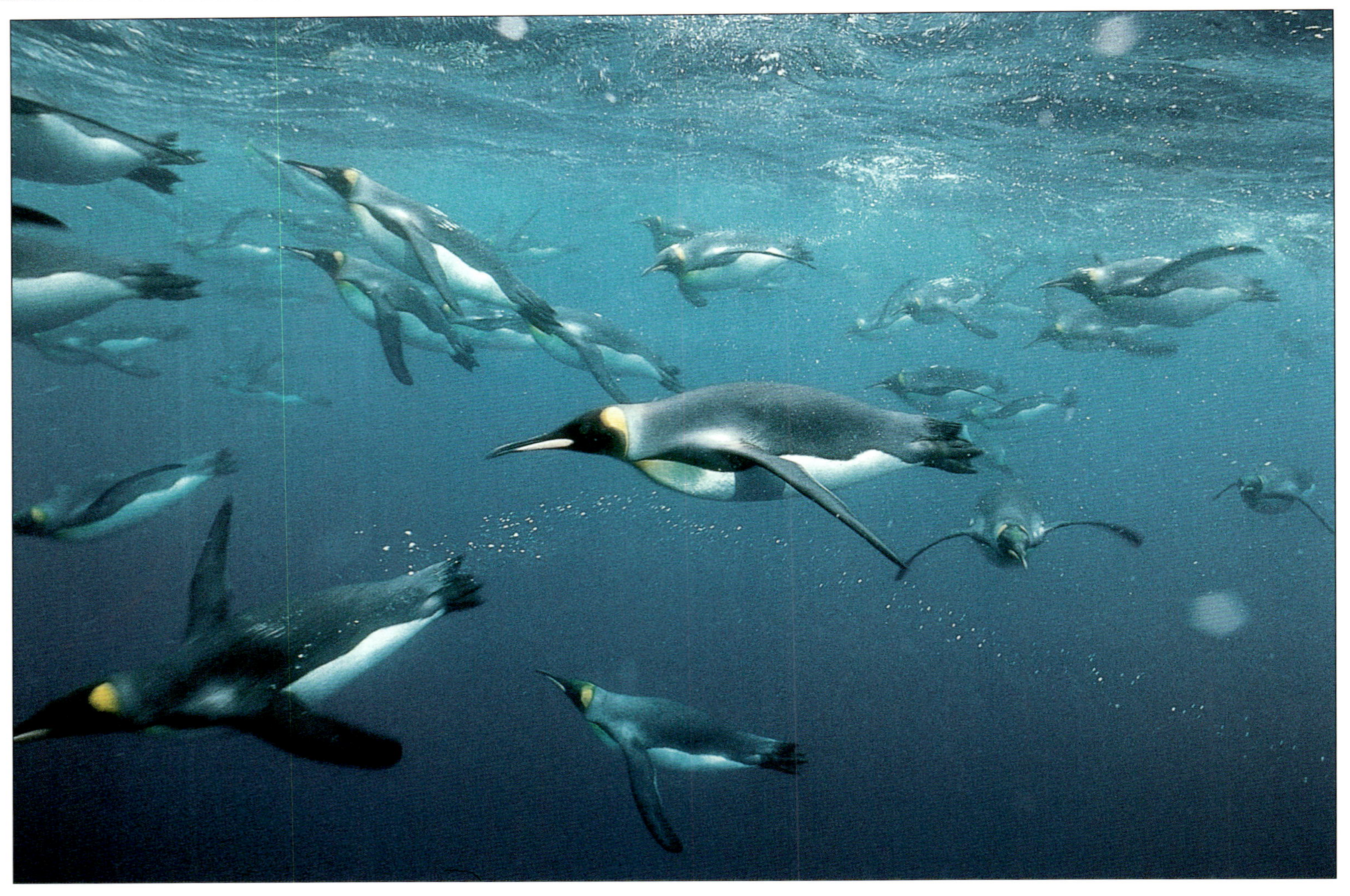

Tui De Roy
New Zealand
RUNNER-UP

King penguins underwater

*"I photographed this group of graceful swimmers in the waters around Macquarie Island.
About 80,000 pairs of king penguins breed on this sub-antarctic island."*

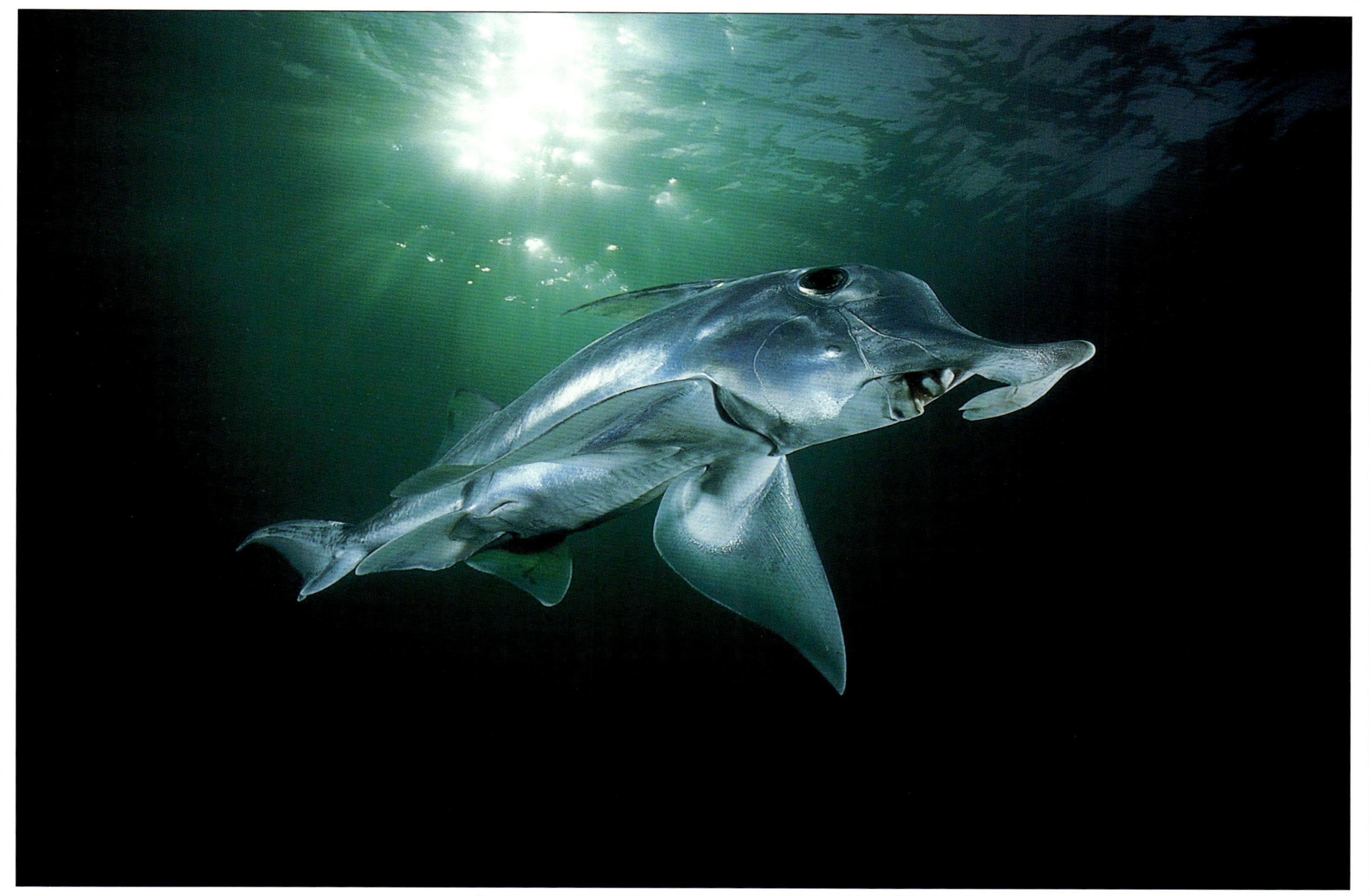

Kelvin Aitken
Australia
SPECIALLY COMMENDED

Elephant fish

"The skin of this delightful and gentle animal is smooth, much like human skin, but it has a silvery finish like aluminium. The plough-shaped snout houses special receptors that help the fish sense its prey. This one was photographed near the entrance of Westernport Bay, Victoria."

Nikonos V with 15mm lens; two strobes; 1/60 sec at f16; Fujichrome Velvia

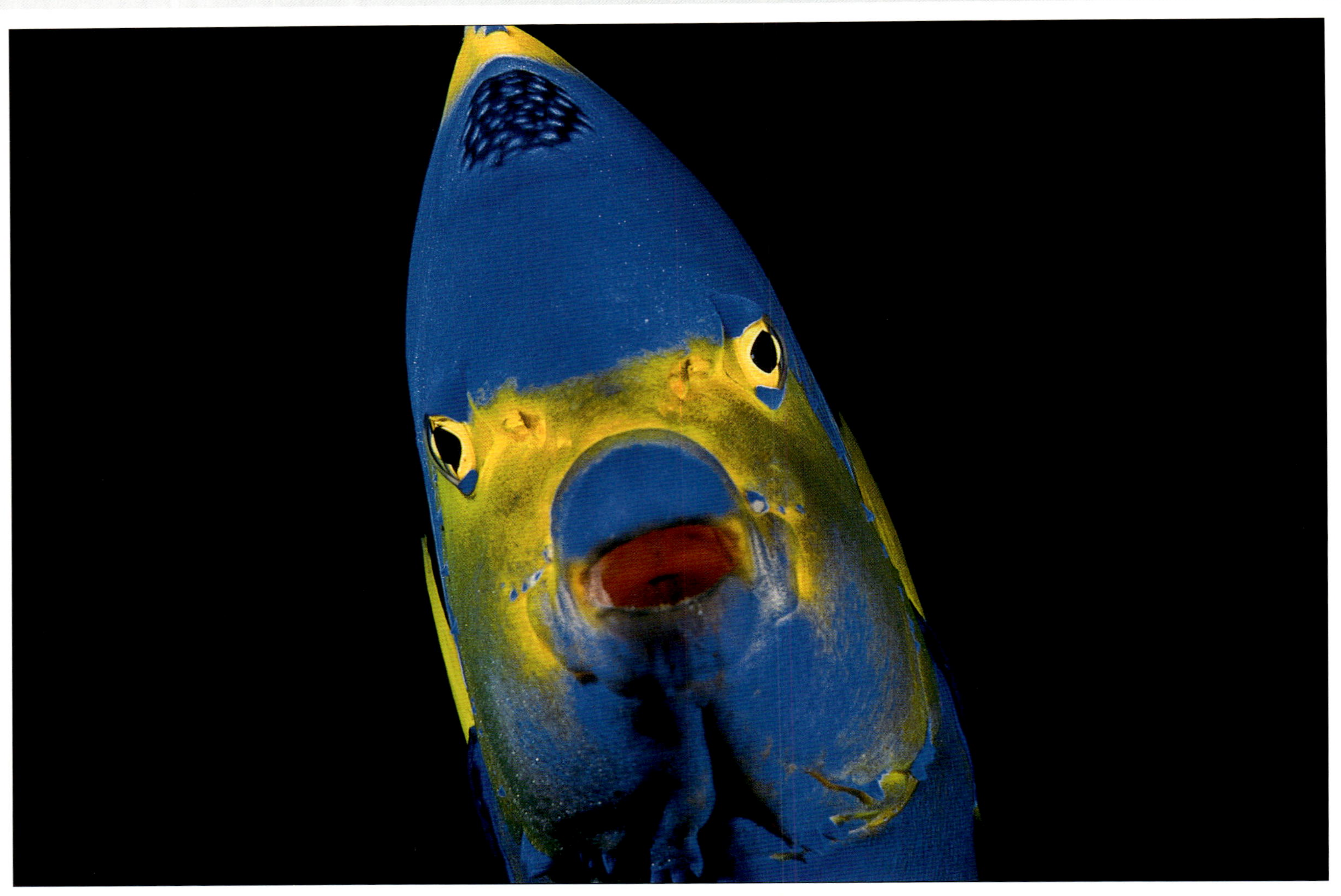

Jay Ireland
& Georgienne Bradley
United States of America
HIGHLY COMMENDED

Queen angelfish

"This Cayman Island fish was captivated by its own reflection in the large glass port of our underwater housing. We didn't know if it had aggressive or amorous intentions, or whether it was just being curious, but the behaviour created a fantastic opportunity to compose an interesting series of shots."

Nikon 8008 with 60mm lens in underwater housing; strobe

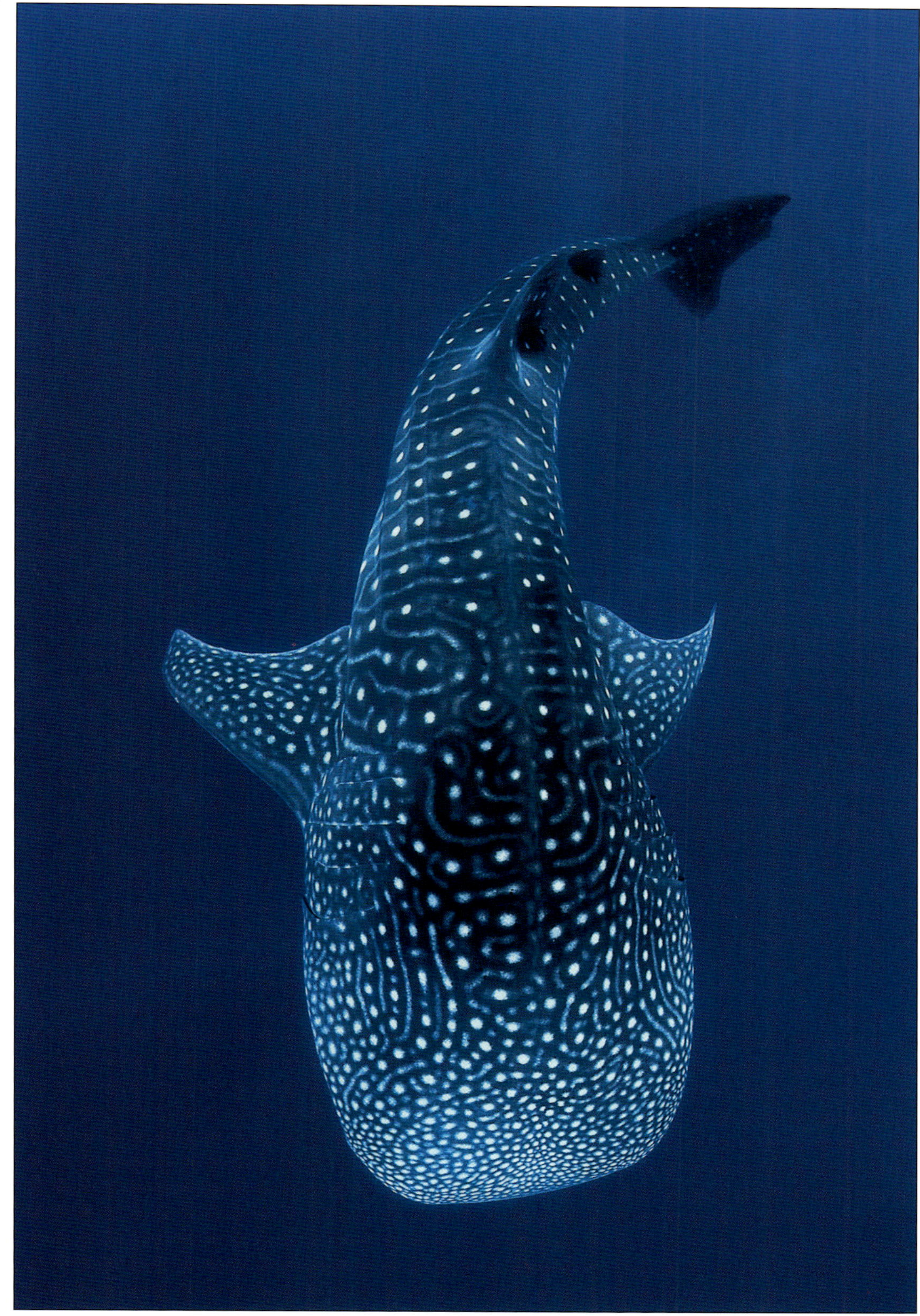

Jürgen Freund
Germany
HIGHLY COMMENDED

Whale shark

"After the annual mass spawning of 120 million land crabs at Christmas Island in the Indian Ocean, whale sharks gather to feed on a banquet of larvae. At other places in the world, people often have to search for whale sharks, but at Christmas Island the sharks found us. In two months we had more than 20 shark encounters."

Nikon F4 with 16mm fisheye lens in underwater housing; strobe; 1/60 sec at f8; Fujichrome Sensia 100

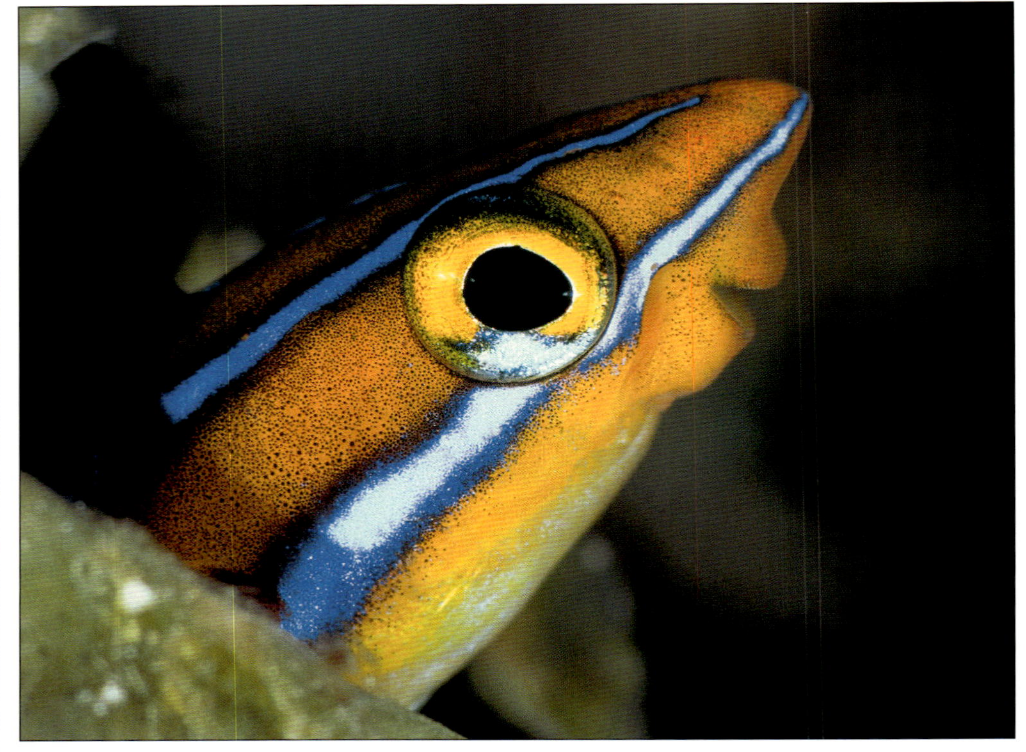

David Hall
United States of America
HIGHLY COMMENDED

Bluestriped fangblenny

"This small fish, which I photographed in the Solomon Islands, looks and behaves like a harmless cleaner wrasse. In this guise it approaches other fish, but instead of removing their parasites it takes a quick bite out of them and then darts back into a small hole for safety."

Nikonos RS with 50mm macro lens and x2 teleconverter; two strobes; 1/125 sec at f11; Fujichrome Velvia

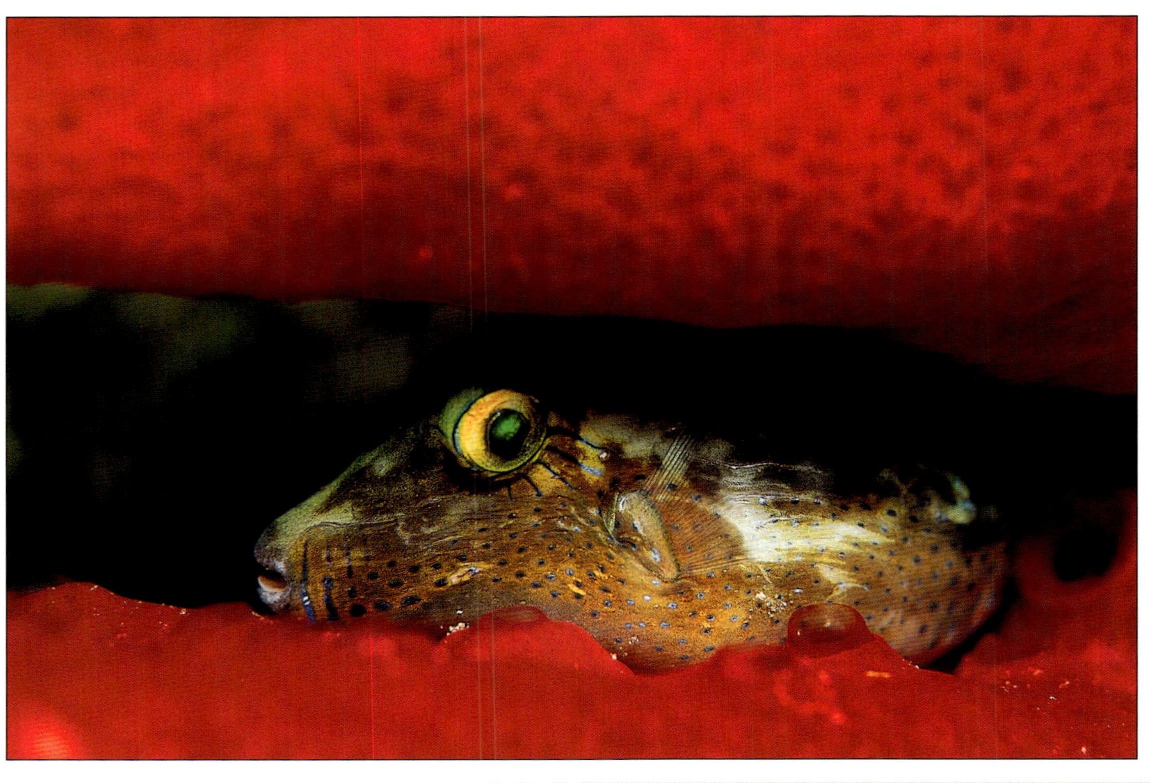

Lawson Wood
United Kingdom
HIGHLY COMMENDED

Pufferfish in red rope sponge

"This photograph was taken during a night dive at Cayos Cochinos, to the south of Roatan in the Bay Islands off Honduras. At a depth of 18 metres I came across this sharpnosed pufferfish, which likes to sleep among sponges."

Nikon F90s with 105mm macro lens; 1/60 sec at f16; Fujichrome Velvia

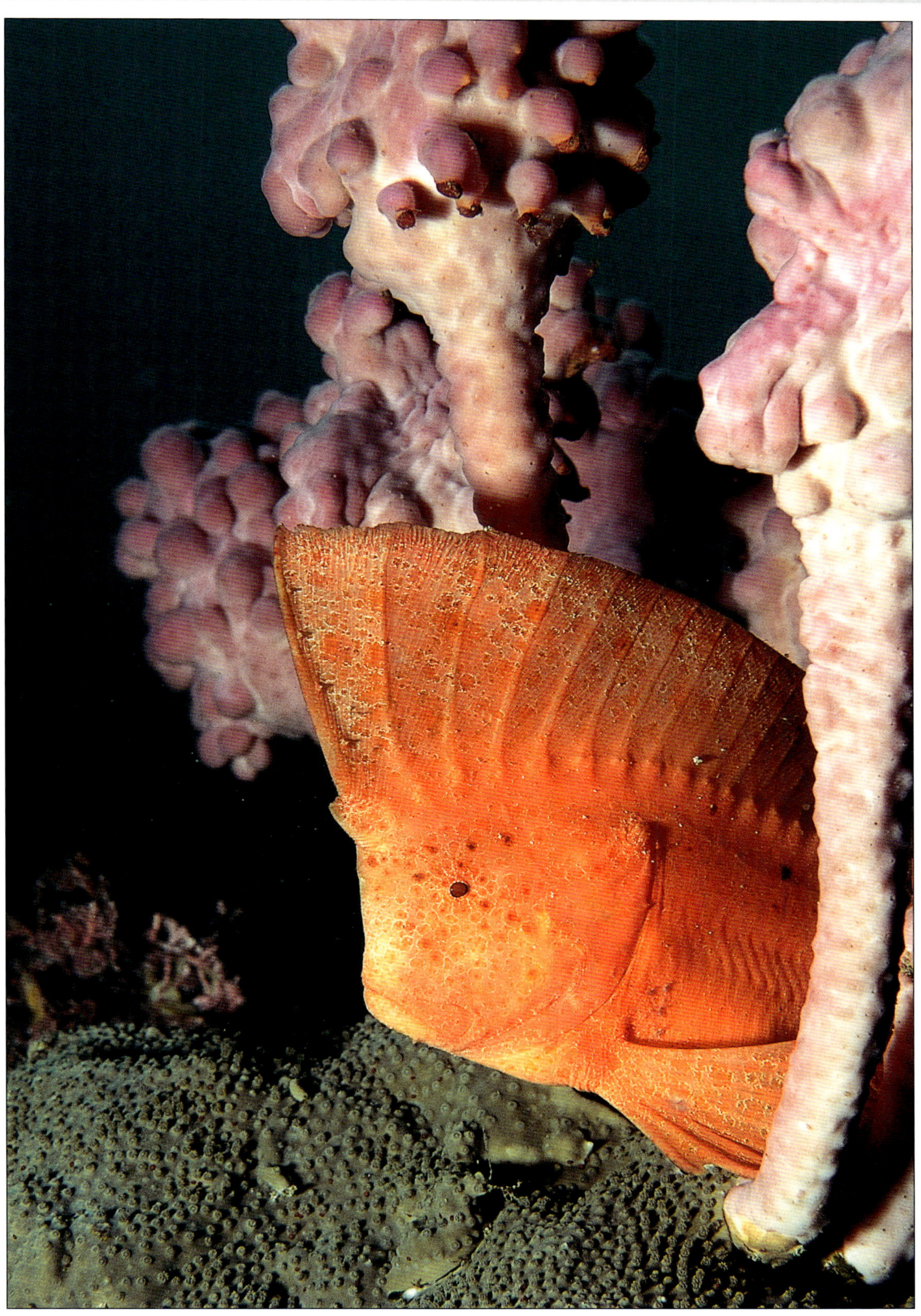

Tony Karacsonyi
Australia
HIGHLY COMMENDED

Red indianfish

I was diving in Jervis Bay, New South Wales, when I found this remarkable fish living among the sponges and sea tulips. Nonchalantly, it just sat there and allowed me to take its photograph. When there's a swell, these fish waft from side to side like orange eucalyptus leaves."

Nikon F3 with 60mm micro lens in underwater housing; strobe; 1/60 sec at f11; Fujichrome Sensia

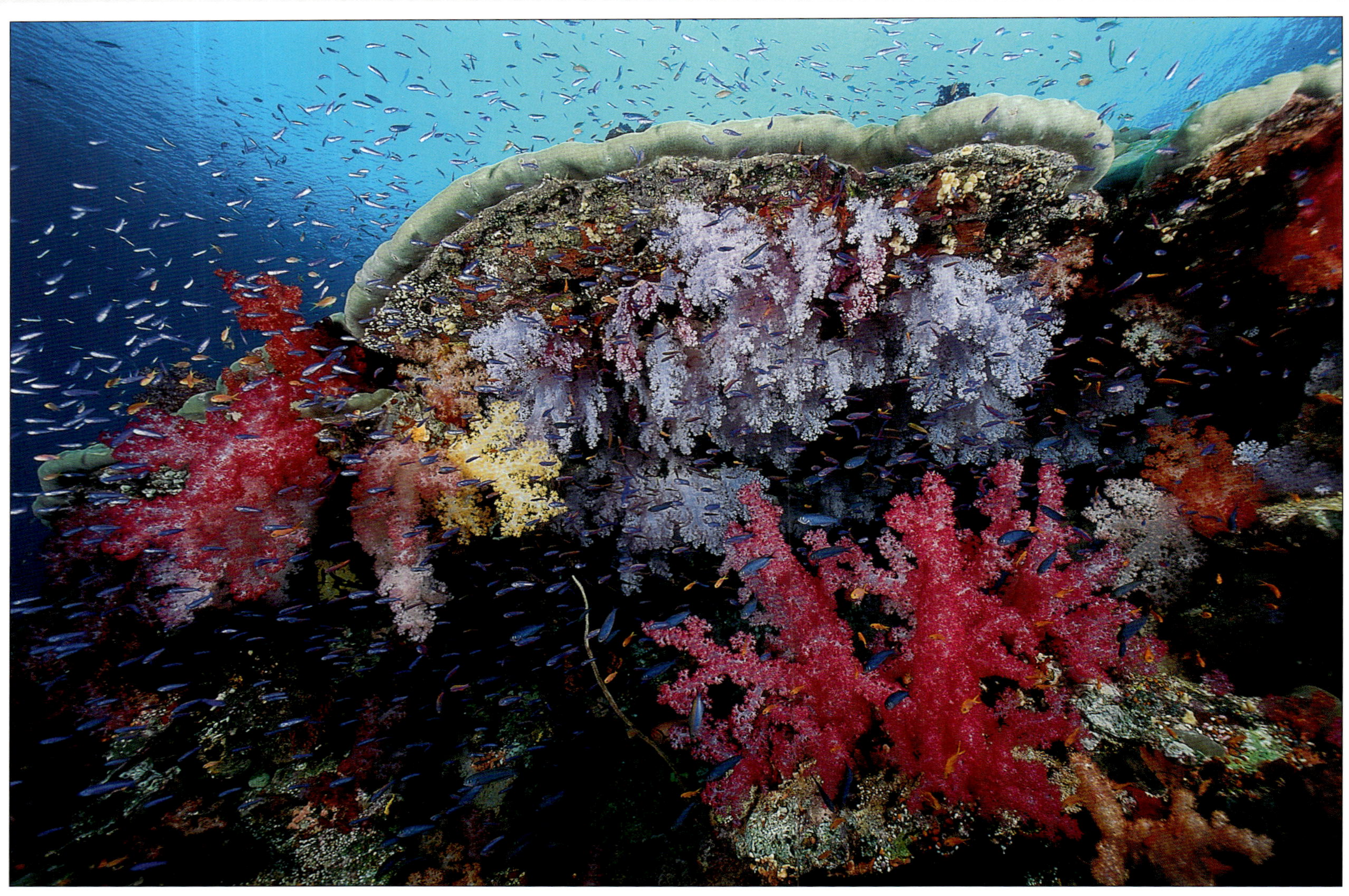

Kelvin Aitken
Australia
HIGHLY COMMENDED

Soft corals

"This picture shows soft corals under a Porites coral mound at Taveuni Island, Fiji. During slack water soft corals deflate, but when the current picks up again they turn into gorgeous blooms. At the same time, various species of Anthias become highly active, darting about to feed on scraps."

Canon F1 with 14mm lens; two strobes; 1/60 sec at f9.5; Fujichrome Velvia

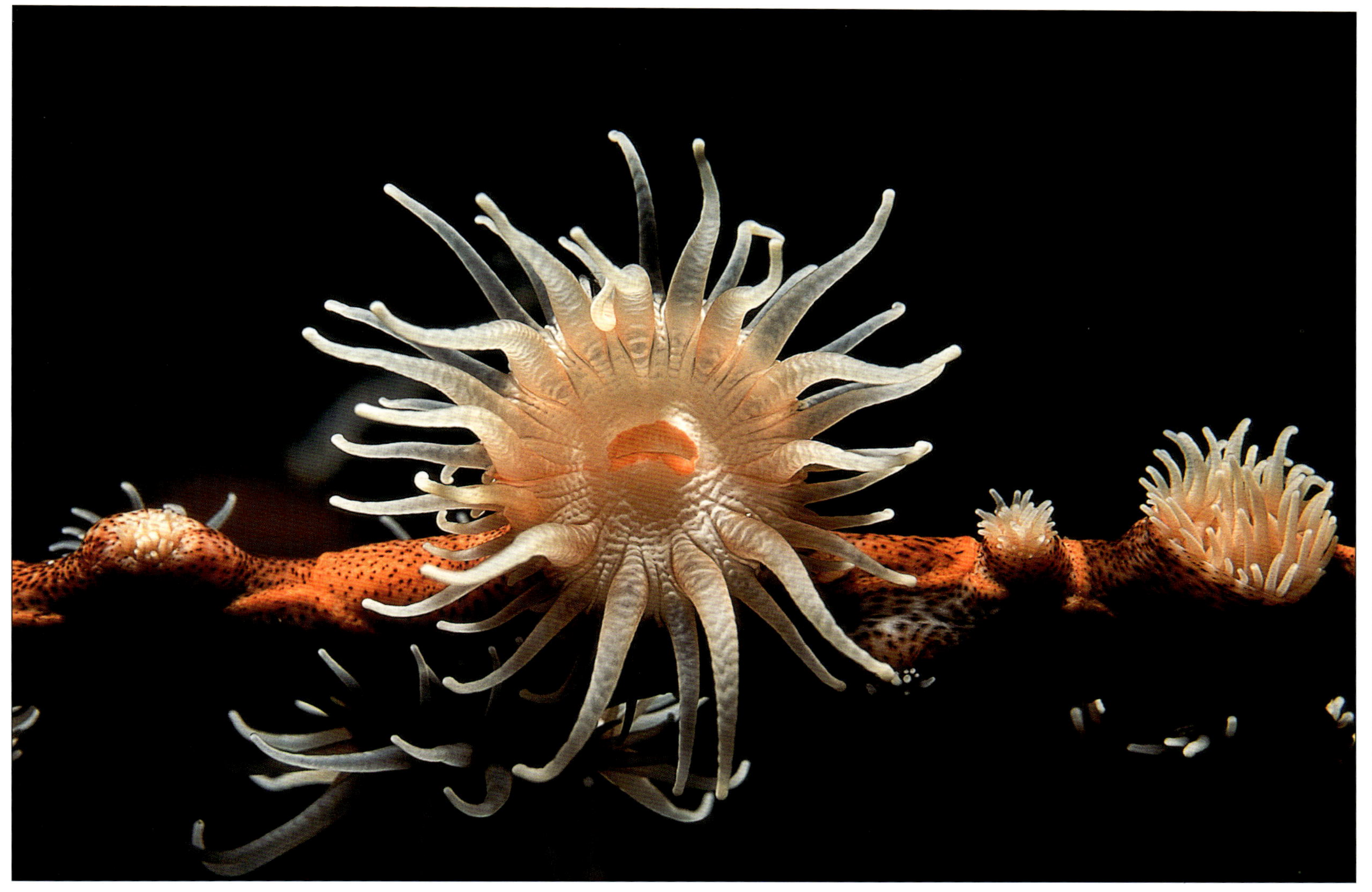

Manfred Pfefferle

Germany

HIGHLY COMMENDED

Tube coral

"This coral usually feeds at night, but there was so little light 49 metres down in the Red Sea off Port Sudan that its polyps were active in the daytime. As the flash caused the polyps to contract, I had to wait for them to expand again, a nerve-racking procedure at that depth."

Nikon F4 with 60mm lens in underwater housing; flash; 1/60 sec at f16; Fujichrome Velvia rated at 40

Urban & Garden Wildlife

Pictures must show animals or plants in a garden or an obviously urban or suburban setting.

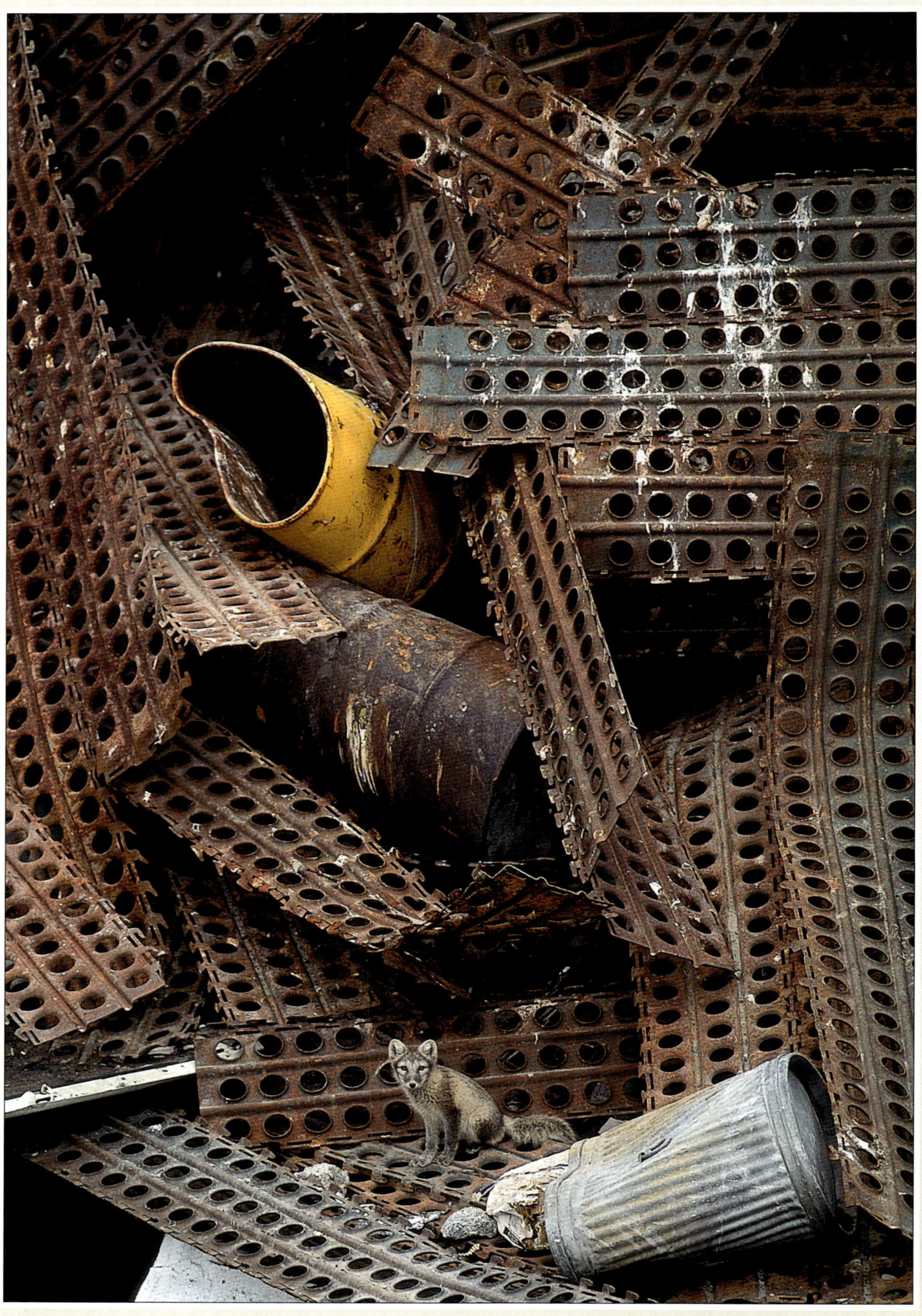

Staffan Widstrand
Sweden
WINNER

Arctic fox in garbage dump

"Arctic foxes are very good at exploiting human leftovers and they can be found in any Arctic garbage dump. At this one, at Kangerlussuaq in Western Greenland, a fox had cleverly hidden its den behind an almost indestructible wall of discarded metal sheets."

Nikon F4 with 300mm lens; tripod; 1/60 sec at f5.6; Fujichrome Velvia

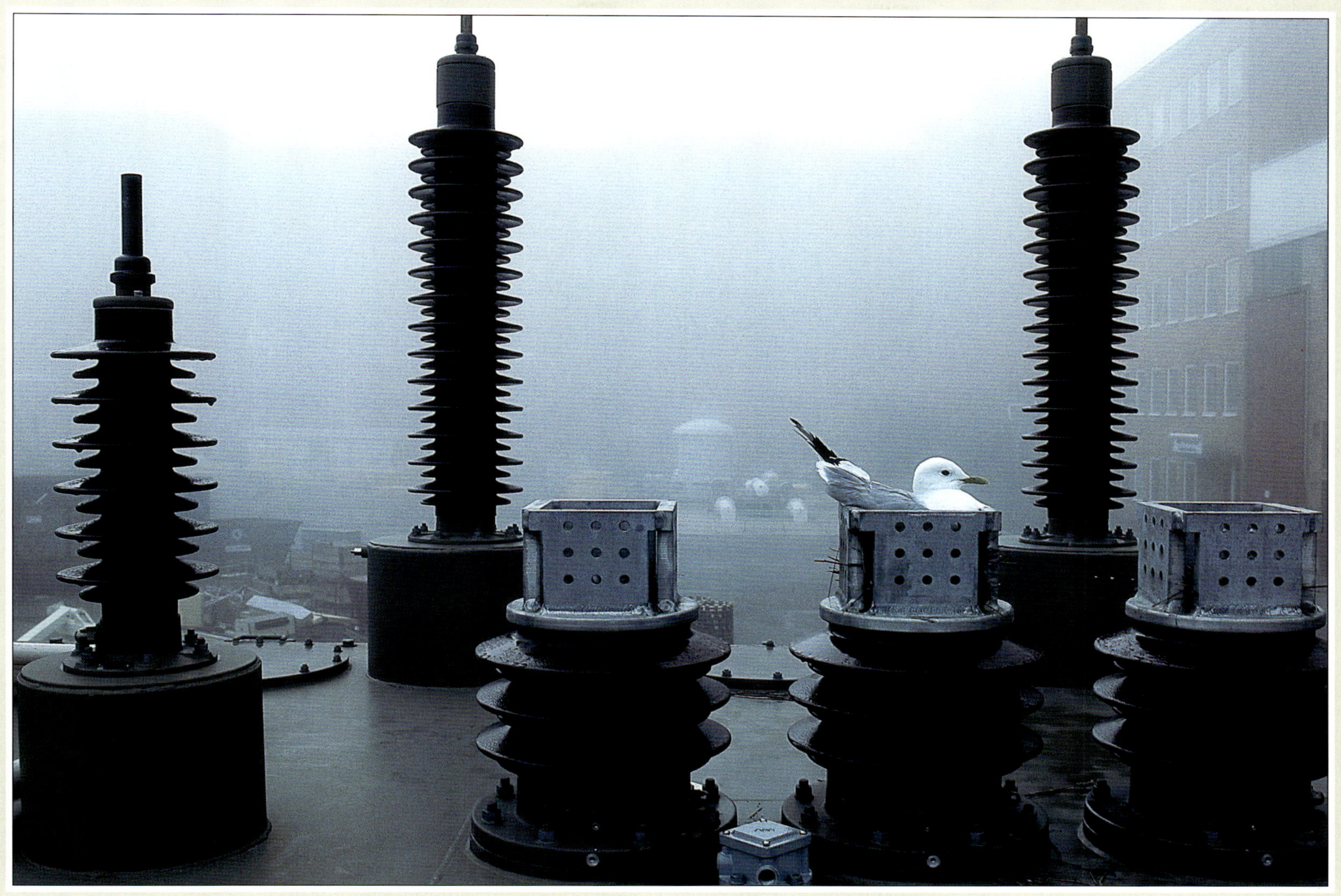

Janos Jurka
Sweden
RUNNER-UP

Common gull

"For the last three years common gulls have nested on these electrical transformers in the Swedish town of Ludvika. Each year they've managed to successfully hatch two young."

Canon F1 with 80-200mm lens; tripod; 1/15 sec at f8

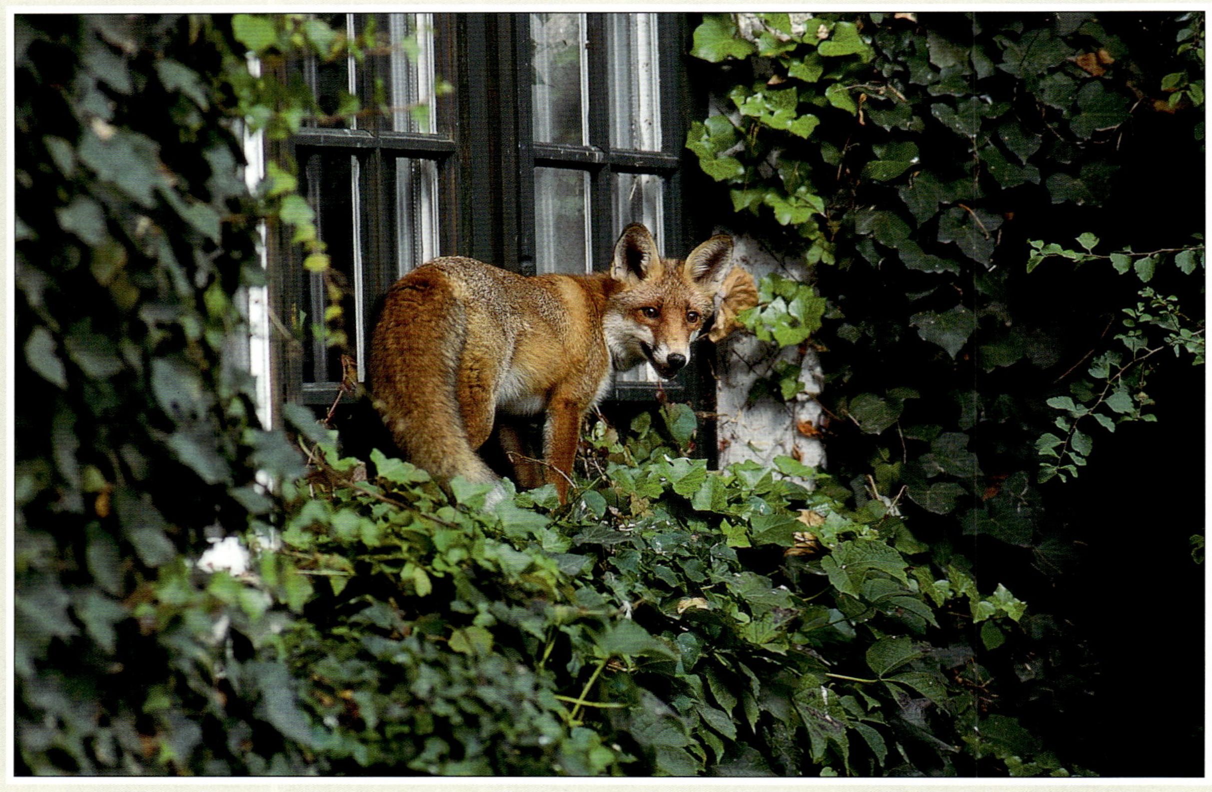

Bèla Berta

Hungary

HIGHLY COMMENDED

Fox on window sill

"This fox was investigating the window sill of a forester's lodge at Gemenc-Keselyüs, near Szekszárd, southern Hungary."

Canon F1 with 300mm lens; 1/30 sec at f5.6; Ektachrome Elite II 100

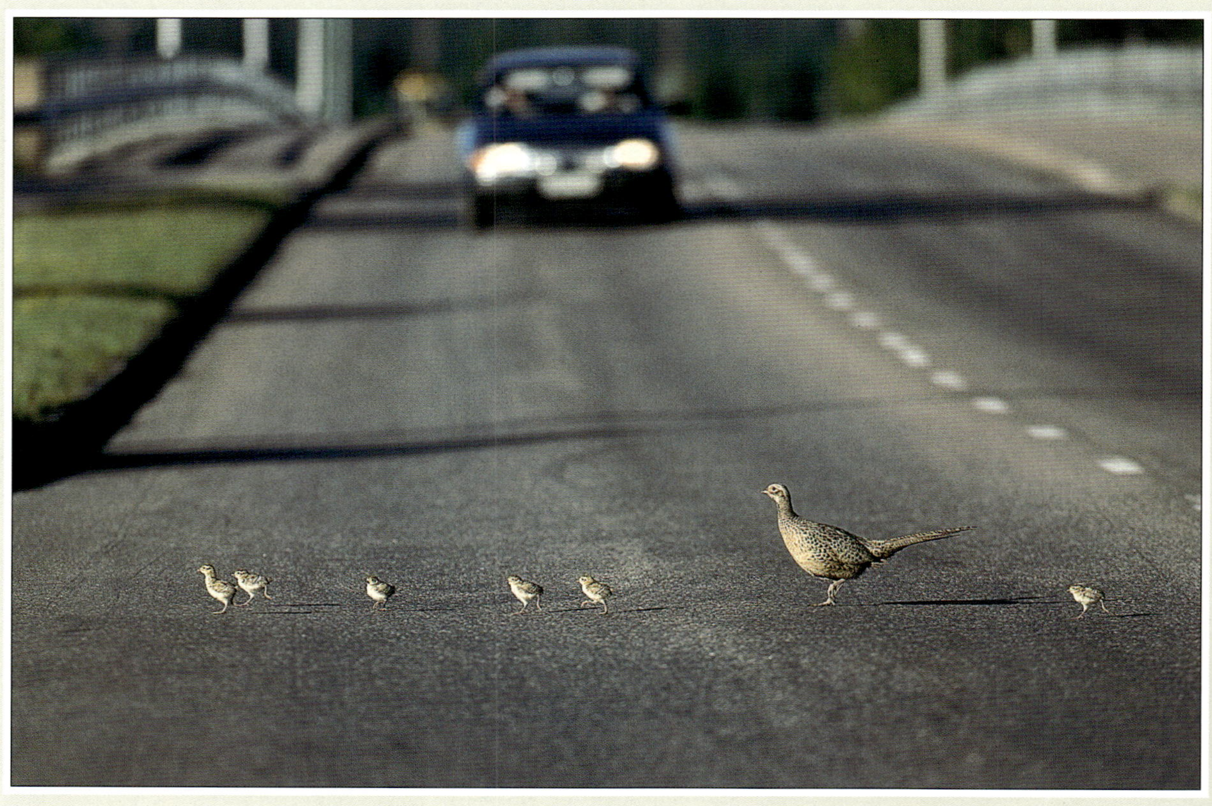

Asko Hämäläinen

Finland

HIGHLY COMMENDED

Common pheasants crossing road

"I was on my way home from a photographic trip when I saw a pheasant with her young on the side of the road. I passed them, stopped, then waited to see if they would cross the road. After a while they did."

Canon EOS 1 with 300mm lens; 1/350 sec at f3.5; Fujichrome 100

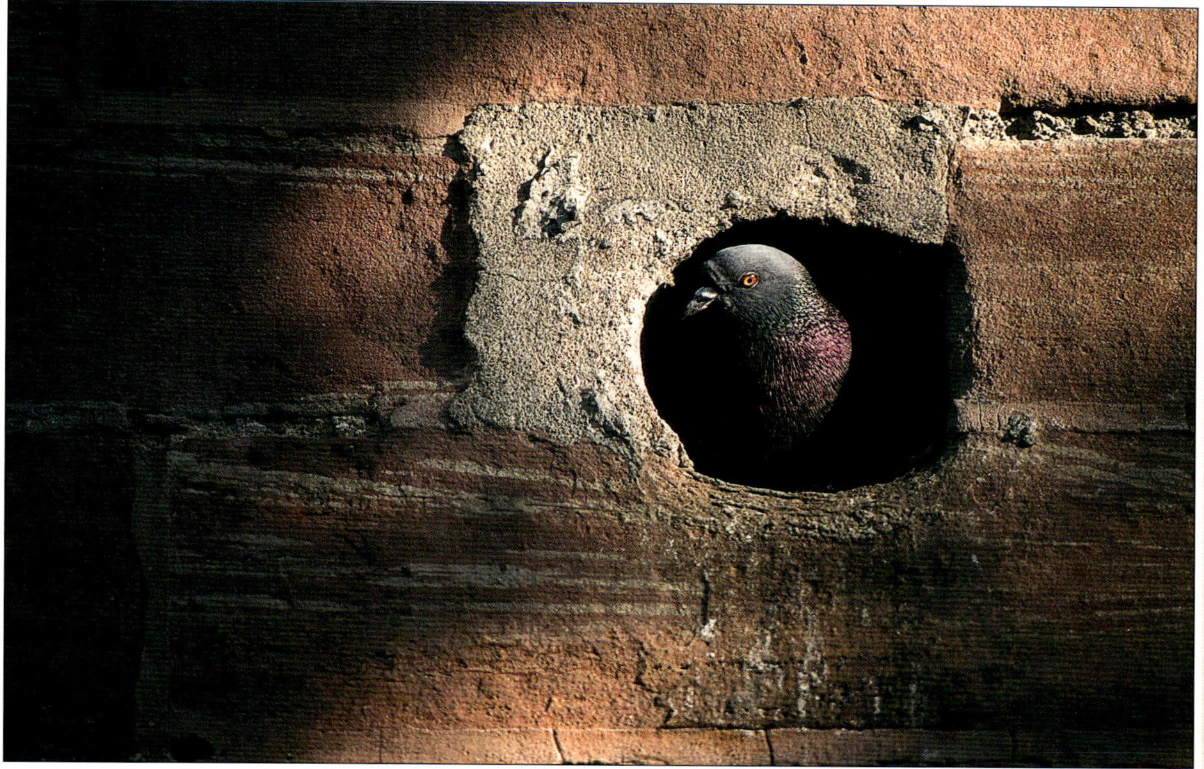

Cay-Uwe Kulzer
Germany
HIGHLY COMMENDED

Dove in sleeping hole

"During a spring walk this year in the city of Mainz, I came across several doves that use holes in the old city wall as their sleeping quarters. While all the other birds immediately disappeared, this one was happy to sit for a portrait."

Contax RTSiii with 500mm lens; tripod; auto at f5.6; Fujichrome Sensia 100

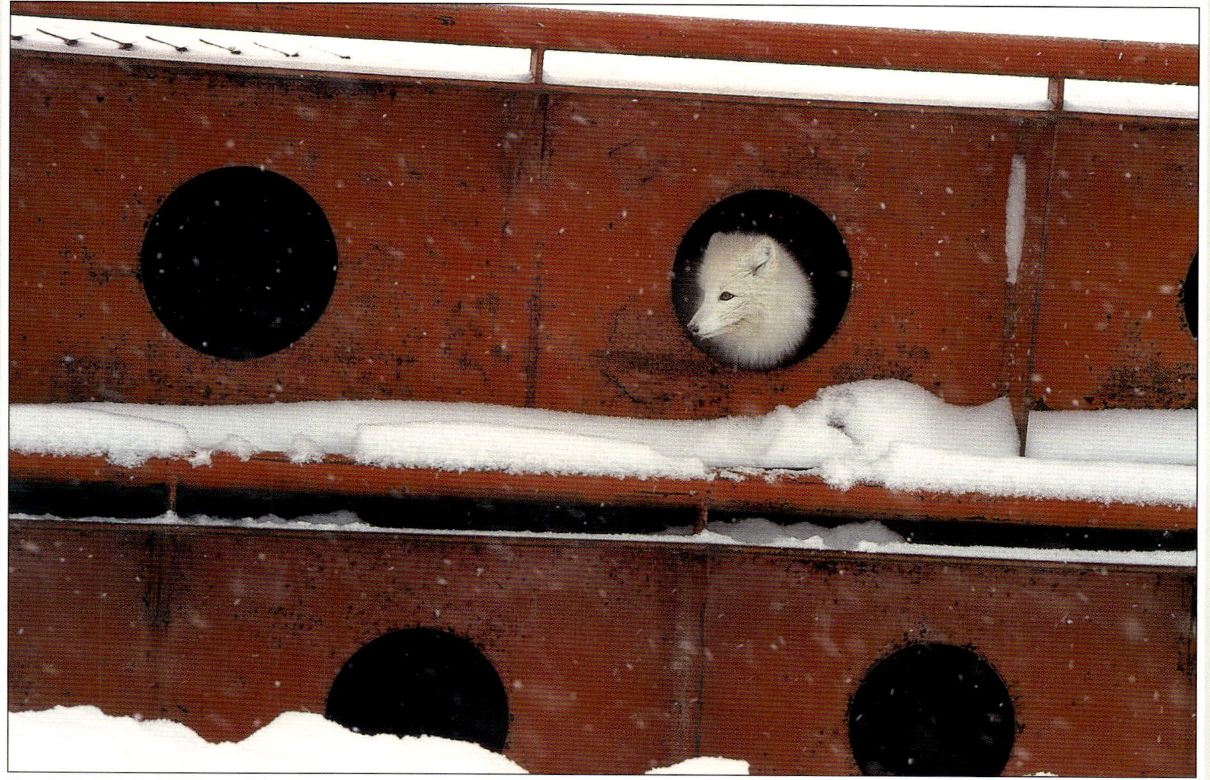

Norbert Rosing
Germany
HIGHLY COMMENDED

Arctic fox among iron bars

"In autumn 1996, sixteen Arctic foxes had taken up residence at Churchill harbour, Canada. I noticed they were hanging around an area where some heavy construction equipment had been stored and I photographed this one as it sheltered from the snow."

Leica R7

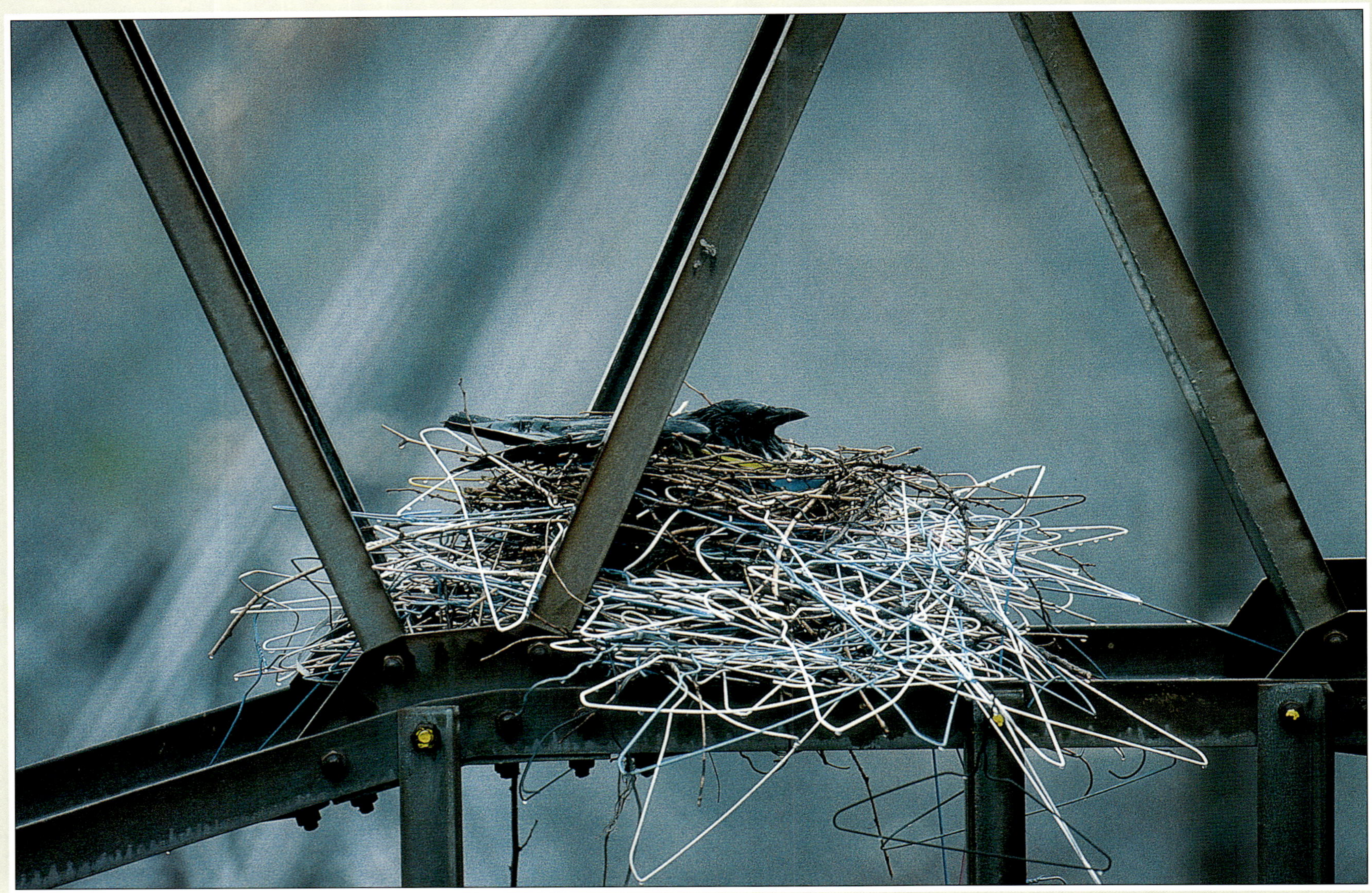

Hideyo Kubota
Japan
HIGHLY COMMENDED

Nesting crow

"One day I found a pair of crows making a nest above railway tracks in the city of Warabi-shi. It isn't unusual to see wire hangers around a crow's nest in Japanese towns, but I have never seen so many in a single nest. When I took the picture it was raining, but the bird kept on incubating, despite being completely soaked."

Canon EOS RT with 300mm lens; tripod; f5.6; Kodachrome 200

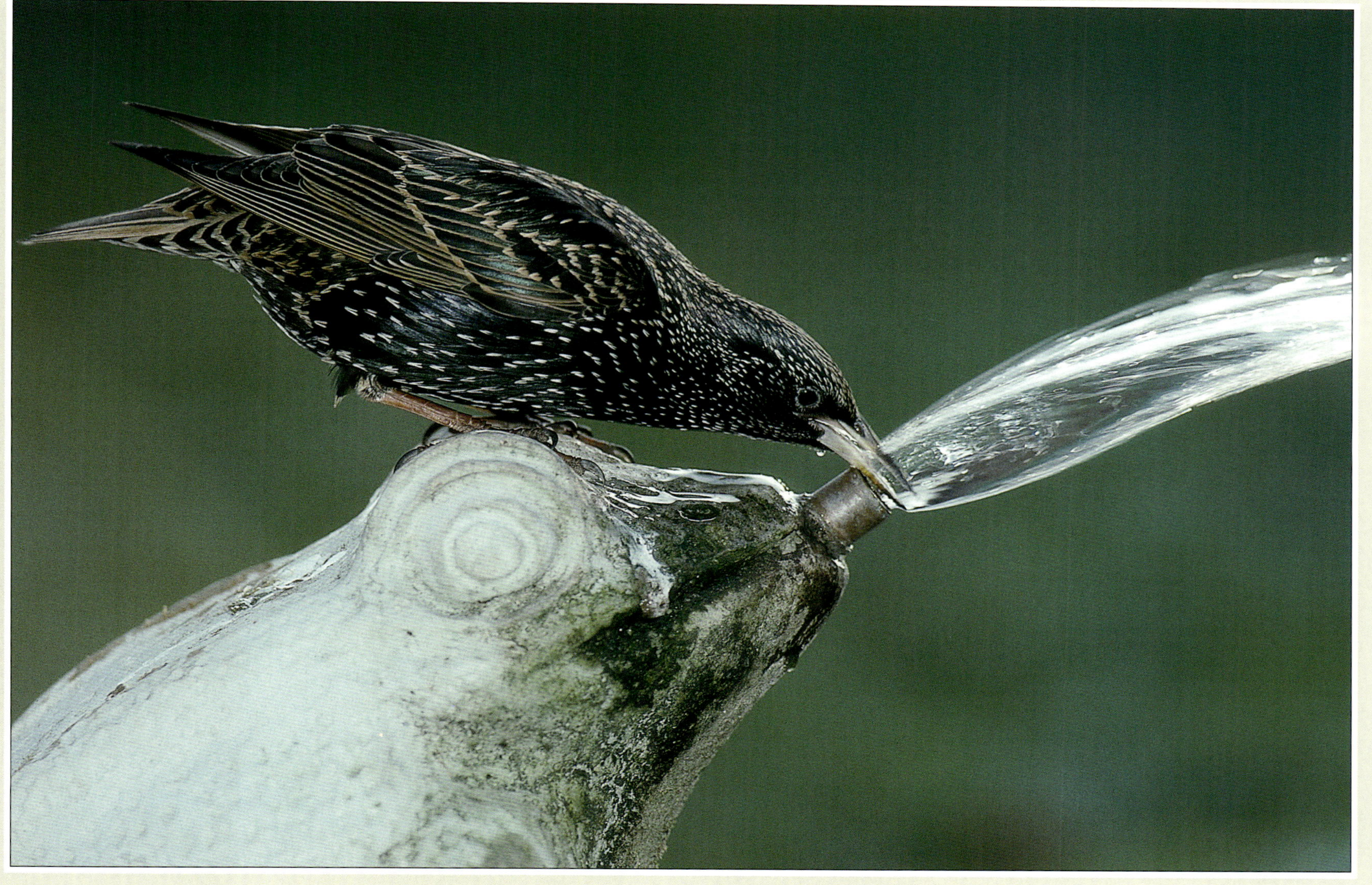

Robert Canis
United Kingdom
HIGHLY COMMENDED

Starling drinking

"During a cold snap two winters ago, nearby ponds and birdbaths iced over, but the ornamental frog in my back garden remained unfrozen. Birds would line up and take turns at drinking. Rather than watch from a hide, I used a long remote cable release and fired the camera from the warmth of my kitchen."

Nikon F3 with 500mm lens and extension tube; flash; 1/60 sec at f8; Kodachrome 64

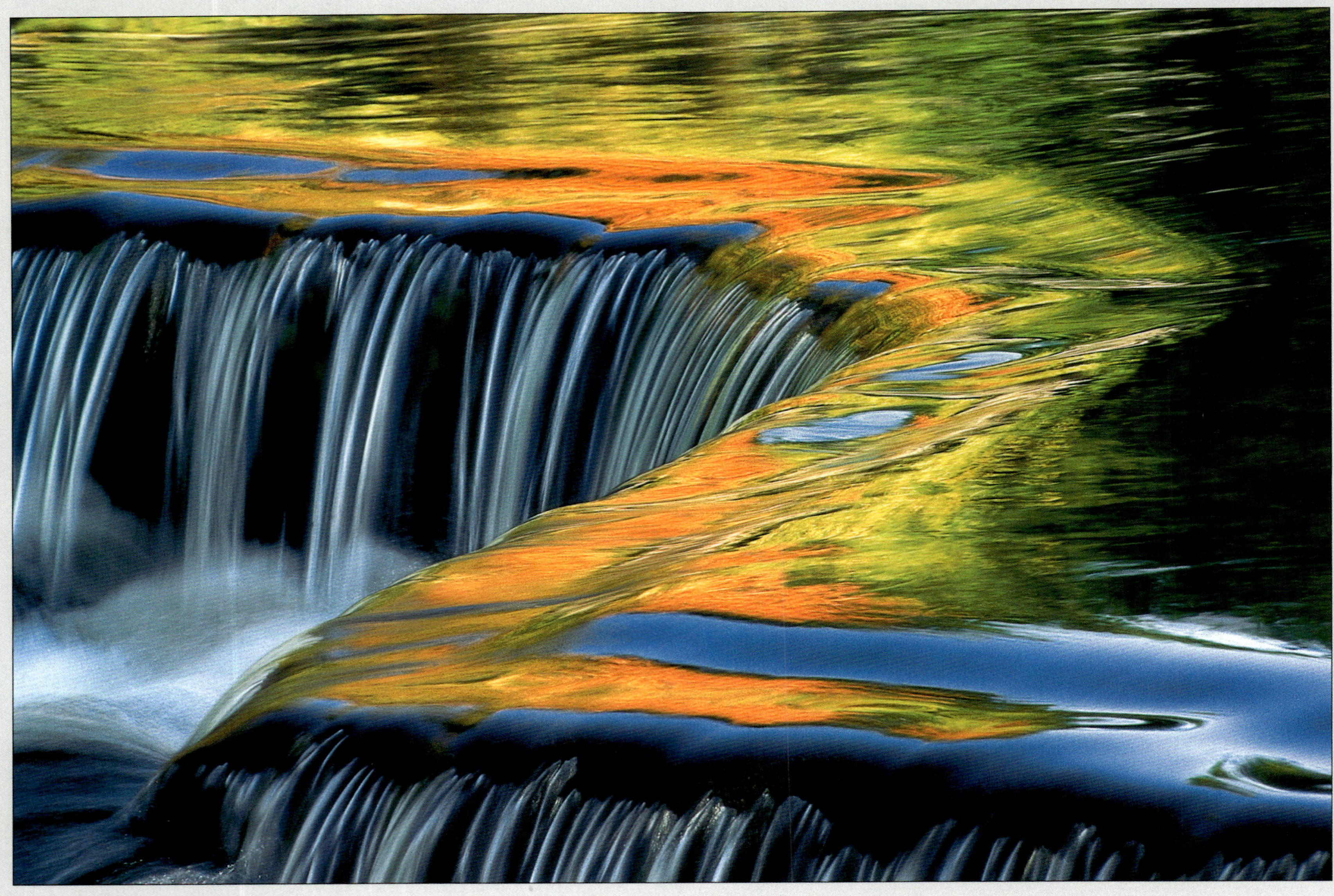

Lawrence A Michael
United States of America
WINNER

Autumn colours on waterfall

"Reflections of autumn leaves and blue sky painted these powerful colours on a shaded waterfall, near Paulding, Michigan. Rather than present the entire scene, I abstracted just a small portion to communicate the essence of the subject."

Nikon F4 with 300 mm lens; tripod; Fujichrome Velvia

Composition and Form

Pictures in this category must illustrate natural subjects in abstract ways, and are judged for their aesthetic values.

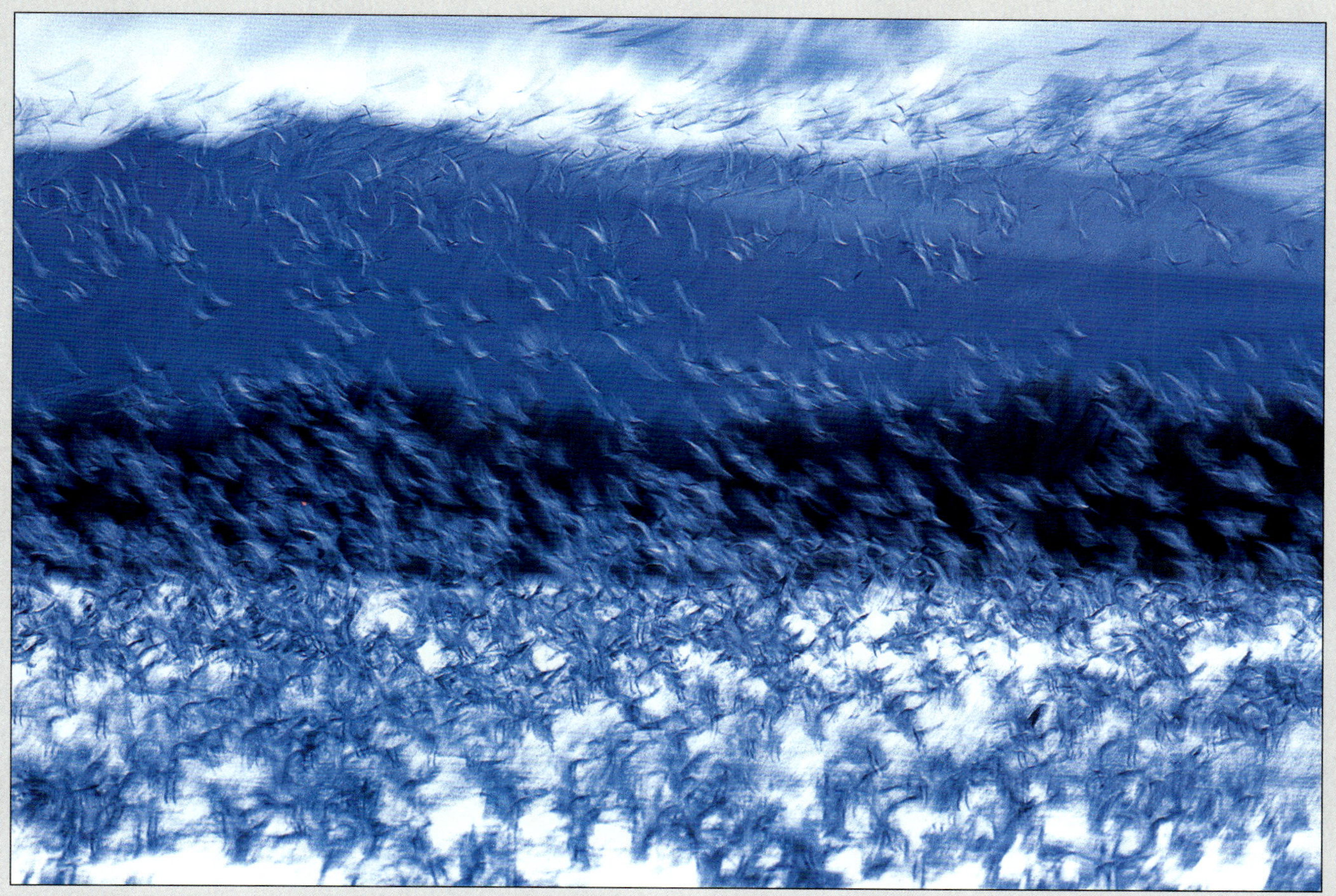

Arthur Morris
United States of America
RUNNER-UP

Snow geese

"It was a very cold, drizzly morning at Bosque del Apache National Wildlife Refuge, New Mexico. The snow geese lifted off before dawn, creating this blizzard in blue."

Canon EOS A2E with 400mm lens; tripod; 1/15 sec at f5.6; Fujichrome Velvia rated at 100

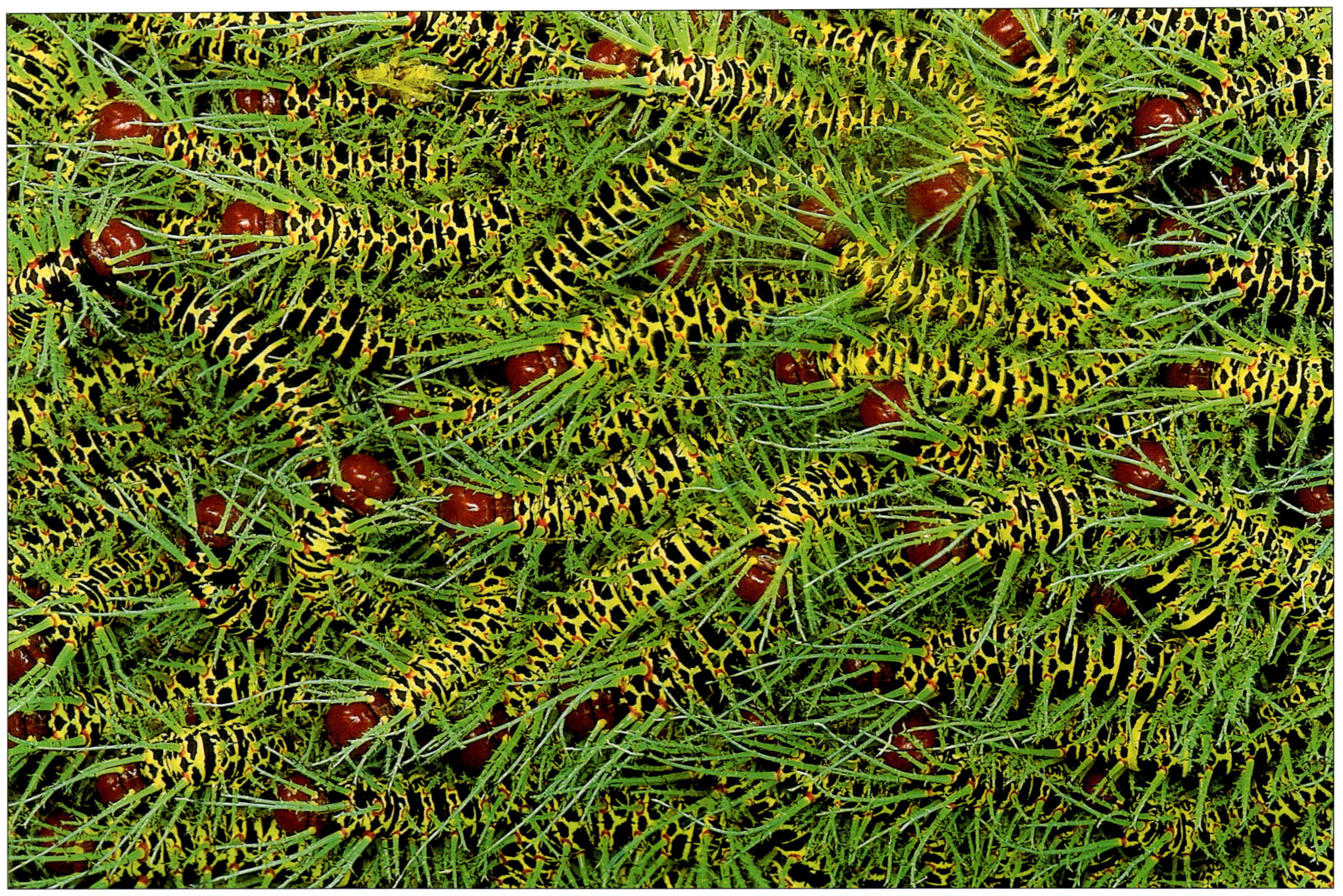

Whit Bronaugh
United States of America
SPECIALLY COMMENDED

Saturnid moth caterpillars

"These caterpillars had congregated on a tree trunk between feeding bouts in the Fautron Rain Forest Reserve, Rondìnia, Brazil. Presumably their warning colouration is more obvious to predators when they are in a large group."

Nikon F3 with 200mm lens; tripod; 2 sec at f22; Fujichrome Velvia

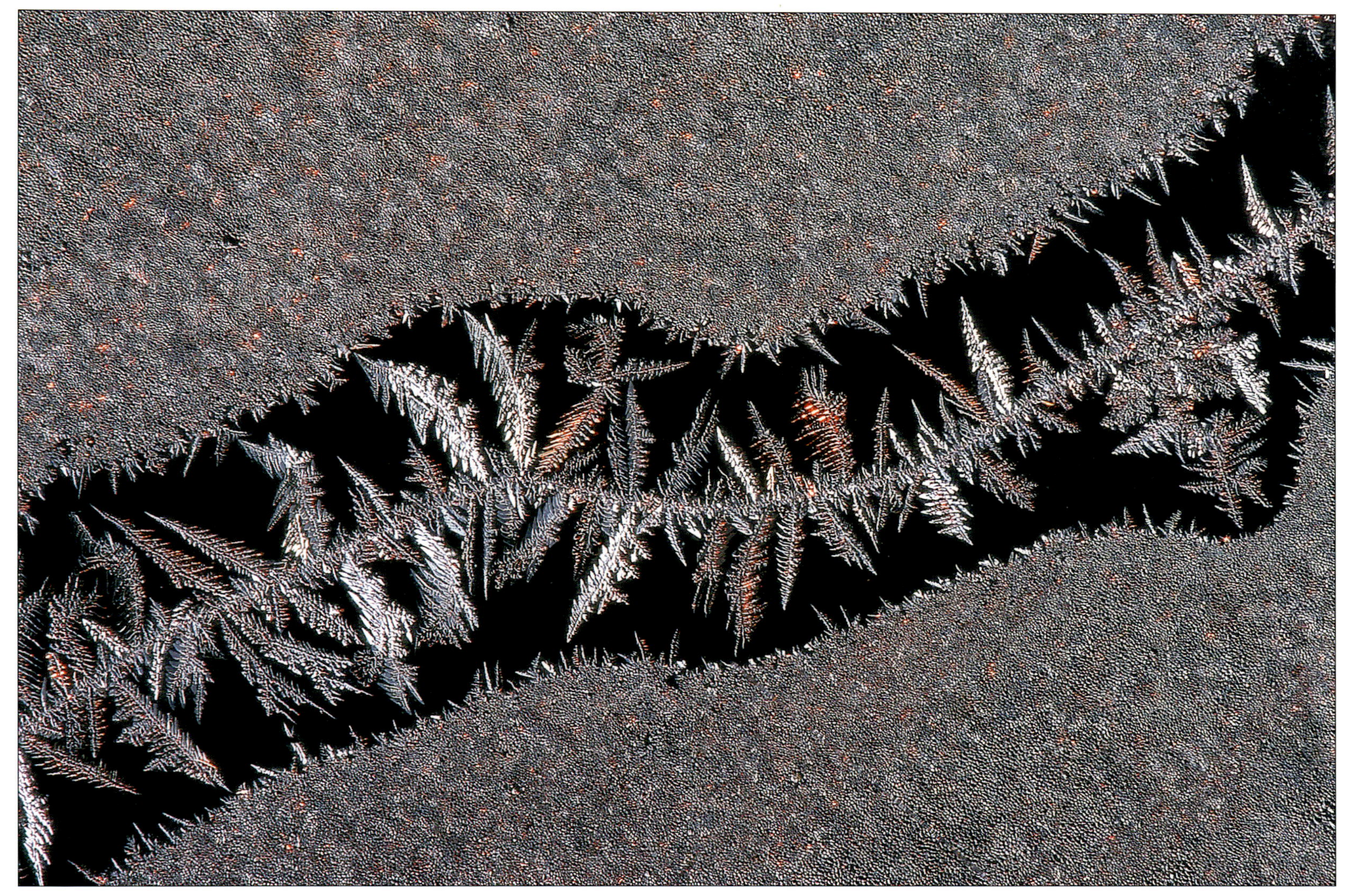

Adam Gibbs
Canada
HIGHLY COMMENDED

Frost pattern on glass

"Frost often creates magical patterns on glass. I came across this example on the window of a greenhouse in a friend's garden in Burnaby, British Columbia. A spider's web had stuck to the window, creating a particularly pleasing display."

Nikon F4 with 200mm macro lens; tripod; Fujichrome Velvia

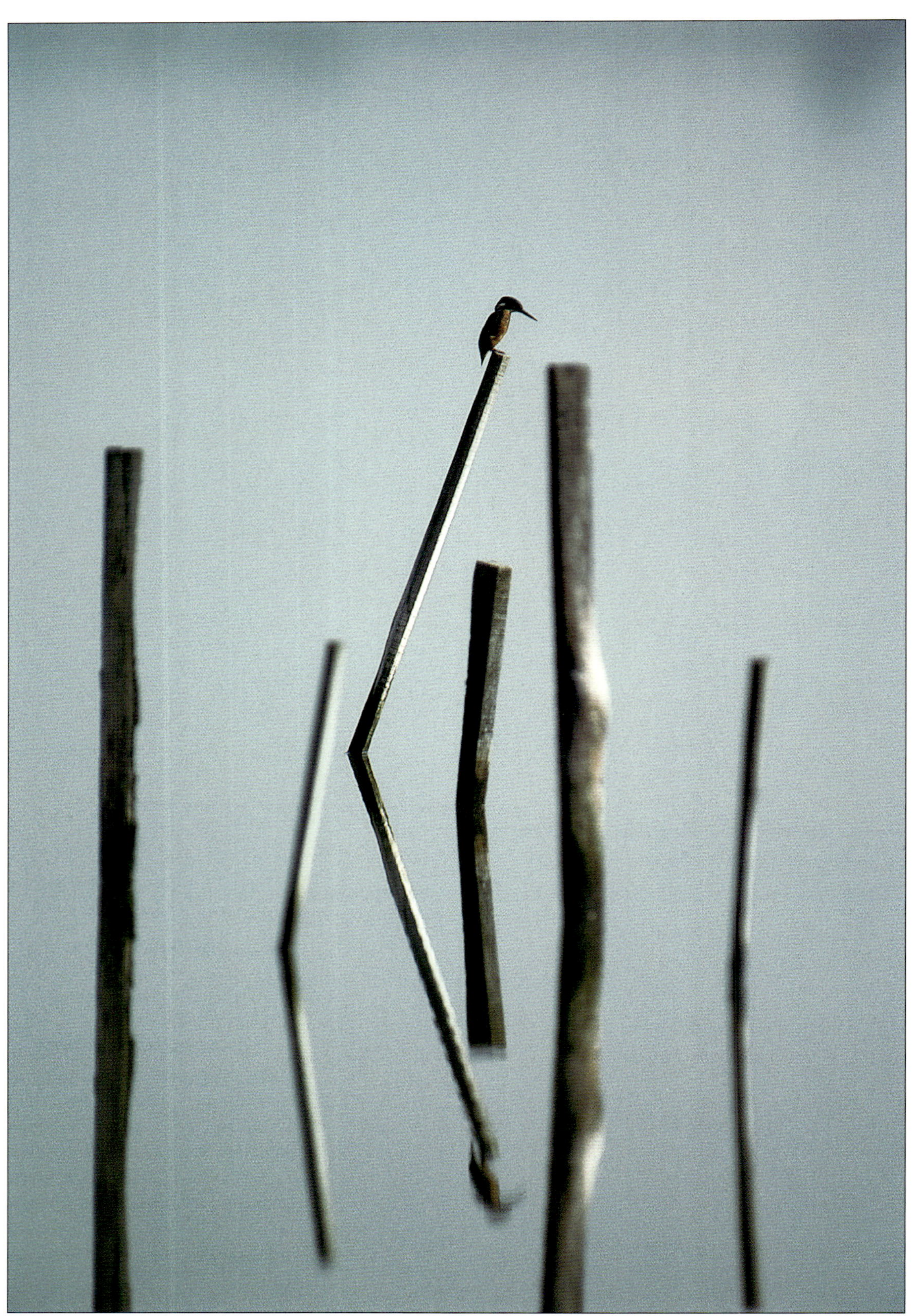

Geoff Doré

United Kingdom

HIGHLY COMMENDED

Kingfisher on post

"I was in a public hide at a nature reserve in Dorset, when this kingfisher appeared. It flew directly to the angled post, glanced down at the water a couple of times and then flew off. I had about a minute to compose the picture and shoot six frames."

Nikon F-801 with 400mm lens and x1.4 teleconverter; tripod; 1/500 sec at f3.5; Kodachrome 64

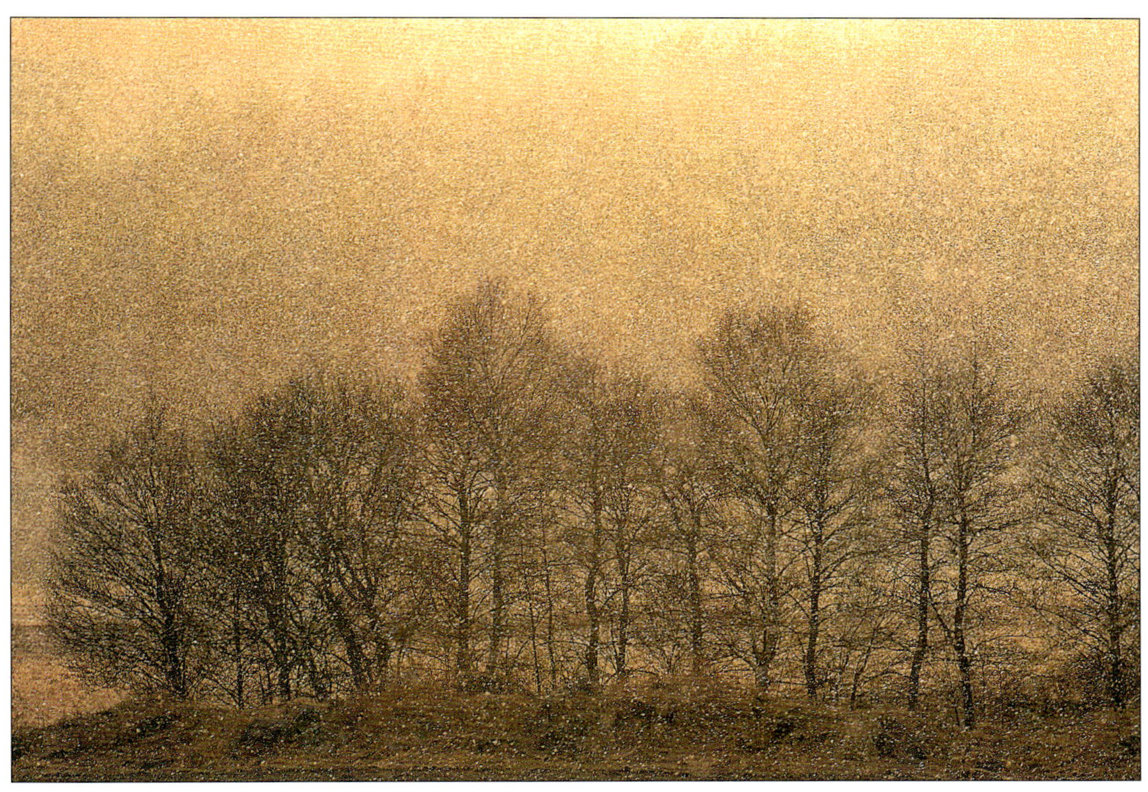

Jan Töve Johansson
Sweden
HIGHLY COMMENDED

Birch trees in snowfall

"The snow came suddenly and fell silently. Backlighting from the low sun gave a golden tone to the whole landscape, while the birch trees stood out like strokes of Indian ink. The picture was taken in Västergötland, Southern Sweden, in April."

Pentax 645 with 600mm lens; tripod; 1/60 sec at f6.7; Fujichrome Velvia

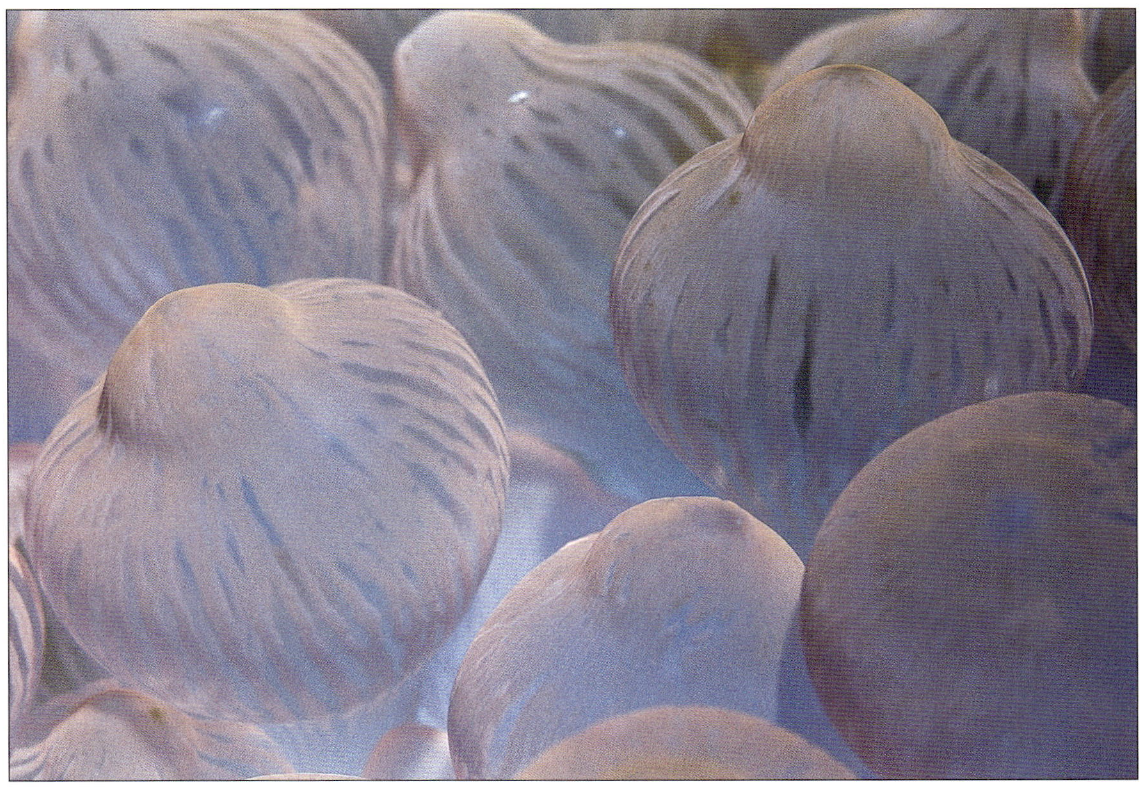

Pete Atkinson
United Kingdom
HIGHLY COMMENDED

Anemone

"I tried photographing this Tongan anemone (Entacmaea quadricolor) with flash, but it came out brown instead of fluorescent orange. So I took a weighted tripod down to a depth of 30 metres and used natural light. This time the anemone came out mauve, but I liked some of the pictures anyway."

Nikon F4 with 105mm micro lens in underwater housing; tripod; 2 sec at f16; Fujichrome Velvia

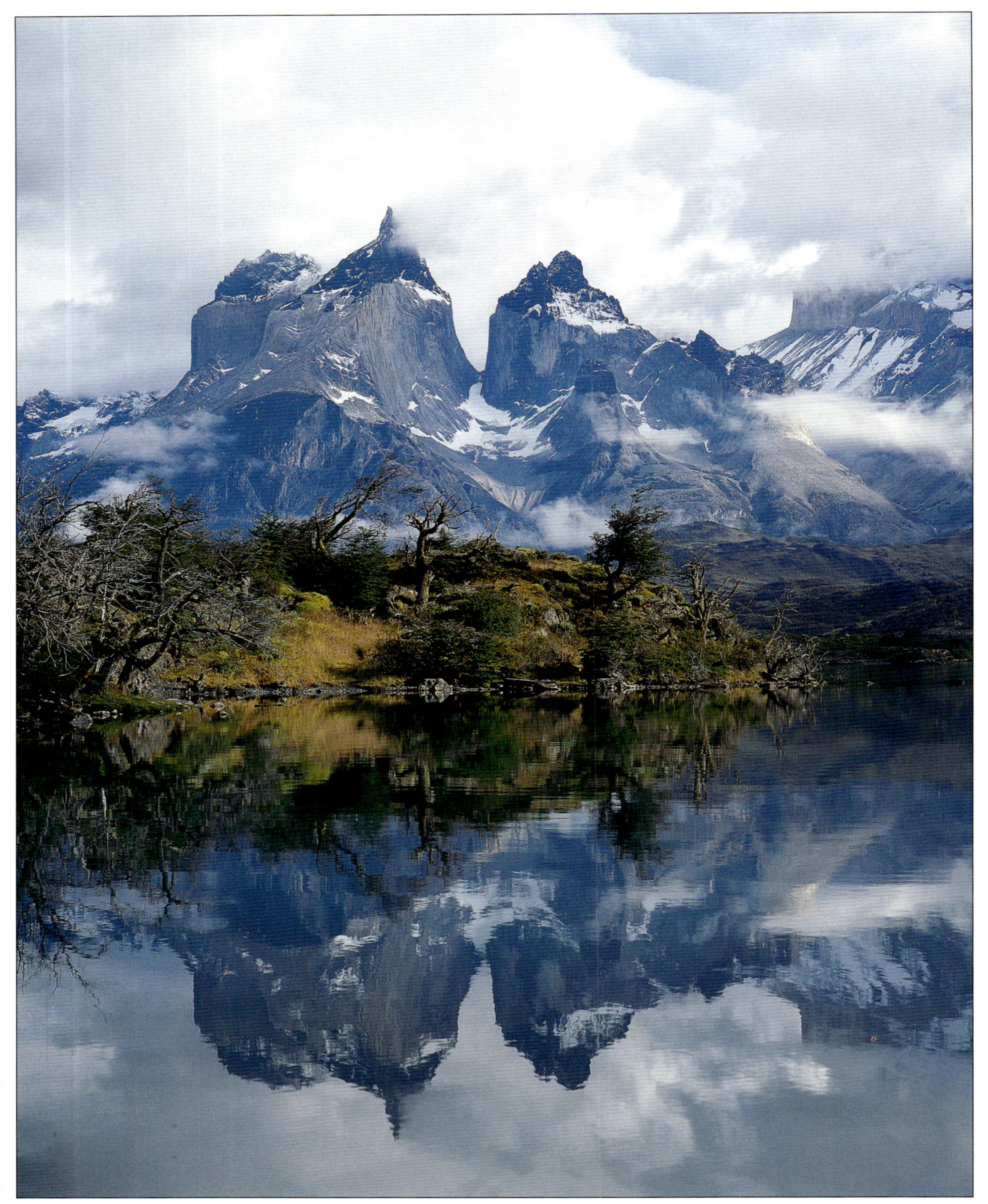

Wild Places

Landscapes must convey a feeling of wildness and create a sense of wonder or awe.

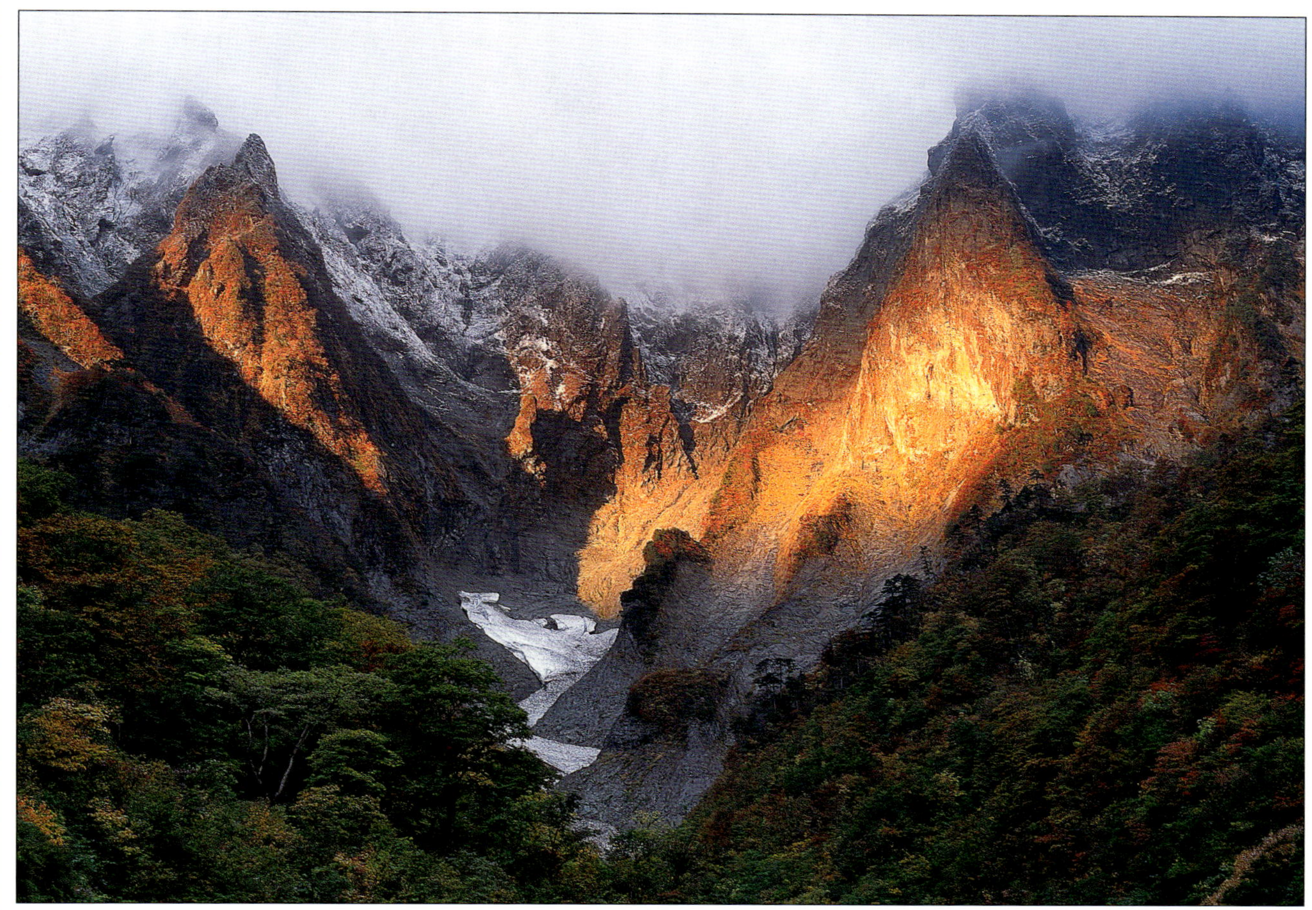

Howie Garber
United States of America
WINNER

Paine Cuernos and reflection

"Torres del Paine National Park, Chile, is known for its extreme weather and high winds. Snow is common, even in summer. As soon as you get off the road you are in the wilderness. Guanacos, flamingos and condors are easily observed."

Pentax 6x7 with 135mm lens; tripod; 1/8 sec at f22; Kodak E100S

Jun Ogawa
Japan
RUNNER-UP

The morning glow

"A fresh layer of snow had fallen at Ichinokura, Japan, but the clouds that had brought the snow were already becoming faint. The first rays of the rising sun broke through the clouds like a spotlight, dyeing the rocky peaks orange."

Pentax 645 with 80-160mm lens; tripod; 4 sec at f22; Fujichrome Velvia rated at 40

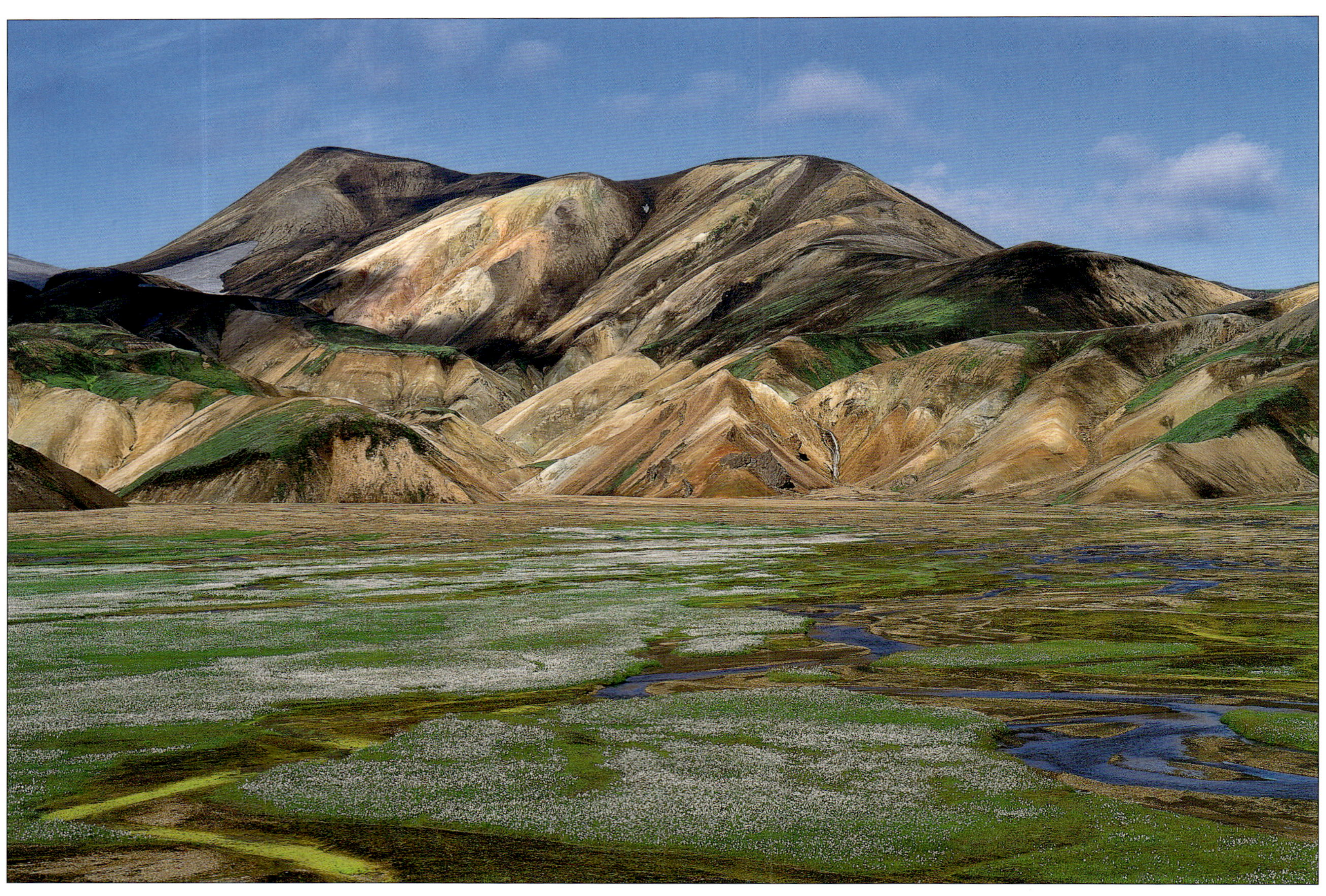

Andreas Leemann
Switzerland
HIGHLY COMMENDED

River plain and mountain, Iceland

"I took this picture of Mount Haalda and the plain of the Namskvisl River while I was on a photographic trip to Iceland. I'd first seen the mountain the day before, but heavy rain had prevented me from getting the picture I wanted. When I went back, conditions were perfect."

Mamiya Universal Press 69 with 150mm lens; tripod; 1/15 sec at f16; Fujichrome Velvia

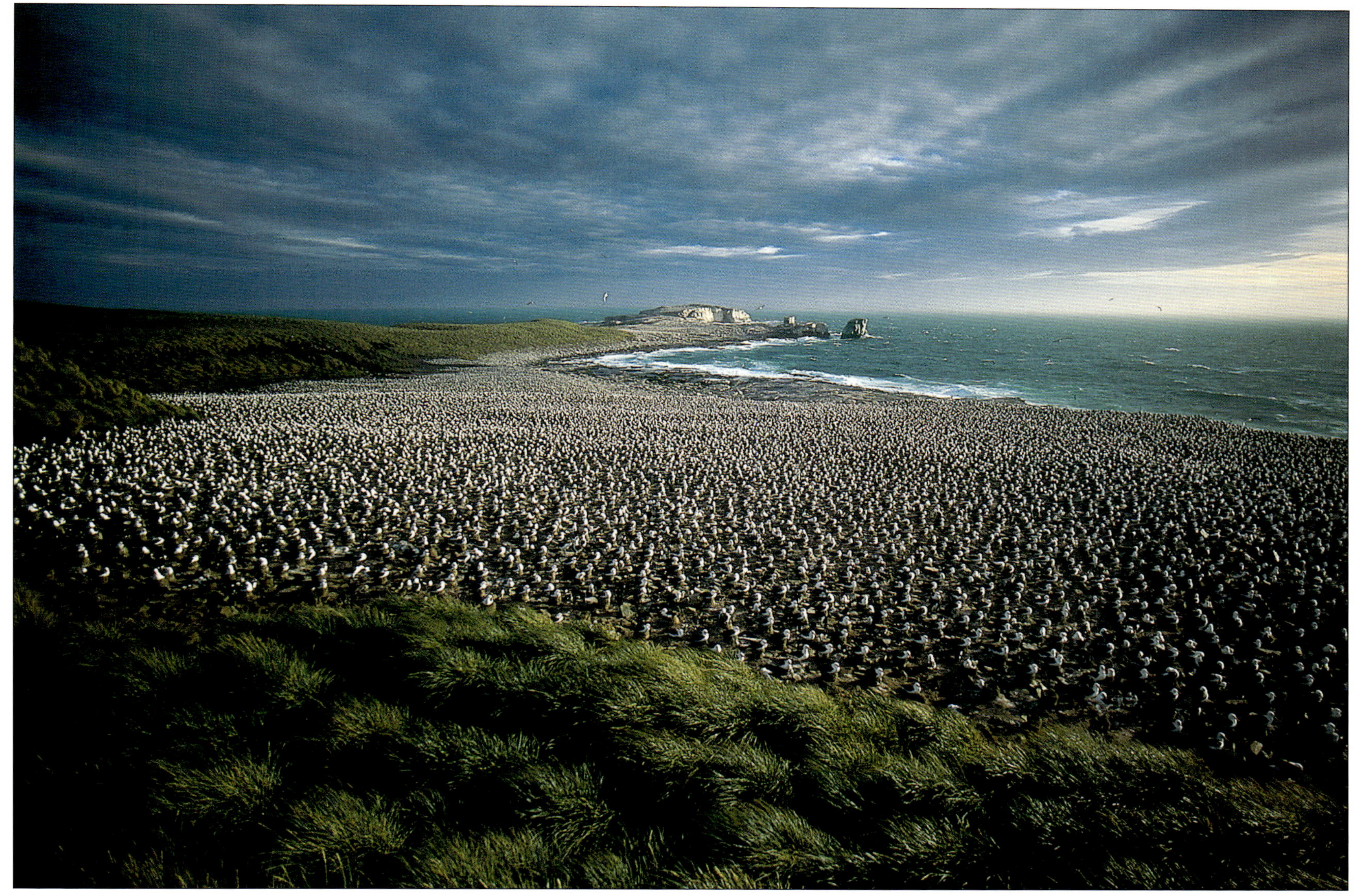

Graham Robertson
Australia
HIGHLY COMMENDED

Black-browed albatross colony

"About 170,000 albatross pairs nest on Beauchene Island in the Falklands. I spent ten days at the colony waiting for the light to be right and for there to be few birds in the sky. I got the shot at about 8pm and left the island an hour later."

Nikon F90x with 28mm lens; tripod; 1/125 sec at f5.6; Fujichrome Velvia

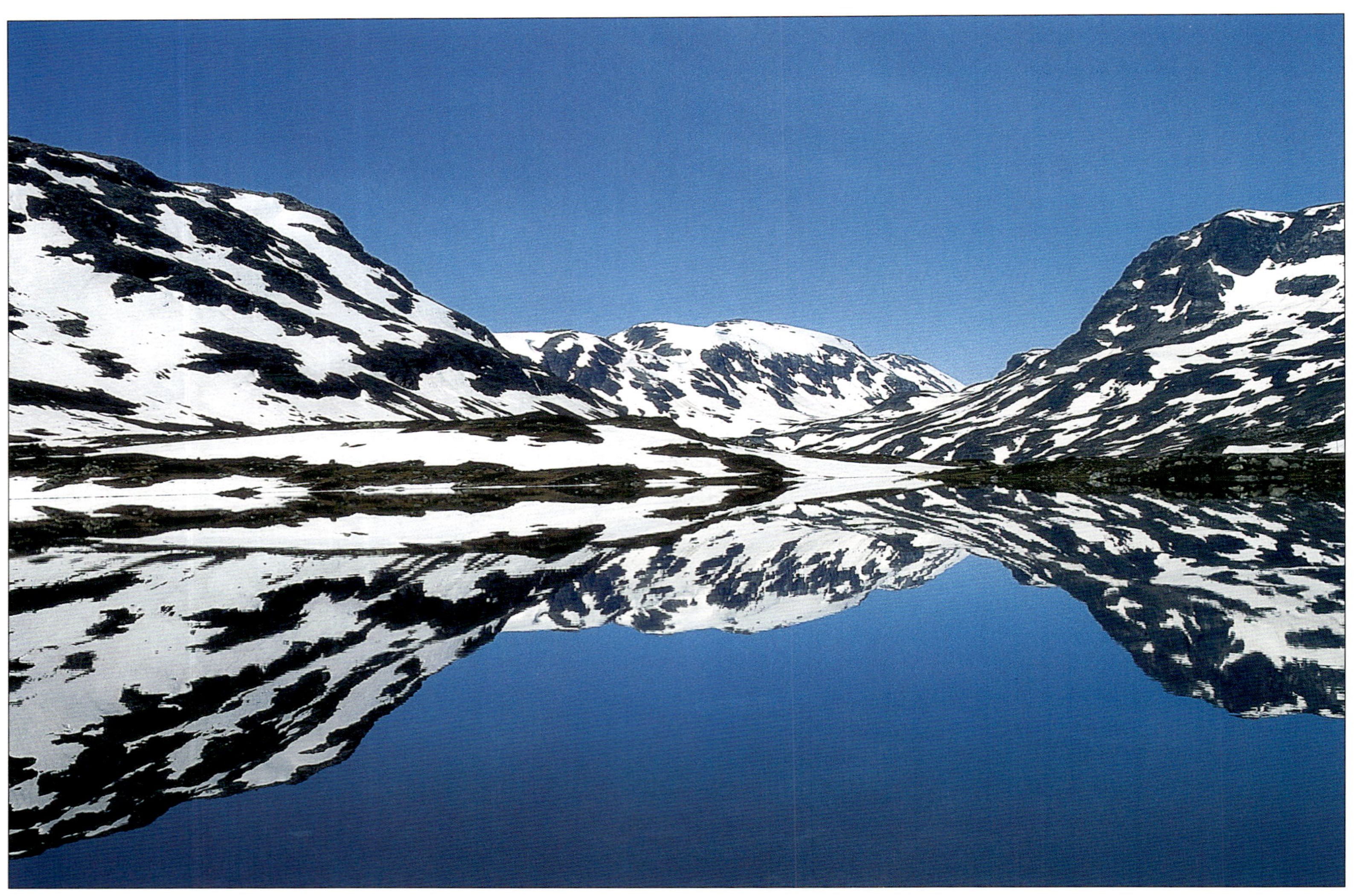

Bernhard Volmer
Germany
HIGHLY COMMENDED

Mountain reflections, Haukeliseter

"Haukeliseter is the starting point for walking tours through the Hardangervidda in Norway. On this occasion there was no wind to ruffle the surface of the lake, and so the mountains in the background were reflected in the water, creating this special effect."

Nikon F4 with 80-200mm lens; polarising filter; 1/125 sec at f11; Fujichrome Sensia 100

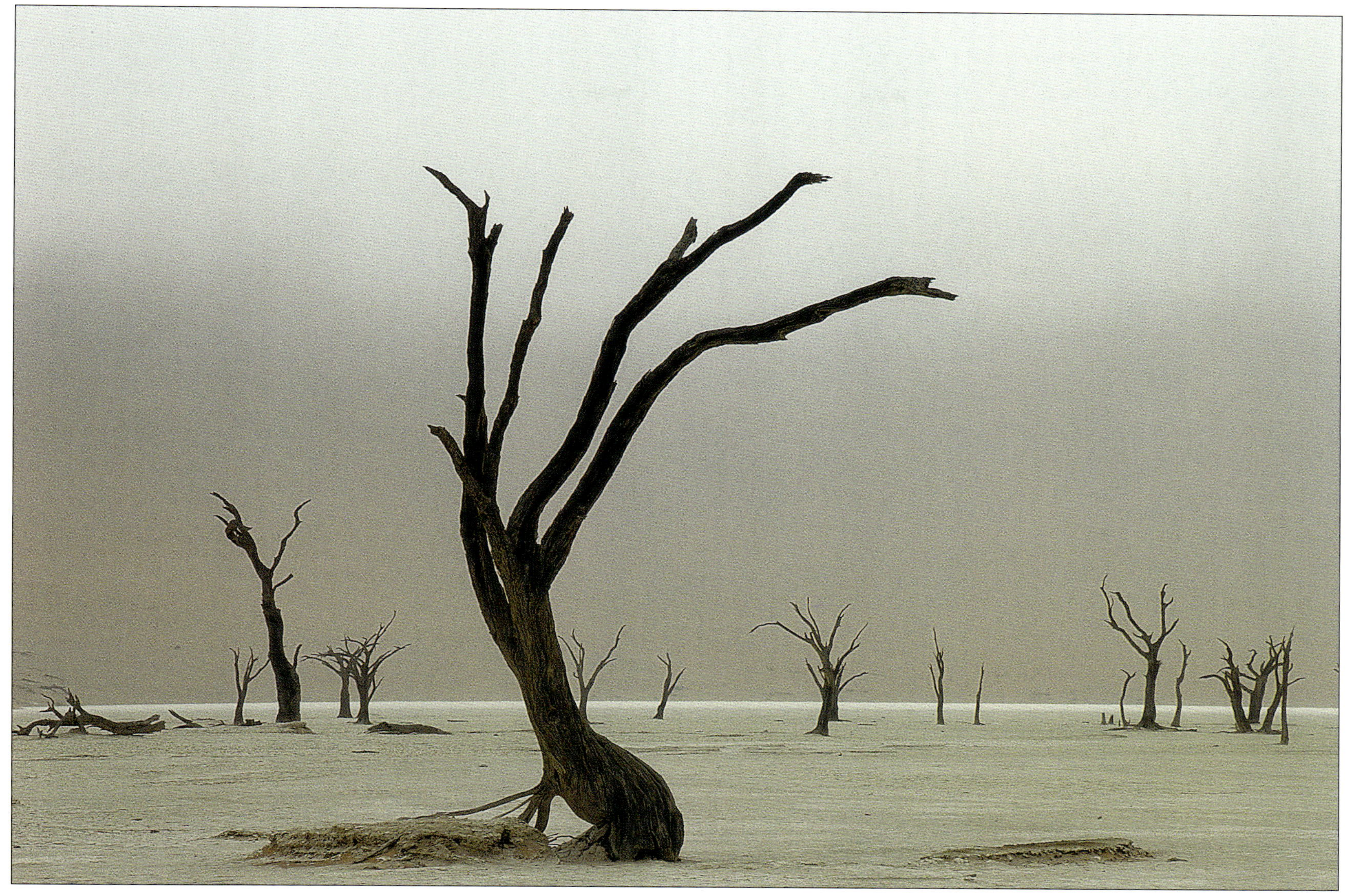

Gil Lopez-Espina
United States of America
HIGHLY COMMENDED

Trees in fog, Namib Desert

"In attempting to reach an impressive section of the Namib Desert named the Dead Pan, I hiked through six kilometres of sand dunes carrying a heavy backpack and tripod. Without warning a thick fog rolled in, causing the temperature to drop suddenly by more than 20 degrees and leaving me extremely chilled."

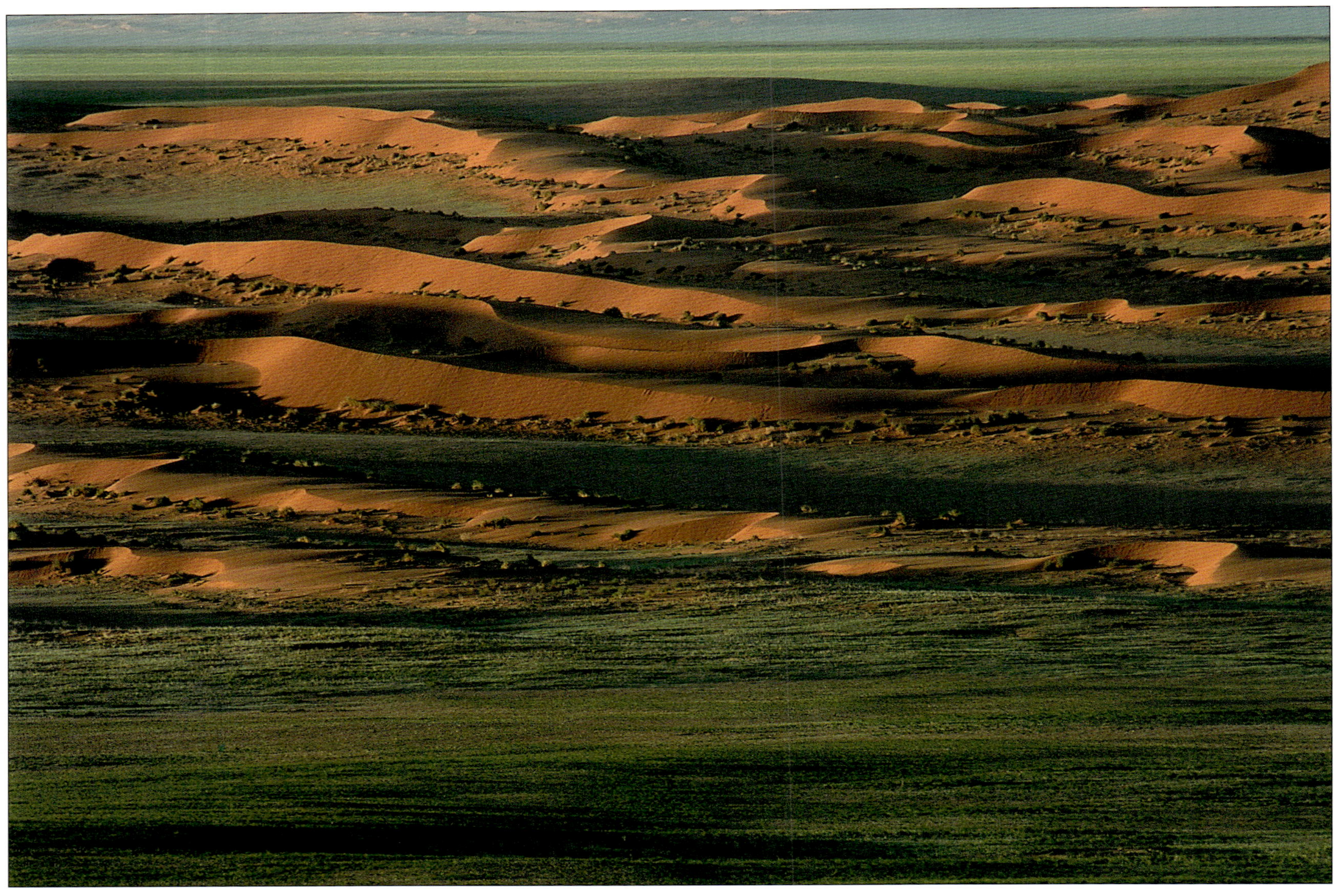

Wynand du Plessis
Namibia
HIGHLY COMMENDED

Greenness in the desert

"My partner and I were driving through a part of the Namib Desert called the Far Eastern Dunes, when we decided to camp by the road. At sunrise the light was even better than it had been the night before. The green grass radiating between orange dunes was a beautiful sight."

Nikon F90x with 70-210mm lens and x2 converter; tripod; 1/60 sec at f11; Fujichrome Velvia

Jeff Foott
United States of America
HIGHLY COMMENDED

Black Rock geysers

"In 1916 a well was dug at this spot in the Black Rock Desert, Nevada. It was left uncapped and, over the years, mineral deposits from the water have created the strange formations shown in the picture."

Arca Swiss 4X5 with 120mm lens; Fujichrome Velvia rated at 40

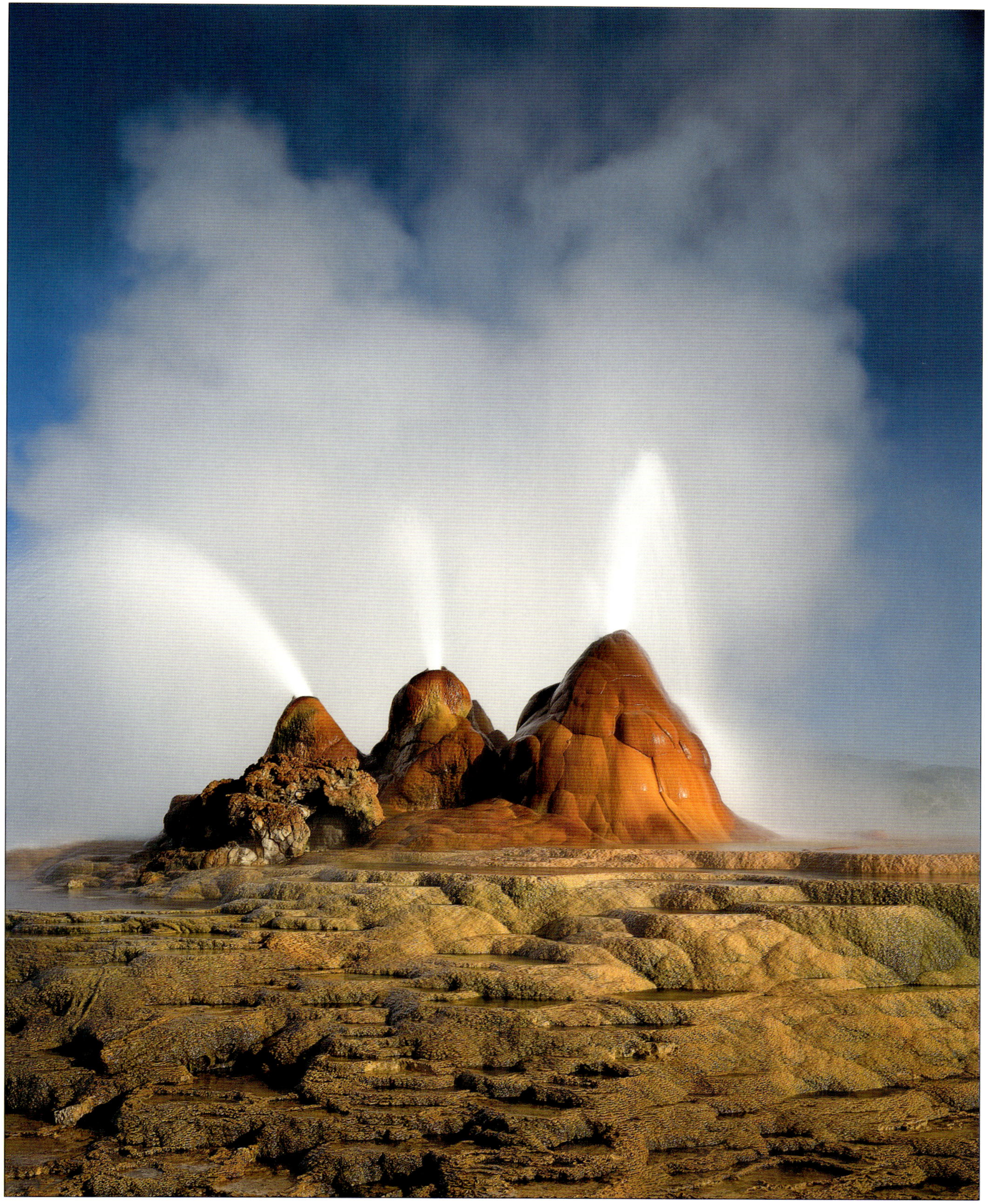

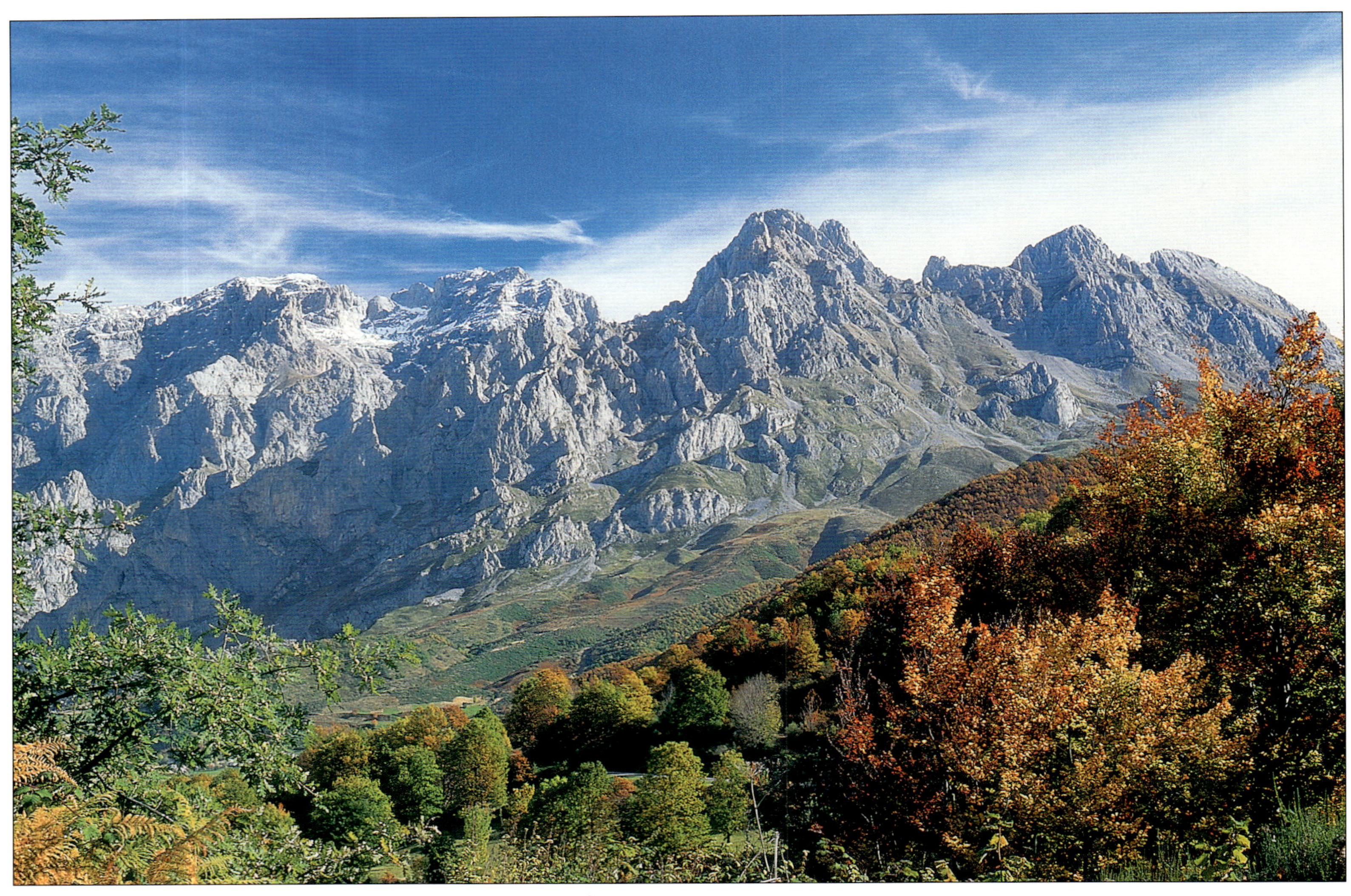

José Delgado
Spain
HIGHLY COMMENDED

Autumn display, Asturias

"Beeches and other deciduous trees joined forces to create this colourful display in the Parque Nacional de los Picos de Europa, Spain. Spanish sailors christened these mountains the Picos de Europa, because they provided a first distant glimpse of home on the journey back from America."

Nikon FM2 with 55mm micro lens; tripod; polarising filter; 1 sec at f32; Fujichrome Velvia rated at 40

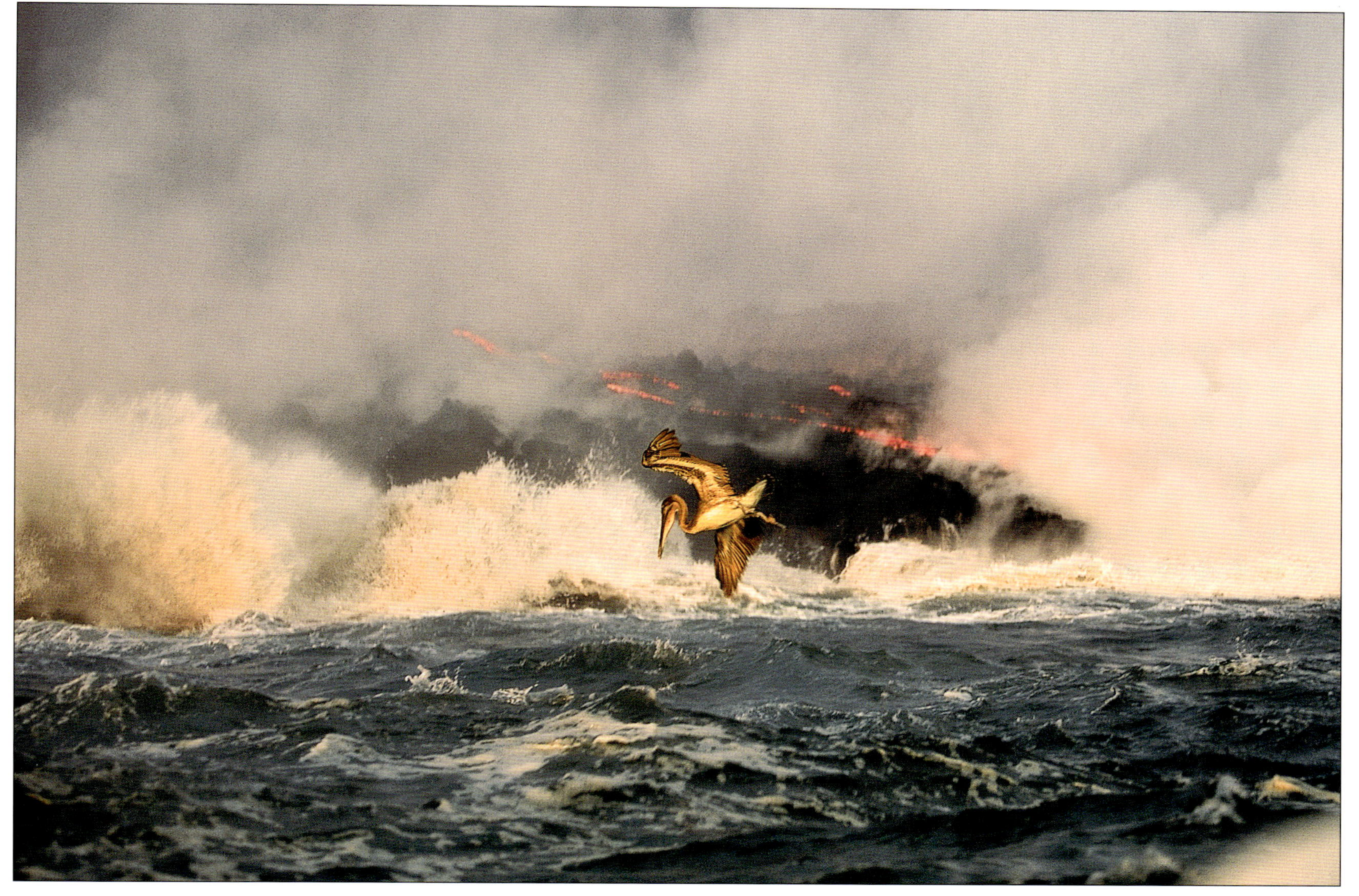

Kelvin Aitken
Australia
HIGHLY COMMENDED

Pelican feeding on fish killed by lava

"For a short time in 1995, a volcanic vent poured lava into the sea around the Galapagos Islands. Fish that went too close were killed. I watched as brown pelicans took advantage of the situation, but I wasn't close enough to get a decent shot. Then late one afternoon a pelican plunged into the sea for an easy meal in front of my camera."

Canon EOS I with 70-200mm lens; 1/400sec at f4; Fujichrome Velvia

The World In Our Hands

Pictures must illustrate in a symbolic or graphic way our dependence on the natural world or our capability of inflicting harm on it.

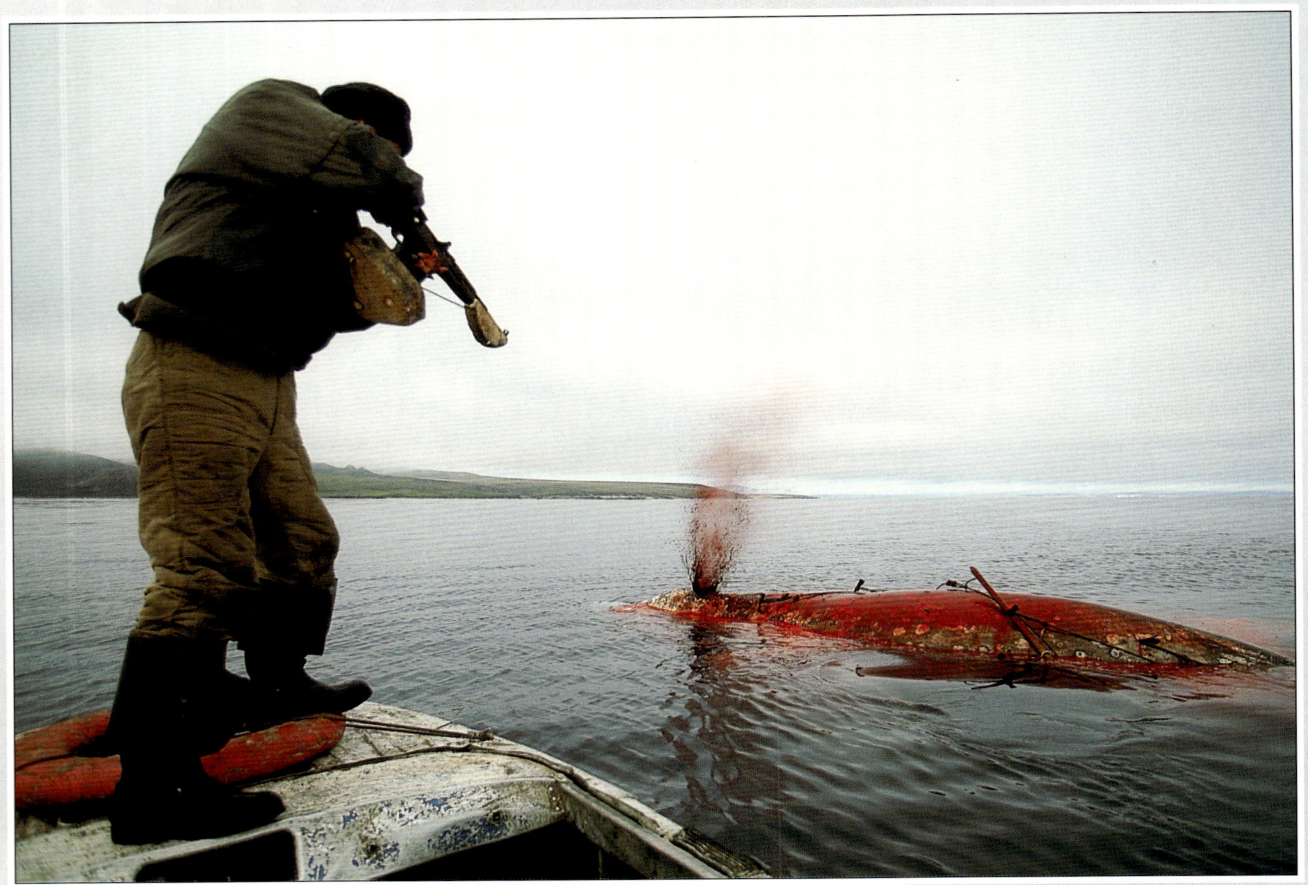

Staffan Widstrand
Sweden
WINNER

Chukchi hunter and grey whale

"About 75 grey whales are taken each year by indigenous Chukchi hunters from the village of Lorino in Chukotka, northeast Siberia. Whale meat has been an important part of the standard diet here for over 3000 years. This whale was first harpooned by hand five times, then finished off with 10-15 bullets from an automatic army rifle. The bloody cloud of spray in the picture was caused by a hit to the lungs."

Nikon F90 with 20-35mm lens; 1/500 sec at f2.8; Fujichrome Velvia

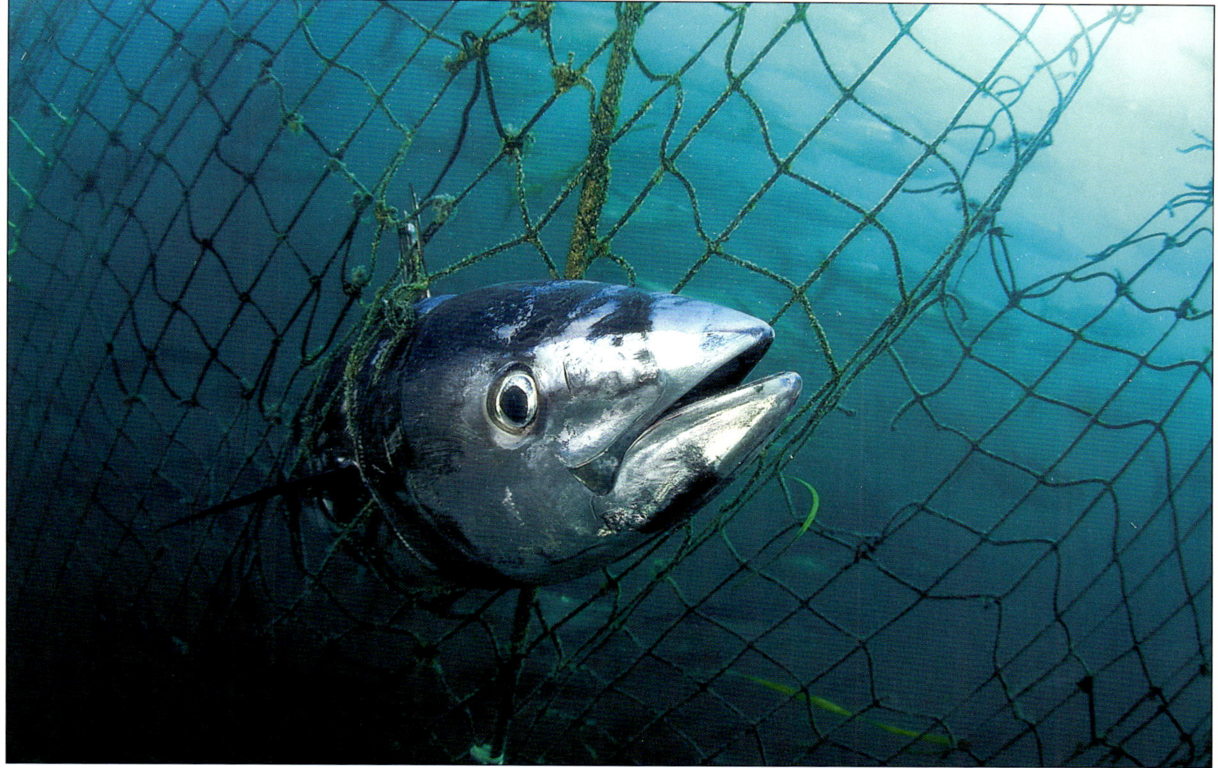

David B Fleetham
Canada
RUNNER-UP

Tuna in net

"This photograph shows a dead southern bluefin tuna, caught in the netting of its holding pen in Spencer Gulf, South Australia. Tuna are fattened in the pens before being shipped to Japan. This species was listed as endangered in 1996."

Canon F1n with 15mm fisheye lens; underwater housing; strobes; 1/30 sec at f5.6; Fujichrome Velvia

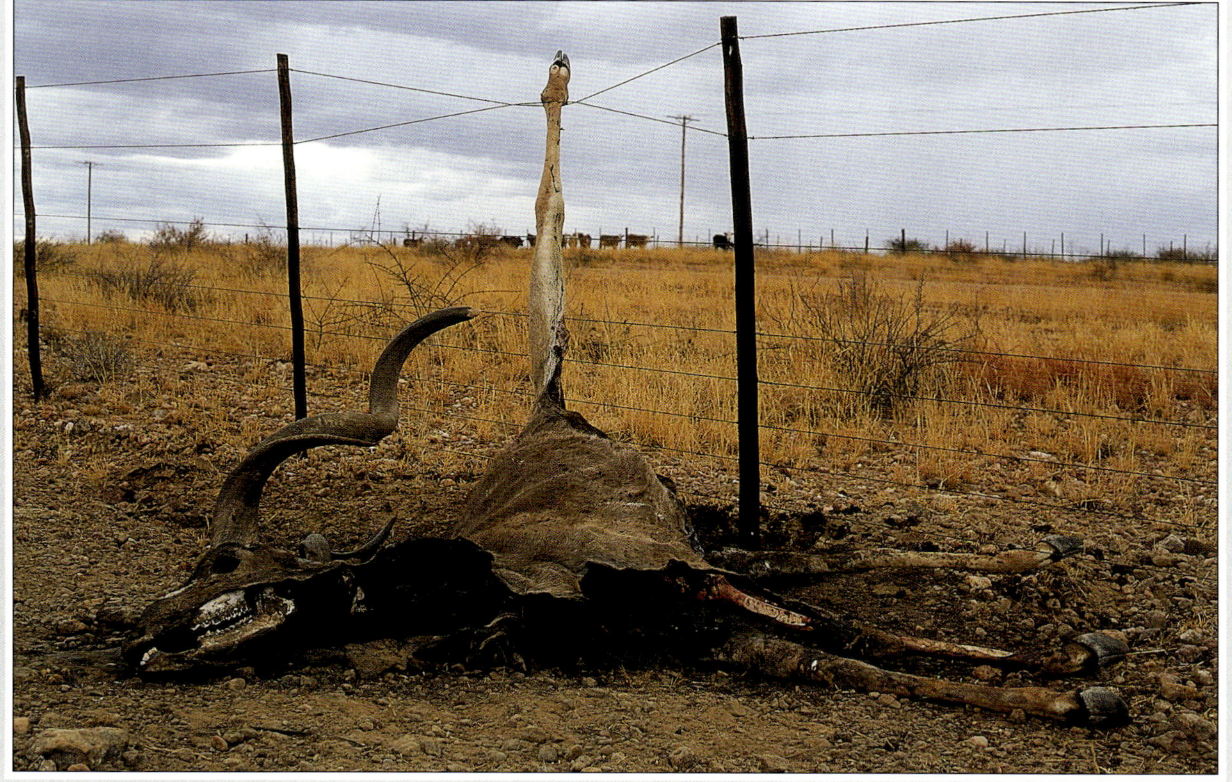

Martin Gabriel
Germany
HIGHLY COMMENDED

Kudu entangled in fence

"This dead kudu bull was one of three carcasses I found on a 500-metre stretch of road in the Khomas Highland, Namibia. The region was in the grip of a severe drought and the kudus must have been in a weakened state. Searching for food and water, they tried to cross the fence, but got entangled and died."

Pentax Super A with 24-40mm lens; tripod; Fujichrome Velvia

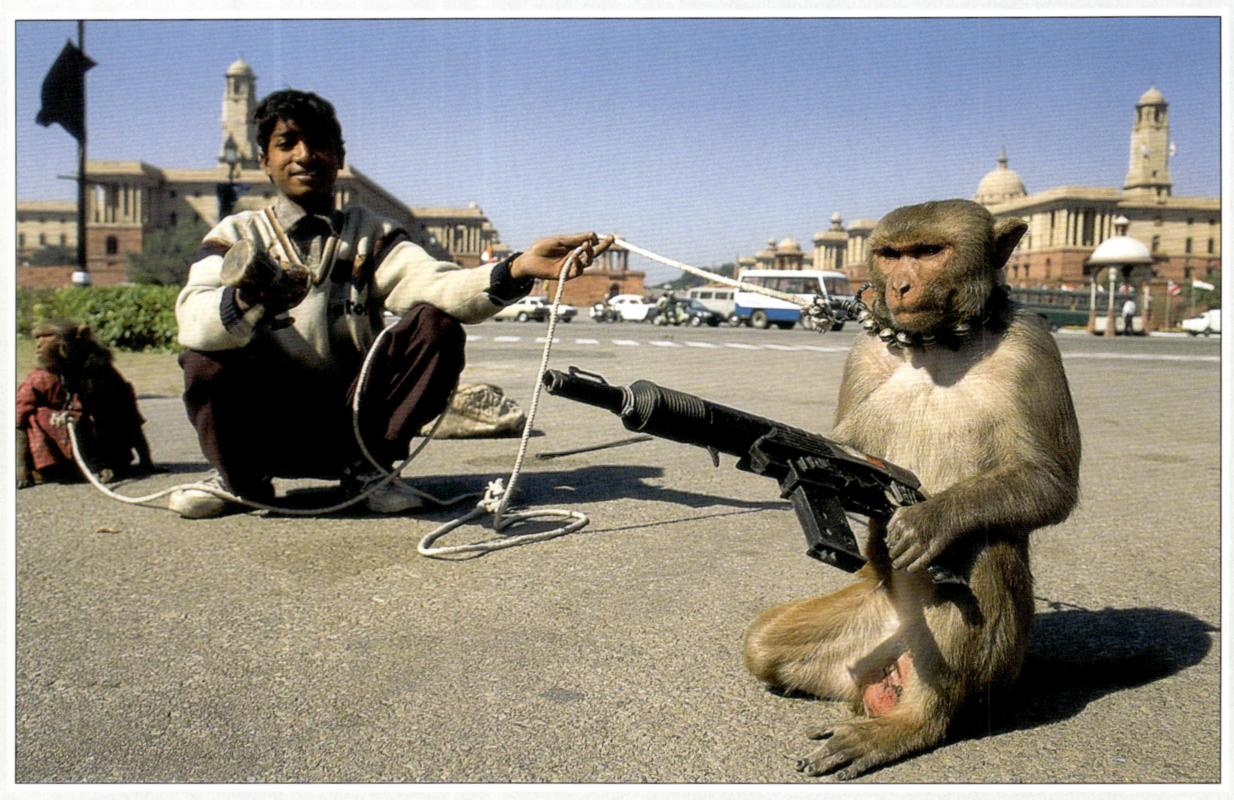

Pete Oxford
United Kingdom
HIGHLY COMMENDED

Machine gun monkey

"Throughout the Indian subcontinent there are many examples of exploitation of animals for the benefit of tourists. These rhesus macaques in New Delhi had been taught various tricks, including dancing and posing with a machine gun. I did not pay to take the photograph."

Nikon F4s with 24mm lens; 1/60 sec at f11; Fujichrome Velvia

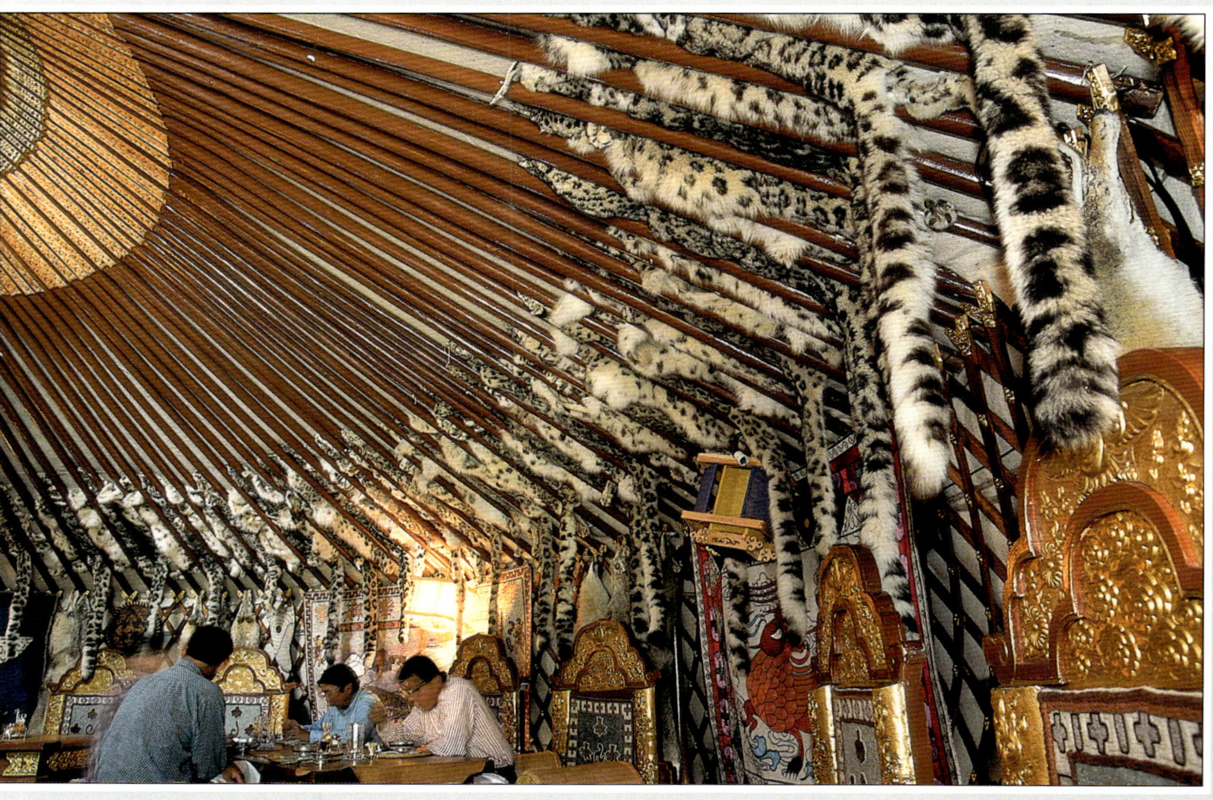

Gertrud & Helmut Denzau
Germany
HIGHLY COMMENDED

Snow leopard furs in restaurant

"In a traditional restaurant in Ulaan Baatar, the Mongolian capital, we found more than 70 snow leopard furs hanging from the ceiling. The furs had been confiscated by customs at the international airport. There was no notice in the restaurant explaining that snow leopards are endangered."

Nikon F4 with 20mm lens; tripod; 1/8 sec at f8; Fujichrome Sensia

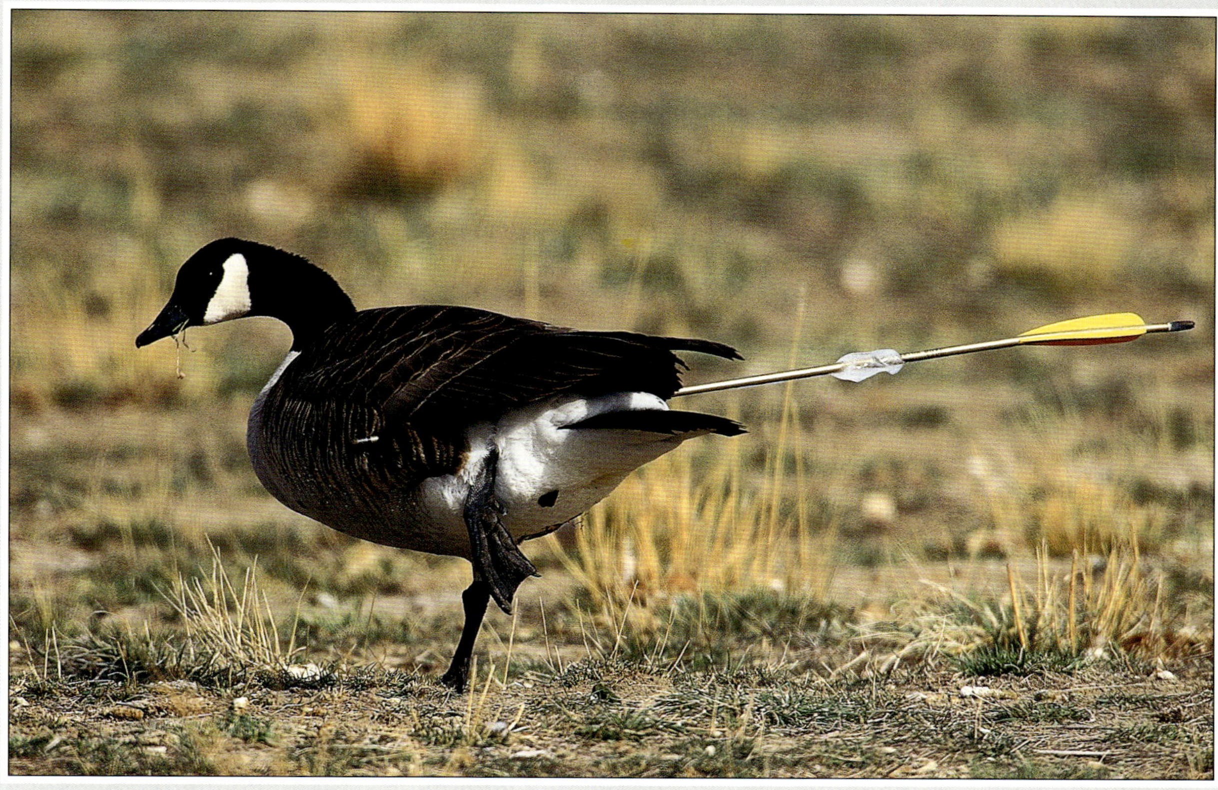

Wendy Shattil & Bob Rozinski
United States of America
HIGHLY COMMENDED

Canada goose pierced with arrow

"We came across this unfortunate Canada goose earlier this year in a suburb of Denver, Colorado. The arrow had passed right through its body. Somehow it was still able to swim, fly and walk, though with difficulty. The State Division of Wildlife tried unsuccessfully to catch the goose to remove the arrow."

Canon EOS 1N with 600mm lens; tripod; 1/125 at f11; Fujichrome Provia

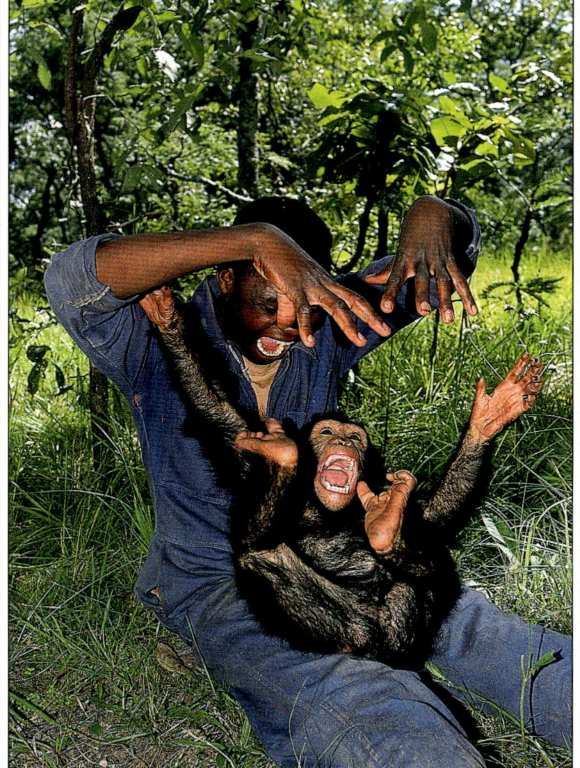

Martin Harvey
South Africa
HIGHLY COMMENDED

Keeper tickling baby chimp

"Chimfunshi Chimpanzee Orphanage, in Zambia, is home to a number of baby chimps, which are taken into the bush each day by keeper Domanik Yewa to learn normal behaviour."

Kurt Amsler
Switzerland
HIGHLY COMMENDED

Coral reef destruction

"For centuries the people of the Maldives have taken building materials from coral reefs without having much effect on the environment. The government has banned the practice but it is still common."

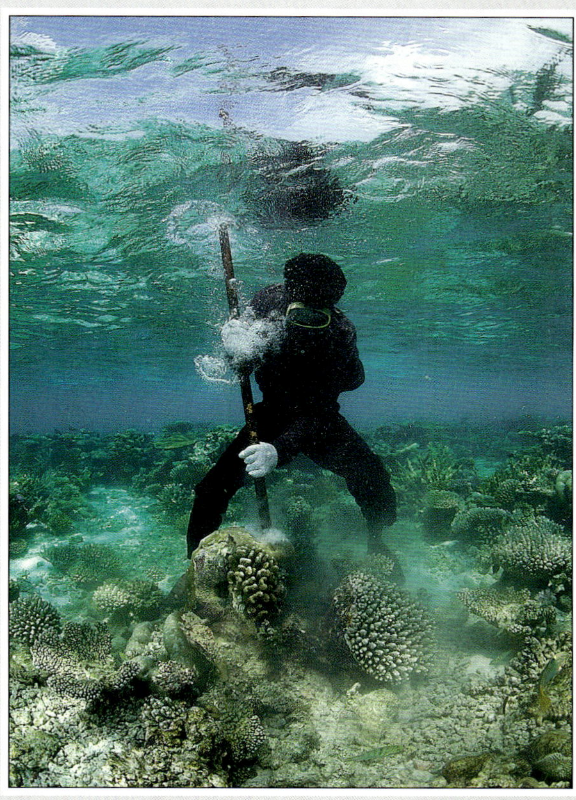

Young Wildlife Photographer of the Year

This section of the competition is open to photographers aged 17 and under. It is divided into three age categories: 10 years and under, 11 to 14 years and 15 to 17 years. Photographers are able to enter up to six images of any wildlife subject. The winner and runner-up in each age-group receives a cash prize.

The overall winner of the competition, 16-year-old Rebecca Dean from the United Kingdom, received the BG plc award - a bronze trophy of an ibis - a cheque for £500 and the opportunity to spend a day on location with wildlife photographer Heather Angel.

Rebecca Dean
United Kingdom
YOUNG WILDLIFE PHOTOGRAPHER OF THE YEAR 1997

Red winged parrot

"We spent four days at Katherine Gorge in Australia's Northern Territory as it was such a good site for birds. Red winged parrots are fairly common in the area, but they usually feed in the upper branches of the trees. This one came much lower and I made the most of the opportunity."

Olympus OM2N with 300mm lens; monopod; 1/125 sec at f8; Kodachrome 200

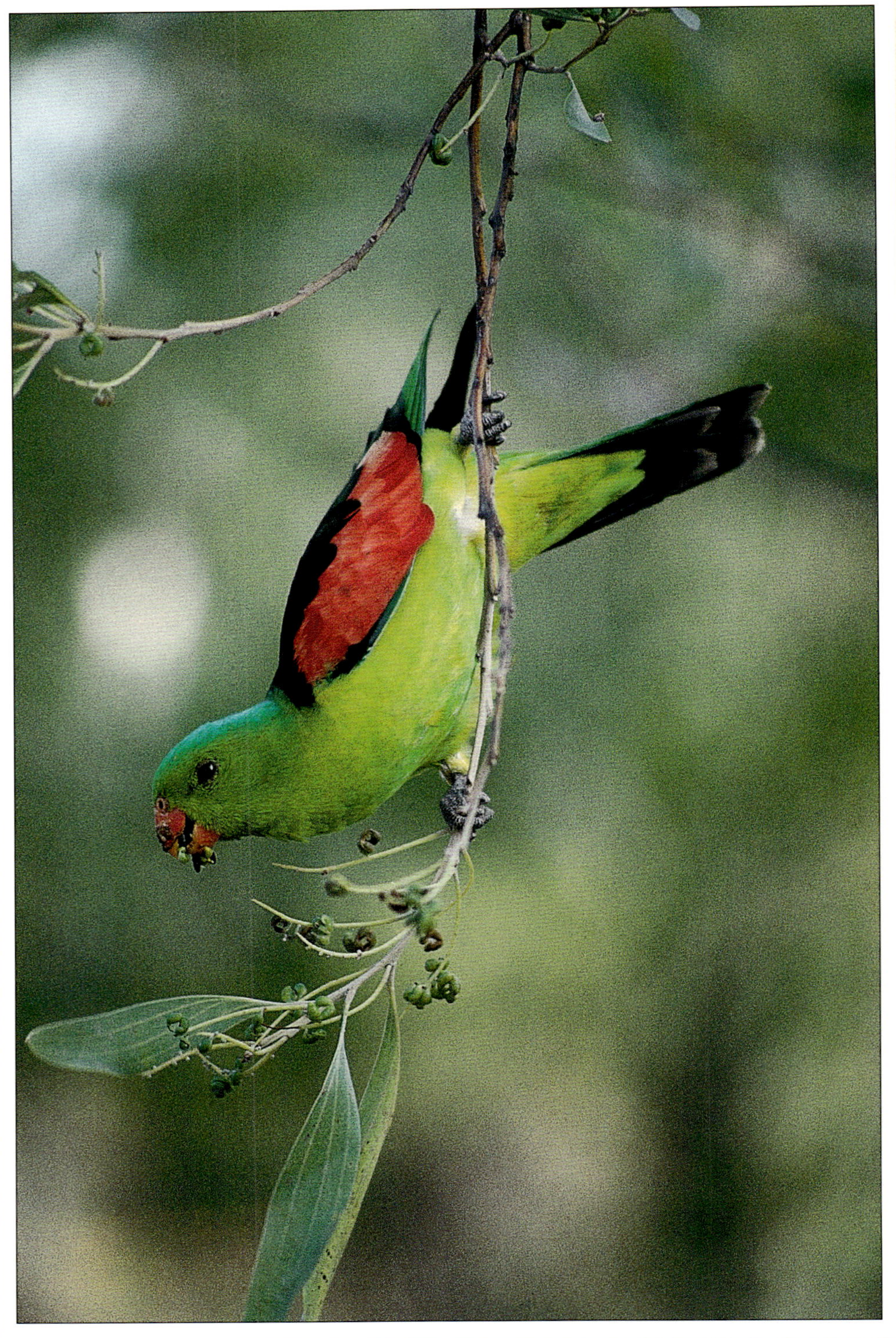

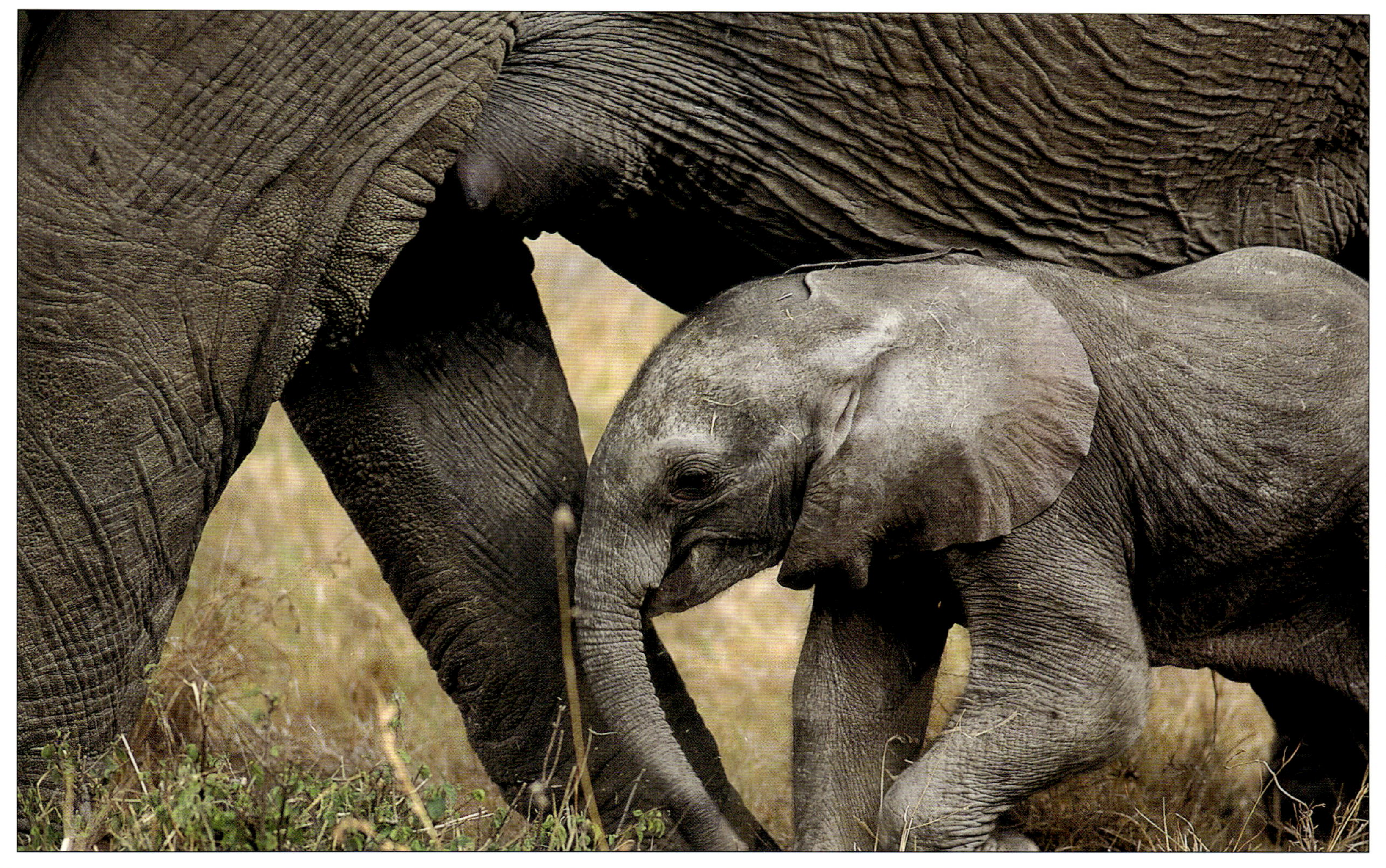

Daniel Gritz
United States of America
WINNER
10 years and under

African elephants with baby

"I took this photograph while I was on safari in Kenya with my parents earlier this year. The elephants were by a swamp in the Maasai Mara Game Reserve. They were in a group of three, made up of a mother, a baby and the baby's sister."

Nikon 8008 with 400mm lens;
Fujichrome Provia 100

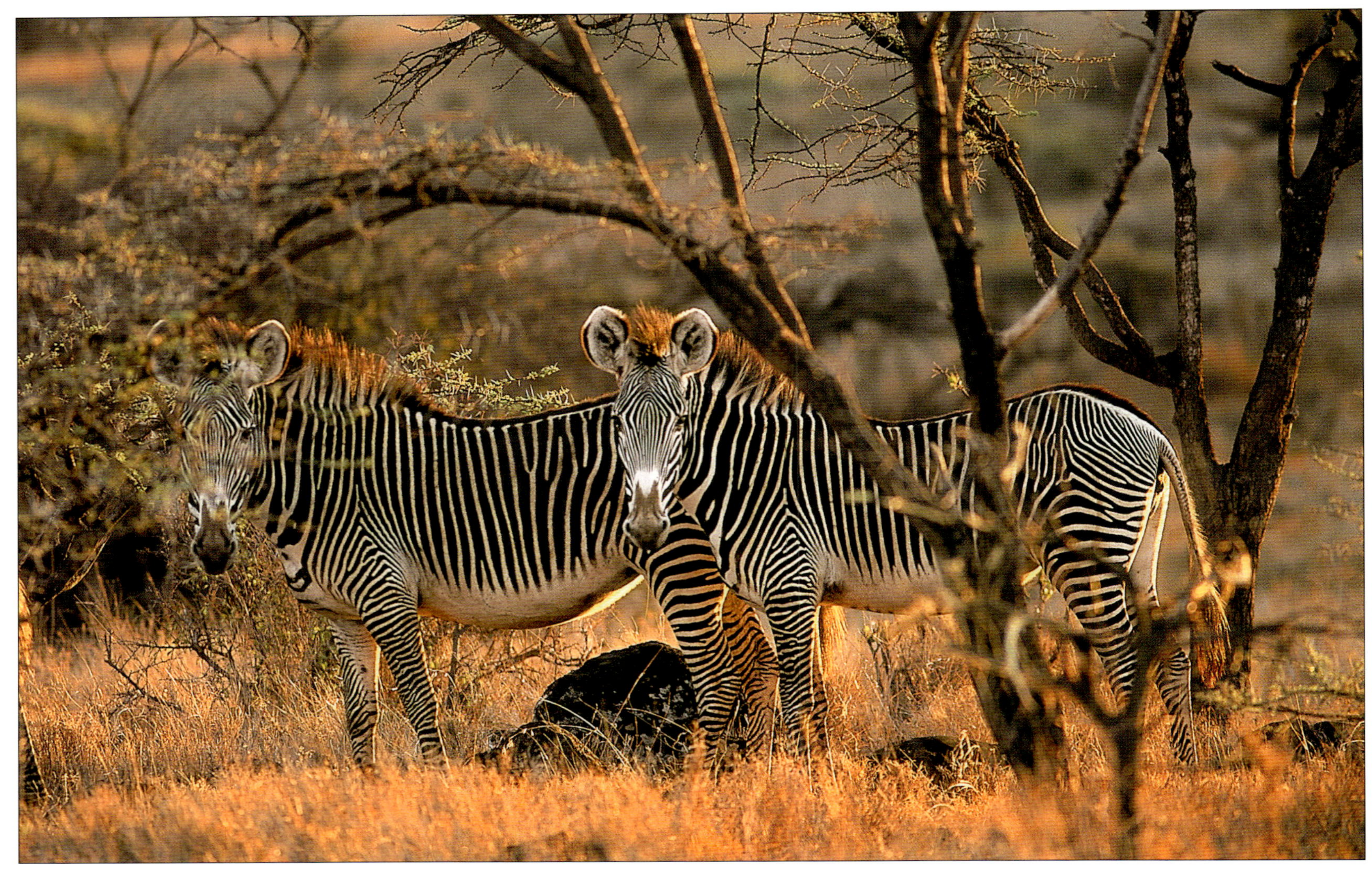

Daniel Gritz
United States of America
RUNNER-UP
10 years and under

Grevy's zebra

"We went to Lewa Downs, Kenya, hoping to see Grevy's zebras. I was lucky to get the photograph because these zebras are rare. Afterwards we got our Landrover stuck and the whole village came to help us get it out."

Nikon 8008 with 100mm lens;
Fujichrome Provia 100

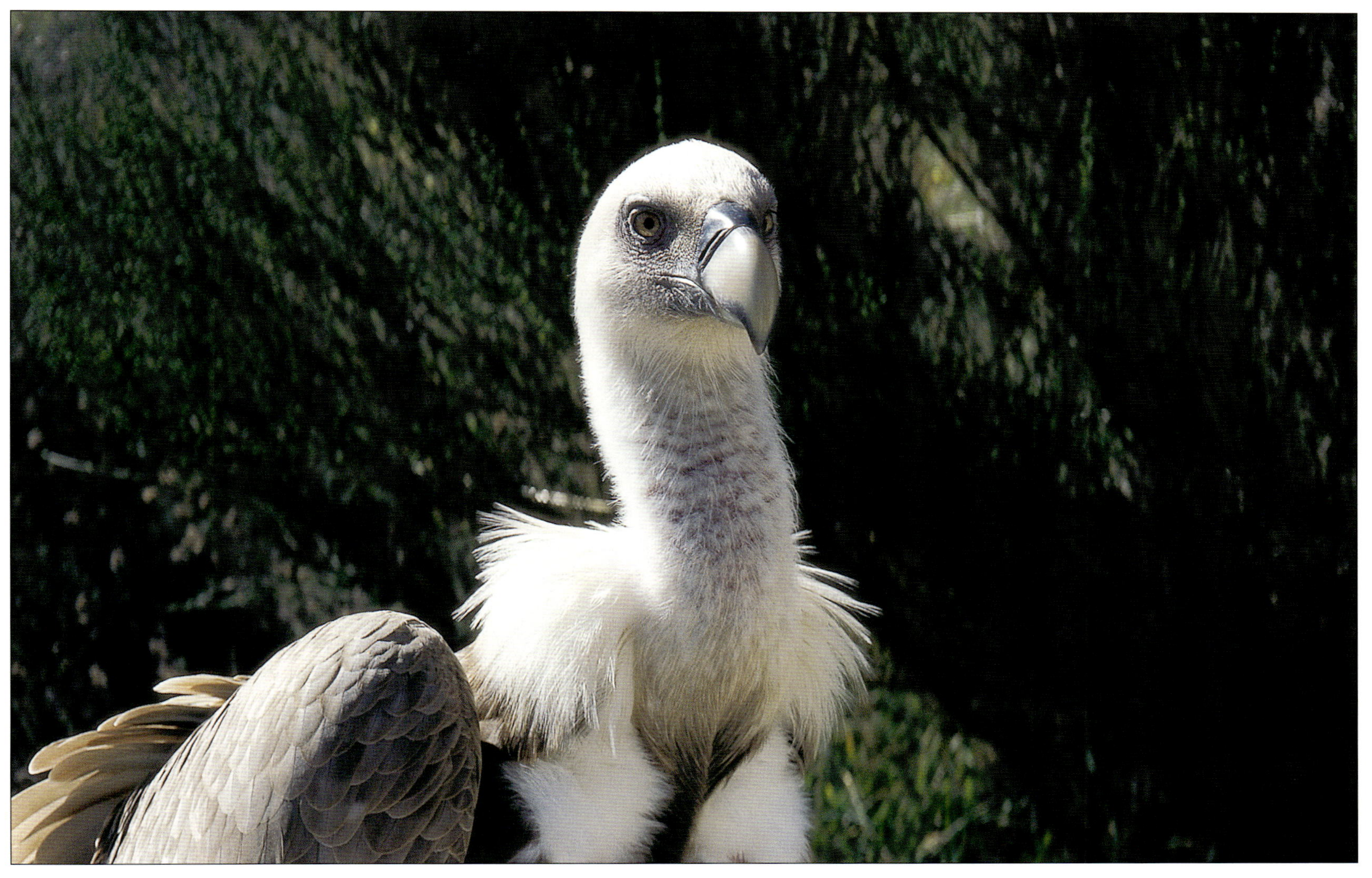

María Cano
Spain
HIGHLY COMMENDED
10 years and under

Griffon vulture

"When we went to La Cañada Real Zoo, Madrid, Nicholas the griffon vulture followed us all day. At the end of our visit he tried to steal sandwiches from my sister Cristina's bag and she got pecked on the hand."

Panasonic C-2200 ZM with 35-70mm lens; Fujichrome Sensia 100

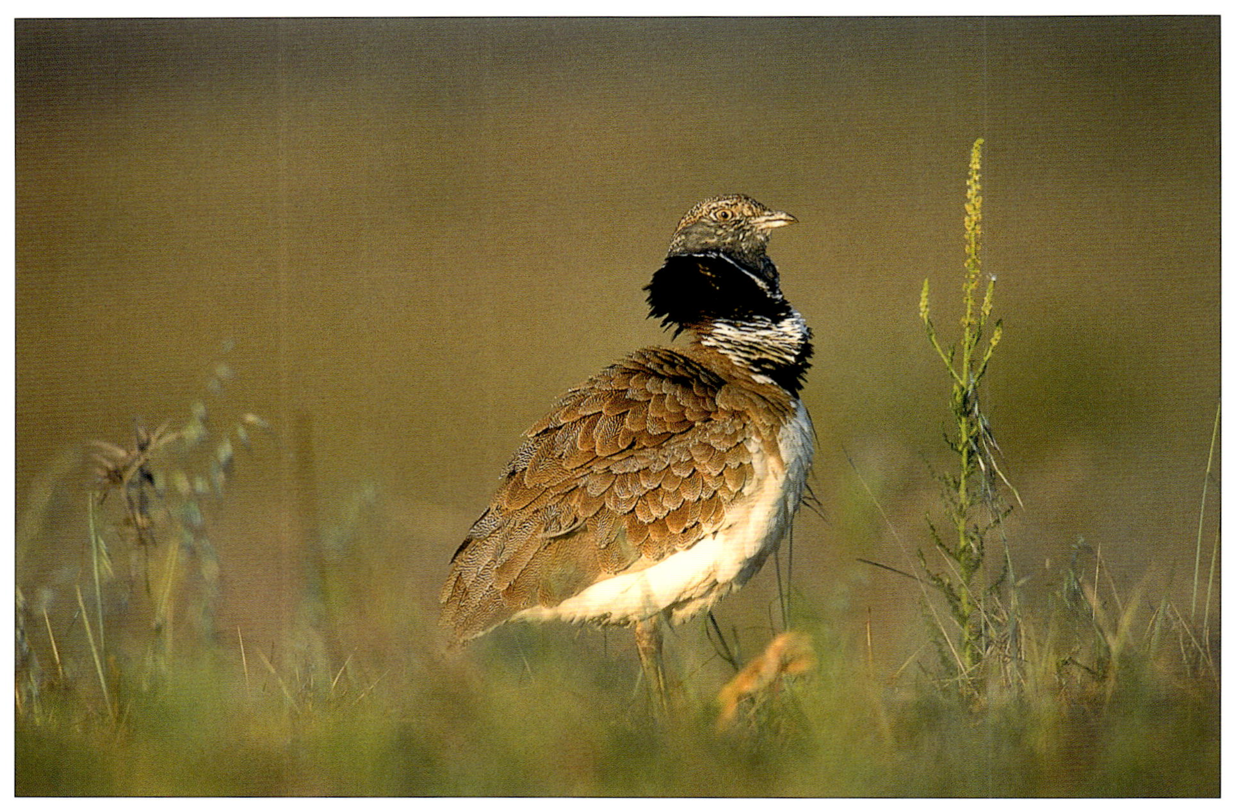

Fabian Fischer

Germany

WINNER

11-14 years

Little bustard displaying

"Little bustards, like this one from the Extremadura region of Spain, can be watched and photographed only from dusk to dawn. To take this picture I installed a hide where the bird had displayed the previous night, then waited until it reappeared."

Nikon F90x with 300mm lens and x2 extender; tripod; 1/60 sec at f5.6; Fujichrome Sensia 100

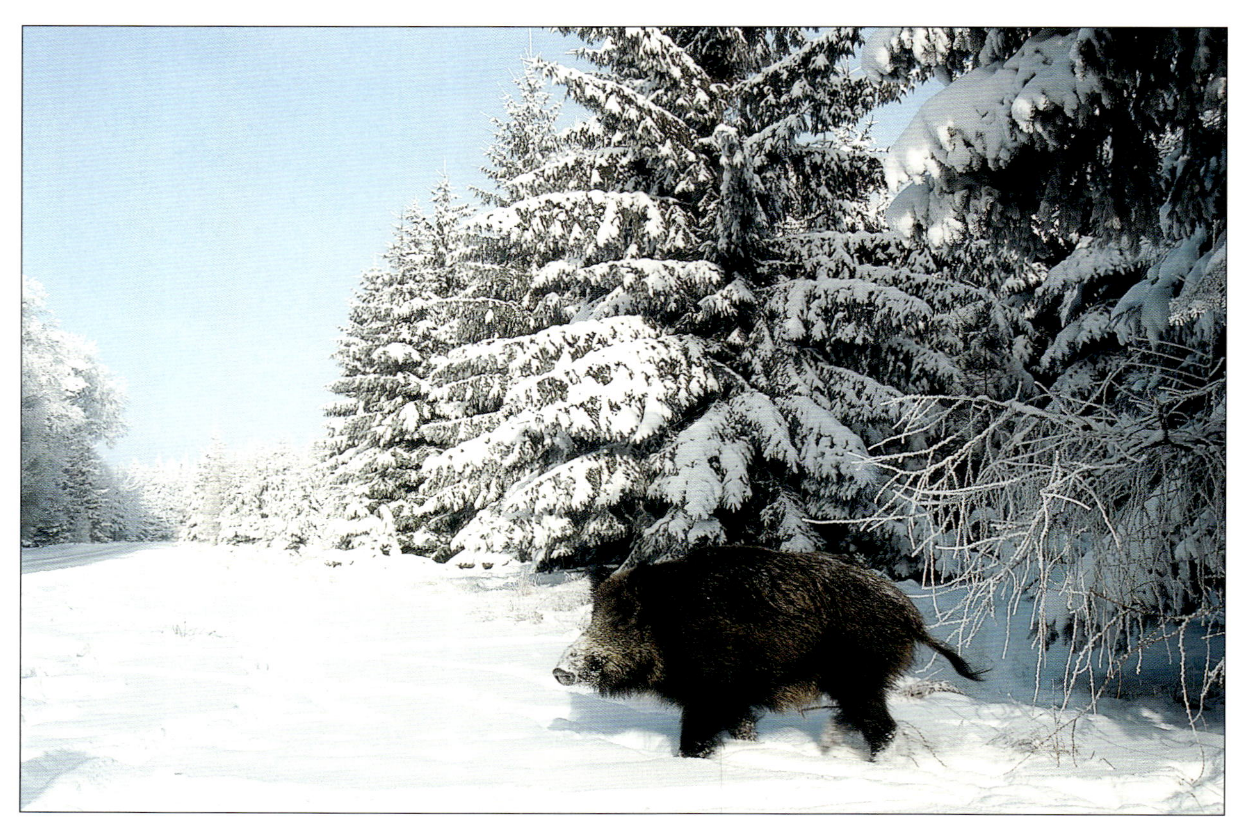

Verena Hahl

Germany

RUNNER-UP

11-14 years

Wild boar

"At Odenwald nature park there is a special place where visitors can watch and feed wild boars. I'd been there a few times before but this was my first visit in the winter season. I struck lucky, because we don't usually have so much snow in southwest Germany."

Nikon FE with 55mm micro lens; tripod; auto at f8; Fujichrome 100

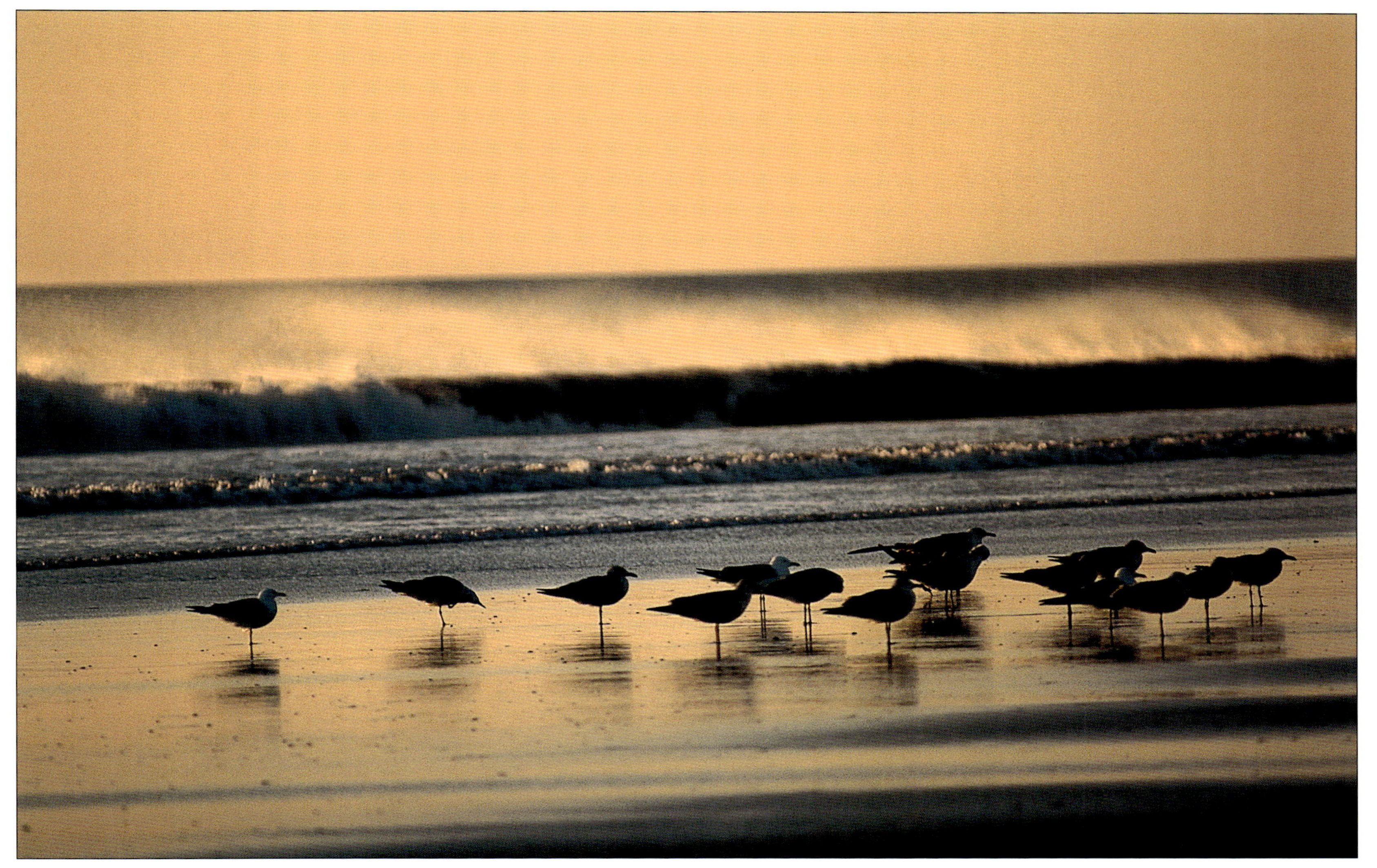

Malcolm Kemp
United Kingdom
WINNER
15-17 years

Herring gulls

"At the end of a wild and blustery day, I found these herring gulls resting on the tide line a mile away from the busy tourist resort of Matalascañas, on the edge of Doñana National Park, Southwest Spain."

Nikkormat with 300mm lens; Fujichrome Velvia

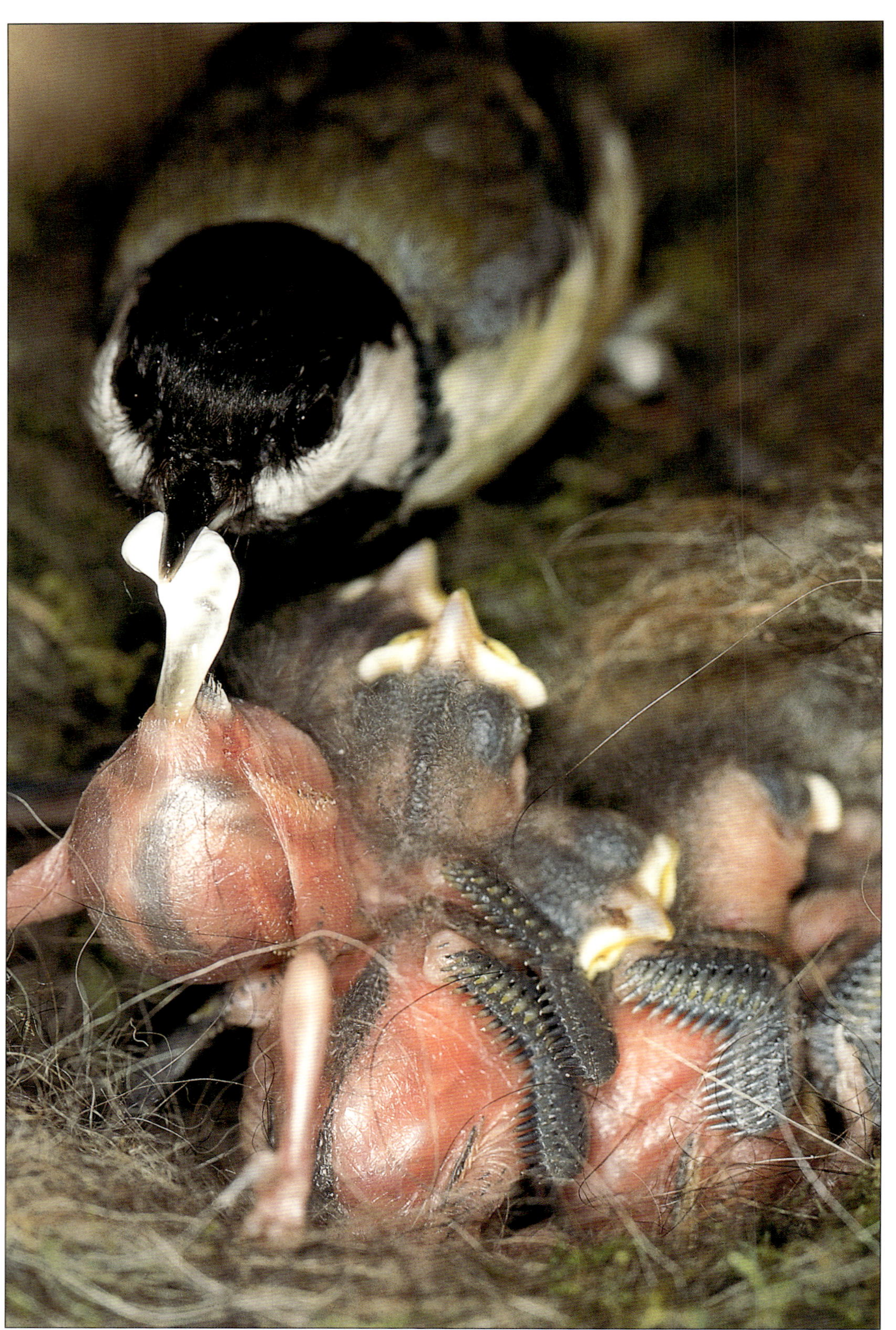

Anne Meyer
France
RUNNER-UP
15-17 years

Great tit removing faecal sac

"A few years ago my father built three special nest boxes in our garage wall so that we could watch and photograph nesting birds. When the chicks have been fed, they present their parents with a faecal sac. I like this funny behaviour and tried to capture this moment."

Nikon F-801 with 105mm macro lens; flash; 1/125 sec at f11-16; Fujichrome Velvia rated at 100

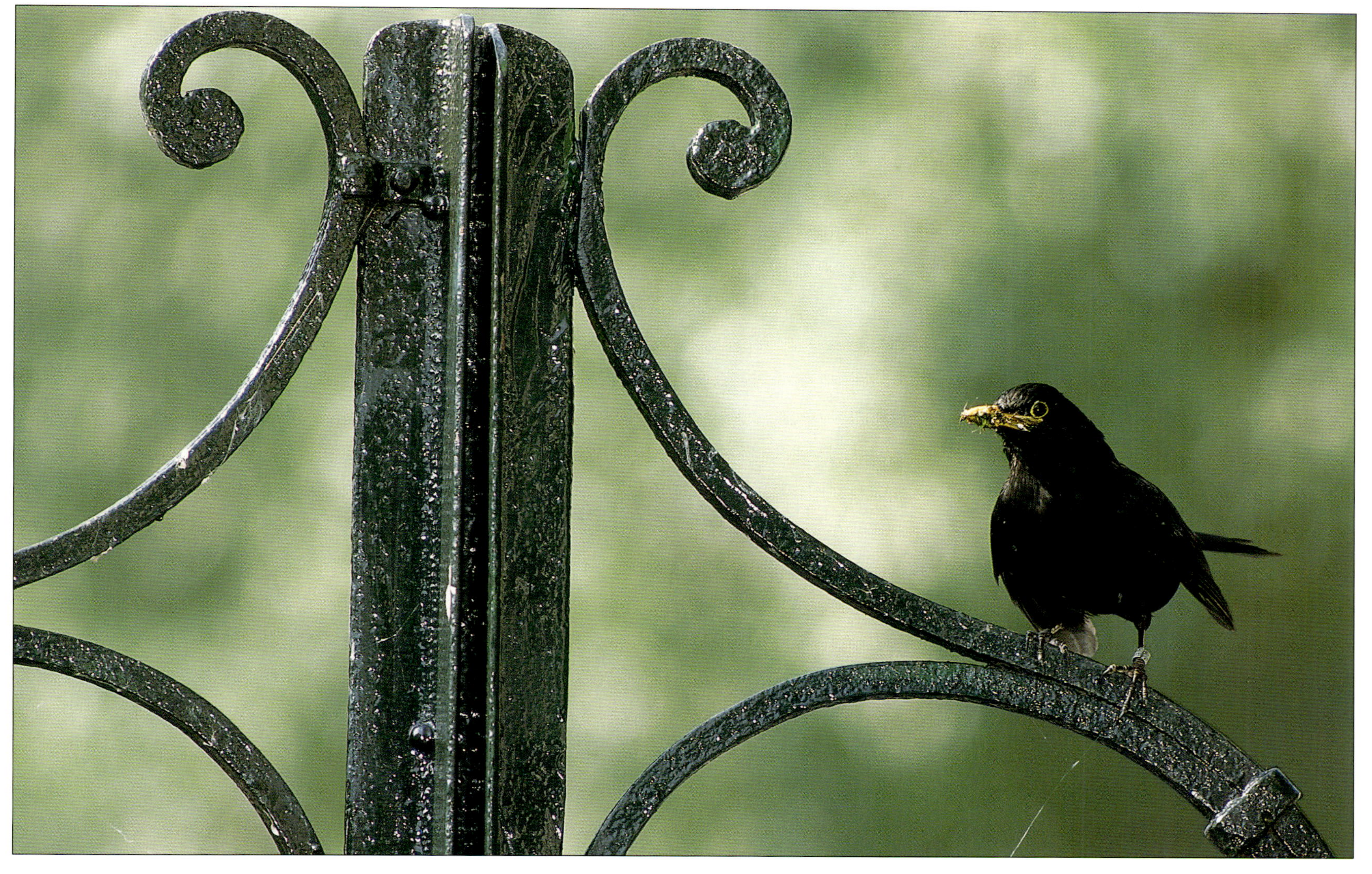

Anne Meyer
France
HIGHLY COMMENDED
15-17 years

Male blackbird

"We share our house and garden in Strasbourg with this ringed blackbird, who is now seven years old. To get this photo I waited in my father's car (the best urban hide) while the blackbird and his mate were feeding their two young in a nest hidden in a nearby hedge."

Nikon F-801 with 300mm lens; flash; 1/125 sec at f11; Fujichrome Velvia rated at 100

From Dusk to Dawn

Pictures must have been taken between sunset and sunrise (the sun may be on but not above the horizon) and must feature animals.

Dale Hancock
South Africa
WINNER

Jackal stretching at dusk

"Knowing that this black backed jackal usually had a good stretch after his long midday sleep, I was able to position myself for the shot in advance. I lay down just a few metres away from him and used the approaching storm as a backdrop. Soon afterwards, the jackal and I were drenched by a typical Etosha downpour."

Canon EOS 1 with 35-350mm lens; beanbag; side light; 1/30 sec at f3.5; Fujichrome Velvia rated at 100

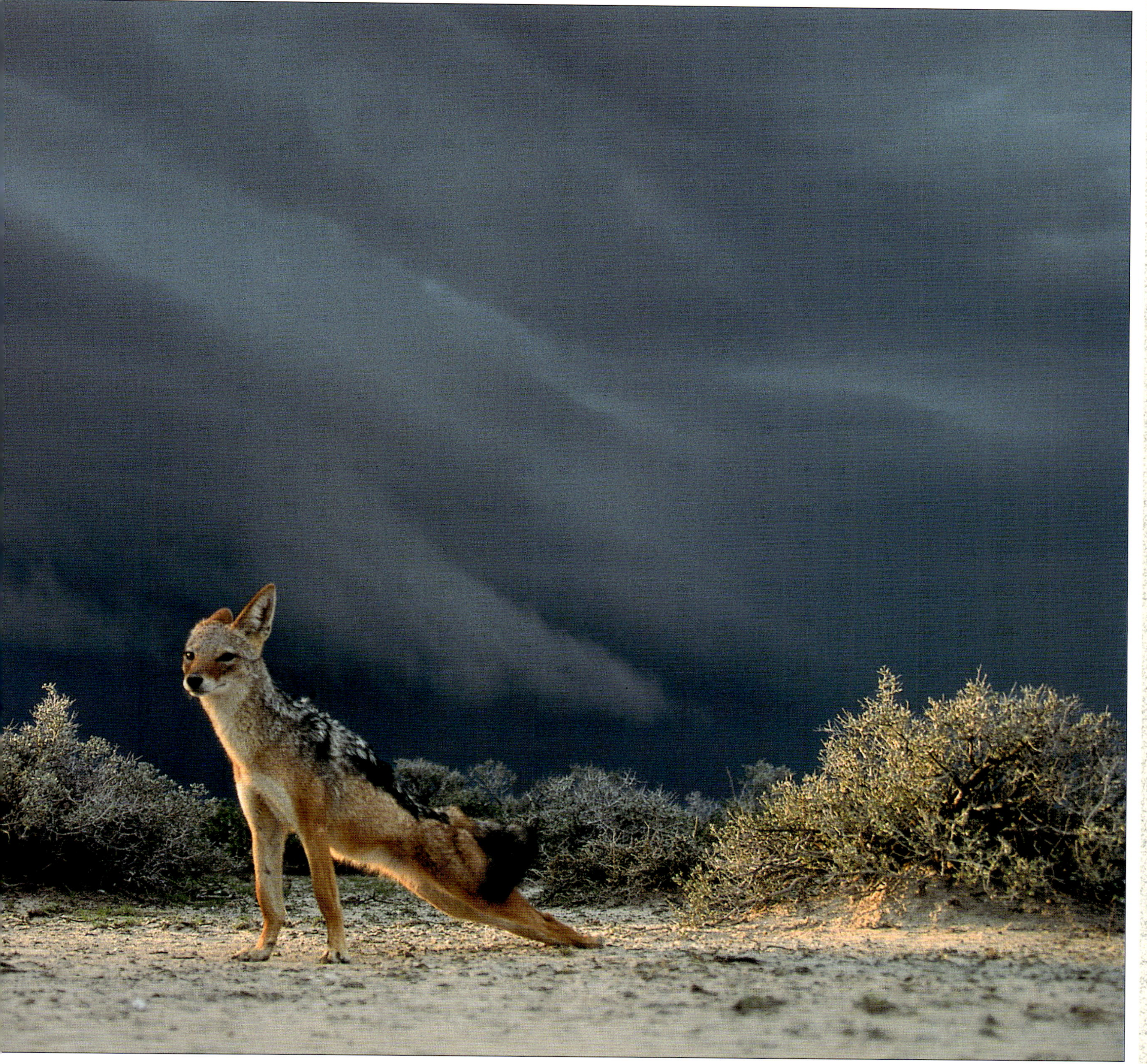

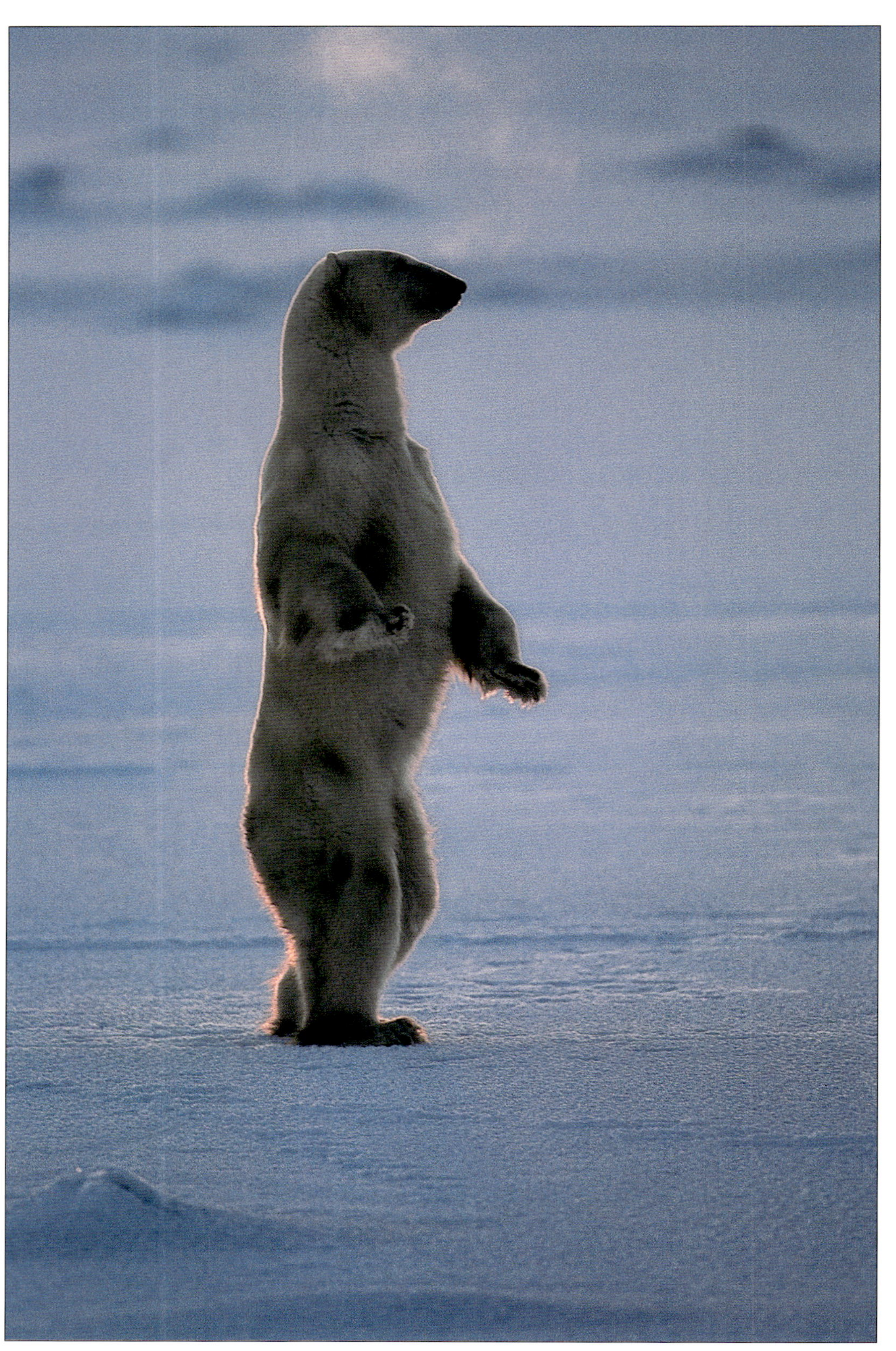

Alice C Garland

United States of America

HIGHLY COMMENDED

Polar bear in evening light

"Polar bears stand upright to watch other bears in the vicinity. This male, from Churchill, Manitoba, had just finished sniffing the air for the scent of a second male, who was entering his territory. As he exhaled, his breath was caught by the last rays of the setting sun."

Canon EOS 1N with 300mm lens and x1.4 teleconverter; window mount; Fujichrome Provia 100

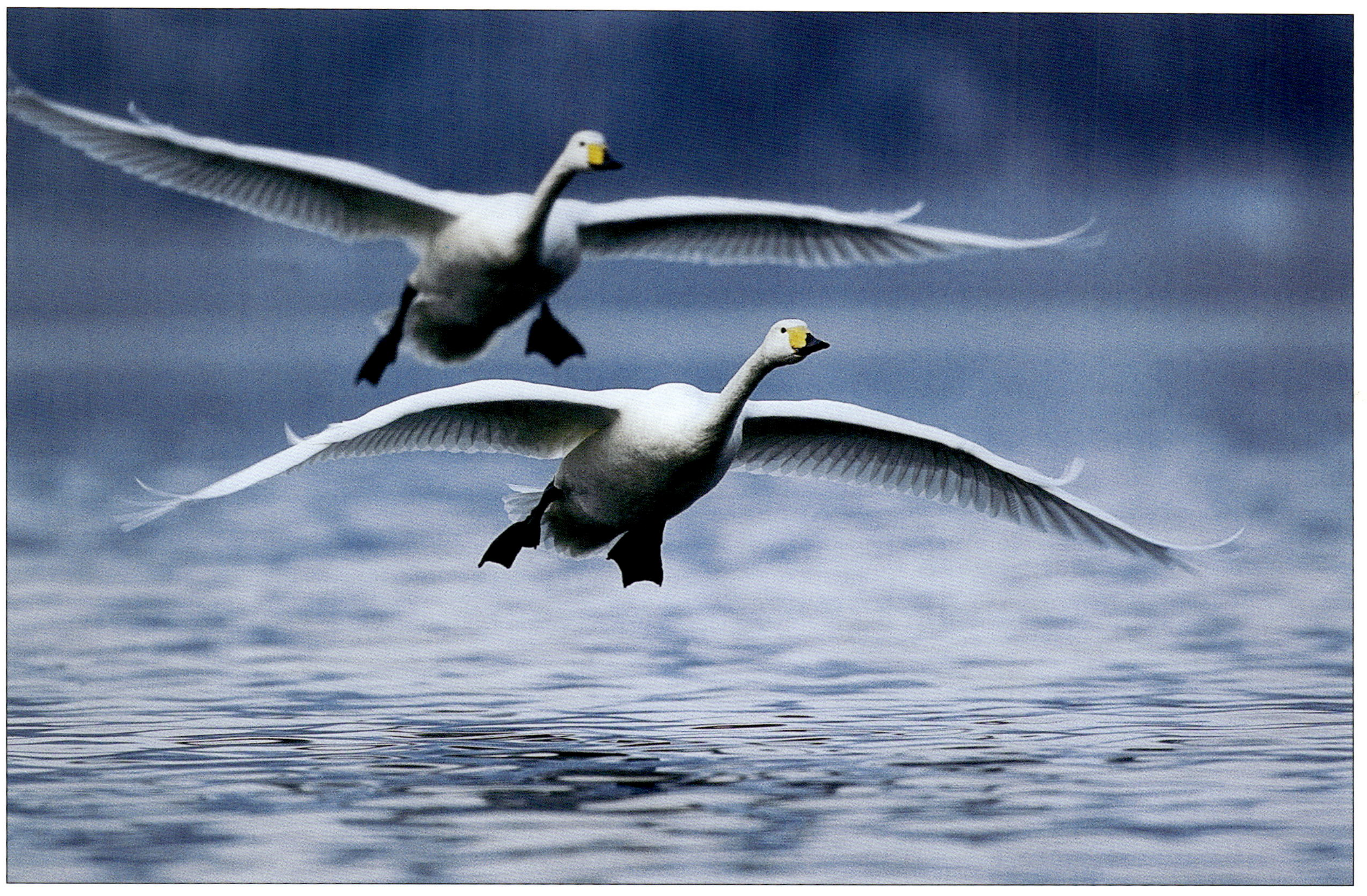

Konrad Wothe
Germany
HIGHLY COMMENDED

Whooper swans

"In January I spent three days photographing whooper swans at Kussharo-ko lake, in Hokkaido. In the evenings, I would watch as these noisy birds took off for their roost sites. One evening, I was in just the right position to get this shot in the bluish light after sunset."

Canon EOS 1N with 600mm lens; tripod; Kodak Ektachrome 100S

Beverly Joubert
Botswana
HIGHLY COMMENDED

Hippo at dusk

"I took this picture at the Zibadianja lagoon, the last remnant of the Savuti channel, Botswana. The channel is now just a dusty depression and the area's hippos are crowded into the lagoon and the Linyanti River. At sunset they begin to leave their schools in the water and wander about on their own to graze."

Canon EOS 1 with 35-350mm lens; tripod; Fujichrome Velvia

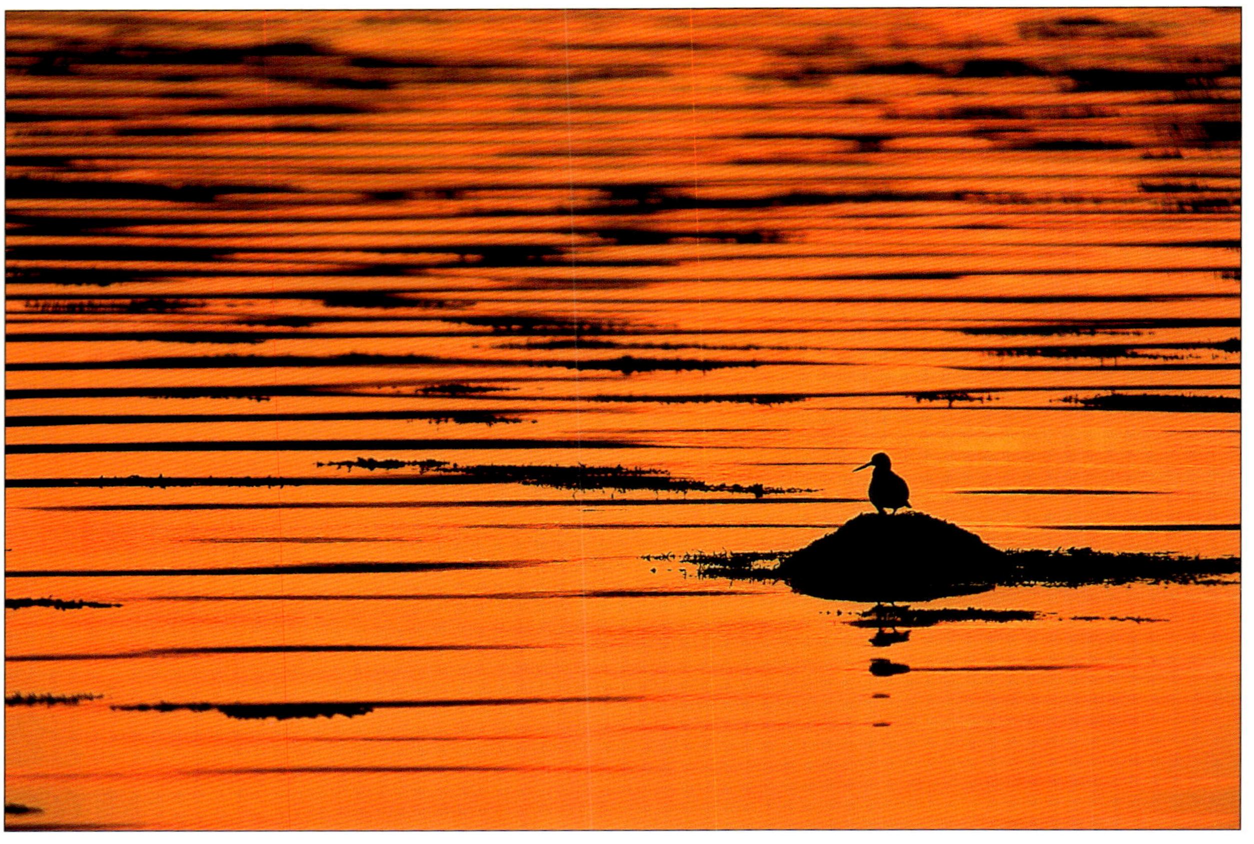

Steve Austin
United Kingdom
SPECIALLY COMMENDED

Oystercatcher at sunset

"A ten minute drive on a November evening took me to the shores of the Moray Firth, where I knew conditions would be ideal for taking pictures. I particularly liked the effect of the long ripples slowly rolling in. They added a sense of movement without destroying the peace of the scene."

Canon T90 with 400mm lens; 1/90 sec at f4; Fujichrome Velvia

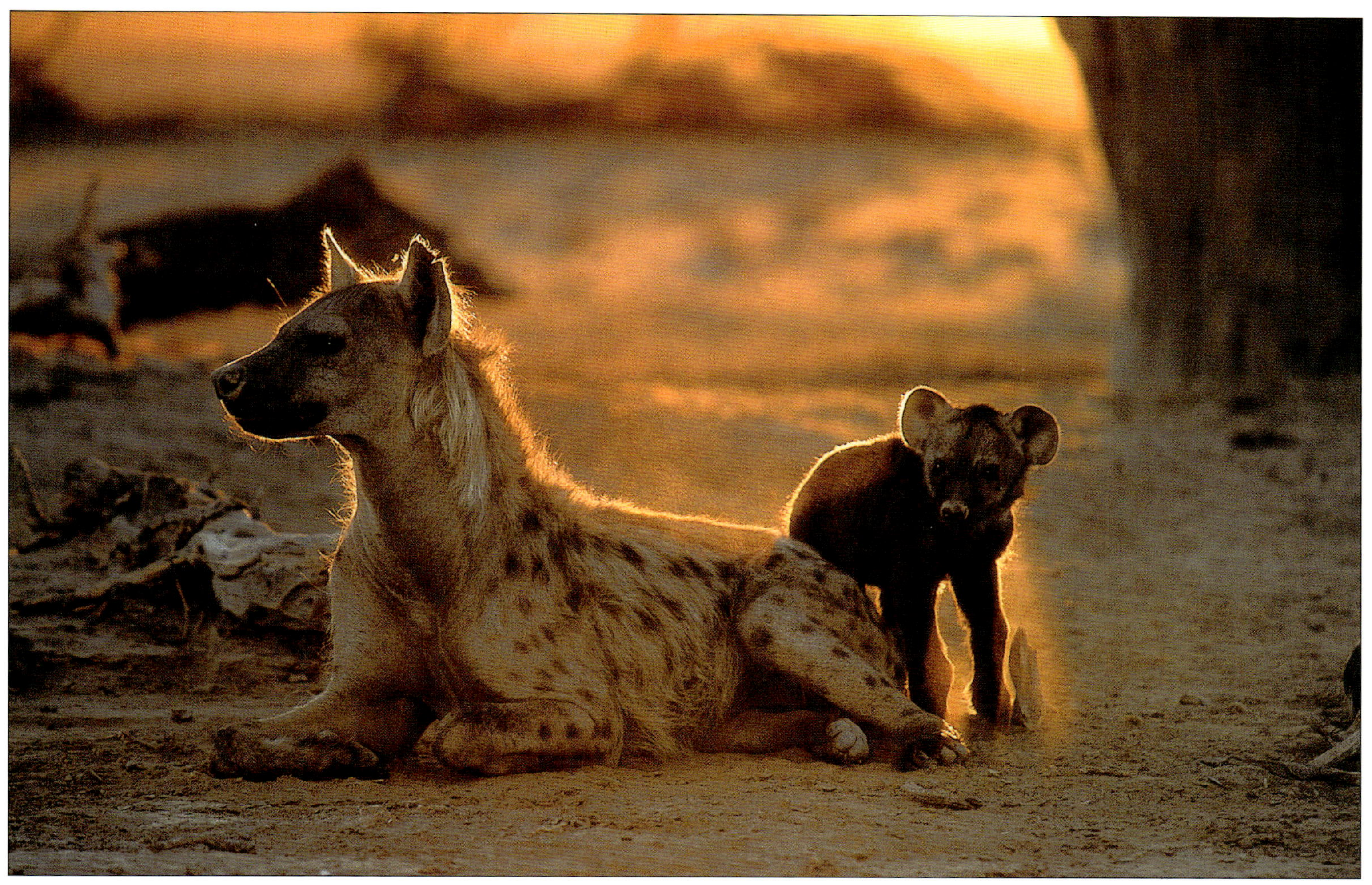

Nigel J Dennis
South Africa
HIGHLY COMMENDED

Hyena and pup at sunset

"I spent ten days taking photographs at this hyena den in the Kalahari Gemsbok National Park, South Africa. Sadly, both the mother and pup in this picture have since been killed by lions."

Canon EOS 5 with 300mm lens; flash; Fujichrome Velvia

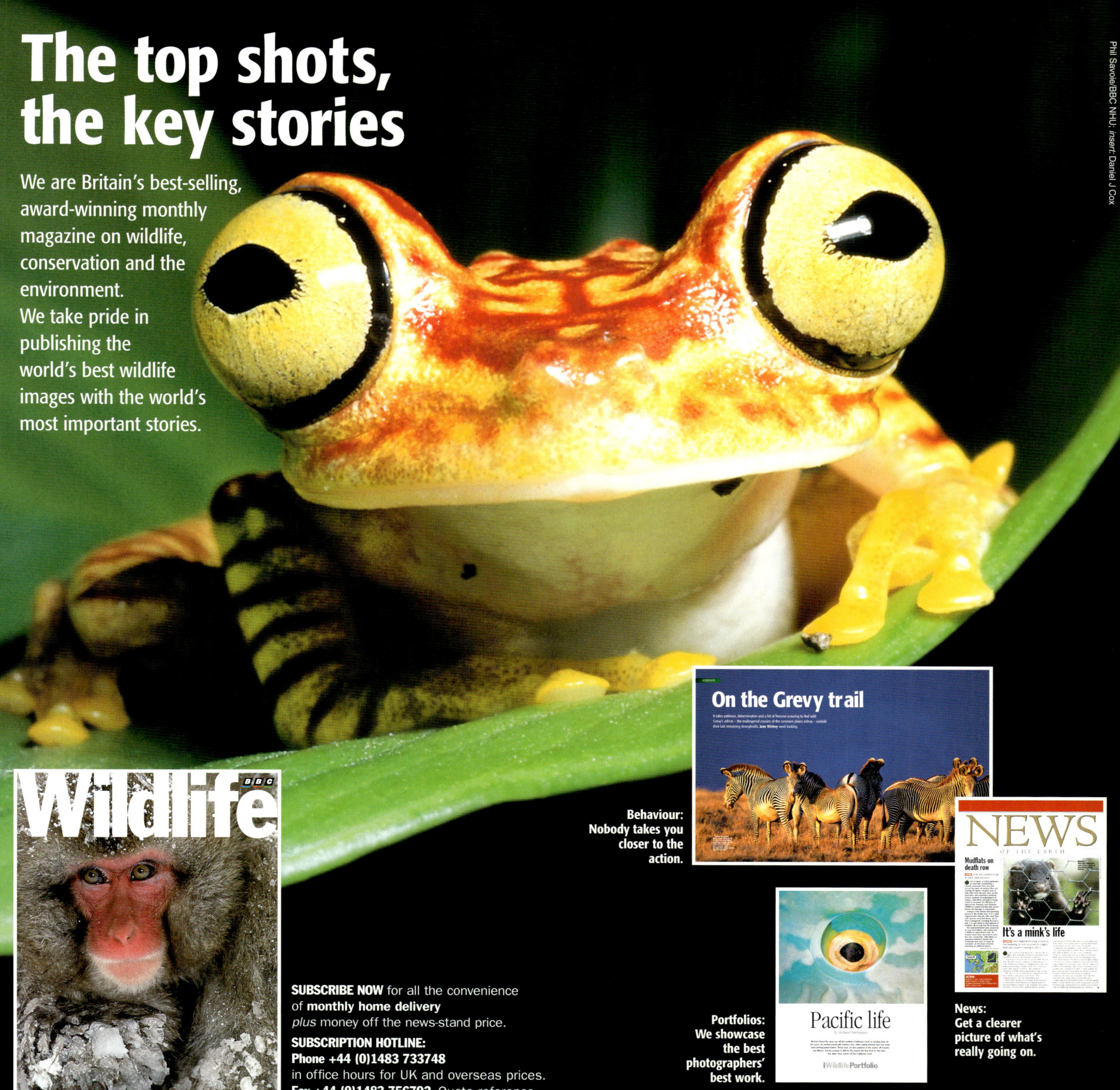
The top shots, the key stories
We are Britain's best-selling, award-winning monthly magazine on wildlife, conservation and the environment.
We take pride in publishing the world's best wildlife images with the world's most important stories.
Phil Savoie/BBC NHU; insert: Daniel J Cox
On the Grevy trail
Behaviour: Nobody takes you closer to the action.
NEWS
Mudflats on death row
It's a mink's life
News: Get a clearer picture of what's really going on.
Pacific life
Portfolios: We showcase the best photographers' best work.
Wildlife
BBC
SUBSCRIBE NOW for all the convenience of monthly home delivery plus money off the news-stand price.
SUBSCRIPTION HOTLINE:
Phone +44 (0)1483 733748
in office hours for UK and overseas prices.
Fax +44 (0)1483 756792. Quote reference WLPF97 for the latest subscription offer.

Index of Photographers

The numbers after the photographers' names indicate the pages on which their work can be found.

Telephone numbers are listed with international dialling codes from the UK in brackets - these should be replaced when dialling from other countries.

OVERALL WINNERS 1984-1996

Cherry Alexander
(Overall Winner 1995) 7
Higher Cottage, Manston,
Sturminster Newton, Dorset, DT10 1EZ
UK
Tel: 01258 473006
Fax: 01258 473333
E-mail: arcticfoto@aol.com

André Bärtschi
(Overall Winner 1992) 6
Bannholzstrasse 10, 9490 Vaduz
LIECHTENSTEIN
Tel: (004175) 232 0338
Fax: (004175) 232 0339
E-mail: 106224.2041@compuserve.com

Rajesh Bedi
(Overall Winner 1986)
Bedi Films,
E-19 Rajouri Gardens, New Delhi
INDIA 110 027

Jim Brandenburg
(Overall Winner 1988)
c/o Minden Pictures,
24 Seascape Village, Aptos, CA 95003
USA
Tel: (001) 408 685 1911
Fax: (001) 408 685 1913

Martyn Colbeck
(Overall Winner 1993) 6
c/o 33 High View, Hempstead,
Gloucester GL2 5LN
UK
Agent:
Oxford Scientific Films Ltd,
Lower Road, Long Hanborough,
Witney, Oxfordshire, OX8 8LL
UK
Tel: 01993 881881
Fax: 01993 882808

Richard & Julia Kemp
(Overall Winner 1984)
Valley Farmhouse, Whitwell, Norwich,
Norfolk, NR10 4SQ
UK
Tel: 01603 872498

Frans Lanting
(Overall Winner 1991) 6
1985 Smith Grade,
Santa Cruz, California 95060
USA
Tel: (001) 408 429 1331
Fax: (001) 408 423 8324

Thomas D Mangelsen
(Overall Winner 1994) 7
Images of Nature
PO Box 2935, 2nd Level, Gaslight Alley,
Jackson, Wyoming 83001
USA
Tel: (001) 307 733 6179
Fax: (001) 307 733 6184
E-mail: stockphoto@mangelsen.com

Jouni Ruuskanen
(Overall Winner 1989)
Ratakatu 31 As 14, 87100 Kajaani
FINLAND
Tel: (00358) 86 133026

Jonathan Scott
(Overall Winner 1987)
PO Box 24499, Nairobi
KENYA
Tel: (00254) 2 216528
Fax: (00254) 2 891162
Agent:
Planet Earth Pictures,
The Innovation Centre,
225 Marsh Wall, London, E14 9FX
UK
Tel: 0171 293 2999
Fax: 0171 293 2998

Wendy Shattil
(Overall Winner 1990)
PO Box 37422, 8325 E Princeton Ave,
Denver, Colorado 80237
USA
Tel: (001) 303 721 1991
Fax: (001) 303 721 1116
E-mail: wshattil@compuserve.com

Charles G Summers Jnr
(Overall Winner 1985)
Wild Images,
6746 N Yucca Trail, Parker, CO 80138
USA
Tel: (001) 303 840 3344
Fax: (001) 303 840 3366

Jason Venus
(Overall Winner 1996) 7
24 Central Acre, Yeovil,
Somerset, BA20 1NU
UK
Tel & Fax: 01935 706834

PORTFOLIO SEVEN

Kelvin Aitken 26, 101, 108, 133
142 Keon St, Thornbury, Victoria 3071
AUSTRALIA
Tel: (0061) 3 9480 4451
Fax: (0061) 3 9480 4452

Karl Ammann 32
Box 437, Nanyuki
KENYA
Tel: (00254) 176 22448
Fax: (00254) 176 32407
E-mail: kamman@form-net.com

Kurt Amsler 137
PO Box 968, 8810 Horgen
SWITZERLAND
Tel & Fax: (0041) 1 725 8314

Uwe Anders 23
Rosenstrasse 10, 38102 Braunschweig
GERMANY
Tel & Fax: (0049) 531 71374

Pete Atkinson 121
Windy Ridge, Hyams Lane,
Holbrook, Ipswich, Suffolk, IP9 2QF
UK
Tel: 01473 328349
Agent:
Planet Earth Pictures,
The Innovation Centre,
225 Marsh Wall, London, E14 9FX
UK
Tel: 0171 293 2999
Fax: 0171 293 2998

Steve Austin 152
17 Burn Brae, Westhill,
Inverness, IV1 2RH
UK
Tel: 01463 790533
Agent:
Woodfall Wild Images,
14 Bull Lane, Denbigh,
Denbighshire, LL16 3SN
UK
Tel: 01745 815903
Fax: 01745 814581

André Bärtschi 20, 31
(*Overall Winner 1992*)
Bannholzstrasse 10, 9490 Vaduz
LIECHTENSTEIN
Tel: (004175) 232 0338
Fax: (004175) 232 0339
E-mail: 106224.2041@*compuserve.com*

Fred Bavendam 30, 105
18 Woodside Lane, Wenham, MA 01984
USA
Tel: (001) 508 468 2354
Fax: (001) 508 468 2365

Andy Belcher 74/75
94 Town Point Road, RD9 *Te Puke*
NEW ZEALAND
Tel: (0064) 7 533 2282
Fax: (0064) 7 533 2283
E-mail: photos-at-legend@xtra.co.nz

Bèla Berta 112
Csobogòs u 4, H-1151 *Budapest*
HUNGARY
Tel: (0036) 1 306 6182

Maurizio Biancarelli 97
via di Porta Romana 164,
06024 *Gubbio* (PG)
ITALY
Tel & Fax: (0039) 75 927 6594

Wayne R Bilenduke 50
PO Box 204, *91 James Street,*
Churchill, Manitoba, R0B 0E0
CANADA
Tel & Fax: (001) 204 675 2834
Agent:
Getty Images,
222 Dexter Avenue North,
Seattle, WA 98109
USA
Tel: (001) 206 622 6262
Fax: (001) 206 622 6662

Sten Björklund 96
Norra Öbyvägen 29, 81832 Valbo
SWEDEN
Tel: (0046) 26 132676

Peter Blackwell 36, 67, 77
PO Box 24, *Thika*
KENYA
Tel: (00254) 151 64032
Fax: (00254) 151 64240
E-mail: stanton@form-net.com

Dr Hermann Brehm 78
Speilbach 90, 74575 Schrozberg
GERMANY
Tel: (0049) 7939 389
Fax: (0049) 7939 1346

Torsten Brehm 60/61
Speilbach 90, 74575 Schrozberg
GERMANY
Tel: (0049) 7939 389
Fax: (0049) 7939 1346

Whit Bronaugh 118
7969 200th Street NE #55,
Arlington, WA 98223
USA
Tel & Fax: (001) 360 435 6082

Laurie Campbell 94
Rosewell Cottage, Paxton,
Berwick-upon-Tweed, TD15 1TE
UK
Tel & Fax: 01289 386736
Agent:
NHPA
57 High Street, Ardingly,
W Sussex, RH17 6TB
UK
Tel: 01444 892514
Fax: 01444 892168

Robert Canis 115
26 Park Avenue, Sittingbourne,
Kent, ME10 1QY
UK
Tel: 01795 477017
Tel & Fax: 01795 431024
Agent:
Planet Earth Pictures,
The Innovation Centre,
225 Marsh Wall, London, E14 9FX
UK
Tel: 0171 293 2999
Fax: 0171 293 2998

María Cano 141
Hernando de Acuña 3-2°A,
47014 Valladolid
SPAIN
Tel: (0034) 83 250450
Fax: (0034) 83 261750

John Conrad 37
1402 E Green Willow Lane,
Littleton, Colorado 80121
USA
Tel: (001) 303 795 2561
Agent:
Sharpshooters,
5000 SW 75th Avenue, 3rd Floor,
Miami, FL 33155
USA
Tel: (001) 305 666 1266
Fax: (001) 305 666 5485

Daniel J Cox 29
16595 Brackett Creek Road,
Bozeman, Montana 59715
USA
Tel & Fax: (001) 406 686 4448
E-mail: danieljcox@naturalexposures.com

Michael Cufer 104
30 Como Road, Oyster Bay, NSW 2225
AUSTRALIA
Tel: (0061) 2 9585 6375
Tel & Fax: (0061) 2 9528 6128
E-mail: mwcufer@ozemail.com.au

Tui De Roy 100
The Roving Tortoise Photography,
Patons Rock Beach,
Box 161 Takaka, Golden Bay
NEW ZEALAND
Tel & Fax: (0064) 3 525 8370

Rebecca Dean 138
Tall Trees, Ellesmere Road,
Weybridge, Surrey, KT13 0HY
UK
Tel: 01932 847418

José Delgado 132
C/Silvano 143 3°D, 28043 Madrid
SPAIN
Tel: (0034) 1 388 9828
Fax: (0034) 1 500 9133 *Attn:* Y Martin

Elio Della Ferrera 51
Via Signorie 3, 23030 Chiuro (SO)
ITALY
Tel & Fax: (0039) 342 213254
E-mail: lvalenti@novanet.it
Agent:
Planet Earth Pictures,
The Innovation Centre,
225 Marsh Wall, London, E14 9FX
UK
Tel: 0171 293 2999
Fax: 0171 293 2998

Michel Denis-Huot 59, 149
1 Bis Rue des Fermes,
F-76310 Sainte Adresse,
FRANCE
Tel: (0033) 2 35 46 29 70
Fax: (0033) 2 35 48 04 30

Nigel J Dennis 53, 153
Nigel Dennis Wildlife Photography,
PO *Box 580,*
Howick 3290, Kwazulu Natal
SOUTH AFRICA
Tel & Fax: (0027) 332 307238
Agent:
NHPA,
57 High Street,
Ardingly, W Sussex, RH17 6TB
UK
Tel: 01444 892514
Fax: 01444 892168

Gertrud & Helmut Denzau 19, 136
Memelstrasse 61, 45259 Essen
GERMANY
Tel & Fax: (0049) 201 465188
E-mail: denzau@t-online.de

Reinhard Dirscherl 98/99
Mendelssohnstrasse 34, D-81245 Munich
GERMANY
Tel: (0049) 89 834 41 63
Fax: (0049) 89 89 62 05 93

Geoff Doré 120
56 Jumpers Avenue, Christchurch,
Dorset, BH23 2ER
UK
Mobile Tel: 0402 364698
Tel & Fax: 01202 485174
Agent:
Getty Images,
101 Bayham Street, London, NW1 0AG
UK
Tel: 0171 267 8988
Fax: 0171 722 9305

Wynand du Plessis 130
PO *Okaukuejo, via Outjo*
NAMIBIA
Tel: (00264) 67 229854
Fax: (00264) 67 229853

Richard du Toit 28
PO *Box 547, Witkoppen 2068*
SOUTH AFRICA
Tel & Fax: (0027) 11 465 9919

Fabian Fischer 142
Reuthstrasse 3b, D-91099 Poxdorf
GERMANY
Tel: (0049) 9133 4960

David B Fleetham
27, 122, 135
PO Box #959, Kihei, Hawaii 96753
USA
Tel: (001) 808 874 9354
Fax: (001) 808 874 5599
E-mail: *photo@maui.net*

Jeff Foott 131
PO Box 2167, 545 S Willow, Jackson, WY 83001
USA
Tel & Fax: (001) 307 739 9383

Jürgen Freund 103
Karolinger Strasse 26, 82205 Gilching
GERMANY
Tel & Fax: (0049) 8105 390460
E-mail: 100766.2753@*compuserve.com*
Agent:
BBC Natural History Unit Picture Library
Broadcasting House, Whiteladies Road, Bristol, BS8 2LR
UK
Tel: 0117 974 6720
Fax: 0117 923 8166

Martin Gabriel 135
Am Hang 7, D-93161 *Sinzing*
GERMANY
Tel & Fax: (0049) 941 31908

Howie Garber 124
Wanderlust Images,
3926 Feramorz Drive,
Salt Lake City, UT 84124
USA
Tel: (001) 801 272 2134
Fax: (001) 801 277 0687
E-mail: *hgphoto@ix.netcom.com*

Alice C Garland 150
13801 N *Riverbluff Lane, Spokane*, WA 99208
USA
Tel: (001) 509 466 0579
Fax: (001) 509 466 3383

Adam Gibbs 119
Unit 83 7501, *Cumberland Street, Burnaby, British Columbia*, V3N 4Y6
CANADA
Tel & Fax: (001) 604 520 0263

Axel Gomille 83
Sandweg 8, D-60316 *Frankfurt*
GERMANY
Tel & Fax: (0049) 69 442523

Jonathan R Green 22, 81
PO Box 17-07-9329, Quito
ECUADOR
Tel & Fax: (00593) 2 890 282
E-mail: *macarena@uio.satnet.net*

Romain Grisius 35
6 Route D'Ettelbruck,
L-7715 Colmar-Berg
LUXEMBOURG
Tel: (00352) 858 331
Fax: (00352) 4015 4004

Daniel Gritz 139, 140
72 Lakeshore Park Road, Boulder, CO 80302
USA
Tel: (001) 303 642 7590
Fax: (001) 303 642 3343

Verena Hahl 142
Goethestr 13a, D-68623 *Lampertheim*
GERMANY
Tel & Fax: (0049) 6206 56421

David Hall 106, 123
257 Ohayo Mountain Road, Woodstock, NY 12498
USA
Tel: (001) 914 679 6138
Fax: (001) 914 679 4085
E-mail: *jamihall@mhv.net*

Asko Hämäläinen 112
Rinnetie 18, 46920 Anjalankoski
FINLAND
Tel: (00358) 5 367 3238

Mark Hamblin 88
63 Waller Road, Walkley Bank, Sheffield, S6 5DP
UK
Tel & Fax: 0114 233 3910
Agent:
Oxford Scientific Films Ltd,
Lower Road, Long Hanborough, Witney, Oxfordshire, OX8 8LL
UK
Tel: 01993 881881
Fax: 01993 882808

Paavo Hamunen 92/93
Lauttalammentie 3 H 24,
93600 Kuusamo
FINLAND
Tel & Fax: (00358) 8 852 3136

Dale Hancock 146/147
4 Kingsbury Park, 20 John Barker Ave, Pelham, Pietermaritzburg, Kwa Zulu-Natal 3201
SOUTH AFRICA
Tel: (0027) 331 460 710
Fax: (0027) 331 77335

Russell Hartwell 84
34 Whitepit Lane, Flackwell Heath, Buckinghamshire, HP10 9HS
UK
Tel: 01628 527996

Martin Harvey 137
PO Box 8945, Centurion 0046, Pretoria
SOUTH AFRICA
Tel & Fax: (0027) 12 664 2241
E-mail: *jonharv@icon.co.za*

Jörg Hauke 58
Nienburgerstr 36A, D-32469 *Lahde*
GERMANY
Tel: (0049) 5702 85697

Hannu Hautala 73
Kiestingintie 12, 93600 Kuusamo
FINLAND
Tel: (00358) 8 8511 056
Fax: (00358) 8 8523 031

Tony Heald 56, 68
23 Elvaston Mews, London, SW7 5HZ
UK
Tel & Fax: 0171 584 1441
Agent:
BBC Natural History Unit Picture Library,
Broadcasting House, Whiteladies Road, Bristol, BS8 2LR
UK
Tel: 0117 974 6720
Fax: 0117 923 8166

Michael Hutchinson 86
Flat 3, 62 Alma Road, Clifton, Bristol, BS8 2DJ
UK
Tel: 0117 973 1011
Fax: 0117 971 9340
E-mail: *Michael.Hutchinson@htv.co.uk*

Jay Ireland & Georgienne Bradley 102
Earth Images,
1511 16th Street, Suite 301, Santa Monica, CA 90404
USA
Tel & Fax: (001) 310 829 4291
E-mail: *EarthImag@aol.com*

Ernie Janes 89
Park House Studio,
Northchurch Common, Berkhamsted, Hertfordshire, HP4 1LR
UK
Tel & Fax: 01442 871342

Chris Johns 41, 79
RT 1 *Box 45A, Woodville*, VA 22749
USA
Tel & Fax: (001) 540 987 9040
Agent:
National Geographic Society, Image Collection,
1145 17th Street NW, Washington DC 20036-4688
USA
Tel: (001) 202 857 7537
Fax: (001) 202 429 5776

Beverly Joubert 52, 152
Wildlife Films,
PO Box 55, Kasane,
BOTSWANA
Fax: (00267) 650 223
Agent:
National Geographic Society, Image Collection,
1145 17th Street NW, Washington DC 20036-4688
USA
Tel: (001) 202 857 7537
Fax: (001) 202 429 5776

Janos Jurka 111
Storängsvägen 5, S-77160 *Ludvika*
SWEDEN
Tel: (0046) 240 39087
Fax: (0046) 240 81125
Agent:
Bruce Coleman Ltd,
16 Chiltern Business Village, Arundel Road, Uxbridge, Middlesex, UB8 2SN
UK
Tel: 01895 257094
Fax: 01895 272357

Tony Karacsonyi 107
PO Box 407, Ulladulla, NSW 2539
AUSTRALIA
Tel & Fax: (0061) 44 554552

Eero Kemilä 48, 63
Kivitie 5, 91700 Vaala
FINLAND
Tel & Fax: (00358) 8 536 1370

Malcolm Kemp 143
Valley Farmhouse, Whitwell, Norwich, Norfolk, NR10 4SQ
UK
Tel & Fax: 01603 872498

Rich Kirchner 71, 82
10 Bronco Drive, Bozeman, Montana 59718
USA
Tel & Fax: (001) 406 388 7724

Hideyo Kubota 114
3-22-18 La Paul Warabi 203, Chuo, Warabi-shi 335, Saitama
JAPAN
Tel: (0081) 48 433 7959

Erich Kuchling 65
Buchenauer Strasse 35, D-82256 Fuerstenfeldbruck
GERMANY
Tel: (0049) 8141 17509
Fax: (0049) 8141 33817

Cay-Uwe Kulzer 113
Waldstr 10, 55599 Stein-Bockenheim
GERMANY
Tel: (0049) 6703 4135
Fax: (0049) 6131 845555

Gary L Lackie 38
6812 Cape Lisburne Loop, Anchorage, Alaska 99504
USA
Tel: (001) 907 338 8220
Fax: (001) 907 278 7467

Andreas Leemann 126
Zürichstr 113, 8123 Ebmatingen
SWITZERLAND
Tel: (0041) 1 980 3163
E-mail: andreas.leemann@empa.ch

Kjell Ljungström 25
Hellzèngatan 14, 87161 Härnösand
SWEDEN
Tel: (0046) 611 22986
E-mail: kjell.ljungstrom@harnosand.mail.telia.com
Agent: Naturbild, Box 3353, Stockholm
SWEDEN
Tel: (0046) 8 411 4330

Gil Lopez-Espina 57, 129
104 Division Avenue, Belleville, NJ 07109
USA
Tel & Fax: (001) 201 751 5641

Thomas D Mangelsen 62
(Overall Winner 1994)
Images of Nature, PO Box 2935, 2nd Level, Gaslight Alley, Jackson, Wyoming 83001
USA
Tel: (001) 307 733 6179
Fax: (001) 307 733 6184
E-mail: stockphoto@mangelsen.com

Anne Meyer 144, 145
21 rue d'Altorf, F-67200 Strasbourg
FRANCE
Tel: (0033) 3 88 30 37 56
Fax: (0033) 3 88 41 39 86

Lawrence A Michael 116
PO Box 498, *Butler,* WI 53007
USA
Tel: (001) 414 965 3344
Fax: (001) 414 790 9009

Arthur Morris 69, 117
Birds as Art, 1455 Whitewood Drive, Deltona, FL 32725
USA
Tel: (001) 407 860 2013
Fax: (001) 407 574 5584

Ewald Neffe 72
Raaballee 284, 8181 St Ruprecht/Raab
AUSTRIA
Tel: (0043) 3178 3189

Frank Neumann 76
Affalterbacher Str 38, D-71686 Remseck
GERMANY
Tel: (0049) 7146 44384

Tero Niemi 39
Bäckvägen 5, S-63369 Skogstorp
SWEDEN
Tel: (0046) 16 26346
Fax: (0046) 16 26341

Klaus Nigge 24
Ernst Becker Strasse 12, D-44534 Lünen
GERMANY
Tel: (0049) 2306 51720
Fax: (0049) 2306 73831

Magnus Nyman 148
Årteryd, S-59041 Rimforsa
SWEDEN
Tel & Fax: (0046) 494 23139

Jun Ogawa 125
2313 LT Yatuka, 77-1 Sezaki-cho, Soka-shi, Saitama Prefecture
JAPAN
Tel & Fax: (0081) 489 27 2213

David N Olsen 55
2237 S Buena Vista Drive, Moab, UT 84532
USA
Tel & Fax: (001) 801 259 2950

John Olsen 81
PO Box 178, *Artarmon,* NSW 2064
AUSTRALIA
Tel: (0061) 2 9428 5969
Fax: (0061) 2 9213 4045
E-mail: jbryant@nsw.redcross.org.au

Pete Oxford 136
Casilla 17-07-9668, Quito
ECUADOR
Tel: (00593) 2 226958
Fax: (00593) 9 465758
E-mail: oxfoto@pi.pro.ec

Manfred Pfefferle 109
Am Prestenberg 4, 79219 Staufen
GERMANY
Tel: (0049) 7633 5620
Fax: (0049) 7633 50876
E-mail: manfred.pfefferle@t-online.de

Allan Potts 91
East Farm, Backworth, Newcastle-upon-Tyne, NE27 0AL
UK
Tel: 0191 268 4706
Agent: Bruce Coleman Ltd, 16 Chiltern Business Village, Arundel Road, Uxbridge, Middlesex, UB8 2SN
UK
Tel: 01895 257094
Fax: 01895 272357

Tapani Räsänen 8/9
Tasalantie 27, Fin-54100 Joutseno
FINLAND
Tel & Fax: (00358) 54 534929

Iñaki Relanzón 42, 64, 80
Guipúscoa 2 2on 2a, 08018 Barcelona, Catalonía
SPAIN
Tel & Fax: (0034) 3 307 4543

Graham Robertson 127
Australian Antarctic Division, Channel Highway, Kingston, Tasmania 7050
AUSTRALIA
Tel: (0061) 3 62 323 337
Fax: (0061) 3 62 323 351
E-mail: graham_rob@antdiv.gov.au

Norbert Rosing 113
Amselweg 15, D-82284 Grafrath
GERMANY
Tel: (0049) 8144 7813
Fax: (0049) 8144 98469

Alan Ross 87
16 Ken Road, Bellfield, Kilmarnock, Scotland, KA1 3QR
UK
Tel: 01563 534919

Kotaro Sano 54
1429-83 Hastusawamachi, Hachioji City, Tokyo
JAPAN
Tel & Fax: (0081) 426 65 5573
Agent: Animals & Earth, 3-14-14-103 Minami-Aoyama, Minato-ku, Tokyo 107
JAPAN
Tel: (0081) 3 3401 5858
Fax: (0081) 3 3401 3737

Kevin Schafer 16/17, 49

2148 Halleck Avenue SW,
Seattle, WA 98116
USA

Tel: (001) 206 933 1668
Fax: (001) 206 933 1659
E-mail: *SchaferPho@aol.com*

Anup Shah 18, 34, 46/47

29 Cornfield Road, Bushey,
Herts, WD2 3TB
UK

Tel & Fax: 0181 950 8705

Agent:

Planet Earth Pictures,
The Innovation Centre,
225 Marsh Wall, London, E14 9FX
UK

Tel: 0171 293 2999
Fax: 0171 293 2998

Manoj Shah 21

PO Box 44219, Nairobi
KENYA

Tel: (00254) 2 743962
Fax: (00254) 2 751692

Agent:
Getty Images,
101 Bayham Street, London, NW1 0AG
UK

Tel: 0171 267 8988
Fax: 0171 722 9305

Wendy Shattil
& Bob Rozinski 137
(Overall Winner 1990)

PO Box 37422, 8325 E Princeton Ave,
Denver, Colorado 80237
USA

Tel: (001) 303 721 1991
Fax: (001) 303 721 1116
E-mail: *wshattil@compuserve.com*

Dr David J Slater 85

Manor Cottage,
Great Rollright, Chipping Norton,
Oxfordshire, OX7 5RH
UK

Tel: 01608 737166

Jill Sneesby
& Barrie Wilkins 40

PO Box 5060, Walmer 6065,
Port Elizabeth
SOUTH AFRICA

Tel: (0027) 41 511214
Fax: (0027) 41 511217
E-mail: *bwilkins@iafrica.com*

Jim Stamates 43

Low Impact Wildlife Photography,
2790 Blitzen Road, PO Box 11211,
South Lake Tahoe, CA 96155
USA

Tel: (001) 916 577 4101
Fax: (001) 916 577 5204
E-mail: *liphoto@oakweb.com*

Jan Töve Johansson 121

Prästgården, Härna,
S-52399 Hökerum
SWEDEN

Tel & Fax: (0046) 33 274028
E-mail:
jt.johansson@ulricehamn.mail.telia.com

Agent:
Planet Earth Pictures,
The Innovation Centre,
225 Marsh Wall, London, E14 9FX
UK

Tel: 0171 293 2999
Fax: 0171 293 2998

Dr Charles Tyler 70

7 Chapel Cottages, Chapel Lane,
Stoke Poges, Bucks, SL2 4QL
UK

Tel: 01753 662695
Fax: 01895 274348
E-mail: *Charles.Tyler@brunel.ac.uk*

Heinrich van den Berg
10–15, 33, 43

HPH Photography,
PO Box 13244,
Cascades, Pietermaritzburg 3202
SOUTH AFRICA

Tel: (0027) 12 309 3240
Tel & Fax: (0027) 331 472728
E-mail: *hberg@ndot.pwv.gov.za*

Jan Vermeer 95

Planetenlaan 10, 7314 KA Apeldoorn
NETHERLANDS

Tel: (0031) 55 355 5803
Fax: (0031) 55 355 7268

Agent:
Foto Natura,
Krommenieërpad 38 a,
1521 HB Wormerveer
NETHERLANDS

Tel: (0031) 75 628 0764
Fax: (0031) 75 640 3409

Bernhard Volmer 128

Rheiner Landstr 82, 49078 Osnabrück
GERMANY

Tel: (0049) 541 432072
Fax: (0049) 541 47148

Mark Webster 90

Photec
42 Trelawney Road, Falmouth,
Cornwall, TR11 3LX
UK

Tel & Fax: 01326 318307

Staffan Widstrand
45, 110, 134

Smedvägen 21, S-17671 Järfälla
SWEDEN

Tel & Fax: (0046) 8 583 51831
E-mail: *photo@staffanwidstrand.se*

Lawson Wood 106

1 The Clouds, Duns,
Berwickshire, TD11 3BB
UK

Tel: 01361 882628
Fax: 01361 882975
E-mail: *lawson@oceaneye.demon.co.uk*

Konrad Wothe 44, 151

Maenherstr 27a, D-81375 München
GERMANY

Tel: (0049) 89 717 453
Fax: (0049) 89 714 7141

Agent:
Look GmbH,
Kapuzinerstr 9D, 80337 München
GERMANY

Tel: (0049) 89 544 2330
Fax: (0049) 89 544 233 22

Dr Mamoru Yoshida 66

4485 St Andrews Drive,
Pine Tree Golf Estates,
Boynton Beach, FL 33436-4427
USA

Tel & Fax: (001) 561 734 5559
E-mail: *DrYoshida@juno.com*